SUICIDE RESEARCH: SELECTED READINGS

Volume 16

May 2016 — October 2016

Y. W. Koo, M. McDonough, V. Ross, D. De Leo

Australian Institute for Suicide Research and Prevention

Griffith
UNIVERSITY

WHO Collaborating Centre for
Research and Training in Suicide Prevention

National Centre of Excellence in Suicide Prevention

First published in 2016
Australian Academic Press
18 Victor Russell Drive,
Samford QLD 4520, Australia
Australia
www.australianacademicpress.com.au

ISBN: 978 1 9221 1784 7

Book and cover design by Maria Biaggini — The Letter Tree.

Contents

Foreword

This volume contains quotations from internationally peer-reviewed suicide research published during the semester May 2016 – October 2016; it is the sixteenth of a series produced biannually by our Institute with the aim of assisting the Commonwealth Department of Health to be constantly updated on new evidences from the scientific community.

As usual, the initial section of the volume collects a number of publications that could have particular relevance for the Australian people in terms of potential applicability. These publications are accompanied by a short comment from us, and an explanation of the motives that justify why we have considered of interest the implementation of studies' findings in the Australian context. An introductory part provides the rationale and the methodology followed in the identification of papers.

The central part of the volume represents a selection of research articles of particular significance; their abstracts are reported in *extenso*, underlining our invitation to read those papers in full text: they represent a remarkable advancement of suicide research knowledge.

The last section reports all items retrievable from major electronic databases. We have catalogued them on the basis of their prevailing reference to fatal and non-fatal suicidal behaviours, with various sub-headings (e.g. epidemiology, risk factors, etc.). The deriving list guarantees a level of completeness superior to any individual system; it can constitute a useful tool for all those interested in a quick update of what was most recently published on the topic.

Our intent was to make suicide research more approachable to non-specialists, and in the meantime provide an opportunity for a *vademecum* of quotations credible also at the professional level. A compilation such as the one that we provide here is not easily obtainable from usual sources and can save a considerable amount of time to readers. We believe that our effort in this direction may be an appropriate interpretation of one of the technical support roles to the Government that the status of National Centre of Excellence in Suicide Prevention — which has deeply honoured our commitment — entails for us.

The significant growth of our centre, the Australian Institute for Suicide Research and Prevention, and its influential function, both nationally and internationally, in the fight against suicide, could not happen without the constant support of Queensland Health and Griffith University. We hope that our passionate dedication to the cause of suicide prevention may compensate their continuing trust in our work.

Diego De Leo AO, DSc
Director, Australian Institute for Suicide Research and Prevention

Acknowledgments

This report has been produced by the Australian Institute for Suicide Research and Prevention, WHO Collaborating Centre for Research and Training in Suicide Prevention and National Centre of Excellence in Suicide Prevention. The assistance of the Commonwealth Department of Health in the funding of this report is gratefully acknowledged.

Introduction

Context

Suicide places a substantial burden on individuals, communities and society in terms of emotional, economic and health care costs. In Australia, about 2000 people die from suicide every year, a death rate well in excess of transport-related mortality. At the time of preparing this volume, the latest available statistics released by the Australian Bureau of Statistics1 indicated that, in 2013, 2,522 deaths by suicide were registered in Australia, representing an age-standardised rate of 10.7 per 100,000.

Despite the estimated mortality, the prevalence of suicide and self-harming behaviour in particular remains difficult to gauge due to the often secretive nature of these acts. Without a clear understanding of the scope of suicidal behaviours and the range of interventions available, the opportunity to implement effective initiatives is reduced. Further, it is important that suicide prevention policies are developed on the foundation of evidence-based empirical research, especially as the quality and validly of the available information may be misleading or inaccurate. Additionally, the social and economic impact of suicide underlines the importance of appropriate research-based prevention strategies, addressing not only significant direct costs on health system and lost productivity, but also the emotional suffering for families and communities.

The Australian Institute for Suicide Research and Prevention (AISRAP) has, through the years, gained an international reputation as one of the leading research institutions in the field of suicide prevention. The most important recognition came via the designation as a World Health Organization (WHO) Collaborating Centre in 2005. In 2008, the Commonwealth Department of Health (DoH) appointed AISRAP as the National Centre of Excellence in Suicide Prevention. This latter recognition awards not only many years of high quality research, but also of fruitful cooperation between the Institute and several different governmental agencies.

As part of this mandate, AISRAP is committed to the creation of a databank of the recent scientific literature documenting the nature and extent of suicidal and self-harming behaviour and recommended practices in preventing and responding to these behaviours. The key output for the project is a critical bi-annual review of the national and international literature outlining recent advances and promising developments in research in suicide prevention, particularly where this can help to inform national activities. This task is not aimed at providing a critique of new researches, but rather at drawing attention to investigations that may have particular relevance to the Australian context. In doing so, we are committed to a user-friendly language, in order to render research outcomes and their interpretation accessible also to a non-expert audience.

In summary, these reviews serve three primary purposes:

1. To inform future State and Commonwealth suicide prevention policies;
2. To assist in the improvement of existing initiatives, and the development of new and innovative Australian projects for the prevention of suicidal and self-harming behaviours within the context of the Living is for Everyone (LIFE) Framework (2008);
3. To provide directions for Australian research priorities in suicidology.

The review is presented in three sections. The first contains a selection of the best articles published in the last six months internationally. For each article identified by us (see the method of choosing articles described below), the original abstract is accompanied by a brief comment explaining why we thought the study was providing an important contribution to research and why we considered its possible applicability to Australia. The second section presents the abstracts of the most relevant literature — following our criteria — collected between May 2016 to October 2016; while the final section presents a list of citations of all literature published over this time-period.

Methodology

The literature search was conducted in four phases.

Phase 1

Phase one consisted of weekly searches of the academic literature performed from May 2016 to October 2016. To ensure thorough coverage of the available published research, the literature was sourced using several scientific electronic databases including: PubMed, ProQuest, Scopus, SafetyLit and Web of Science, using the following key words: *suicide OR suicidal OR self-harm OR self-injury OR parasuicide.*

Results from the weekly searches were downloaded and combined into one database (deleting duplicates).

Specific inclusion criteria for Phase 1 included:

- Timeliness: the article was published (either electronically or in hard-copy) between May 2016 to October 2016;
- Relevance: the article explicitly referred to fatal and/or non-fatal suicidal behaviour and related issues and/or interventions directly targeted at preventing/treating these behaviours;
- The article was written in English.

Articles about euthanasia, assisted suicide, suicide terrorist attacks, and/or book reviews, abstracts and conference presentations were excluded.

Also, articles that have been previously published in electronic versions (ahead of print) and included in the previous volumes (Volumes 1 to 15 of *Suicide Research: Selected Readings*) were excluded to avoid duplication.

Phase 2

Following an initial reading of the abstracts (retrieved in Phase 1), the list of articles was refined down to the most relevant literature. In Phase 2 articles were only included if they were published in an international, peer-reviewed journal.

In Phase 2, articles were excluded when they:

- were not particularly instructive or original
- were of a descriptive nature (e.g. a case-report)
- consisted of historical/philosophical content
- were a description of surgical reconstruction/treatment of self-inflicted injuries
- concerned biological and/or genetic interpretations of suicidal behaviour, the results of which could not be easily adoptable in the context of the LIFE Framework.

In order to minimise the potential for biased evaluations, two researchers working independently read through the full text of all articles selected to create a list of most relevant papers. This process was then duplicated by a third researcher for any articles on which consensus could not be reached.

The strength and quality of the research evidence was evaluated, based on the *Critical Appraisal Skills Programme (CASP) Appraisal Tools* published by the Public Health Resource Unit, England (2006). These tools, publically available online, consist of checklists for critically appraising systematic reviews, randomized controlled trials (RCT), qualitative research, economic evaluation studies, cohort studies, diagnostic test studies and case control studies.

Phase 3

One of the aims of this review was to identify research that is both evidence-based and of potential relevance to the Australian context. Thus, the final stage of applied methodology focused on research conducted in countries with populations or health systems sufficiently comparable to Australia. Only articles in which the full-text was available were considered. It is important to note that failure of an article to be selected for inclusion in Phase 3 does not entail any negative judgment on its 'objective' quality.

Specific inclusion criteria for Phase 3 included:

- applicability to Australia
- the paper met all criteria for scientificity (i.e., the methodology was considered sound)
- the paper represented a particularly compelling addition to the literature, which would be likely to stimulate suicide prevention initiatives and research
- inevitably, an important aspect was the importance of the journal in which the paper was published (because of the high standards that have to be met in order to obtain publication in that specific journal); priority was given to papers published in high impact factor journals
- particular attention has been paid to widen the literature horizon to include sociological and anthropological research that may have particular relevance to the Australian context.

After a thorough reading of these articles ('Key articles' for the considered timeframe), a written comment was produced for each article detailing:

- methodological strengths and weaknesses (e.g., sample size, validity of measurement instruments, appropriateness of analysis performed)
- practical implications of the research results to the Australian context
- suggestions for integrating research findings within the domains of the LIFE framework suicide prevention activities.

Phase 4

In the final phase of the search procedure all articles were divided into the following classifications:

- *Fatal suicidal behaviour* (epidemiology, risk and protective factors, prevention, postvention and bereavement)
- *Non-fatal suicidal/self-harming behaviours* (epidemiology, risk and protective factors, prevention, care and support)

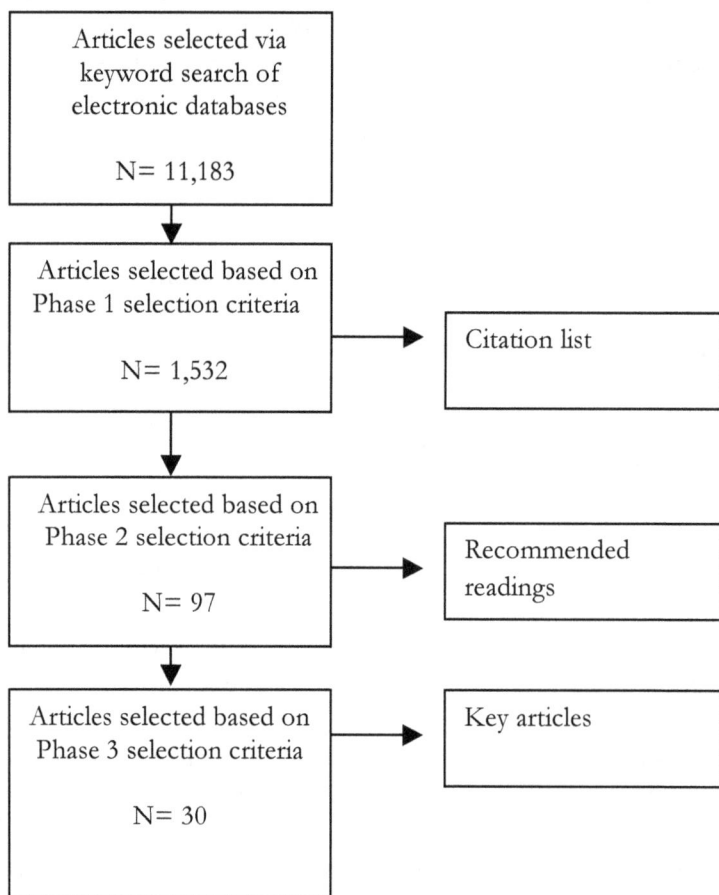

Figure 1

- *Case reports* include reports of fatal and non-fatal suicidal behaviours
- *Miscellaneous* includes all research articles that could not be classified into any other category.

Allocation to these categories was not always straightforward, and where papers spanned more than one area, consensus of the research team determined which domain the article would be placed in. Within each section of the report (i.e., Key articles, Recommended readings, Citation list) articles are presented in alphabetical order by author.

Endnotes

1   Australian Bureau of Statistics (2015). *Causes of death, Australia, 2013. Suicides.* Cat. no. 3303.0. Canberra: ABS.

Key Articles

Predicting suicidal behavior from longitudinal electronic health records

Barak-Corren Y, Castro VM, Javitt S, Hoffnagle AG, Dai Y, Perlis RH, Nock MK, Smoller JW, Reis BY (Australia)

American Journal of Psychiatry. Published online: 9 September 2016. doi: 10.1176/appi.ajp.2016.16010077

Objective: The purpose of this article was to determine whether longitudinal historical data, commonly available in electronic health record (EHR) systems, can be used to predict patients' future risk of suicidal behavior.

Method: Bayesian models were developed using a retrospective cohort approach. EHR data from a large health care database spanning 15 years (1998-2012) of inpatient and outpatient visits were used to predict future documented suicidal behavior (i.e. suicide attempt or death). Patients with three or more visits (N=1,728,549) were included. ICD-9-based case definition for suicidal behavior was derived by expert clinician consensus review of 2,700 narrative EHR notes (from 520 patients), supplemented by state death certificates. Model performance was evaluated retrospectively using an independent testing set.

Results: Among the study population, 1.2% (N=20,246) met the case definition for suicidal behavior. The model achieved sensitive (33%-45% sensitivity), specific (90%-95% specificity), and early (3-4 years in advance on average) prediction of patients' future suicidal behavior. The strongest predictors identified by the model included both well-known (e.g. substance abuse and psychiatric disorders) and less conventional (e.g. certain injuries and chronic conditions) risk factors, indicating that a data-driven approach can yield more comprehensive risk profiles.

Conclusions: Longitudinal EHR data, commonly available in clinical settings, can be useful for predicting future risk of suicidal behavior. This modeling approach could serve as an early warning system to help clinicians identify high-risk patients for further screening. By analyzing the full phenotypic breadth of the EHR, computerized risk screening approaches may enhance prediction beyond what is feasible for individual clinicians.

Comment

Main findings: There is currently no model for understanding how risk factors work together to cause suicidal behaviour. This poses a problem for clinicians as there is no single objective algorithm to help determine whether a patient will make a suicide attempt. Clinicians often use intuition as a result and this method is no better than chance at predicting suicidal behaviours. Therefore this study aimed to develop and test new models of suicide risk using large samples of longitudinal data from electronic health records (ERHs). Data were obtained from the Partners Healthcare Research Patient Data Registry, a warehouse of EHR data containing 4.6 million patients from two large academic medical centres in Boston, and community and specialty hospitals in the Boston area.

Two separate models were developed to account for gender differences to estimate a patient's risk for suicidal behaviour (i.e., a male and female model). These models included data on demographic characteristics, diagnostic codes, laboratory results and prescribed medications. For each independent input variable, a partial risk score was assigned based on the ratio of its prevalence among case subjects compared to control. Scores were positive (protective) if they were not associated with suicidal behaviour, and negative (adverse) if they had higher prevalence among cases compared to controls). There was a total of 1,728,549 patients who met the inclusion criteria of three or more visits, 30 days or more between the first and last visits, and the existence of records after age 10 and before age 90, with all demographic, diagnostic, procedure, laboratory and medical data recorded at each visit. However, due to lack of historical data and gender information, 3,764 patients were excluded. A final number of 16,588 case subjects and 1,708,197 control subjects were included in the modelling. Suicidal behaviour was defined according to ICD-9 diagnostic codes and death certificates from the Commonwealth of Massachusetts. In order to validate case definitions over 2,700 notes for 520 patients were reviewed to establish codes that accurately described suicide attempt cases.

Suicidal behaviour was more common among males than females (odds ratio: 1.75, 95% confidence interval [CI]=1.68-1.82). For both males and females, suicide cases were more likely to be Hispanic or African American. Moreover, for both males and females suicide cases, martial statuses such as separated, divorced or single were also more prevalent. Suicidal behaviour was more likely to occur in females under 25 years of age, while for males suicidal behaviours were more likely to occur in those aged 25-45 years. Results revealed that with 90% specificity (i.e., ability of a test to correctly identify those without suicidal behaviour) and 45% sensitivity (i.e., the ability of a test to correctly identify those with suicidal behaviour), these models detected 44% and 46% of the suicidal cases among men and women respectively, with an average of 3-4 years in advance. Moreover running the model by gender for specific age groups with 90% specificity improved prediction for narrower subpopulations, such as women ages 45-65 which achieved 54% sensitivity. In addition, results revealed that the model predicted suicidal behaviour an average of 4 years before the case-defining code was recorded in the EHR for 45% of cases at 90% specificity. When increasing specificity to 95%, the model predicted suicidal events an average of 3.5 years prior to diagnosis for 33% of cases identified by the model at this level.

Implications: When compared to clinician predictions based on an 18-point suicide assessment checklist, this EHR-based model was more successful in stratifying risk at 30-180 days. These findings suggest that the vast quantities of available longitudinal EHR data present a largely untapped opportunity for improving medical screening and diagnosis through the development of risk-stratification models. Nevertheless, the authors noted that this approach is designed as a screening tool for decision support rather than to give a specific prediction of suicide risk. They suggested that this tool should be used to create an alarm system so that when patients exceed thresholds of predicted risk, clinicians can conduct more targeted assessments of suicide risk to ensure safety of the patient. However, as this study only included patients that were screened for suicidal risk and in a relatively short time frame (3-4 years), these findings may not generalise to individuals who do not attend hospitals for suicidal behaviours or those with chronic suicidality. Thus future studies should aim to replicate this prediction model in an Australian setting in order to ensure generalisability, as well as applicability to the National Suicide Prevention Strategy[1]. This would help improve healthcare systems and provide tailored and timely care for those under psychiatric care for suicidal behaviours.

Endnotes

1. Department of Health (2016). National suicide prevention strategy. Retrieved 13 October 2016 from http://www.health.gov.au/internet/main/publishing.nsf/content/mental-nsps.

Sex and age trends in Australia's suicide rate over the last decade: Something is still seriously wrong with men in middle and late life

Burns RA (Australia)

Psychiatry Research 245, 224-229, 2016

Despite significant investment in mental health and suicide intervention strategies in Australia, the extent of change in suicide rates over the last decade is unclear. This paper analyses sex and age trajectories in suicide rates over the last decade in Australia. Age Standardized Suicide Rates from 2004 – 2013 were obtained from the Australian Bureau of Statistics and reflect rates of suicide per 100,000 within age and sex cohorts. Age-related suicide rates were consistent over the last decade. For both males and females, there were increases in mid-life suicide rates before declining around 55-65 years of age. However, rates of suicide in men increased in late-life with rates for those aged 70-79 comparable with those in mid-life. Rates amongst men aged 85+ were consistently the highest rates over the decade. Positively, there was decline in suicide rates among younger men aged 20-34 years. However, more consistently, for both sexes across most age cohorts, there were either increases or no change in suicide rate. Apart from declines in younger-adult males, analysis of age-standardized suicide rates indicate no improvement in suicide rates. High suicide rates amongst middle-aged and older males remain a significant public health issue that needs to be addressed.

Comment

Main findings: Despite the introduction of the Australian National Suicide Prevention Strategy (NSPS), there has been continued debate as to whether the strategies under the NSPS have been effective. Moreover, there has been little quantifiable examination of differences in suicide rates between age and sex cohorts over the last decade in Australia. Thus, this paper aimed to quantify the extent to which suicide rates have been moderated as a function of the NSPS. Specifically, age-cohort trends and sex differences in suicide rates over the last 10 years in Australia were analysed. Age standardised suicide rates from 2004-2014 were obtained from the Australian Bureau of Statistics. Analyses were also stratified by sex due to expected sex differences across life span.

Results showed that there was a general overall trend of increasing rates of suicide for men. The lowest rates of suicide were for the 15-19 year age group (10.67 per 100,000), with rates peaking at 35-39 years (24.79 per 100,000), 40-44 years (25.72 per 100,000) and 44-49 years (24.89 per 100,000), with the highest suicide rates among those aged 85+ (33.44 per 100,000). For females, suicide rates were substantially lower when compared to males, with the lowest rates at 15-19 years (4.73 per 100,000), with rates peaking at 35-39 years (7.20 per 100,000), 40-44 years (7.44 per 100,000), 45-49 years (7.04 per 100,000) and 50-54 years (7.41 per 100,000). Contrary to male suicide rates, these female suicide rates declined and became stable in the older age groups (4.20 to 5.35 per 100,000). Across the 10-year period, there were significant declines in suicide rates among younger males aged 20-24 (-0.48 per 100,000) and 30-34 (-0.80 per 100,000). However, there were no change in suicide rates for the other age groups, but rather a significant increase among those aged 50-54 (0.40 per 100,000) and 55-59 (0.66 per 100,000). Additionally, suicide rates for older males aged 85+ were the highest consistently over the last decade. Meanwhile for females there was no evidence for a decline in rates, with small increases in suicide rates for those aged 20-24 (0.23 per 100,000), 35-39 (0.18 per 100,000), 40-44 (0.29 per 100,000), 50-54 (0.26 per 100,000), 55-59 (0.26 per 100,000) and 85+ (0.34 per 100,000).

Implications: This study provides a clear picture of suicide trajectories in age-sex cohorts in Australia in the past 10 years. The increased availability of services and implementation of public mental health initiatives to reduce suicide across the nation[1,2] is not reflected in the relative stability or increase in suicide rates in different age cohorts for both males and females. This is especially evident in the observed 6-10 fold increase in suicide rates among middle-aged and older males compared to females, and the 2-3 fold increase among middle-aged and older male groups compared to those in their teens and those aged between 55-69 years. The author cautions against complacency regarding the low rates of suicide in females and highlight the need to emphasise that benefits to existing public health initiatives may impact less directly on these low suicide rates, but rather indirectly on suicide ideation and attempts, or general reduction in mental health burden. These findings suggest that there is an urgent need for suicide prevention activities to target males aged 35-54 and 70+ years of age. This is important as Australia's population is ageing due to both a large baby boomer cohort and increased life expectancy, increasing the proportion of population reaching older adulthood. The author noted that the decline among younger males could be a reflection of teenagers and younger adults being more aware of and more attuned to public health strategies[3]. However, for most age-sex cohorts, no improvement in suicides rate was observed. A significant limitation of this study was the method by which national suicide data are recorded and collated, which may be subject to errors due to misclassifications of death and differences between centres reporting deaths. These trends show alarming numbers and warrant further investigation into underlying factors (e.g., social, psychological and physical health factors) that contribute to these gender and age differences in suicide rates. It is also important to examine the underlying factors affecting these persistently high suicide rates among men. This will help address gaps and improve current strategies under NSPS to target those at risk.

Endnotes

1. Commonwealth Government (2010). *The Hidden Toll: Suicide in Australia. Report of the Senate Community Affairs Reference Committee.* Commonwealth of Australia: Canberra.
2. Department of Health and Ageing (2014). *Evaluation of Suicide Prevention Activities.* Commonwealth of Australia: Canberra.
3. Jorm AF (2009). Australian young people's awareness of headspace, beyondblue and other mental health organizations. *Australasian Psychiatry* 17, 472-474.

Variation between hospitals in inpatient admission practices for self-harm patients and its impact on repeat presentation

Carroll R, Corcoran P, Griffin E, Perry I, Arensman E, Gunnell D, Metcalfe C (Ireland)

Social Psychiatry and Psychiatric Epidemiology. Published online: 14 June 2016. doi: 10.1007/s00127-016-1247-y

Purpose: Self-harm patient management varies markedly between hospitals, with fourfold differences in the proportion of patients who are admitted to a medical or psychiatric inpatient bed. The current study aimed to investigate whether differences in admission practices are associated with patient outcomes (repeat self-harm) while accounting for differences in patient case mix.

Methods: Data came from the National Self-Harm Registry Ireland. A prospective cohort of 43,595 self-harm patients presenting to hospital between 2007 and 2012 were included. As well as conventional regression analysis, instrumental variable (IV) methods utilising between hospital differences in rates of hospital admission were used in an attempt to gain unbiased estimates of the association of admission with risk of repeat self-harm.

Results: The proportion of self-harm patients admitted to a medical bed varied from 10 to 74 % between hospitals. Conventional regression and IV analysis suggested medical admission was not associated with risk of repeat self-harm. Psychiatric inpatient admission was associated with an increased risk of repeat self-harm in both conventional and IV analyses. This increased risk persisted in analyses stratified by gender and when restricted to self-poisoning patients only.

Conclusions: No strong evidence was found to suggest medical admission reduces the risk of repeat self-harm. Models of health service provision that encourage prompt mental health assessment in the emergency department and avoid unnecessary medical admission of self-harm patients appear warranted. Psychiatric inpatient admission may be associated with a heightened risk of repeat self-harm in some patients, but these findings could be biased by residual confounding and require replication.

Comment

Main findings: There is limited evidence regarding the impact that hospitalisation has on self-harm. Some research suggests that hospital admission in itself has therapeutic benefits[1], whereas other research suggests that psychiatric admission may be associated with an increased risk of suicide[2]. The current study examined variations in hospital admission practices and their association with the risk of repeat self-harm following hospitalisation. Data were collected from the National Self-Harm Registry in Ireland which gathers information on people's hospital presentation following self-harm. Data were included for patients who first presented to hospital between 2007 and 2012, with follow-up data collected until the end of 2013. The registry recorded data on age, sex, method of self-harm, whether alcohol was used as part of the episode and the hospital of attendance. Information was also recorded on the aftercare following hospital presentation. This included data on whether a patient was admitted to a medical bed, admitted to a psychiatric inpatient bed, or not admitted. Data on presentations made by individuals under 16 years of age were excluded. The main exposures of interest were medical and psychiatric inpatient admission following treatment in the emergency department. The outcome variable of interest was repeat hospital attendance for self-harm within 12 months following their first presentation to hospital. Analyses were conducted using conventional regression analysis, as well as instrumental variable methods utilising between hospital differences in rates of hospital admission. Instrumental variable methods were used in an attempt to gain unbiased estimates of the association between hospital admission and risk of repeat self-harm.

A total of 43,595 people in Ireland presented to hospitals with self-harm during the study period. Intentional drug overdose was the most common self-harm method (67.9%), followed by self-cutting (14.4%). Other high lethality methods, including hanging and drowning made up 14.3% of cases, with the remainder using both intentional drug overdose and self-cutting (3.8%). Overall, 30.6% of patients were admitted to a medical bed compared to 9.3% admitted to a psychiatric inpatient bed. Repeat self-harm was present in 14.8% of the cohort within 12 months of their initial presentation to hospital. For patients admitted to a medical bed, self-harm repetition decreased in comparison to those not admitted, however this relationship was attenuated after controlling for potential confounding variables. There was a higher risk of repeat self-harm amongst those admitted to psychiatric inpatient beds (21.6%) versus those who were not (14.1%). This was the case even after controlling for potential confounding variables.

Implications: This study raises concerns as to the effectiveness and potential harm of hospital admission for self-injury. Medical admission not only fails to reduce self-harm but is also costly, with a United Kingdom study estimating that 112 extra patients would need to be medically admitted to avoid one repeat attendance[3]. This indicates a need for an alternative to medical admissions, such as psychosocial assessment and treatment. Psychiatric admission was also shown to increase the risk of repeat self-harm, with authors asserting that the circumstances and environment associated with psychiatric admission potentially leads to repeat self-harm. This study's methodological strengths were its large sample size and use of a prospective design. However, the study also had some limitations. The authors were unable to assess the impact that potential confounding variables such as psychiatric diagnoses had on repeat self-harm due to limited information. Information on whether a patient received a psychosocial assessment during their hospital presentation was also unavailable. This is problematic because previous studies have highlighted mental health assessment as a possible key intervention in terms of repeat self-harm[4].

Endnotes

1. Waterhouse J, Platt S (1990). General hospital admission in the management of parasuicide. A randomised controlled trial. *British Journal of Psychiatry* 156, 236–242.

2. Hjorthoj CR, Medsen T, Agerbo E, Nordentoft M (2014). Risk of suicide according to level of psychiatric treatment: A nationwide nested case-control study. *Social Psychiatry and Psychiatric Epidemiology* 49, 1357–1365.

3. Excellence NICE (2011). *Self-harm: Longer-term management costing report*. Department of Health, London: United Kingdom.

4. Bergen H, Hawton K, Waters K, Cooper J, Kapur N (2010). Psychosocial assessment and repetition of self-harm: The significance of single and multiple repeat episode analyses. *Journal of Affective Disorders* 127, 257–265. doi:10.1016/j.jad.2010.05.001.

Association between gun law reforms and intentional firearm deaths in Australia, 1979–2013

Chapman S, Alpers P, Jones M (Australia)
JAMA 316, 291-299, 2016

Importance: Rapid-fire weapons are often used by perpetrators in mass shooting incidents. In 1996 Australia introduced major gun law reforms that included a ban on semiautomatic rifles and pump-action shotguns and rifles and also initiated a program for buyback of firearms.

Objective: To determine whether enactment of the 1996 gun laws and buyback program were followed by changes in the incidence of mass firearm homicides and total firearm deaths.

Design: Observational study using Australian government statistics on deaths caused by firearms (1979-2013) and news reports of mass shootings in Australia (1979-May 2016). Changes in intentional firearm death rates were analyzed with negative binomial regression, and data on firearm-related mass killings were compared.

Exposures: Implementation of major national gun law reforms.

Main Outcomes and Measures: Changes in mass fatal shooting incidents (defined as ≥5 victims, not including the perpetrator) and in trends of rates of total firearm deaths, firearm homicides and suicides, and total homicides and suicides per 100,000 population.

Results: From 1979-1996 (before gun law reforms), 13 fatal mass shootings occurred in Australia, whereas from 1997 through May 2016 (after gun law reforms), no fatal mass shootings occurred. There was also significant change in the preexisting downward trends for rates of total firearm deaths prior to vs after gun law reform. From 1979-1996, the mean rate of total firearm deaths was 3.6 (95% CI, 3.3-3.9) per 100,000 population (average decline of 3% per year; annual trend, 0.970; 95% CI, 0.963-0.976), whereas from 1997-2013 (after gun law reforms), the mean rate of total firearm deaths was 1.2 (95% CI, 1.0-1.4) per 100,000 population (average decline of 4.9% per year; annual trend, 0.951; 95% CI, 0.940-0.962), with a ratio of trends in annual death rates of 0.981 (95% CI, 0.968-0.993). There was a statistically significant acceleration in the preexisting downward trend for firearm suicide (ratio of trends, 0.981; 95% CI, 0.970-0.993), but this was not statistically significant for firearm homicide (ratio of trends, 0.975; 95% CI, 0.949-1.001). From 1979-1996, the mean annual rate of total non-firearm suicide and homicide deaths was 10.6 (95% CI, 10.0-11.2) per 100,000 population (average increase of 2.1% per year; annual trend, 1.021; 95% CI, 1.016-1.026), whereas from 1997-2013, the mean annual rate was 11.8 (95% CI, 11.3-12.3) per 100,000 (average decline of 1.4% per year; annual trend, 0.986; 95% CI, 0.980-0.993), with a ratio of trends of 0.966 (95% CI, 0.958-0.973). There was no evidence of substitution of other lethal methods for suicides or homicides.

Conclusions and Relevance: Following enactment of gun law reforms in Australia in 1996, there were no mass firearm killings through May 2016. There was a more rapid decline in firearm deaths between 1997 and 2013 compared with before 1997 but also a decline in total nonfirearm suicide and homicide deaths of a greater magnitude. Because of this, it is not possible to determine whether the change in firearm deaths can be attributed to the gun law reforms.

Comment

Main findings: In 1996, Australia introduced extensive gun law reforms, including bans on the sale of rapid-fire long guns following the Port Arthur massacre. In the subsequent years mandatory buybacks of prohibited firearms, further prohibitions on weapons and large criminal penalties for possession of these weapons were also introduced. Since then no mass shootings have occurred in the years following these reforms[1]. In the current study the authors aimed to determine the broader impact of these reforms with regards to firearm-related deaths. Also of interest was the impact of the reforms on firearm suicide. Information pertaining to intentional (suicides and homicide) firearm deaths for the 1979-2013 period were obtained from the National Injury Surveillance Unit (which sources data from the Australian Bureau of Statistics). Population data representing person-years at risk of death were obtained from the Australian Bureau of Statistics (ABS) for the same period, and intentional firearm death rates per 100,000 were calculated. Firearm death rates for years (1979-1996) prior to gun reform were compared to the years following the reforms (1997-2013). Mortality rates in post reform years were also examined for all non-firearm homicides and suicides in order to determine whether other lethal means were substituted in place of guns.

Total firearm deaths decreased following the gun reforms, with annual firearm deaths falling from 3.6 per 100,000 in 1979-1996 to 1.2 per 100,000 in 1997-2013. Overall suicide (firearm and non-firearm) rates had been increasing by 1.0% per year prior to the gun reforms, but declined following their introduction by 1.5% per year between 1997-2013. Between 1979-2013 firearm suicides represented the largest component cause of total intentional firearm deaths in Australia (83.9%). In the 18 years between 1979- 1996 the mean annual rate of firearm suicide was 3.0 per 100,000, with this falling to 0.99 per 100,000 in the 17 years following the introduction of the reforms. Interestingly, firearm suicides had already been declining by an average of 3% per year prior to the reforms; however this decline accelerated to 4.8% per year following their implementation. Total non-firearm suicides had been increasing by 2.3% per year before the introduction of the gun control laws and then declined by 1.2% per year following their implementation. After the introduction of the 1996 gun laws the subsequent decline in suicide by firearms was not offset by substitution to other lethal means, or if there was substitution, it may have been into less lethal methods. For example, a previous examination of this decline in suicides in Australia concluded that much of it could be explained by changes towards the use of less fatal methods[2].

Implications: The authors concluded that in the 20 years since the gun law reforms and buyback programs, no mass shootings have occurred in Australia, and that there was a more rapid decline in total firearm deaths after gun law reforms than before the reforms. The prelaw reform decline in firearm suicides also increased significantly after the reforms. This has important implications for other jurisdictions with elevated rates of firearm suicide and it speaks to the need to maintain Australia's ban on rapid-fire long guns and other gun restrictions. However, the study is not without some limitations. The observational nature of the study restricts one from drawing causal inferences between the gun reform laws and reductions in firearm suicide as other explanations cannot be excluded. Data on accidental deaths were also not included because the number of those deaths as a proportion of total firearm deaths in Australia was small (<5%) and because the main intent of the 1996 gun reforms was to prevent mass shootings. The authors were unable to compare the validity of their findings to other studies because they were unaware of any other nations that had enacted such substantial changes in gun laws.

Endnotes

1. Chapman S, Alpers P, Agho K, Jones M (2006). Australia's 1996 gun law reforms: faster falls in firearm deaths, firearm suicides, and a decade without mass shootings. *Injury Prevention* 12, 365- 372.
2. Spittal MJ, Pirkis J, Miller M, Studdert DM (2012). Declines in the lethality of suicide attempts explain the decline in suicide death in Australia. *PLoS One* 7, e44565.

How does gatekeeper training improve suicide prevention for elderly people in nursing homes? A controlled study in 24 centres

Chauliac N, Brochard N, Payet C, Margue Y, Bordin P, Depraz P, Dumont A, Kroupa E, Pacaut-Troncin M, Polo P, Straub S, Boissin J, Burtin C, Montoya G, Rivière A, Didier C, Fournel C, Durand C, Barrellon M, Amigues O, Brosson A, Mahé E, Haxaire O, Bonnot C, Defaux M, Rougier D, Gaultier A, Gutierrez A, Pozo M, Lefèvre V, Nier A, Bolzan S, Liautaud M, Barbosa S, Garcia S, Anfreville A, Mazille S, Durantet C, Morlon M, Gaboriau C, Halbert C, Cholvy M, Milinkovich P, Martin L, Maury-Abello L, Toulier B, Kerleguer V, Gabriel S, Duclos A, Terra JL (France)

European Psychiatry 37, 56-62, 2016

Background: The death rate due to suicide in elderly people is particularly high. As part of suicide selective prevention measures for at-risk populations, the WHO recommends training "gatekeepers".

Methods: In order to assess the impact of gatekeeper training for members of staff, we carried out a controlled quasi-experimental study over the course of one year, comparing 12 nursing homes where at least 30% of the staff had undergone gatekeeper training with 12 nursing homes without trained staff. We collected data about the residents considered to be suicidal, their management further to being identified, as well as measures taken at nursing home level to prevent suicide.

Results: The two nursing home groups did not present significantly different characteristics. In the nursing homes with trained staff, the staff were deemed to be better prepared to approach suicidal individuals. The detection of suicidal residents relied more on the whole staff and less on the psychologist alone when compared to nursing homes without trained staff. A significantly larger number of measures were taken to manage suicidal residents in the trained nursing homes. Suicidal residents were more frequently referred to the psychologist. Trained nursing homes put in place significantly more suicide prevention measures at an institutional level.

Conclusions: Having trained gatekeepers has an impact not only for the trained individuals but also for the whole institution where they work, both in terms of managing suicidal residents and routine suicide prevention measures.

Comment

Main findings: Gatekeeper training is recognised internationally as an important measure in preventing elderly suicide[1] and has been implemented in many nursing homes. However to date no studies have investigated the impact this training has on the identification and management of suicidality in the elderly. As a result, the authors conducted a study examining the effect that gatekeeper training has on the management of suicidal crises (SC) in nursing homes. It compared trained nursing homes to untrained nursing homes in terms of the suicide prevention measures they implemented at an institutional level and their identification of suicidal individuals. A quasi-experimental intervention study was conducted across 24 nursing homes, with 12 receiving gatekeeper training and the other 12 receiving none. A total of 310 staff were trained across the nursing homes over nineteen 2-day sessions. This equated to a mean of 53% of staff receiving training across the 12 nursing homes. The authors collected data from nursing homes on a bi-monthly basis over a 12-month period. Data were collected on the following: staff competence regarding their approach to suicidal residents; detection of SC; management of SC; and nursing home suicide prevention measures. Both qualitative and quantitative data were collected. Staff competence was assessed using a self-report scale which measured the ability of staff to directly ask residents if they were having any suicidal ideas.

Preliminary analyses found that nursing home groups were similar in nature prior to the intervention, with no significant differences existing in terms of staff or nursing home characteristics (e.g., gender ratio, mean age of residents). When the authors assessed staff competence for the whole of staff, the mean competence score was 6.0 for trained nursing homes and 3.0 for untrained nursing homes ($p<0.001$). However, there was no significant difference between nursing homes in their ability to detect SC, with 36 SC detected in trained nursing homes and 33 in untrained nursing homes ($p = 0.14$). In untrained nursing homes over 20% of SC led to no specific suicide intervention measure being taken, whereas trained nursing homes took at least one suicide measure in all SC. This finding reflects an overall propensity of trained staff to utilise more suicide intervention measures, with trained nursing homes on average employing 2.7 measures compared to non-trained nursing homes employing 1.9 measures. For example, trained nursing home staff referred suicidal residents to psychologists more often. Furthermore, the trained nursing homes implemented more institutional suicide prevention measures during the course of the study. Overall, the authors found that gatekeeper training had an impact on the management of nursing homes even where only a proportion of the team received training.

Implications: The results of this study suggest that gatekeeper training is an effective tool for increasing nursing home staff competence, the use of suicide intervention measures and the implementation of suicide prevention measures across nursing homes. The findings align with WHO recommendations that gatekeeper training is an important tool for addressing suicide risk in elderly populations[1]. The attractiveness of gatekeeper training is further enhanced by its ease of use and relatively low cost to implement. The study found no difference between nursing home groups in their ability to identify suicidality in residents, possibly indicating that nursing home staff are already competent in doing this. It suggests that where gatekeeper training is implemented in nursing homes it is effective in improving staff responsiveness to SC and their feelings of competence. This study was not without some limitations. The nursing homes could not be randomly selected, and the researchers were not able to establish a baseline for judgement criteria before the study commenced. This limits the inferences one can draw regarding the actual efficacy of gatekeeper training in reducing suicidality.

Endnote

1. World Health Organization (2012). *Public health action for the prevention of suicide: A framework.* Retrieved 25 October 2016 from http://apps.who.int/iris/bitstream/10665/75166 /1/9789241503570 _eng.pdf?ua= 1.

Parental suicide attempt and offspring educational attainment during adolescence in the Avon Longitudinal Study of Parents and Children (ALSPAC) birth cohort

Geulayov G, Metcalfe C, Gunnell D (United Kingdom)
Psychological Medicine 40, 2097-2107, 2016

Background: Few studies have investigated the impact of parental suicide attempt (SA) on offspring outcomes other than mental health. We investigated the association of parental SA with offspring educational attainment in the Avon Longitudinal Study of Parents and Children (ALSPAC).

Method: Parental SA was prospectively recorded from pregnancy until the study children were 11 years old. National school test results (ages 11-16 years) were obtained by record linkage. Multilevel regression models quantified the association between parental SA and offspring outcomes.

Results: Data were available for 6667 mother-child and 3054 father-child pairs. Adolescents whose mothers had attempted suicide were less likely than their peers to achieve the expected educational level by age 14 years [adjusted odds ratio (aOR) 0.63, 95% confidence interval (CI) 0.41-0.95] in models controlling for relevant confounders, including parental education and depression. At age 16 years, adolescents whose mothers had attempted suicide were less likely to obtain the expected educational level (five or more qualifications at grade A*-C) (aOR 0.66, 95% CI 0.43-1.00) in models controlling for relevant confounders and parental education; however, after additionally controlling for maternal depression the results were consistent with chance (aOR 0.74, 95% CI 0.48-1.13). Findings in relation to paternal SA were consistent with those of maternal SA but power was limited due to lower response rate amongst fathers.

Conclusions: Maternal SA was associated with diminished educational performance at age 14 years. Educational attainment during adolescence can have substantial effect on future opportunities and well-being and these offspring may benefit from interventions.

Comment

Main findings: Research suggests that for every completed suicide there are at least 20 suicides attempts[1]. This means that every year a significant number of children are exposed to non-fatal suicidal acts by their parents. These children are said to be at an increased risk of psychopathology, particularly suicidal behaviours and affective disorders[2], but little is known about the impact of parental suicidal behaviours on other aspects of children's well-being. To date no research has directly investigated the impact that parental suicide attempts have on children's educational attainment over time. Therefore, the authors conducted a UK-based prospective cohort study examining the educational attainment of children following a parent's suicide attempt. Data were collected from mother-offspring and father-offspring dyads by questionnaire. Dyads were included in the study where they provided sufficient information regarding their suicide attempt. This led to 6667 mother-child and 3054 father-child dyads being included in the analysis. Parents were sent questionnaires on 10 separate occasions, from before the birth of their child and up until they were 11 years old. Parents who responded affirmatively to suicide attempt questions were categorised as suicide attempters and parents who responded negatively were classified as non-suicide attempters. Offspring educational attainment was examined using the KS3 and KS4 national assessment exercises, a series of tests which measure adolescent (ages 11-16 years) school performance. Potential confounding variables were also examined, including marital status during pregnancy, socioeconomic position, parental symptoms of depression, child ethnicity, child gender and the child's age when completing the respective key stages of the KS3 and KS4.

Results showed that children aged 14 years who were exposed to maternal suicide attempts were less likely than their peers to achieve the expected educational level by age 14 years. At age 16 years, adolescents whose mothers attempted suicide were less likely to obtain the expected educational level in models controlling for relevant confounders and parental education; however, after additionally controlling for maternal depression the results were consistent with chance. Findings were similar in relation to suicide attempts by fathers, however the smaller sample size meant that statistical evidence for the associations was weak.

Implications: This paper highlights the negative affect that maternal suicide has on educational attainment in children. Existing literature provides indirect support for this finding suggesting that exposure to parental psychopathology is associated with adverse developmental[3] and academic[4] outcomes. This study's strengths were its longitudinal design and use of an objective measure of offspring educational attainment. Information on parental suicide attempts was collected directly and repeatedly from parents, limiting potential recall bias. However, this paper did have several limitations. The study restricted its analyses to parents who responded to 70% or more of the information on suicide attempts across the 10 assessments. This conservative approach resulted in a participant sample of healthier and more socio-economically advantaged families, limiting the inferences one can draw from the study's findings to less socio-economically advantaged families. These findings suggest that treatments for maternal suicide attempts should consider not only the needs of the mother but also the needs of the child, particularly with respect to potential academic difficulties. Support services could help identify educational deficits in these children early on and where necessary provide educational interventions.

Endnote

1. World Health Organization (2014). Suicide prevention (SUPRE). Retrieved 14 September 2016 from http://www.who.int/mental_health/prevention/suicide/suicideprevent/en/
2. Geulayov G, Gunnell D, Holmen TL, Metcalfe C (2012). The association of parental fatal and non-fatal suicidal behaviour with offspring suicidal behaviour and depression: A systematic review and meta-analysis. *Psychological Medicine* 42, 1567–1580.
3. Grace SL, Evindar A, Stewart DE (2003). The effect of postpartum depression on child cognitive development and behavior: A review and critical analysis of the literature. *Archives of Women's Mental Health* 6, 263–274.
4. Murray L, Arteche A, Fearon P, Halligan S, Croudace T, Cooper P (2010). The effects of maternal postnatal depression and child sex on academic performance at age 16 years: A developmental approach. *Journal of Child Psychology and Psychiatry* 51, 1150–1159.

Psychosocial interventions for self-harm in adults

Hawton K, Witt KG, Taylor Salisbury TL, Arensman E, Gunnell D, Hazell P, Townsend E, van Heeringen K (United Kingdom)

Cochrane Database of Systematic Reviews 5, CD012189, 2016

Background: Self-harm (SH; intentional self-poisoning or self-injury) is common, often repeated, and associated with suicide. This is an update of a broader Cochrane review first published in 1998, previously updated in 1999, and now split into three separate reviews. This review focuses on psychosocial interventions in adults who engage in self-harm.

Objectives: To assess the effects of specific psychosocial treatments versus treatment as usual, enhanced usual care or other forms of psychological therapy, in adults following SH.

Search Methods: The Cochrane Depression, Anxiety and Neurosis Group (CCDAN) trials coordinator searched the CCDAN Clinical Trials Register (to 29 April 2015). This register includes relevant randomised controlled trials (RCTs) from: the Cochrane Library (all years), MEDLINE (1950 to date), EMBASE (1974 to date), and PsycINFO (1967 to date).

Selection Criteria: We included RCTs comparing psychosocial treatments with treatment as usual (TAU), enhanced usual care (EUC) or alternative treatments in adults with a recent (within six months) episode of SH resulting in presentation to clinical services.

Data Collection and Analysis: We used Cochrane's standard methodological procedures.

Main Results: We included 55 trials, with a total of 17,699 participants. Eighteen trials investigated cognitive-behavioural-based psychotherapy (CBT-based psychotherapy; comprising cognitive-behavioural, problem-solving therapy or both). Nine investigated interventions for multiple repetition of SH/probable personality disorder, comprising emotion-regulation group-based psychotherapy, mentalisation, and dialectical behaviour therapy (DBT). Four investigated case management, and 11 examined remote contact interventions (postcards, emergency cards, telephone contact). Most other interventions were evaluated in only single small trials of moderate to very low quality. There was a significant treatment effect for CBT-based psychotherapy compared to TAU at final follow-up in terms of fewer participants repeating SH (odds ratio (OR) 0.70, 95% confidence interval (CI) 0.55 to 0.88; number of studies k = 17; N = 2665; GRADE: low quality evidence), but with no reduction in frequency of SH (mean difference (MD) -0.21, 95% CI -0.68 to 0.26; k = 6; N = 594; GRADE: low quality). For interventions typically delivered to individuals with a history of multiple episodes of SH/probable personality disorder, group-based emotion-regulation psychotherapy and mentalisation were associated with significantly reduced repetition when compared to TAU: group-based emotion-regulation psychotherapy (OR 0.34, 95% CI 0.13 to 0.88; k = 2; N = 83; GRADE: low quality), mentalisation (OR 0.35,

95% CI 0.17 to 0.73; k = 1; N = 134; GRADE: moderate quality). Compared with TAU, dialectical behaviour therapy (DBT) showed a significant reduction in frequency of SH at final follow-up (MD -18.82, 95% CI -36.68 to -0.95; k = 3; N = 292; GRADE: low quality) but not in the proportion of individuals repeating SH (OR 0.57, 95% CI 0.21 to 1.59, k = 3; N = 247; GRADE: low quality). Compared with an alternative form of psychological therapy, DBT-oriented therapy was also associated with a significant treatment effect for repetition of SH at final follow-up (OR 0.05, 95% CI 0.00 to 0.49; k = 1; N = 24; GRADE: low quality). However, neither DBT vs 'treatment by expert' (OR 1.18, 95% CI 0.35 to 3.95; k = 1; N = 97; GRADE: very low quality) nor prolonged exposure DBT vs standard exposure DBT (OR 0.67, 95% CI 0.08 to 5.68; k = 1; N =18; GRADE: low quality) were associated with a significant reduction in repetition of SH. Case management was not associated with a significant reduction in repetition of SH at post intervention compared to either TAU or enhanced usual care (OR 0.78, 95% CI 0.47 to 1.30; k = 4; N = 1608; GRADE: moderate quality). Continuity of care by the same therapist vs a different therapist was also not associated with a significant treatment effect for repetition (OR 0.28, 95% CI 0.07 to 1.10; k = 1; N = 136; GRADE: very low quality). None of the following remote contact interventions were associated with fewer participants repeating SH compared with TAU: adherence enhancement (OR 0.57, 95% CI 0.32 to 1.02; k = 1; N = 391; GRADE: low quality), mixed multimodal interventions (comprising psychological therapy and remote contact-based interventions) (OR 0.98, 95% CI 0.68 to 1.43; k = 1 study; N = 684; GRADE: low quality), including a culturally adapted form of this intervention (OR 0.83, 95% CI 0.44 to 1.55; k = 1; N = 167; GRADE: low quality), postcards (OR 0.87, 95% CI 0.62 to 1.23; k = 4; N = 3277; GRADE: very low quality), emergency cards (OR 0.82, 95% CI 0.31 to 2.14; k = 2; N = 1039; GRADE: low quality), general practitioner's letter (OR 1.15, 95% CI 0.93 to 1.44; k = 1; N = 1932; GRADE: moderate quality), telephone contact (OR 0.74, 95% CI 0.42 to 1.32; k = 3; N = 840; GRADE: very low quality), and mobile telephone-based psychological therapy (OR not estimable due to zero cell counts; GRADE: low quality). None of the following mixed interventions were associated with reduced repetition of SH compared to either alternative forms of psychological therapy: interpersonal problem-solving skills training, behaviour therapy, home-based problem-solving therapy, long-term psychotherapy; or to TAU: provision of information and support, treatment for alcohol misuse, intensive inpatient and community treatment, general hospital admission, or intensive outpatient treatment. We had only limited evidence on whether the intervention had different effects in men and women. Data on adverse effects, other than planned outcomes relating to suicidal behaviour, were not reported.

Authors' Conclusions: CBT-based psychological therapy can result in fewer individuals repeating SH; however, the quality of this evidence, assessed using GRADE criteria, ranged between moderate and low. Dialectical behaviour therapy for people with multiple episodes of SH/probable personality disorder may lead to a reduction in frequency of SH, but this finding is based on low quality evidence. Case management and remote contact interventions did not appear to have any benefits in terms of reducing repetition of SH. Other therapeutic approaches were mostly evaluated in single trials of moderate to very low quality such that the evidence relating to these interventions is inconclusive.

Comment

Main findings: Self-harm (SH) includes intentional self-poisoning/overdose and self-injury, and is a major problem in many countries as it is strongly linked to suicide. It is important to investigate the effectiveness of interventions for SH patients, thus the aim of this review is to further evaluate the evidence for the effectiveness of psychosocial treatments for patients with SH. Randomised control trials of psychosocial interventions compared to treatment as usual for adults who had recently engaged in SH were reviewed. A total of 55 studies were found, including a total of 17,699 participants. Of these, 18 trials investigated cognitive-behavioural-based psychotherapy (CBT-based psychotherapy; comprising cognitive-behavioral, problem-solving therapy or both), nine investigated interventions for multiple repetition of SH/probable personality disorder, comprising emotion-regulation group-based psychotherapy, mentalisation, and dialectical behaviour therapy (DBT). Four examined case management, while 11 investigated remote contact interventions (post cards, emergency cards, telephone contact). The remaining thirteen interventions were evaluated in small single trials with only moderate to very low quality.

There was only moderate quality evidence to suggest that CBT-based psychotherapy compared to treatment as usual may help prevent SH repetition despite not reducing overall SH frequency. However, there was no clear evidence supporting the effectiveness of: prolonged exposure to DBT, case management, approaches to improve treatment adherence, mixed multimodal interventions, remote contact interventions, interpersonal problem-solving skills training, behaviour therapy, provision of information and support, treatment for alcohol misuse, home-based problem-solving therapy, intensive inpatient and community treatment, general hospital admission, intensive outpatient treatment or long-term psychotherapy compared to treatment as usual. Similarly, DBT for people with multiple episodes of SH was not associated with a significant reduction in SH repetition at final follow-up, however there was low quality evidence to suggest a reduction in frequency of SH.

Implications: These findings highlight the need for further research into psychotherapy for adults who SH. Despite results indicating that DBT and CBT-based psychotherapy may be effective in reducing future SH repetition, this is limited by the quality of evidence in these trials. The evidence as to whether the remaining interventions are effective is still inconclusive due to the low quality of evidence in the literature. Moreover, many trials were too small to detect significant differences in proportions of patients. Future research should aim to replicate randomised control trials of high quality with adequate sample sizes in order to conclusively examine the effectiveness of these interventions. This will shed more light on what effective treatments are available for SH patients. Another limitation highlighted was high risk of bias with respect to trial design, as not all trials blinded both participants and clinical personnel. However, it is generally not possible to blind participants or clinical personnel to psychological therapy. Therefore performance or detection bias cannot be ruled out. It is also possible that self-reported data might under or overestimate the occurrence of SH. In addition, there was imprecision in observed results, as indicated by the wide confidence intervals around the effect size estimates for many outcomes in this meta-analysis. The authors also concluded that there is a need for more information about which types of patients are most likely to benefit from CBT-based psychotherapy and other treatment approaches, and whether there are gender differences in the effectiveness of interventions. These findings may help inform the Australian and New Zealand Clinical Practice Guideline for the Management of Adult Deliberate Self-Harm[1] which was last updated in 2004.

Endnotes

1. Royal Australian and New Zealand College of Psychiatrists (2004). Australian and New Zealand clinical practice guideline for the management of adult deliberate self-harm. *Australian & New Zealand Journal of Psychiatry 38*, 868-884.

Suicide risk and absconding in psychiatric hospitals with and without open door policies: A 15 year, observational study

Huber CG, Schneeberger AR, Kowalinski E, Fröhlich D, von Felten S, Walter M, Zinkler M, Beine K, Heinz A, Borgwardt S, Lang UE (Switzerland, USA, Germany)

Lancet Psychiatry 3, 842-849, 2016

Background: Inpatient suicide and absconding of inpatients at risk of self-endangering behaviour are important challenges for all medical disciplines, particularly psychiatry. Patients at risk are often admitted to locked wards in psychiatric hospitals to prevent absconding, suicide attempts, and death by suicide. However, there is insufficient evidence that treatment on locked wards can effectively prevent these outcomes. We did this study to compare hospitals without locked wards and hospitals with locked wards and to establish whether hospital type has an effect on these outcomes.

Methods: In this 15 year, naturalistic observational study, we examined 349 574 admissions to 21 German psychiatric inpatient hospitals from Jan 1, 1998, to Dec 31, 2012. We used propensity score matching to select 145 738 cases for an analysis, which allowed for causal inference on the effect of ward type (ie, locked, partly locked, open, and day clinic wards) and hospital type (ie, hospitals with and without locked wards) on suicide, suicide attempts, and absconding (with and without return), despite the absence of an experimental design. We used generalised linear mixed-effects models to analyse the data.

Findings: In the 145 738 propensity score-matched cases, suicide (OR 1.326, 95% CI 0.803-2.113; p=0.24), suicide attempts (1.057, 0.787-1.412; p=0.71), and absconding with return (1.288, 0.874-1.929; p=0.21) and without return (1.090, 0.722-1.659; p=0.69) were not increased in hospitals with an open door policy. Compared with treatment on locked wards, treatment on open wards was associated with a decreased probability of suicide attempts (OR 0.658, 95% CI 0.504-0.864; p=0.003), absconding with return (0.629, 0.524-0.764; p<0.0001), and absconding without return (0.707, 0.546-0.925; p=0.01), but not completed suicide (0.823, 0.376-1.766; p=0.63).

Interpretation: Locked doors might not be able to prevent suicide and absconding.

Comment

Main findings: The main rationale for locking psychiatric wards is safety - to prevent completion of suicide and absconding with possible self-harm or harm to others after the patients have left the ward. However, no study has examined whether locked wards actually lead to a reduction in suicide and absconding compared with hospitals with an open-door policy. Thus, this study assessed the safety of locking psychiatric wards by investigating the occurrence of suicide, suicide attempts and absconding in 21 German hospitals with open-door or locked-door policies. This study compared the effect of hospital type (hospital with vs. hospital without locked wards) and ward type (locked vs partly locked, open or day clinic) on suicide occurrence, suicide attempts and absconding during psychiatric treatment. The inclusion criteria were treatment on locked, partly locked, open or day clinic wards in one of the 21 hospitals that gave consent to use of data within the period from 1 January 1998 to 31 December 2012. Of these, 16 hospitals had at least one locked ward (locked-door policy) during the entire study duration, while four had no locked wards during the whole study duration (open-door policy). One hospital had no locked wards at the beginning of the study period but introduced locked wards in 2000 for legal reasons. The final dataset comprised of 349,574 hospital admissions from 177,295 patients. The primary outcome was completed suicide, and secondary outcomes were suicide attempt during treatment, absconding with return and absconding without return. Patients were matched on their propensity score, which is their probability of having been admitted to a hospital with an open-door policy rather than a locked-door policy. This was to prevent potential confounds that may affect both the probability of relevant outcomes and the probability a case having been admitted to a specific hospital type. From 1998 to 2012 there were a total of 271,128 admissions to hospitals with locked-door policy and 78,446 admissions to hospitals with open-door policy. Pyschopharmacological medication (except benzodiapines) were more frequently used in hospitals without locked wards compared to patients in hospitals with locked wards. Moreover, patients admitted to open-door policy hospitals had a longer average treatment duration compared to locked-door policy hospitals (29.2 days vs. 26 days). There were no significant differences between hospitals with locked-door policy and hospitals with open-door policy on occurrence of death by suicide, suicide attempts and self-harm. However, in locked-door policy wards, absconding with return was more frequent than absconding without return. Additionally, ward type (i.e., between being treated on partly locked, open or day clinic ward vs. to being treated in closed-door policy ward) was not a significant predictor of death by suicide (OR 0.823, 95% CI 0.376-1.766; p=0.63). However, compared with being treated in a locked ward, being treated in an open ward was associated with significantly lower probability of suicide attempts (OR 0.658, 95% CI 0.504-0.864; p=0.003). Moreover, patients treated in open and day clinic wards had lower probability of absconding with return (OR 0.629, 95% CI 0.524-0.764; p<0.0001 and OR 0.166 95%CI 0.121-0.230, p<0.0001, respectively) and absconding without return (OR 0.707, 95% CI 0.546-0.925; p=0.01 and OR 0.089, 95% CI 0.046-0.171; p=0.0001, respectively).

Implications: Overall, these findings from this 15-year study showed that hospital type and ward type were not significant predictors of death by suicide, suicide attempt, absconding with return, or absconding without return. That is, securing doors in acute psychiatric care may not be sufficient to protect patients from suicide and suicide attempts, or in prevention of absconding. It is important to note that this large sample size may have produced significant differences even with minor differences (with questionable clinical relevance). For example, significant differences for substance use disorder 36.9% vs 36.2% in exploratory analyses. Therefore, these results should be interpreted with caution. The authors noted that absconding may occur due to restrictive ward climate, which may strengthen patients' motivation to abscond to regain personal freedom. They suggested that open and day clinics might counter their reduced ability to retain patients physically by providing an improved therapeutic atmosphere; for example, adapting day clinic settings to the needs of severely ill patients rather than referring to hospital wards. Future research should aim to replicate this study in Australia in order to ensure generalisability and application of these findings This may inform the National Suicide Prevention Strategy[1] as these findings challenge current practices in various states in Australia[2,3,4].

Endnotes

1. Department of Health (2016). *National Suicide Prevention Strategy*. Retrieved 8 October 2016 from http://www.health.gov.au/internet/main/publishing.nsf/content/mental-nsps.
2. NSW Department of Health (2004). *Framework for Suicide Risk Assessment and Management for NSW Health Staff.* Retrieved 8 October 2016 from http://www.health.nsw.gov.au/mental-health/programs/mh/Publications/mental-health-in-patient-unit.pdf.
3. Queensland Mental Health Commission (2013). Decision to lock Adult Acute Mental Health facilities in Queensland's public hospitals. Retrieved 8 October 2016 from https://www.qmhc.qld.gov.au/wp-content/uploads/2013/12/QMHC-statement-201213.pdf.
4. Health Department of Western Australia (1998). Guidelines for the construction, establishment and maintenance of private hospital and day procedure facilities. Retrieved 8 October 2016 from http://ww2.health.wa.gov.au/~/media/Files/Corporate/general%20documents/Licensing/PDF/Private%20Hospital%20Guidelines%20%201999.ashx.

Health workers' views of help seeking and suicide among Aboriginal people in rural Victoria

Isaacs AN, Sutton K, Hearn S, Wanganeen G, Dudgeon P (Australia)

Australian Journal of Rural Health. Published online: 14 April 2016. doi: 10.1111/ajr.12303

Objective: To explore Aboriginal health workers' views about help seeking and suicide.

Design: One-to-one semi-structured interviews were conducted with participants. Data were analysed thematically.

Setting: Njernda Aboriginal Corporation and the Yorta Yorta Aboriginal Community of Echuca, Victoria. *Participants*: Twenty seven participants (15 men and 12 women) over the age of 18 years were interviewed, of which 24 were Aboriginal workers employed by Njernda Aboriginal Corporation.

Results: Four themes emerged from the data: 'Difficulty in talking about one's problems'; 'Reasons for not talking with family and peers'; 'Lack of access to suitable formal supports' and 'Consequences of not talking about one's problems'.

Conclusion: This study unpacks the problem of help seeking for psychological distress among rural Aboriginal people and highlights its association with suicide and self-harm. The findings suggest that the barriers faced by Aboriginal people in sharing their traumatic emotions exist from childhood to older age groups and this inability to seek and obtain help can lead to self-harm and suicide. Similar studies on Aboriginal help seeking and suicide will help shed more light on this challenging issue.

Comment

Main findings: Australian and international studies demonstrate that Aboriginal people do not seek help prior to suicide[1,2]. This is problematic given that help-seeking facilitates many of the protective factors associated with suicide prevention, such as increased wellbeing and support. The current study explored the reasons for Aboriginal Australian suicide and minimal help-seeking from the prospective of Aboriginal health workers. The study was part of a larger Victorian Government pilot project which evaluated an Aboriginal suicide prevention program in Echuca. The authors adopted a participatory approach, where they spent 2-3 hours supporting Aboriginal project workers every three months during the course of the three year project. At completion of the project, health workers who were closely involved in the project were invited to participate in one-to-one semi-structured interviews. A total of 27 participants (15 men and 12 women) aged 18 years and older were interviewed, of which 24 were Aboriginal workers employed by Njernda Aboriginal Corporation. Aboriginal workers represented medical services, family and childcare services, social and emotional wellbeing services as well as justice and youth services. There was also a senior clinician from the local mental health service, a police officer and an Aboriginal Elder from the community. Participants were asked to reflect on why young people in their communities died by suicide, and were also provided the opportunity to share any personal experiences related to suicide or suicidal ideation. Interviews were recorded, transcribed and thematically analysed.

Four key themes emerged from the analysis: difficulty in talking about one's problems; reasons for not talking to family and peers; lack of access to suitable formal supports; and consequences of not talking about one's problems. Difficulty in talking about one's problems refers to the difficulties Aboriginal people face in sharing their problems with their peers. Participants reported that non-help seeking behaviour is learnt early in life, with children being taught to hold onto their problems and not share them. This socialisation inhibits an Aboriginal person's ability to share and discuss problems throughout their lives. Participants also indicated that Aboriginal people do not seek help even though they are aware their problems are shared by others. Non-help seeking was also prevalent among older people, with reports of some elders not seeking help even when experiencing abuse from their grandchildren or children. Reasons for not talking to family and peers also emerged as an important theme. Participants described a distinct fear amongst Aboriginal people that discussing one's problems could lead to negative social repercussions for both themselves and their families. Family members did not encourage problem sharing, with one participant stating "I wouldn't go and tell my family because they'd look down on me". Another reason given for non-help seeking is that Indigenous Australians perceive problem sharing to be a sign of weakness, particularly for men. The results also highlighted lack of access to suitable formal supports as a barrier to help seeking. It was reported that young people and adult men don't have access to appropriate people to safely share their problems with. Furthermore, even where Aboriginal people do seek help from mainstream services, these services are often unable to provide prompt assistance. Finally, the consequences Indigenous Australians face for not talking about their problems were also discussed. Participants asserted that non-help seeking leads to an increasing emotional burden (including intergenerational trauma) for Aboriginal people which could eventually lead to self-harm and suicide.

Implications: This paper describes the sociocultural and practical barriers to Aboriginal help seeking. It is one of the few papers that unpacks and describes the difficulties for Aboriginal people in sharing traumatic experiences, something which leads to psychological distress and potentially self-harm or suicide. Given the high Indigenous suicide rates in Australia[3], these findings should be used to inform the development of suicide prevention strategies that are socio-culturally appropriate. The paper was not without some limitations. Its anecdotal nature and small sample size restricts the conclusions that one can draw regarding the general Aboriginal population. It is also possible that not all communities will consider an inability to share traumatic experiences to be a matter that requires urgent attention. Therefore, suicide prevention measures need to be tailored according to the needs identified in each community. Future research should seek to identify these distinct community needs.

Endnote

1. Malchy B, Enns MW, Young TK, Cox BJ (1997). Suicide among Manitoba's aboriginal people, 1988 to 1994. *Canadian Medical Association Journal* 156, 1133–1138.

2. De Leo D, Milner A, Sveticic J (2012). Mental disorders and communication of intent to die in indigenous suicide cases, Queensland, Australia. *Suicide & Life-Threatening Behavior* 42, 136–146.

3. McHugh C, Campbell A, Chapman M, Balaratnasingam S (2016). Increasing Indigenous self-harm and suicide in the Kimberley: An audit of the 2005-2014 data. *Medical Journal of Australia 205*, 33.

Suicide methods in children and adolescents

Kõlves K, De Leo D (Australia)

European Child and Adolescent Psychiatry. Published online: 9 May 2016. doi: 10.1007/s00787-016-0865-y

There are notable differences in suicide methods between countries. The aim of this paper is to analyse and describe suicide methods in children and adolescents aged 10-19 years in different countries/territories worldwide. Suicide data by ICD-10 X codes were obtained from the WHO Mortality Database and population data from the World Bank. In total, 101 countries or territories, have data at least for 5 years in 2000-2009. Cluster analysis by suicide methods was performed for countries/territories with at least 10 suicide cases separately by gender (74 for males and 71 for females) in 2000-2009. The most frequent suicide method was hanging, followed by poisoning by pesticides for females and firearms for males. Cluster analyses of similarities in the country/territory level suicide method patterns by gender identified four clusters for both gender. Hanging and poisoning by pesticides defined the clusters of countries/territories by their suicide patterns in youth for both genders. In addition, a mixed method and a jumping from height cluster were identified for females and two mixed method clusters for males. A number of geographical similarities were observed. Overall, the patterns of suicide methods in children and adolescents reflect lethality, availability and acceptability of suicide means similarly to country specific patterns of all ages. Means restriction has very good potential in preventing youth suicides in different countries. It is also crucial to consider cognitive availability influenced by sensationalised media reporting and/or provision of technical details about specific methods.

Comment

Main findings: Despite suicide being a rare occurrence in children, it is still a leading cause of death in young people[1]. However, there are limited studies which analyse differences in suicide methods in young people between countries. Thus this paper aimed to analyse and describe suicide methods in children and adolescents aged 10-19 years in different countries worldwide. Suicide methods for the age group 10-19 years by gender were obtained from the WHO Mortality Database and population data from the World Bank. In total, 101 countries or territories that have data at least for 5 years in 2000-2009 were included. This yielded a total of 86,280 suicide cases. Cluster analysis by suicide methods was performed for countries/territories with at least 10 suicide cases separately by gender (74 for males and 71 for females) in 2000-2009. 14.7% of all suicide cases were in the 10-14 age group and 85.3% were in the 15-19 age group. Hanging was the most frequent suicide method for both age groups and genders (highest in males aged 10-14 years). Hanging was found to be the only method significantly more prevalent in the younger age group for both genders (OR = 2.31, 95% CI: 2.19-2.44 for males and OR=1.57, 95%CI: 1.48-1.68 for females). Cluster analysis revealed four clusters each for both genders. Clusters were defined by the suicide methods of hanging and poisoning by pesticides for both genders, a mixed method and a jumping from height cluster for females only and two mixed methods for males. Geographical similarities were also observed in the clusters.

Implications: The prevalence of hanging in country specific suicide rates and its prevalence in the age group 10-14 years may be due to the accessibility of such methods. For example, younger age groups may have limited access to means such as firearms, drugs, and pesticides in their households compared to the older group. Means restriction is therefore a potentially effective method of prevention. Nevertheless, a major limitation of this study is the unequal availability of data. While European and American countries use ICD-10 X codes to report deaths, Africa and particularly heavily populated Asian countries such as China and India do not. Thus, these results may have been biased, since countries were excluded if they were not able to provide data due to lack of death registrations systems, or did not report using ICD-10 X codes. It is also possible that the prevalence of suicide among younger age groups may be underreported as suicides are more likely to be recorded as accidental or undetermined for children and adolescents. Lastly, the authors noted that the media and internet may have had an influence in exposing children and adolescents to suicide methods[2]. Although suicide in children is a rare occurrence, future research should aim to further investigate suicide methods of children by country in order to inform specific countries on appropriate suicide prevention initiatives.

Endnotes

1. World Health Organization (2014). *Preventing suicide: A global imperative*. WHO, Geneva.
2. Dunlop SM, More E, Romer D (2011). Where do youth learn about suicides on the Internet, and what influence does this have on suicidal ideation? *Journal of Child Psychology and Psychiatry* 52, 1070-1080.

Meta-analysis of longitudinal cohort studies of suicide risk assessment among psychiatric patients: Heterogeneity in results and lack of improvement over time

Large M, Kaneson M, Myles N, Myles H, Gunaratne P, Ryan C (Australia)

PLoS One 11, e0156322, 2016

Objective: It is widely assumed that the clinical care of psychiatric patients can be guided by estimates of suicide risk and by using patient characteristics to define a group of high-risk patients. However, the statistical strength and reliability of suicide risk categorization is unknown. Our objective was to investigate the odds of suicide in high-risk compared to lower-risk categories and the suicide rates in high-risk and lower-risk groups.

Method: We located longitudinal cohort studies where psychiatric patients or people who had made suicide attempts were stratified into high-risk and lower-risk groups for suicide with suicide mortality as the outcome by searching for peer reviewed publications indexed in PubMed or PsychINFO. Electronic searches were supplemented by hand searching of included studies and relevant review articles. Two authors independently extracted data regarding effect size, study population and study design from 53 samples of risk-assessed patients reported in 37 studies.

Results: The pooled odds of suicide among high-risk patients compared to lower-risk patients calculated by random effects meta-analysis was of 4.84 (95% Confidence Interval (CI) 3.79-6.20). Between-study heterogeneity was very high (I2 = 93.3). There was no evidence that more recent studies had greater statistical strength than older studies. Over an average follow up period of 63 months the proportion of suicides among the high-risk patients was 5.5% and was 0.9% among lower-risk patients. The meta-analytically derived sensitivity and specificity of a high-risk categorization were 56% and 79% respectively. There was evidence of publication bias in favour of studies that inflated the pooled odds of suicide in high-risk patients.

Conclusions: The strength of suicide risk categorizations based on the presence of multiple risk factors does not greatly exceed the association between individual suicide risk factors and suicide. A statistically strong and reliable method to usefully distinguish patients with a high-risk of suicide remains elusive.

Comment

Main findings: It is generally assumed that those presenting to psychiatric services should undergo a suicide risk assessment in order to identify high-risk patients to receive close monitoring, and whether more clinical resources should be offered. However, there is some controversy of whether it is clinically meaningful to categorise individuals as high suicide risk. This meta-analysis aimed to calculate overall strength of the effect size of suicide risk assessment of suicide in high risk groups compared to lower-risk groups. It was hypothesised that the effect size associated with suicide risk assessment would: 1) be reliable between studies and resulting in low between study heterogeneity, and 2) have improved over time with stronger results in more recent studies. Studies were included if they reported on longitudinal cohorts of psychiatric patients; measured patient factors at baseline (either in a validation study of a suicide risk scale or in an exploratory study of multiple variables); reported subsequent death by suicide as the outcome variable; and used two or more variables other than age and sex to define a high suicide risk group. Studies were excluded if they were retrospective case controlled; reported suicide attempts as the outcome variable; examined general populations rather than patient groups; did not describe a high-risk group, or described a high-risk group on the basis of single characteristic or solely demographic characteristics, or examined potential biological markers (due to the focus on clinical practice). Reporting strength was also assessed using six variables: whether the study was a validation study; the study was drawn from a defined catchment area; the suicides were obtained using mortality databases/coronial findings; the study did not exclusively report inpatient suicides; the study had a length of follow up that was greater than the median length of follow up; the study reported more suicides than the median number of suicides reported. Any study that included any of these characteristics was awarded one point, allowing each study to be awarded a maximum of six points.

A total of 37 relevant studies was included, with a sample of 315,309 persons, of which 3,114 died by suicide. Eighteen studies recruited patients in a psychiatric treatment setting and 19 studies included patients who presented after suicide attempts and/or episodes of self-harm. Of these 53 tests of suicide risk categorisation, 24 were validation studies (those that determine risk categories through the use of scales) and 29 were exploration studies (those that combine potential risk factors observed at baseline to develop a post-hoc risk model based on eventual suicide at follow-up). Analyses of pooled odds of suicide in high risk suicide groups was 4.84 compared to the lower risk groups, indicating a strong effect size. There was evidence of publication bias for studies reporting a stronger association between high risk strata and suicide; however, the publication date was not significantly associated with the effect size of the 53 samples. The pooled sensitivity of high-risk categorisation was 56%, indicating that just over half of the suicides occurred in the high-risk groups. Meanwhile the pooled sensitivity of lower-risk categorisation was 79%, whereby four in five of the survivors were in the low risk group. In addition, the pooled estimate for the crude suicide rate in the high-risk group was 5.5%, compared to 0.9% in the low-risk group. Validation and exploratory studies reported similar pooled effect sizes, with both very high between-study heterogeneity. Studies including general psychiatric patients and studies of patients who were recruited after a suicide attempt or an episode of deliberate self-harm had a similar effect size. Moreover, studies with a reporting strength of four or more had a similar effect size to studies with lower strength reporting scores.

Implications: This is one of the first studies to investigate the relationship between categorising high-risk patients and death by suicide in a large and representative body of research over the past 40 years. These findings show that there was no difference between studies that used more variables to define high-risk categories compared to those who had less. The finding that heterogeneity in effect size could not be explained by year suggests a lack of improvement over 40 years in the ability of published models to identify high-risk groups of patients. Although the authors noted that this does not mean that such developments are impossible. Nevertheless there were several limitations in this study. First, these results cannot be generalisable as the between-study heterogeneity was not well explained by the predetermined moderator variables, or measures of reporting strength. Second, there may be publication biases in favour of studies reporting stronger association between high-risk and suicide. Third, the large sample sizes pooled together to estimate the effect size may have inflated the significance. Finally, the design of this study is a meta-analysis and therefore studies which greatly differed on sample size and methodology were included. The authors noted that the value of risk categorisation should be judged by whether it can actually contribute to a reduction in patient suicides. Further investigation into reliable methods to clearly distinguish between high-risk from lower-risk patients are warranted. These could then be used in combination with other innovative methods of predicting suicidal behaviour (e.g., predicting suicidal behaviour from longitudinal electronic health records)[1] in order to ensure that those at high risk are adequately cared for.

Endnotes

1. Barak-Corren MS, Castro VM, Javitt, S, ... Reis BY (2016). Predicting suicidal behaviour from longitudinal electronic health records. *American Journal of Psychiatry.* doi: 10.1176/appi.ajp.2016.16010077.

Improving prediction of suicide and accidental death after discharge from general hospitals with natural language processing

McCoy TH, Jr. Castro VM, Roberson AM, Snapper LA, Perlis RH (USA)

JAMA Psychiatry 73, 1064-1071, 2016

Importance: Suicide represents the 10th leading cause of death across age groups in the United States (12.6 cases per 100000) and remains challenging to predict. While many individuals who die by suicide are seen by physicians before their attempt, they may not seek psychiatric care.

Objective: To determine the extent to which incorporating natural language processing of narrative discharge notes improves stratification of risk for death by suicide after medical or surgical hospital discharge.

Design, Setting, and Participants: In this retrospective health care use study, clinical data were analyzed from individuals with discharges from 2 large academic medical centers between January 1, 2005, and December 31, 2013.

Main Outcomes and Measures: The primary outcome was suicide as a reported cause of death based on Massachusetts Department of Public Health records. Regression models for prediction of death by suicide or accidental death were compared relying solely on coded clinical data and those using natural language processing of hospital discharge notes.

Results: There were 845417 hospital discharges represented in the cohort, including 458053 unique individuals. Overall, all-cause mortality was 18% during 9 years, and the median follow-up was 5.2 years. The cohort included 235 (0.1%) who died by suicide during 2.4 million patient-years of follow-up. Positive valence reflected in narrative notes was associated with a 30% reduction in risk for suicide in models adjusted for coded sociodemographic and clinical features (hazard ratio, 0.70; 95% CI, 0.58-0.85; P < .001) and improved model fit (chi22 = 14.843, P < .001 by log-likelihood test). The C statistic was 0.741 (95% CI, 0.738-0.744) for models of suicide with or without inclusion of accidental death.

Conclusions and Relevance: Multiple clinical features available at hospital discharge identified a cohort of individuals at substantially increased risk for suicide. Greater positive valence expressed in narrative discharge summaries was associated with substantially diminished risk. Automated tools to aid clinicians in evaluating these risks may assist in identifying high-risk individuals.

Comment

Main findings: Epidemiological studies provide insight into demographic characteristics, symptoms or diagnoses associated with suicide risk, while other small-scale studies show certain biomarkers or psychosocial features associated with high-risk individuals. The optimal time for risk-stratification and interventions is post-hospital discharge because this period constitutes elevated risks for suicide and risk events. Previous research by the authors has shown that using a natural language processing method, which aggregates words conveying positive or negative emotion (valence) has improved prediction of all-cause mortality and hospital admission[1]. Therefore this study aimed to determine whether incorporating natural language processing of narrative discharge notes will improve stratification of risk for death by suicide after medical or surgical hospital discharge. A curated list of 3,000 subjectively valence-conveying terms was used. For example, positive valence terms include glad, pleasant and lovely, while negative terms included gloomy, unfortunate and sad. Each word had a polarity score (negative to positive scored as -1 to 1) and a subjectivity score (not subjective to subjective scored as 0 and 1). Post-discharge narrative notes were scored based on the mean value for all recognised valence terms after accounting for preceding negations (e.g., to distinguish happy from not happy). The primary outcome was suicide as cause of death; however, as some suicides may be misclassified as accidental death, these were also included as a secondary composite outcome. Two regression models were generated for the analyses. The first model used only coded clinical data including age, sex, self-reported ethnicity, recent health care use and overall medical morbidity. The second model included all clinical data from the first model in addition to aggregated measures of positive and negative valence (natural language processing method).

There were a total of 845,417 hospital discharges represented in the cohort, with 458,053 unique individuals. Of the total cohort, 2,026 individuals died by either suicide or accidental death during follow-up. This included 712 people in the first year of follow-up and 178 within the first 30 days after discharge. In model 1, greater suicide risk was associated with white ethnicity, male gender and more emergency department visits and psychiatric outpatient visits 12 months prior admission. Inclusion of accidental deaths yielded similar coefficients across the two outcomes definitions, except for age, and comorbidity index. This suggests accidental deaths were disproportionally affecting that older and sicker patients rather than misclassified suicide. In model 2, which included natural language processing, positive valence was associated with the lower suicide risk (hazard ratio: 0.70, 95% CI: 0.58-0.85). That is, a 1 standard deviation increase was associated in a reduction of 30% in risk for suicide. Addition of the valence feature into the model of composite outcome improved fit whereby, a 1 standard deviation increase was associated with 20% in risk (hazard ratio: 0.80, 95% CI: 0.75-0.85). Thus, an intervention targeting the top 50% of risk could prevent up to 78% of suicides or accidental deaths, while an intervention targeting the highest-risk quartile could prevent up to 52%.

Implications: This is one of the first studies to investigate post-discharge risk among large nonpsychiatric cohorts. These findings suggest that the addition of natural language process adds predictive value when modelling suicide risk. Moreover, these narrative notes are readily collected post-discharge in a patients' electronic health record, and are able to identify re-admissions. It is important to develop risk identification models in order to successfully intervene when patients are most at-risk. Nevertheless, it must be noted that cause of death was not reported for some patients and therefore misclassification of death cannot be ruled out and may have affected these results. Moreover, clinician-level features in discharge notes were not examined due to the fact that there are multiple admitting and discharging physicians. Despite these limitations, these findings show that this approach is a feasible and cost-effective way to improve stratification of risk for death by suicide after hospital discharge. The authors suggested that under a population management strategy, scores could be generated for each patient, and those with the highest-risk should be targeted for follow-up telephone calls, letters to primary care practice, or office visit to reassess risk and assist with psychiatric referral if needed. These findings should be replicated in an Australian setting to ensure generalisability. This would allow for tailoring of intervention to the needs of the patient, which is in line with the LIFE framework[2] in Australia.

Endnotes

1. McCoy TH, Castro VM, Cagan A, Roberson AM, Kohane IS, Perlis RH (2015). Sentiment measured in hospital discharge notes is associated with readmission and mortality risk: An electronic health record study. *PloS One* 10, e0136341.
2. Department of Health and Ageing (2007). A framework for prevention of suicide in Australia. Retrieved 8 October 2016 from http://www.livingisforeveryone.com.au/uploads/docs /LIFE_framework-web.pdf.

Dialectical behavior therapy compared with enhanced usual care for adolescents with repeated suicidal and self-harming behavior: Outcomes over a one-year follow-up

Mehlum L, Ramberg M, Tormoen AJ, Haga E, Diep LM, Stanley BH, Miller AL, Sund AM, Groholt B (Norway)

Journal of the American Academy of Child Adolescent Psychiatry 55, 295-300, 2016

Objective: We conducted a 1-year prospective follow-up study of posttreatment clinical outcomes in adolescents with recent and repetitive self-harm who had been randomly allocated to receive 19 weeks of either dialectical behavior therapy adapted for adolescents (DBT-A) or enhanced usual care (EUC) at community child and adolescent psychiatric outpatient clinics.

Method: Assessments of self-harm, suicidal ideation, depression, hopelessness, borderline symptoms, and global level of functioning were made at the end of the 19-week treatment period and at follow-up 1 year later. Altogether 75 of the 77 (97%) adolescents participated at both time points. Frequencies of hospitalizations, emergency department visits and other use of mental health care during the 1-year follow-up period were recorded. Change analyses were performed using mixed effects linear spline regression and mixed effect Poisson regression with robust variance.

Results: Over the 52-week follow-up period, DBT-A remained superior to EUC in reducing the frequency of self-harm. For other outcomes such as suicidal ideation, hopelessness, and depressive or borderline symptoms and for the global level of functioning, inter-group differences apparent at the 19-week assessment were no longer observed, mainly due to participants in the EUC group having significantly improved on these dimensions over the follow-up year, whereas DBT-A participants remained unchanged.

Conclusion: A stronger long-term reduction in self-harm and a more rapid recovery in suicidal ideation, depression, and borderline symptoms suggest that DBT-A may be a favorable treatment alternative for adolescents with repetitive self-harming behavior.

Comment

Main findings: Self-harm is a strong predictor of completed suicide in adolescents, particularly in those who have a pattern of repetitive self-harm[1]. It is therefore surprising that until recently there have been no randomized-controlled trials (RCTs) examining the effectiveness of self-harm treatments for adolescents. An RCT recently examined the efficacy of dialectical behaviour therapy (DBT), which is a type of cognitive-behavioural therapy designed to treat self-harm and suicidality. In this study DBT adapted for adolescents (DBT-A) was found to be superior to enhanced usual care (EUC) in reducing participants' self-harm frequency, severity of suicidal ideations and depressive symptoms[2]. The current study follows up this RCT, evaluating the efficacy of DBT one year after treatment.

As in the original study, frequency of suicidal and self-harm episodes, severity of depressive symptoms and suicidal ideation were used as the primary outcome measures. In addition, measures of psychiatric symptoms, use of health care services, borderline pathology and overall functioning were also included.

Of the 77 original RCT participants who had a mean age of 15.6 and were mostly female (88.3%), 75 participated in the one year follow-up evaluation. Inclusion criteria for the original RCT were fluency in Norwegian; a history of at least 2 episodes of self-harm, with 1 episode occurring in last 16 weeks; and at least 2 criteria of DSM-IV borderline personality disorder, or alternatively at least 1 criterion and a minimum of 2 subthreshold-level criteria. Participants were randomly assigned to either the DBT-A or EUC conditions to receive 19 weeks of treatment. Treatment was provided free of charge by therapists working at 10 publicly funded child and adolescent psychiatric outpatient clinics. Participants were assessed through interviews and self-report measures at 19 and 71 weeks (one year follow-up). Participants were assessed by independent interviewers blinded to treatment allocation at the one year follow up. There were no differences between the treatment groups in baseline demographic variables, diagnoses or pre-treatment suicidal or non-suicidal self-harm behaviours.

At both 19 weeks post-treatment and one year follow-up participants in the DBT-A group had significantly fewer self-harm episodes than EUC participants, with DBT-A participants reporting an average of 9 (95% CI = 4.8–13.2) episodes of self-harm at 19 weeks and 5.5 (95% CI = 1.7–9.1) episodes at the one year follow-up. Whereas, EUC participants reported an average of 22.5 (95% CI = 11.4–33.5) self-harm episodes at 19 weeks and 14.8 (95% CI = 7.3–22.3) episodes at the one year follow-up. For suicidal ideation, DBT-A participants had significantly lower ideation levels at 19 weeks compared to EUC, however at the one year follow-up improvements in the EUC group eliminated these between-group differences. This pattern of results was repeated for measures of depression, hopelessness, borderline symptoms and general level of functioning, with DBT-A participants performing significantly better than EUC participants at 19 weeks, although these differences were no longer significant at the one year follow-up.

Implications: This study suggests that DBT-A appears to be superior to EUC, in long-term reduction of self-harm, and more rapid clinical improvements in suicidal ideation, depression, and borderline symptoms. Given its effectiveness, DBT-A stands out as the intervention of choice for treating self-harm and suicidality in adolescents. The implementation of programs using DBT-A could form a part of a response to both the Queensland Government's mental health action plan[3] and the Australian Government's mental health review[4]. The study was not without its limitations. The small sample size means that findings should be interpreted with some caution. Furthermore, like most self-harm trials, the patient sample was predominately female, meaning that gender differences in treatment outcomes could not be examined. Among the study's strengths are the prospective follow-up design, the application of rigorous procedures for data collection, the use of standardised instruments and a very high follow-up rate.

Endnotes

1. Madge N, Hewitt A, Hawton K, Wilde EJD, Corcoran P, Fekete S, van Heeringen K, De Leo D, Ystgaard M (2008). Deliberate self-harm within an international community sample of young people: comparative findings from the Child and Adolescent Self-harm in Europe (CASE) Study. *Journal of Child Psychology Psychiatry* 49, 667-677.

2. Mehlum L, Tormoen AJ, Ramberg M, Haga H, Diep LM, Laberg S, Larsson BS, Stanley BH, Miller, AL, Sund AM, Groholt B (2014). Dialectical behavior therapy for adolescents with repeated suicidal and self-harming behavior: A randomized trial. *Journal of American Academy of Child & Adolescent Psychiatry* 53, 1082-1091.

3. Queensland Mental Health Commission (2015). *Queensland Suicide Prevention Action Plan 2015-17*. Retrieved 28 April 2016 from https://www.qmhc.qld.gov.au/wp-content/uploads/2015/09/Queensland-Suicide-Prevention-Action-Plan-2015-17_WEB.pdf.

4. Department of Health (2015). *Australian government response to contributing lives, thriving communities – review of mental health programmes and services*. Retrieved 27 May 2016 from http://www.health.gov.au/internet/main/publishing.nsf/Content/0DBEF2D78F7CB9E7CA257F07001ACC6D/$File/response.pdf.

Suicide by health professionals: A retrospective mortality study in Australia, 2001-2012

Milner AJ, Maheen H, Bismark MM, Spittal MJ (Australia)
Medical Journal of Australia 205, 260-265, 2016

Objectives: To report age-standardised rates and methods of suicide by health professionals, and to compare these with suicide rates for other occupations.

Study Design: Retrospective mortality study.

Setting, Participants: All intentional self-harm cases recorded by the National Coronial Information System during the period 2001-2012 were initially included. Cases were excluded if the person was unemployed at the time of death, if their employment status was unknown or occupational information was missing, or if they were under 20 years of age at the time of death. Suicide rates were calculated using Australian Bureau of Statistics population-level data from the 2006 census.

Main Outcome Measures: Suicide rates and method of suicide by occupational group.

Results: Suicide rates for female health professionals were higher than for women in other occupations (medical practitioners: incidence rate ratio [IRR], 2.52; 95% CI, 1.55-4.09; P < 0.001; nurses and midwives: IRR, 2.65; 95% CI, 2.22-3.15; P < 0.001). Suicide rates for male medical practitioners were not significantly higher than for other occupations, but the suicide rate for male nurses and midwives was significantly higher than for men working outside the health professions (IRR, 1.50; 95% CI 1.12-2.01; P = 0.006). The suicide rate for health professionals with ready access to prescription medications was higher than for those in health professions without such access or in non-health professional occupations. The most frequent method of suicide used by health professionals was self-poisoning.

Conclusion: Our results indicate the need for targeted prevention of suicide by health professionals.

Comment

Main findings: Previous research has identified elevated rates of suicidal ideation and death by suicide among certain groups of health professionals including nurses, doctors and dentists. In Australia, research on suicide by health professionals has only been conducted in Queensland, Therefore, this study investigated health professional suicide deaths nationally from 2001 to 2012. This study aimed to compare suicide deaths between health professionals and other occupations; examine whether female health professionals had higher suicide rates than their male colleagues and examine the effect of occupational access to prescription medicines (i.e., registered professions whose members are legally allowed to prescribe, supply or administer prescription medication compared to those who do not have access). Suicide cases were obtained using the National Coronial Information System. Individuals who were employed adults with a known occupation aged at least 20 years old at time of death were included. Occupations were divided into two broad groups: health professions (e.g., medical practitioners, midwifery and nursing professionals, other health professions such as health diagnostic and promotion professions, pharmacists, optometrists, physiotherapists, occupational therapists and psychologists) and all other professions. Health professions were not included if they were community and personal service workers (e.g., paramedics and Indigenous health workers).

A total of 9,828 suicides were identified in Australia during the 12-year period by employed adults aged 20-70 years. Of these, 369 were suicide deaths of health professionals. The age-standardised suicide rate for male medical practitioners was 14.8 per 100,000 person-years and 22.7 per 100,000 for male nurses and midwives. The rate for men in non-health occupations was 14.9 per 100,000. Among females, age-standardised suicide rates for health professionals was 6.4 per 100,000 for medical practitioners, 8.2 per 100,000 for midwives and nurses, and 4.5 per 100,000 for other health professionals. Meanwhile the rate in non-health occupations was 2.8 per 100,000. Hanging was least common method of suicide in doctors (24%), nurses and midwives (28%) compared to other non-health professionals (48%) and other health professionals (43%). Self-poisoning was more common in doctors (51%), and nurses and midwives (40%) compared to other occupations. Further analyses revealed a significantly higher suicide rate for males working as nurses and midwives compared to men in other non-health occupations (IRR: 1.50, p=0.006). Meanwhile, the suicide rate for male "other health professionals" was lower than for men in non-health care occupations (IRR: 0.75, p=0.061). For females, doctors (IRR: 2.52, p<0.001) and nurses or midwives (IRR: 2.65, p<0.001) were associated with significantly higher suicide rates than for women in non-health care occupations. Additionally, suicide rates among health care professions with ready access to prescription medication were 1.62 times higher than that for health professionals without access (p<0.001).

Implications: This is the first national study to analyse suicide deaths in health professionals in Australia. These findings indicate that access to prescription medication as a lethal means is a risk factor for suicide by health professionals. Moreover, the authors suggested that gender-related stressors may also play a role in contributing to these deaths. For example, some male nurses experience anxiety about the perceived stigma associated with their non-traditional career choice, while female professionals may feel pressure to fulfil child care and household roles. Moreover, previous research has shown that work-related stressors such as experiencing trauma vicariously through their patients and families, and psychosocial work stressors (e.g., long working hours, high job demands, fear of making mistakes at work) may also be risk factors for suicide[1]. However, a number of limitations should be noted, such as the possibility of underreporting and misclassification of deaths. Moreover, only those who had a known occupation at time of death were included, thus these results may be only generalisable to only those who were working at the time of death. In addition, this study did not investigate reasons as to why these suicide rates differ between occupations and genders, therefore further studies are warranted to explore specific stressors and risk factors. This knowledge could help inform targeted suicide prevention activities for vulnerable individuals, which is in line with the Australia's National Suicide Prevention Strategy[2]. The higher rates of suicide for those occupations with access to prescription medication suggest that methods of monitoring and regulating access should be explored since means restriction is an effective preventative method[3].

Endnotes

1. Milner A, Spittal MJ, Pirkis J, Chastang J-F, Niedhammer I, LaMontagne A (2016). Low control and high demands at work as risk factors for suicide: An Australian national population-level case control study. *Psychosomatic Medicine*. doi: 10.1097/PSY.0000000000000389.

2. Department of Health (2014). *National Suicide Prevention Strategy.* Retrieved 6 October 2016 from http://www.health.gov.au/internet/publications/publishing.nsf/Content/suicide-prevention-activities-evaluation~background~national-suicide-prevention-strategy.

3. Yip P, Caine E, Yousuf S, Chang S, Wu K, Chen, Y (2012). Means restriction for suicide prevention. *Lancet* 379, 2393-2399.

Psychosocial working conditions and suicide ideation: Evidence from a cross-sectional survey of working Australians

Milner A, Page K, Witt K, LaMontagne A (Australia)

Journal of Occupational & Environmental Medicine 58, 584-587, 2016

Objectives: This study examined the relationship between psychosocial working factors such as job control, job demands, job insecurity, supervisor support, and workplace bullying as risk factors for suicide ideation.

Methods: We used a logistic analytic approach to assess risk factors for thoughts of suicide in a cross-sectional sample of working Australians. Potential predictors included psychosocial job stressors (described above); we also controlled for age, gender, occupational skill level, and psychological distress.

Results: We found that workplace bullying or harassment was associated with 1.54 greater odds of suicide ideation (95% confidence interval 1.64 to 2.05) in the model including psychological distress. Results also suggest that higher job control and security were associated with lower odds of suicide ideation.

Conclusions: These results suggest the need for organizational level intervention to address psychosocial job stressors, including bullying.

Comment

Main findings: Research indicates that both psychosocial job stressors and workplace bullying are linked to poor mental health outcomes[1]. However, limited research has examined the impact of psychosocial stressors and workplace bullying on suicidal ideation, particularly in the Australian context. Therefore, the authors examined this relationship utilising a cross-sectional survey. The survey consisted of structured telephone interviews conducted with a nationally representative sample of Australia's working population. Survey questions pertained to experiences of bullying and harassment at work, psychosocial working conditions (job control, job insecurity, social support, job demands) and suicidal thoughts (i.e., thoughts or plans about suicide). Bullying questions included physical, sexual and verbal abuse, as well as intimidation. Potential confounding variables were also examined, including: relationship status, age, gender, occupational skill level and psychological distress. The authors recognised that psychological distress could act as both a cause and a result of suicidal ideation and therefore conducted analyses with this variable both included and not included.

Nine hundred and thirty-two participants were included in the analysis. Logistic regression was utilised to examine the relationship between psychosocial job stressors and suicidal thoughts, controlling for other variables. When adjusting for psychological distress, higher job control (OR 0.99, 95% CI 0.98 to 1.00, p = 0.036) and security (OR 1.01, 95% CI 1.00 to 1.02, p = 0.041) was found to be associated with lower odds of suicidal ideation, however the size of these relationships were quite small. Bullying was shown to increase the odds of suicidal intent by 1.54 (95% CI 1.16 to 2.05) when adjusting for psychological distress and

1.94 (95% CI 1.50 to 2.50) when not adjusting for it. Ordinary least square regression analyses found that low supervisor support, high job demands and high job insecurity were all predictive of bullying.

Implications: This is one of the first studies to investigate the impact of psychological stressors and bullying on suicidal ideation in the Australian workplace. The link between workplace bullying and suicide ideation is particularly concerning given that suicidal ideation increases one's odds of future suicide attempts[2]. These findings highlight the need for workplace interventions that reduce bullying, such as organisational level initiatives which target the environmental and structural factors that are predictive of bullying[3]. This paper has several limitations. It is possible that the study's relatively small sample size hindered the ability to observe statistically significant effects. The study's cross-sectional design also limits the causal inferences one can draw from the findings, particularly regarding the direction of the relationship between the exposure variables and suicide ideation. Future research is clearly needed to explain the relationship between working environments, psychosocial job stressors and suicide, in order to inform future prevention efforts.

Endnote

1. Takada M, Suzuki A, Shima S, Inoue K, Kazukawa S, Hojoh M (2009). Associations between lifestyle factors, working environment, depressive symptoms and suicidal ideation: A large-scale study in Japan. *Industrial Health* 47, 649–655.

2. Miranda R, Ortin A, Scott M, Shaffer D (2014). Characteristics of suicidal ideation that predict the transition to future suicide attempts in adolescents. *Journal of Child Psychology and Psychiatry* 55, 1288–1296.

3. Vartia M, Leka S (2011). Interventions for the prevention and management of bullying at work. In S Einarsen, H Hoel, D Zapf, CL Cooper (Eds.), *Bullying and Harassment in the Workplace: Developments in Theory, Research, and Practice* (pp.359-380). Boca Raton, FL: CRC Press.

Low control and high demands at work as risk factors for suicide: An Australian national population-level case-control study

Milner A, Spittal MJ, Pirkis J, Chastang J-F, Niedhammer I, Lamontagne AD (Australia)

Psychosomatic Medicine. Published online: 31 August 2016. doi: 10.1097/PSY.0000000000000389

Objectives: Previous research suggests that psychosocial job stressors may be plausible risk factors for suicide. This study assessed the relationship between psychosocial job stressors and suicide mortality across the Australian population.

Methods: We developed a job exposure matrix to objectively measure job stressors across the working population. Suicide data came from a nationwide coronial register. Living controls were selected from a nationally representative cohort study. Incidence density sampling was used to ensure that controls were sampled at the time of death of each case. The period of observation for both cases and controls was 2001 to 2012. We used multilevel logistic regression to assess the odds of suicide in relation to 2 psychosocial job stressors (job control and job demands), after matching for age, sex, and year of death/survey and adjusting for socioeconomic status.

Results: Across 9,010 cases and 14,007 matched controls, our results suggest that low job control (odds ratio [OR], 1.35; 95% confidence interval [CI], 1.26-1.44; p <.001) and high job demands (OR, 1.36; 95% CI, 1.26-1.46; p <.001) were associated with increased odds of male suicide after adjusting for socioeconomic status. High demands were associated with lower odds of female suicide (OR, 0.81; 95% CI, 0.72-0.92; p =.002).

Conclusions: It seems that adverse experiences at work are a risk factor for male suicide while not being associated with an elevated risk among females. Future studies on job stressors and suicide are needed, both to further understand the biobehavioral mechanisms explaining the link between job stress and suicide, and to inform targeted prevention initiatives.

Comment

Main findings: Despite a number of studies demonstrating the adverse effects of job stressors on mental health, there is a lack of systematically available exposure information on psychosocial job stressors (such as low job control, high psychological demands) in death records. The current study developed a job exposure matrix (JEM) to assess the relationship between psychosocial job stressors and suicide mortality across the Australian population. The JEM, which was designed to objectively measure psychosocial job stressors, was comprised of occupation (rows) and exposure to job stressors (columns). Suicide data were obtained from the National Coroners Information System (NCIS), and controls were obtained from the Household, Income and Labour Dynamics in Australia cohort. Data from 2001 to 2012 was analysed using multilevel logistic regression in order to determine the odds of suicide in relation to psychosocial job stressors (job control and job demands). Suicide deaths were matched with controls on age, sex, year of death/year of survey taken and socioeconomic status.

A total of 9,010 cases and 14,007 controls were included in this study. Results revealed that 63.7% of the suicide cases were exposed to low job control, compared to 59.7% in the control group, and 75.6% of suicide cases were exposed to high job demands compared to 71% of controls. In addition, suicide cases were more likely to be employed as technical or trade workers or machinery operators or drivers, but less likely to be employed as professionals, in clerical and administrative jobs, or as sales workers. The first sensitivity analysis revealed that there were no significant differences in the relationship between psychosocial job stressors for case patients and controls for female cases after adjusting for occupational skill and SES. Meanwhile the male cases had higher odds than controls of being exposed to low job control (OR 1.24; 95% CI 1.14-1.34, p<.001) and high psychological demands (OR 1.33; 95% CI, 1.23-1.45; p <.001). The second sensitivity analyses using a continuous job stressor variable indicated no significant effects for job control for both sexes (males OR: 1.00, 95% CI, 0.98-1.02; p=0.938, females OR: 1.00, 95% CI, 0.97-1.03; p=0.956). However, higher psychological demands were associated with significantly higher odds of suicide for males (OR 1.10; 95% CI, 1.07-1.14; p <.001), and conversely, with lower odds of suicide for women (OR 0.96; 95% CI, 0.94-0.97; p<.001).

Implications: This is one of the first studies to analyse a whole working population in a country. Thus, these findings are generalisable across all occupations in Australia. Moreover a strength of this study is the use of an objective measure of psychological job stressors, calculated using a JEM specifically designed for the same country context that the suicide data are drawn from. Psychological job stressors were found to be significant risk factors for male suicide but associated with lower risk of suicide for women in Australia. However, the authors noted that this may have been due to the greater number of suicides in the male groups compared to the female groups. Moreover, it is possible that other pressures outside of the workplace may be more important to females (e.g., family/home). For example, previous research investigating suicide in female nurses found that a combination of stress at home and work was associated with the greatest suicide risk[1]. Future studies should aim to understand the relationship between adverse work factors and suicide. One limitation is that this study only measured two psychosocial job stressors (control and demands) and thus the impact of other work stressors (e.g., bullying) in combination with control and demands are unknown. It should also be noted that occupations and suicide deaths may have been misreported in police reports or miscoded by the research team, which may have occurred due to the use of a structured approach to classification. These findings are important as they can inform workplace directed prevention strategies that specifically target males and take their working conditions into account.

Endnotes

1. Feskanich D, Hastrup JL, Marshall JR, Colditz GA, Stampfer MJ, Willett WC, Kawachi I (2002). Stress and suicide in the Nurses' Health Study. *Journal of Epidemiology and Community Health* 56, 95-98.

Stimulating community action for suicide prevention: Findings on the effectiveness of the Australian R U OK? Campaign

Mok K, Donovan R, Hocking B, Maher B, Lewis R, Pirkis J (Australia)

International Journal of Mental Health Promotion 18, 213-221, 2016

R U OK? is an Australian-based organisation that aims to prevent suicide by empowering and encouraging community members to have regular, meaningful conversations with those around them by asking, 'Are you ok?' One of the organisation's main activities is 'R U OK? Day', a national day of action held in Australia every year to remind people of the importance of connecting with and supporting those around them who may be troubled. This paper primarily examines data from a 2014 Australia-wide population survey evaluating the effectiveness of the R U OK? campaign in promoting its message. Following R U OK? Day in 2014, approximately two-thirds of participants reported being aware of R U OK?, with one in five of these participating in R U OK? Day activities. Overall, people believed that the R U OK? campaign has a positive impact on people's willingness to talk to others about their problems and seek professional help, and in reducing the stigma associated with help-seeking. The findings were positive, but future work should also investigate outcomes such as knowledge, stigma and help-seeking in order to demonstrate the efficacy of the campaign.

Comment

Main findings: R U OK? day has expanded its activities to promote its message, including providing resources and tips for connecting with someone in various settings (i.e., classroom, workplace). There are three main strategic goals in this campaign: 1) proving the value of meaningful conversation in helping someone who is struggling and building peoples' capacity to meaningfully connect with those around them; 2) getting people to commit to having these conversations; and 3) inspiring people to actually have these conversations regularly. This study aimed to assess the effectiveness of R U OK? campaign in promoting its message, specifically the public's awareness of, participation in, and perceptions of the value and impact of R U OK? campaign.

Data were obtained from an annual cross-sectional survey conducted across Australia through online survey companies' databases. The annual survey included questions about awareness of R U OK?, participation in R U OK? Day and perceptions of R U OK? However, survey content differed across years, reflecting the continuing development of R U OK?'s activities and goals. A total of 2,000 participants completed the 2014 post-campaign survey (female=1013, male=987). Over half (65.7%) of the sample reported having heard of R U OK? Day, which was an increase from 28% of awareness for R U OK? Day in 2010. There was a significantly higher proportion of females aware of the campaign compared to males (p<0.001). Those aged 16-24 had significantly higher awareness while those aged 65+ had significantly lower awareness. Moreover, 81.7% of those who selected R U OK? as an organisation associated this campaign with encouraging people to talk about things that are troubling them, and 58.8% associated R U OK? with suicide prevention. There were no significant differences in participation in R U OK? day across gender. However those aged 25-34 reported significantly higher rates of participation and those aged 65+ reported significantly lower levels of participation. The most common type of activities participated in were: 1) asking if others were ok face-to-face (56.4%); 2) asking if others were ok via online messaging (22.4%); 3) asking if others were ok using SMS messaging (21.2%); 4) asking if others were ok through telephone (17.6%); and 5) asking if others were ok on email (11.6%). The perceived impact of the campaign was generally positive, as the majority of those aware of the campaign believed that it has made people more willing to ask their friends about their struggles, while 20.3% thought it made no difference and 20.9% did not know. Meanwhile 47.1% believed it made people more willing to share their troubles if asked, 25.4% thought it made no difference and 26.4% did not know. Nearly half (41%) of the participants also believed that this campaign made people more willing to seek professional for their troubles. Negative unintended effects were very low, with a minority of participants believing the campaign made people less willing to ask their friends about their problems.

Implications: The gender differences in R U OK? awareness suggests that future campaigns should aim to develop and tailor campaigns according to their target audience. For example, men are less willing to seek-help for both mental and physical illnesses[1]. What is most concerning is that those aged 65+ reported lowest levels of awareness and lower levels of participation compared to other age groups, given that suicide rates are highest among that those aged 85 years and over[2]. However, this may be due to the fact that there are lower rates of Internet use among older adults[3] which may limit their exposure to the campaign, as well as the ability to contact friends online to ask if they 'are ok'. The authors suggested that it may be effective to target those who are most likely to come into contact with this older age group such as GPs. Together, these findings suggest that different marketing strategies should be used for different age groups and gender. Nevertheless, a few limitations must be noted. First, participants may not be representative of the Australian population since this survey was distributed online, and thus only those with Internet access were able to participate. Moreover, although surveys have been conducted annually, changes across years were difficult to ascertain due to differences in survey content in previous years. It is important to continually improve public health campaigns that aim to reduce risk factors and enhance protective factors across the entire population, which aligns with the recommendations of Australia's National Suicide Prevention Strategy[4].

Endnotes

1. Galdas PM, Cheater F, Marshal P (2005). Men and health help-seeking behaviour: Literature review. *Journal of Advanced Nursing* 49, 616-623.

2. Australian Bureau of Statistics (2015). Causes of Death, Australia, 2015. Cat No. 3303.0. Retrieved 14 October from http://www.abs.gov.au/ausstats/abs@.nsf/Lookup/by%20Subject/ 3303.0~2015~Main%20Features~Intentional%20self-harm:%20key%20characteristics~8.

3. Zickuhr K, Madden M (2012). *Older adults and internet use. Pew Internet & American Life Project.* Retrieved 14 October 2016 from http://www.pewinternet.org/files/old-media/Files/Reports/2012/PIP_Older_adults_and_internet_use.pdf.

4. Department of Health (2014). *National Suicide Prevention Strategy.* Retrieved 6 October 2016 from http://www.health.gov.au/internet/publications/publishing.nsf/Content/suicide-prevention-activities-evaluation~background~national-suicide-prevention-strategy.

Who goes online for suicide-related reasons?

Mok K, Jorm AF, Pirkis J (Australia)
Crisis 36, 112-120, 2016.

Background: Although people who use the Internet for suicide-related reasons have been found to report significantly higher levels of suicidal ideation, little is known about the characteristics of these users.

Aims: To examine the differences between suicidal people who use the Internet for suicide-related reasons and those who do not.

Method: Participants were 205 Australian citizens and permanent residents aged 18–24 years who had felt suicidal within the past year. Participants were recruited online through non-mental health-related websites and asked to complete an anonymous online survey.

Results: In univariate analyses, suicide-related users reported significantly higher levels of social anxiety and lifetime and past year suicidal ideation than non-suicide-related users, as well as a higher likelihood of future suicide and overall higher risk for suicide. There were no differences on depressive symptoms and perceived social support. Both groups were unlikely to anticipate seeking help from any source and generally perceived similar barriers to offline help-seeking. Multivariate analyses showed that past year suicidal ideation and likelihood of future suicide significantly predicted suicide-related Internet use.

Conclusions: Individuals may choose to go online for alternative methods of coping when their suicidal feelings become more severe, demonstrating the need for more online suicide prevention efforts.

Comment

Main findings: Previous research has examined the potential impact of Internet on suicide. For example, some studies have investigated the impact of pro-suicide websites as they may be used to facilitate or encourage suicidal behaviour. Although there is a growing body of literature investigating the impact of suicide-related Internet use, research is yet to be done on the characteristics of the users themselves, which may assist our understanding of the impact of the Internet on suicide[1]. This study aimed to explore the differences between suicidal people who go online for suicide-related reasons and suicidal people who do not go online for suicide-related reasons in order to examine the factors associated with suicide-related Internet use. The two groups were also compared on measures of depressive symptoms, suicide risk, perceived social support, social anxiety, anticipated help-seeking behaviours and perceived barriers to offline help-seeking. Data were collected through an online survey which was not advertised on mental health or suicide-related websites to ensure that both suicide-related and non-suicide-related users were recruited. To avoid potential confounds due to factors such as age and culture, the sample was limited to Australian citizens and permanent residents aged 18-24 years who had felt suicidal within the past year. Participants were categorised as suicide-related Internet users if they had gone online for suicide-related reasons within the past year.

A total of 205 eligible participants were recruited (156 females, 45 males, and 4 other gender), the mean age was 20.17 years. There were 102 suicide-related users and 103 non-suicide related users, and these groups did not differ on any of the sociodemographic variables. This sample reported moderate levels of suicide ideation and perceived social support, and were unlikely to report that they had disclosed their suicidal thoughts to others. Between group analyses revealed that suicide-related users reported significantly more lifetime suicidal ideation and attempts, past year suicidal ideation, a higher likelihood of future suicide and an overall higher risk for suicide. Additionally, suicide-related users also reported higher levels of social anxiety. No significant differences were found on depressive symptoms or perceived social support. Meanwhile suicide-related users scored significantly higher on all online help-seeking sources, and also scored significantly lower on the likelihood of seeking help from a friend, minister or religious leader. Both groups perceived similar barriers to help-seeking, with the most common being preference to deal with issues on their own, questioning how serious their needs are, not knowing what to say about their problems and worrying about what others would think of them. Non-suicide related users reported one help-seeking barrier significantly more than suicide-related users (i.e., "I worry my actions will be documented in my academic record"). There were no significant differences in the remaining barriers between the two groups.

Implications: These results of this study showed no significant differences between suicide-related Internet users and non-suicide-related Internet users on measures of depressive symptoms and perceived social support. Despite results indicating that both groups are unlikely to seek help from any source suicide-related users were more likely to consider seeking help from all of the online sources. This suggests that the Internet may be particularly useful for targeting this population for interventions. However, since data were collected through an online survey and a convenience sample (mostly university students), the generalisability of these results may be limited. Thus, future research should aim to examine this relationship in a wider and more general population in order to generalise these findings and inform suicide prevention initiatives on a higher level. Moreover, it was unclear whether suicide-related users were seeking help or motivated by potentially harmful reasons such as looking for suicide methods. A recent review revealed that there are only two professional online-based interventions that significantly reduce suicidal thoughts[2]. Thus further research into the characteristics of suicide-related Internet users and their online behaviours would be useful in informing Australia's current suicide prevention strategy[3]. The authors also noted that online suicide prevention should be targeted toward both individuals looking for help and individuals looking to die by suicide.

Endnotes

1. Bell V (2007). Online information, extreme communities and internet therapy: is the internet good for our mental health? *Journal of Mental Health* 16, 445-457.

2. Mok K, Jorm AF, Pirkis J (2015). Suicide-related Internet use: A review. *Australian and New Zealand Journal of Psychiatry, 49*(8), 697–705.

3. Department of Health (2015). *Australian government response to contributing lives, thriving communities – review of mental health programmes and services.* Retrieved 15 August 2016 from http://www.health.gov.au/internet/main/publishing.nsf/Content/0DBEF2D78F7CB9E7CA257F07001ACC6D/$File/response.pdf.

Short-term suicide risk after psychiatric hospital discharge

Olfson M, Wall M, Wang S, Crystal S, Liu SM, Gerhard T, Blanco C (USA)

JAMA Psychiatry. Published online: 21 September 2016. doi: 10.1001/jamapsychiatry.2016.2035

Importance: Although psychiatric inpatients are recognized to be at increased risk for suicide immediately after hospital discharge, little is known about the extent to which their short-term suicide risk varies across groups with major psychiatric disorders.

Objective: To describe the risk for suicide during the 90 days after hospital discharge for adults with first-listed diagnoses of depressive disorder, bipolar disorder, schizophrenia, substance use disorder, and other mental disorders in relation to inpatients with diagnoses of nonmental disorders and the general population.

Design, Setting, and Participants: This national retrospective longitudinal cohort included inpatients aged 18 to 64 years in the Medicaid program who were discharged with a first-listed diagnosis of a mental disorder (depressive disorder, bipolar disorder, schizophrenia, substance use disorder, and other mental disorder) and a 10% random sample of inpatients with diagnoses of nonmental disorders. The cohort included 770643 adults in the mental disorder cohort, 1090551 adults in the nonmental disorder cohort, and 370 deaths from suicide from January 1, 2001, to December 31, 2007. Data were analyzed from March 5, 2015, to June 6, 2016.

Main Outcomes and Measures: Suicide rates per 100000 person-years were determined for each study group during the 90 days after hospital discharge and the demographically matched US general population. Adjusted hazard ratios (ARHs) of short-term suicide after hospital discharge were also estimated by Cox proportional hazards regression models. Information on suicide as a cause of death was obtained from the National Death Index.

Results: In the overall population of 1861194 adults (27% men; 73% women; mean [SD] age, 35.4 [13.1] years), suicide rates for the cohorts with depressive disorder (235.1 per 100000 person-years), bipolar disorder (216.0 per 100000 person-years), schizophrenia (168.3 per 100000 person-years), substance use disorder (116.5 per 100000 person-years), and other mental disorders (160.4 per 100000 person-years) were substantially higher than corresponding rates for the cohort with nonmental disorders (11.6 per 100000 person-years) or the US general population (14.2 per 100000 person-years). Among the cohort with mental disorders, AHRs of suicide were associated with inpatient diagnosis of depressive disorder (AHR, 2.0; 95% CI, 1.4-2.8; reference cohort, substance use disorder), an outpatient diagnosis of schizophrenia (AHR, 1.6; 95% CI, 1.1-2.2), an outpatient diagnosis of bipolar disorder (AHR, 1.6; 95% CI, 1.2-2.1), and an absence of any outpatient health care in the 6 months preceding hospital admission (AHR, 1.7; 95% CI, 1.2-2.5).

Conclusions and Relevance: After psychiatric hospital discharge, adults with complex psychopathologic disorders with prominent depressive features, especially patients who are not tied into a system of health care, appear to have a particularly high short-term risk for suicide.

Comment

Main findings: Approximately one-third of all suicides among psychiatric patients occur within the three months following their discharge from an inpatient psychiatric unit[1]. Whilst research has investigated this short-term risk in the context of individual psychiatric disorders, little is known about the relative risk of suicide across groups with major psychiatric disorders. Therefore, the authors examined suicide risk during the 90 days following hospital discharge for a cohort of patients with psychiatric disorders. Information was collected from the National Medicaid Analytic database for the 1 January 2001 to 31 December 2007 period. Patients aged 18-64 years who had been admitted to hospital from one to 30 days were selected. Patients were partitioned into groups based on their first listed psychiatric diagnosis. These were depressive disorder, bipolar disorder, schizophrenia, substance use disorder, other mental health disorders and non-mental health disorders. A sample of patients with nonmental health disorders served as the comparison group. The primary outcome measure was suicide within 90 days of hospital discharge.

The study consisted of 1,861,194 adults (27% men, 73% female), of which 770,643 were from the mental health cohorts and 1,090,551 were from the nonmental health cohorts. The 90 day suicide rate for the mental health group was 178.3 per 100,000 person-years, whereas the suicide rate for the non-mental health group was 11.6 per 100,000 person-years. This equates to mental health patients being 15.4 times more likely to die by suicide in the short term than nonmental health patients. Suicide rates were shown to be the highest for depressed patients (235.1 per 100 000 person-years), followed by bipolar patients (216 per 100,000 person-years), schizophrenic patients (168.3 per 100,000 person-years), those with other mental disorders (160.4 per 100,000 person-years) and patients with substance use disorders (116.5 per 100,000 person-years). The overall 90-day suicide rate was nearly twice as high for men compared to women in the mental illness cohort, and approximately four times as high for men than for women in the nonmental disorder cohort. Furthermore, young adults aged 18-34 years with mental health disorders were at the greatest risk of short-term suicide. Other risk factors for short-term suicide included an absence of outpatient health care in the six months prior to hospital admission, a high number of outpatient visits in the six months before admission, and a recent history of deliberate self-harm.

Implications: The results of this study highlight the elevated suicide risk facing psychiatric patients immediately following their discharge from hospital. Depression in particular was shown to be a significant risk factor, a finding which aligns with prior research on suicide risk factors[2,3]. These findings have serious implications for the elevated suicide risk for psychiatric patients if prematurely discharged from hospital. However, given the financial pressures being placed on hospitals to shorten inpatient stays, inpatient psychiatrists commonly face clinical uncertainties in determining when patients are no longer at short-term risk of suicide. This study must be interpreted in light of its limitations. The study only reports on suicide mortality data for the 2001-2007 period, and did not include young or elderly psychiatric patients, potentially limiting its relevance in assessing current suicide trends. In addition, the authors did not have the means to validate the accuracy of the first-listed diagnoses of mental disorders from the Medicaid data.

Endnote

1. Huisman A, Kerkhof AJ, Robben PB (2011). Suicides in users of mental health care services: treatment characteristics and hindsight reflections. *Suicide and Life-Threatening Behavior* 41, 41-49.
2. Mann JJ, Waternaux C, Haas GL, Malone KM (1999). Toward a clinical model of suicidal behavior in psychiatric patients. *American Journal of Psychiatry 156*, 181-189.
3. Kessler RC, Borges G, Walters EE (1999). Prevalence of and risk factors for lifetime suicide attempts in the National Comorbidity Survey. *Archives of General Psychiatry 56*, 617-626.

Nocturnal wakefulness as a previously unrecognized risk factor for suicide

Perlis ML, Grandner MA, Brown GK, Basner M, Chakravorty S, Morales KH, Gehrman PR, Chaudhary NS, Thase ME, Dinges DF

Journal of Clinical Psychiatry 77, e726-e733, 2016

Objective: Suicide is a major public health problem and the 10th leading cause of death in the United States. The identification of modifiable risk factors is essential for reducing the prevalence of suicide. Recently, it has been shown that insomnia and nightmares significantly increase the risk for suicidal ideation, attempted suicide, and death by suicide. While both forms of sleep disturbance may independently confer risk, and potentially be modifiable risk factors, it is also possible that simply being awake at night represents a specific vulnerability for suicide. The present analysis evaluates the frequency of completed suicide per hour while taking into account the percentage of individuals awake at each hour.

Methods: Archival analyses were conducted estimating the time of fatal injury using the National Violent Death Reporting System for 2003-2010 and the proportion of the American population awake per hour across the 24-hour day using the American Time Use Survey.

Results: The mean ± SD incident rate from 06:00-23:59 was 2.2% ± 0.7%, while the mean ± SD incident rate from 00:00-05:59 was 10.3% ± 4.9%. The maximum incident rate was from 02:00-02:59 (16.3%). Hour-by-hour observed values differed from those that would be expected by chance (P <.001), and when 6-hour blocks were examined, the observed frequency at night was 3.6 times higher than would be expected by chance (P <.001).

Conclusions: Being awake at night confers greater risk for suicide than being awake at other times of the day, suggesting that disturbances of sleep or circadian neurobiology may potentiate suicide risk.

Comment

Main findings: Recent research has found sleep disturbance to be an indicator of risk for suicidal ideation, attempts and suicides. However, little attention has been paid to the circadian patterning of suicide or whether at-risk individuals are more vulnerable at specific times of the day or night. For example, it is possible that sleep disturbance results in being awake at night, and being awake at night itself may confer a risk. Although previous studies found that the peak frequency for completed suicide occurs during the day, they did not adjust for the proportion of the population awake at each time interval. Thus, the current study aimed to evaluate the incidence of suicide by time while accounting for the proportion of the population that is awake at each given hour. It was hypothesised that suicides should disproportionately occur at night, when controlling for the proportion of population that is likely to be awake. The research question was operationalised as "how common is suicide at each hour of the day, given how many people tend to be awake at that hour?". Data from 2003-2010 were obtained from the National Violent Death Reporting System to investigate suicide deaths by time and the American Time Use Survey was used to assess the proportion of the population that is awake each hour. Time was categorised into 1-hour segments, and morning, afternoon, evening and night were binned into 6 hour segments (e.g., morning = 06:00-11:59, afternoon = 12:00-17:59, evening = 18:00-23:59, and night = 0:00-05:59).

There was a total of 71,282 documented suicides, however only 35,332 suicides were included which had time of fatal injury data. Results indicated that the majority of suicides (63.9%) were more likely to occur at night (between midnight and 06:00) than during the morning, afternoon or evening, and this was consistent across age, sex, race, and for depressed and nondepressed individuals. Moreover, gender differences were observed whereby these temporal effects for men were larger compared to women. Across ethnicities, the largest effect was observed in Hispanic/Latinos and smallest effect sizes were seen among African-Americans.

Implications: These findings suggest that being awake at night confers suicide risk compared to being awake at other times of the day. The authors suggested being awake at night may be associated with reduced social support and increased use of alcohol and other substances, or that insomnia and/or nightmares may contribute to suicidal ideation and behaviour by intensifying feelings of hopelessness, isolation and distress associated with inability to sleep. Moreover, being awake at night may decrease frontal lobe function due to hypoactivation of frontal lobes due to sleep loss or deprivation[1]. Thus, a way to reduce suicide risk may be to ensure that individuals are not awake when they are disproportionately vulnerable (i.e., at night, when one is not biologically predisposed to be awake). These findings suggest that treatments should be targeted for insomnia and nightmares, and that there should be an increase of psychosocial resources (i.e., availability of peer and professional support) for those who are at-risk. Despite these novel findings, several limitations should be noted. The National Violent Death Reporting System data does not contain information as to why individuals who die by suicide were awake between midnight and 06:00. Moreover, the data obtained did not allow assessment of individual factors such as social isolation, access to means, alcohol and other substances or decreased frontal lobe function. It is also possible that the American Time Use Survey may have not accurately captured the population of depressed and/or suicidal individuals who are awake during the traditional sleep period. Thus, future studies should apply a largescale psychological autopsy method to assess the relative contribution of insomnia, nightmares, social isolation, and access to means, and substances to this observed finding. Further investigation into the use of cognitive behavioural therapy for insomnia and reducing suicidal ideation in a representative sample would help consolidate these findings and ensure applicability. It would also be meaningful to explore how suicidal ideation and impulsive behaviour may vary as a function of hour of day in at-risk individuals.

Endnotes

1. Vandewalle G, Archer SN, Wuillaume C, Balteau E, Degueldre C, Luxen A, Maquet P, Dijk, DJ (2009). Functional magnetic resonance imaging-assessed brain responses during an executive task depend on interaction of sleep homeostasis, circadian phase, and PER3 genotype. *Journal of Neuroscience* 29, 7948-7956.
2. Trockel M, Karlin BE, Taylor CB, Brown GK, Manber R (2015). Effects of cognitive behavioural therapy for insomnia on suicidal ideation in veterans. *Sleep* 38, 259-265.

The communication of suicidal intentions: A meta-analysis

Pompili M, Belvederi Murri M, Patti S, Innamorati M, Lester D, Girardi P, Amore M (Italy)

Psychological Medicine 46, 2239-2253, 2016

Background: Among the myths that are often cited about suicide is that "people who talk about killing themselves rarely die by suicide", but the evidence seems to contradict this statement. The aim of this study was to conduct a meta-analysis of studies reporting a prevalence of suicide communication (SC), and to examine the diagnostic accuracy of SC towards suicide in case-control reports.

Method: Eligible studies had to examine data relative to completed suicides and report the prevalence of SC. Data relative to sample characteristics, study definition, modality and recipient of the SC were coded.

Results: We included 36 studies, conducted on a total of 14 601 completed suicides. The overall proportion of SC was 44.5% [95% confidence interval (CI) 35.4-53.8], with large heterogeneity ($I2 = 98.8\%$) and significant publication bias. The prevalence of SC was negatively associated with the detection of verbal communication as the sole means of SC and, positively, with study methodological quality. Based on seven case-control studies, SC was associated with an odds ratio of 4.66 for suicide (95% CI 3.00-7.25) and was characterized by sufficient diagnostic accuracy only if studies on adolescents were removed.

Conclusion: Available data suggest that SC occurs in nearly half of subjects who go on to die by suicide, but this figure is likely to be an underestimate given the operational definitions of SC. At present, SC seems associated with overall insufficient accuracy towards subsequent suicide, although further rigorous studies are warranted to draw definite conclusions on this issue.

Comment

Main findings: Contrary to popular belief, research suggests that as many as two-thirds of completed suicide cases communicate their intent prior to death. Communication can involve a direct statement regarding one's intention to die, or indirect communications, such as telling a spouse not to buy new things for them[1]. No consensus exists as to which factors influence an individual's decision to communicate their suicidal intent, as well as the extent to which suicidal communication predicts completed suicide. The authors therefore conducted a meta-analysis in order to examine the proportion of suicide cases with previous communication of their intent, and the factors affecting the proportion of communicators. The search strategy involved searching a number of databases for papers pertaining to suicidal communication, reviewing bibliographies of identified papers (with access sought to published research not found in the previous search), as well as consulting international experts in the field to retrieve further relevant citations. Two of the authors independently reviewed the retrieved papers and consensus was reached as to which papers to include. Papers were included where: 1) they examined data relevant to completed suicides and reported the number of subjects who communicated their suicidal intent; 2) reported infor-mation describing the setting of the study and the type of population involved; and 3) adopted and utilised an unequivocal definition of suicidal communication consistently.

Thirty-eight papers were identified, comprising a total of 14,601 (25% female) completed suicides, with samples sizes ranging from 14 to 7126 subjects. Twenty studies gathered data from multiple information sources, six from chart reviews only, eight from next of kin (NOK) and in two studies the information source was unknown. Twenty-eight studies provided information concerning psychiatric diagnoses of subjects. Most studies did not define suicide communication in a detailed and systematic way. Ten studies did not specify the modality of suicide communication, 21 reported verbal communications, eight reported data on written notes, three included both written and verbal communication, and four included suicidal behaviours.

The overall proportion of suicidal communication by suicide cases was 44.5% across all papers in the meta-analysis. Prevalence rates differed by modality of communication, with the proportion of communicators being lower for both verbal and written communication (32.8%), compared to studies only reporting verbal (40.5%) or written communication (43.8%). Where suicidal behaviours were also included in the definition of suicide communication, the proportion of communicators was greater (61.1%). However, these differences were not statisti-cally significant. Participant characteristics such as gender, age and psychological diagnosis were not associated with the proportion of suicide communication. The authors conducted a multiple meta-regression and found that the proportion of suicide communicators was negatively associated with verbal communication as the sole means of communication, and positively associated with the study's methodological quality. Of the few case-control studies available, suicide commu-nication was associated with a 4.66 times greater risk of suicide completion than no communication. Interestingly, when examining only adults, suicide risk was 4.99 times greater (95% CI 3.13–7.96, Q test $\chi2 = 30.8$, df = 3, $p < 0.001$, I^2 =90.3%), whereas with adolescents there was no significant impact on suicide risk (OR 1.83, 95% CI 0.57–5.89, Q test $\chi2 = 21.7$, df = 1, $p < 0.001$, $I^2 = 95.4\%$). Case-control studies were also analysed to determine the diagnostic accuracy of suicide communications and found that suicide communication was not associated with diagnostic accuracy for suicide. However, after removing studies with adolescent subjects, the diagnostic accuracy of suicide communications became significant.

Implications: This meta-analysis was the first to investigate the incidence of suicide communication prior to suicide, and found that about half of suicide cases communicate their intention before death. These findings contradict the belief that people who communicate their suicidal intent rarely die by suicide. This was particularly evident when suicidal behaviour was included as a form of suicide communication. These findings highlight the importance of suicide communica-tion in identifying suicide risk and need for society to take such communications seriously. It is important that mental health and suicide prevention training reflect this reality. For example, mental health practitioners should be trained in awareness of the association between suicide communications and actual suicide. Future mental health initiatives must reflect this research and help bring further awareness to suicide communication. This meta-analysis was not without some limitations. Firstly, results are based on studies with generally low methodological quality, and there was little consensus on the definitions of suicide communication, making it difficult to accurately compare the results. Data were also collected from a wide variety of information sources, such as case histories, public records and written reports. This is problematic because each data source by itself is likely to underestimate the incidence of suicide communication. Interview methodology in particular is prone to underreporting as NOK may not be aware of suicide communications made to others.

Endnote

1. Robins E, Gassner S, Kayes J, Wilkinson Jr RH, Murphy GE (1959). The communication of suicidal intent: A study of 134 consecutive cases of successful (completed) suicide. *American Journal of Psychiatry* 115, 724–733.

Why do adolescents self-harm? An investigation of motives in a community sample

Rasmussen S, Hawton K, Philpott-Morgan S, O'Connor RC (United Kingdom)
Crisis 37, 176-183, 2016

Background: Given the high rates of self-harm among adolescents, recent research has focused on a better understanding of the motives for the behavior.

Aims: The present study had three aims: to investigate (a) which motives are most frequently endorsed by adolescents who report self-harm; (b) whether motives reported at baseline predict repetition of self-harm over a 6-month period; and (c) whether self-harm motives differ between boys and girls.

Method: In all, 987 school pupils aged 14-16 years completed a lifestyle and coping questionnaire at two time points 6 months apart that recorded self-harm and the associated motives.

Results: The motive "to get relief from a terrible state of mind" was the most commonly endorsed reason for self-harm (in boys and girls). Interpersonal reasons (e.g. "to frighten someone") were least commonly endorsed. Regression analyses showed that adolescents who endorsed wanting to get relief from a terrible state of mind at baseline were significantly more likely to repeat self-harm at follow-up than those adolescents who did not cite this motive.

Conclusion: The results highlight the complex nature of self-harm. They have implications for mental health provision in educational settings, especially in relation to encouraging regulation of emotions and help-seeking.

Comment

Main findings: Few studies have examined the motivations that cause adolescents to self-harm in the community. This is concerning as the majority of adolescents who self-harm do not attend clinical services[1]. The aim of this study was to examine in a community setting whether or not adolescent self-harm was more likely to be driven by intrapersonal or interpersonal motives, whether differences in motivations existed between males and females, and whether motives at baseline were predictive of future self-harming behaviour. This study used a subsample from the Northern Ireland Lifestyle and Coping Survey, a survey conducted in Northern Irish schools. The participant sample included 987 school pupils aged 14-16 years, of which 423 were males and 564 were females. The authors reported on survey questions pertaining to self-harm, intrapersonal motivations (e.g., "I wanted to get relief from a terrible state of mind") and interpersonal motivations (e.g., "I wanted to find out whether someone really loved me"). Surveys were completed at baseline and six months follow-up, with the follow-up response rate varying between 19-79% within schools. Adolescents who self-harmed at baseline were less likely to complete the follow-up survey than those who did not, however these two groups did not significantly differ in the motives they reported.

Overall, 8.9% of respondents reported at least one self-harm episode in their lifetime, with females 2.5 times more likely to report than males. Intrapersonal motivations were the most frequent drivers of self-harming behaviour (79.5%) compared to interpersonal motivations (40.9%). Both males and females reported "wanting to get relief from a terrible state of mind" as the most common motivation (62.5%). Gender differences were present, with more boys reporting the interpersonal motive "wanting to frighten someone", whereas more girls reported the intrapersonal motive "wanting to die". Additionally, more males (59.1%) than females (34.8%) reported at least one interpersonal motive. Although, there were no significant difference between males and females with respect to the frequency of intrapersonal motives reported ($\chi2 = .84$, $df = 1, 14$; $p = ns$). At 6-month follow-up 26.1% of participants who self-harmed at baseline reported having self-harmed again. Univariate logistic regression found two motives to be independently associated with repeat self-harm. When directly comparing these two motivations, adolescents who stated "I wanted to get relief from a terrible state of mind" were 17 times more likely ($OR = 17.77$, 95% CI = 1.63–190.70) to repeat self-harm, whereas adolescents who stated "I wanted to find out whether someone really loved me" were less likely to repeat self-harm ($OR = 0.047$, 95% CI = .004–.569).

Implications: These findings highlight the intrapersonal nature of self-harm and contradict the damaging belief that self-harm is primarily driven by a desire to manipulate others and seek attention. In fact, these damaging beliefs combined with the intrapersonal nature of self-harm may help explain why young people do not attend clinical services following self-harm[1]. The presence of some gender differences suggests that adolescent females and males need to be treated differently for self-harm and suggest that there may be value in the tailoring of interventions and treatments for self-harm differently for boys and girls. Training in emotional regulation and effective coping skills will also be critical in intervention and treatment programs. The study's findings must be interpreted in light of its limitations. Despite the large sample, the number of adolescents who self-harmed was only modest at baseline and small at the 6-month follow-up, limiting the inferences one can draw from the study. The strength of people's motivations, such as reporting a wish to die, were not measured, possibly underestimating the ability of certain motivations to predict repeat self-harm. Finally, the study was unable to explore whether any differences in motivations existed between younger and older adolescents.

Endnote

1. Groholt B, Ekeberg O, Wichstrom L, Haldorsen T (2000). Young suicide attempters: A comparison between a clinical and an epidemiological sample. *Journal of the American Academy of Child and Adolescent Psychiatry, 39*, 868–875.

Developing a school-based preventive life skills program for youth in a remote Indigenous community in North Australia

Robinson G, Leckning B, Midford R, Harper H, Silburn S, Gannaway J, Dolan K, Delphine T, Hayes C (Australia)

Health Education 116, 510-523, 2016

Purpose: The purpose of this paper is to describe the process of development and the pilot implementation of a preventive life skills curriculum for Indigenous middle school students in a very remote community college in the West Arnhem region of North Australia. The curriculum integrates proven educational and psychological techniques with culturally informed notions of relatedness and was developed as a contribution to efforts to prevent alarming rates of suicide among remote Indigenous youth. In this paper, the term, Indigenous refers to Australians of Aboriginal or Torres Strait Islander descent.

Design/methodology/approach: Based on reviews of research literature on school-based suicide prevention and social and emotional learning in both general and Indigenous populations, and following detailed community consultations, a 12 week curriculum was drafted and implemented in two middle school classes (combined years 7-9). Lessons were videotaped and later analyzed and detailed commentary was sought from participating school staff.

Findings: The pilot program has yielded important insights into requirements of a curriculum for young people with low English literacy levels and with variable school attendance patterns. It confirmed the need to adjust both pedagogical approach and curriculum content for the program to have resonance with students from this linguistic and cultural background and with varying levels of exposure to multiple stressors in disadvantaged community settings.

Practical implications: The project has identified and resolved key questions for sustainable implementation of a preventive curriculum in challenging community circumstances.

Originality/value: There are to date no examples of the systematic adaptation and design of a universal preventive intervention specifically for remote Australian Indigenous youth. The project is the first step toward the formal evaluation of the efficacy of a classroom-based approach to suicide prevention in remote community schools.

Comment

Main findings: Indigenous youth suicide rates in the Northern Territory have increased significantly, from negligible levels in 1990 to the highest levels nation-wide today. Social and emotional life skills programs have been posited as a potential intervention to address these elevated rates, with a meta-analysis demonstrating that school-based programs lead to significant improvements in social and emotional skills and behaviours and substantial gains in academic attainment[1]. Social learning theory underpins elements of school-based learning activities such as providing information about the helpful and harmful behaviours of certain behaviours, modelling target skills, rehearsing behaviours for skills acquisition and providing feedback for skills refinement. However, to date teaching methods and curriculum content based on social learning approaches have not been developed for Indigenous youth in remote Australian communities. The current article describes the process of developing and piloting a preventive life skills curriculum aimed at Indigenous youths to integrate educational and psychological techniques with culturally informed notions of relatedness.

The study was set in a very remote Northern Territory government-run school, Maningrida Community College. Researchers working alongside college staff and local youth services developed a life skills curriculum aimed at Aboriginal youth in middle school (years 7-9). The program was delivered in class every week for 2 hours from week 5 of term 2 to week 7 of term 3. Lessons were videotaped for qualitative analysis, with detailed commentary also provided by participating school staff. The aim of the pilot was to develop a 12-week curriculum that could promote both resilience and prevention strategies relevant to known risks in Aboriginal communities. Eleven lessons were delivered encapsulating the following themes: strengths in the community; character strengths; emotional literacy and managing strong emotions; positive thinking and problem solving; passive, aggressive and assertive communication; dealing with grief and loss; saying "no" to alcohol; help seeking and working together with friends.

Fifty-one students took part in the pilot, with exposure to the program varying considerably across the 12 weeks. The average attendance in the girls' class was 10.9 students per week and 8.8 students per week for boys. Only a minority of students attended at least half of the lessons. This was problematic given that the program structure required continued attendance from students in order for program ideas to be properly developed. Low levels of literacy and reading confidence were found to inhibit student learning. The pilot also caused some disruption to students' routines, inhibiting their capacity to learn. The program utilised scenarios and activities employing visual aids and narrative prompts written to enable limited exploration of issues such as grief, loss, anger and dispute resolution. However, the authors noted that openness to community themes and cultural patterns needed more careful balancing with conventional provision of factual content and evidence-based information to students (e.g., mental health and illness information). The pilot also demonstrated that staff need to be prepared to respond appropriately to students who have witnessed destructive and suicidal behaviours in their community and to refer students to school psychologists where necessary. Indigenous facilitators were also highlighted as being important to program delivery as they can provide insight into students' communication styles and help to break down cultural barriers.

Implications: This paper provides a roadmap for the development of life skills programs aimed at reducing suicidality in Indigenous youth. It was the first study to design and pilot a universal intervention specifically for remote Aboriginal youth. It is also the first step towards the formal evaluation of classroom-based suicide prevention in remote community schools. The authors suggested that students would benefit from life skills programs being implemented across all year levels, as this would lead to the reinforcement of and further development of key themes and skills. This study had a number of limitations. Firstly, it was unable to analyse the effect that the pilot program had on student self-harm or suicidality, making it difficult to evaluate its actual effectiveness in reducing destructive behaviours. Furthermore, the study only focused on Indigenous youths living on regulated Aboriginal land, limiting the conclusions that can be drawn regarding the program's effectiveness in other indigenous communities.

Endnotes

1. Durlak JA, Weissberg RP, Dymnicki AB, Taylor RD, Schellinger KB (2011). The impact of enhancing students' social and emotional learning: A meta-analysis of school-based universal interventions. *Child Development* 82, 405-432.

Teachers' perspectives on preventing suicide in children and adolescents in schools: A qualitative study

Ross V, Kõlves K, De Leo D (Australia)

Archives of Suicide Research. Published online: 31 August 2016. doi: 10.1080/13811118.2016.1227005

Given the important role teachers play as gatekeepers in school suicide prevention, this study explored teachers' perspectives on what should be done to improve current suicide prevention efforts. The study, in Queensland, Australia, was part of a large-scale survey examining teachers' knowledge, attitudes and experience of suicidality. One hundred and fifteen teachers responded to an online survey question regarding their views on the requirements for school suicide prevention. Qualitative analysis identified five themes from teachers' responses: awareness and stigma reduction, support services for students, education and training, bullying and the role of social media. The results of this study provide some profound insights into teachers' perspectives on suicide and highlight the critical need for improved suicide prevention efforts in schools.

Comment

Main findings: School settings are an ideal location for targeting youth prevention initiatives, given the large proportion of time spent there by children and adolescents. Within the school environment, teachers are in a unique position to potentially act as gatekeepers in recognising warning signs, and providing first line support and referrals to appropriate services. However, research on teachers' attitudes towards suicide prevention in schools has shown mixed results. Thus, this qualitative study aimed to investigate Australian teachers' perspectives on youth suicide and their personal insights on what is necessary to improve suicide prevention initiatives. The study was part of a wider online survey disseminated through the Queensland Government Department of Education and Training Bulletin Board and School Update, and Queensland Teachers' Union Professional Magazine via emails to schools that used the directory. Participants for this study were presented with an open-ended question: "Please share your thoughts regarding what you believe is required in the future for suicide prevention in children and adolescents both in the wider context (society) and in the school environment?"

Of the 138 Queensland primary and secondary school teachers who participated in the wider survey, 115 (83.3%) responded to the question of relevance for this study. The sample was comprised of teachers from metropolitan areas (47.8%), regional areas (47.8%), and remote or very remote areas (4.4%). Of the sample of teachers, 33.3% reported having been exposed to a student suicide. Three key dominant and interrelated themes were identified: the need for awareness and stigma reduction, the need for suicide prevention education and training, and the need for improved support services for students. Additionally, two less prevalent themes of bullying and the role of social media were identified. Over 50% of teachers identified greater awareness and de-stigmatisation of mental illness and suicide as essential to youth suicide prevention initiatives. Stigma was also viewed as a barrier to help-seeking for students. However, views on creating suicide awareness were polarised regarding the potential benefits and dangers to vulnerable students. The need for suicide prevention training for students, teachers, parents and the wider community was also cited by more than 50% of teachers. Teachers highlighted the importance of education for students and parents on the available channels to find help and support within schools and in the community. Respondents also identified the need for suicide prevention training for teachers, as generally this was not current practice. However, some teachers reported that they were already "overloaded" with work responsibilities and do not have time to respond to student issues. Teachers also stressed the need to improve support services for students, such as the provision of more school councillors trained to assist those with depression and suicidal ideation. Broader approaches to improving students' mental health such as meditation and yoga were also recommended. The issue of bullying and its impact on youth suicide was also a concern for teachers. Respondents acknowledged that vulnerable children, particularly those who are perceived as "different" (e.g., lesbian, gay, bisexual or transgender, or those who are obese) are targeted by bullies, with harmful psychological effects on students. From many teachers' perspectives, not enough was currently being done in schools to act on cases of bullying. The impact of social media on youth suicide was described, both in a positive and negative light. Teachers reported the dangers of glamorising suicide through "celebrity suicide", and the psychologically damaging effects of bullying through social media. Nevertheless, teachers also believed that social media could also have a potentially positive role as a communication tool for targeting children and adolescents.

Implications: Despite young people being vulnerable and at-risk for suicide, there is still a lack of evidence for effective school-based interventions[1]. The findings from this study may help inform and improve on national mental health programs such as Mindmatters[2] and KidsMatter[3], which are currently delivered to secondary school and primary schools through the *beyondblue* organisation. A strength of this study was that it provided a rich qualitative account of a representative sample of Queensland's teachers' perspectives on youth suicide prevention. Future research should aim to also explore a more diverse range of school staff (e.g., principals and school guidance officers) and investigate differences in gender and career length, as well as the impact of suicide on teachers. This will provide a more holistic account and help inform future youth suicide prevention strategies.

Endnotes

1. Robinson J, Cox G, Malone A, Williamson M, Baldwin G, Fletcher K, O'Brien M (2013). A systematic review of school-based interventions aimed at preventing, treating, and responding to suicide-related behaviour in young people. *Crisis* 34, 164–182.

2. Wyn J, Cahill H, Holdsworth R, Rowling L, Carson S (2000). MindMatters, a whole-school approach promoting mental health and wellbeing. *Australian and New Zealand Journal of Psychiatry* 34, 594–601.

3. Graetz B, Littlefield L, Trinder M, Dobia B, Souter M, Champion C, Boucher S, Killick-Moran C, Cummins R (2008). KidsMatter: A population health model to support student mental health and well-being in primary schools. *International Journal of Mental Health Promotion* 10, 13-20.

Factors related to suicide in LGBT populations: A Psychological Autopsy Case-Control Study in Australia

Skerrett DM, Kõlves K, De Leo D (Australia)

Crisis. Published online: 23 September 2016. doi: 10.1027/0227-5910/a000423

Background: There is evidence of heightened vulnerability to nonfatal suicidal behaviors among LGBT populations yet a paucity of studies into fatal behaviors.

Aim: The specific aim of this article was to identify factors related to suicide in LGBT individuals in Australia.

Method: The psychological autopsy (PA) method with a matched case-control study design was used. PA interviews were conducted with 27 next-of-kin of an LGBT person that had died by suicide. Three living LGBT controls per suicide case, matched by age and gender, were also interviewed.

Results: The key factors relating to suicide in LGBT people were a lack of acceptance by family and self (reflected in higher internalized homophobia and shame), negative feelings about own sexuality/gender, and dissatisfaction with appearance. LGBT people who died by suicide also tended to go through coming out milestones 2 years earlier than controls. There was a higher prevalence of aggressive behaviors and a more predominant history of physical and sexual abuse. Additionally, there was greater incidence of depression and anxiety and alcohol and substance use disorders.

Conclusion: Specific predictive factors for suicide in LGBT populations in Australia were identified, including significantly poorer mental health outcomes and more violence across an array of measures.

Comment

Main findings: There is limited research discussing the suicide risk factors non-heterosexual people face. The literature that does exist is equivocal, with some studies finding that no differences exist[1,2] between non-heterosexual and heterosexual suicides and others finding that differences do exist[3]. Given the elevated suicide risk LGBT (lesbian, gay, bisexual and transgender) people face, there is a need to identify the specific characteristics that lead to this increased risk.

The authors conducted a matched case-control study, collecting data through a psychological autopsy (PA) method, which involved interviewing the next-of-kin (NOK) of LBGT people who had died by suicide. The purpose of a PA is to gather information pertaining to the events leading up to a suicide and examine how these events affected the deceased's life. Interviewers asked questions concerning demographics, sexuality, gender, history of suicidality, aggressive behaviour, history of mental and physical health problems, experiences of bullying and victimisation, recent life events, shame, personality, social support, internalised homophobia/transphobia, hobbies and friendships. Three living LGBT controls were interviewed for each suicide case and were matched by age and gender. Interviews with NOKs were conducted either in person or by telephone.

Suicide cases consisted of 20 males, five females and two trans-females. Numerous factors were found to be associated with these suicides. In particular, LGBT suicide cases were 6.85 times more likely to have been on medication and 6.15 times more likely to have seen a psychiatrist than non-suicide cases. They were also 23.41 times more likely to have a current major depressive episode and 9.9 times more likely to have previously attempted suicide. Furthermore, suicide cases were 9.19 times more likely to have posttraumatic stress disorder, 6.02 times more likely to be substance users and 8.40 times more likely to be unable to work due to mental health problems. Other risk factors included a lack of acceptance by family and self, reflected by higher internalized homophobia and shame; negative feelings about their sexuality/gender; and dissatisfaction with their appearance. There was also a higher prevalence of aggressive behaviours and a more predominant history of physical and sexual abuse in LGBT people who died by suicide.

Implications: This is the first Australian study to investigate the range of factors that influence LGBT suicides with living matched controls. As with heterosexual suicide cases, LGBT people suffering from psychological disorders were at a greater risk of suicide, with all suicide cases having a diagnosable mental health disorder present. LGBT-specific factors included internalised homophobia and transphobia, lack of family acceptance, and internalised shame. Given the elevated risk of suicidality in LGBT communities[4], mental health initiatives should seek to target these specific risk factors. Specifically, the authors recommend the application of targeted prevention and intervention measures that promote acceptance around sexual and gender diversity, and promoting inclusive mental health services to promote health seeking. This study was not without some limitations. The small sample size limited the choice of statistical analysis that could be applied, as well as the inferences that could be drawn from the study to the wider LGBT population. Furthermore, the PA method is subject to recall bias from NOKs and a potentially skewed understanding of the deceased's thoughts, feelings and behaviours.

Endnote

1. Rich CL, Fowler RC, Young D, Blenkush M (1986). San Diego suicide study: Comparison of gay to straight males. *Suicide and Life-Threatening Behavior 16*, 448-457.
2. Shaffer D, Fisher P, Hicks RH, Parides M, Gould M (1995). Sexual orientation in adolescents who commit suicide. *Suicide and Life-Threatening Behavior 25*, 64-71.
3. Renaud J, Berlim MT, Begoll, M, McGirr A, Turecki G (2010). Sexual orientation and gender identity in youth suicide victims: An exploratory study. *Canadian Journal of Psychiatry 55*, 29-34.
4. Haas AP, Eliason M, Mays VM, Mathy RM, Cochran SD, D'Augelli AR, ... Russell ST (2010). Suicide and suicide risk in lesbian, gay, bisexual, and transgender populations: review and recommendations. *Journal of Homosexuality 58*, 10-51.

Pathways to suicide in lesbian and gay populations in Australia: A life chart analysis.

Skerrett DM, Kõlves K, De Leo D (Australia)

Archives of Sexual Behavior. Published online: 6 May 2016. doi: 10.1007/s10508-013-0827-y

Given the continued paucity of research into suicide in lesbian and gay (LG) people, there is a need to investigate the characteristics of those LG suicides that are able to be identified. The aim of this article was to analyze pathways to suicide in lesbian and gay individuals by way of life charts. Data were gathered through of 24 psychological autopsy interviews with next-of-kin of an LG person who had died by suicide. The female (n = 5) and male (n = 19) cases in this study clustered into younger and older suicides. The defining feature of the younger suicides was lack of acceptance by family and, to a lesser extent, self, and that of the older suicides was romantic relationship conflict, although this was also common in younger suicides. There appears to have been, furthermore, an accumulation of risk factors, particularly in the period prior to death where these specific risk factors combined with other life stressors, such as work problems. Initiatives to reduce stigma around diversity in sexuality and to support families and young people through the "coming out" process as well as services designed to assist those experiencing problems in same-sex relationships, in particular, would appear to be the most relevant within the trajectories presented.

Comment

Main findings: Currently in Australia, the majority of research on LGBTI (lesbian, gay, bisexual, transgender and intersex) and suicide are represented by "grey" literature, that is, generally academic but unpublished research. Given the increased vulnerability to non-fatal suicidal behaviour among LGBTI populations, and fatal behaviours, there is a need to investigate the characteristics of LGBTI suicides. The aim of this study was to analyse pathways to suicide in LG individuals (as a more accessible subset of the LGBTI community) using life charts. Life charts map out and identify critical time points in the lives of those who had died by suicide. This study employed a psychological autopsy (PA) design, whereby a knowledgeable informant is interviewed to gain information about the deceased, and to reconstruct the events leading up to the suicide death, and how these events impacted on the life of the deceased. Participants were recruited using a snowball method and thus, constituted a convenience sample. The inclusion criteria was that, the deceased self-identified as LG or was unsure/conflicted about their sexuality, and that suicide death occurred after 2005 to reduce recall bias. A total of 24 interviews were conducted with next-of-kin (NOK) of an LG individual who died by suicide. The mean age for LG individuals who died by suicide was 34.8 years, and consisted of 19 males and five females. The cases were found to cluster into two groups of younger and older age groups at time of death, with particular patterns of life events associated with the groups.

Those in the younger group were aged from 19 to 30 years (n=10). The younger group was characterised by lack of acceptance of sexuality from self or family, and in half these cases, the father was specifically mentioned. All but one individual in this group experienced chronic suicidality or a suicide attempt. The younger suicides appeared to be particularly influenced by the "coming out" process. Other typical trajectories included physical and mental health problems (anxiety, depression, bipolar disorder and alcohol and substance use disorders). The older group were aged from 32-61 years (n=14). The presence of romantic relationship problems in the period immediately leading up to death characterised this group. This was true for all cases except those who made up a subgroup (n=3) who experienced a lack of acceptance (by self, parents, and partner's parents). This subgroup was also characterised by non-romantic relationship conflict, work problems, and physical health problems at the time of death. Four individuals in the older group were gay males with HIV. Seven older individuals experienced romantic relationship subgroup all were experiencing work problems and majority had life event or ongoing problems related to suicide. Meanwhile four had physical health problems and two further cases included problems with acceptance of sexuality (by family or by self).

Implications: This is one of the first studies in Australia and internationally to analyse pathways to suicide in LG people. These results highlight the importance of acceptance for younger LG individuals and romantic relationship difficulties across all LG age groups (9 out of 10 younger suicides and 11 out of 14 older suicides). Together, these findings emphasise the need for targeted approaches in mental health services for the LG population. For example, relationship and counselling, school-based programs, and public health and reducing stigma around diversity in sexuality and to support families and young people through the "coming out" process will help support a healthy development of an LGBT identity. However, as the sample size was relatively small, caution should be exercised in generalising to the wider LG population, specifically for the lesbian community as they constituted only five out of the 24 cases in this study. Thus, future research should aim to employ a non-LG control group, and have a larger representative sample in order to ensure generalisability. A key limitation is that the nature of this study (PA design) relies on an LG person's NOK to recall information, which is subject to recall bias and potential skewed understanding of the deceased person's thoughts, feelings and behaviours. Lastly, a limitation that is not within the control of the researchers is that sexuality is seldom documented at death, and thus LGBTI deaths are suspected to be largely under-reported. Nevertheless these results are important in building knowledge to inform evidence-based interventions for this vulnerable group. LGBTI people are currently a priority area of "vulnerable groups" in the Queensland Suicide Prevention Action Plan[1], thus, these findings and future research in this area will help inform the unique needs and circumstances of this subgroup in the action plan. Research in this area will ensure that the underlying structural inequities and social disadvantages which contribute to the heightened risk of harm in this group are minimised.

Endnotes

1. Queensland Mental Health Commission (2015). *Queensland Suicide Prevention Action Plan 2015-2017*. Retrieved 8 September 2016 from https://www.qmhc.qld.gov.au/wp-content/uploads /2015/09/Queensland-Suicide-Prevention-Action-Plan-2015-17_WEB.pdf

Is a person thinking about suicide likely to find help on the internet?
An evaluation of google search results

Thornton L, Handley T, Kay-Lambkin F, Baker A (Australia)

Suicide and Life-Threatening Behavior. Published online: 25 April 2016. doi: 10.1111/sltb.12261

It is unclear whether individuals searching the Internet for assistance with thoughts of suicide are likely to encounter predominantly helpful or harmful resources. This study investigated websites retrieved by searching Google for information and support for suicidal thoughts. Google searches retrieved a high percentage of irrelevant websites (26%, n = 136). Of the 329 relevant websites retrieved, the majority were suicide preventive (68%); however, a considerable proportion of sites expressed mixed (22%) or neutral (8%) suicide attitudes, and 1% were explicitly pro-suicide. The results highlight a need for suicide prevention organization websites to be made more easily accessible. In the meantime, clinicians should be aware of appropriate websites to recommend to clients.

Comment

Main findings: There has been an increase of user-generated suicide content (e.g., personal websites, interactive discussion forums, chat rooms), allowing opportunities for users to exchange information on a global scale. However, previous research investigating the kind of content that might be found on the internet for those who were suicidal[1] was designed to explore research results using "pro-suicide" search terms. It is still unclear how commonly potentially harmful resources appear in more generic or "suicide preventative" searches for an individual using the Internet to seek help. Thus this study aimed to employ more neutral and suicide preventative search terms, rather than "pro-suicide". The study also investigated how easily accessible online treatments for mental health problems are to lay-people who may not search for them specifically, in an Australian context. The Google search engine was employed as it is the most commonly used search engine in Australia. Thirteen search terms were generated with consideration from previous studies, discussions between authors, and consultation with experts in the field (e.g., "better off dead", "do away with myself", "end my life", "how to kill myself", "I don't want to live", "I want to die", "I want to kill myself", "no reason to live", "suicidal", "suicide", "take my own life", "thoughts of death", and "wish I was dead"). In addition, each term was combined with the term "help", creating an additional 13 terms. The first two pages of the search results for each term were recorded and analysed.

A total of 520 search results were obtained, of which two were not rated as the links were no longer valid. Of the remaining 518 websites, 136 were irrelevant, 49 were newspaper stories, and 4 were academic articles. The majority of the remaining relevant websites were suicide preventative (n=225) while only 6 were explicitly pro-suicide. A considerable proportion of sites expressed mixed (n=72) or neutral suicide attitudes (n=26). Only thirteen of the websites were Australian; Lifeline, beyondblue, and Suicide Prevention Australia only appeared four times, while Living is for Everyone appeared once. A significantly higher proportion of websites retrieved using only the original search terms were irrelevant, compared to those including "help" in combination with the original search term (search term only=43.46%, search term with help=29.46%, p<.001). Eight search terms prompted an automatic response from Google encouraging the user to seek assistance from Lifeline.

Implications: This was the first study to examine how likely it would be for an Australian internet user to encounter helpful or potentially dangerous resources online. While the majority of the websites retrieved were suicide preventative, and several of these were Australian, it is concerning that only eight search terms prompted an automated response from Google urging the user to seek help, and specifically that only two of the terms including the word "help" received this response. This shows that small modifications in the wording used by an at-risk individual could be the difference between receiving access to help and generic search results only. Thus, adjusting the automated system to be more sensitive to a wider range of suicide-related terms may be of assistance to vulnerable internet users. Moreover, the authors stress the urgent need for Australian suicide prevention organisations to adapt their search optimisation strategies so that their websites can be more easily found. However, it should be noted that the search terms used in this study were generated by experts to mimic suicide ideation and thus may not accurately reflect the search terms used by a person experiencing suicide ideation. To clarify whether these search terms accurately reflect terms a suicidal individual would use, future research should aim to extend the potential search terms used by this population. Given that online support is an important part of Australia's current suicide prevention intiatives[2], it is imperative that this research area is not neglected.

Endnotes

1. Biddle L, Derges J, Mars B, Heron J, Donovan JL, Potokar J, Piper M, Wyllie C, Gunnell D (2016). Suicide and the internet: changes in the accessibility of suicide-related information between 2007 and 2014. *Journal of Affective Disorders* 190, 370-375.

2. Department of Health (2015). *Australian government response to contributing lives, thriving communities – review of mental health programmes and services.* Retrieved 15 August 2016 from http://www.health.gov.au/internet/main/publishing.nsf/Content/0DBEF2D78F7CB9E7 CA257F07001ACC6D/$File/response.pdf.

Individual and community factors for railway suicide: A matched case-control study in Victoria, Australia

Too LS, Spittal MJ, Bugeja L, McClure R, Milner A (Australia)

Social Psychiatry and Psychiatric Epidemiology. Published online: 30 March 2016. doi: 10.1007/s00127-016-1212-9

Purpose: This study aims to simultaneously examine individual- and community-level factors associated with railway suicide.

Methods: We performed a case-control study in Victoria, Australia between 2001 and 2012. Data on cases of railway suicide were obtained from the National Coronial Information System (a database of coronial investigations). Controls were living individuals randomly selected from the Household, Income and Labour Dynamics in Australia study, matching to cases on age groups, sex and year of exposures. A conditional logistic regression model was used to assess the individual-level and community-level influences on individual odds of railway suicide, controlling for socioeconomic status.

Results: Individual-level diagnosed mental illness increased railway suicide odds by six times [95 % confidence interval (CI) 4.5, 9.2]. Community-level factors such as living in an area with a presence of railway tracks [odds ratio (OR) 1.8, 95 % CI 1.2, 2.8], within a city (OR 3.2, 95 % CI 1.9, 5.4), and with a higher overall suicide rate (OR 1.02, 95 % CI 1.01, 1.04) were independently associated with greater individual odds of railway suicide compared to living in an area without a presence of railway tracks, outside a city, and with a relatively lower overall suicide rate.

Conclusions: The effects of mental illness and high incidence of overall suicides are prominent, but not specific on railway suicide. The effects of presence of railway tracks and city residence suggest the importance of accessibility to the railways for individual risk of railway suicide. Prevention efforts should focus on vulnerable people live in areas with easy access to the railways.

Comment

Main findings: Railway suicides cause significant emotional distress to both the friends and families of deceased, the person driving the train and any witnesses to the suicide. At the individual level, research shows that people who die by rail suicide are predominately male, young, single and not in the labour force[1]. In Australia however, no studies have investigated both the individual, community level and rail-specific factors that are associated with rail suicide risk. Therefore, the authors sought to address this research gap, running a case control study comparing those who died by rail suicide in Victoria between 2001 and 2012 to living controls.

Information was obtained from the National Coronial Information System (NCIS). Deaths classified as intentional self-harm by railway vehicle or involving a rail vehicle were extracted and cross-referenced with railway suicides provided by the Coroners Court of Victoria. The NCIS also provided toxicology, coroners and autopsy reports, as well as sociodemographic information and residential addresses. Data for living controls were randomly sampled from the Household, Income and Labour Dynamics in Australia (HILDA) Survey, who resided in Victoria during the study period. Utilising HILDA, the authors matched on average, 1.9 living controls to each suicide case by date (year of suicide to date of survey), age and sex. Exposure variables included individual-level variables, which included marital status and employment status at the time of death, and mental illness diagnosis. Environmental measures were also included, such as community-level social fragmentation, socioeconomic status, train-related measures, number of assaults in area, density of alcohol outlets in area, number of mental health services and overall suicide rate. There were nine train-related measures which were categorised into train frequency, accessibility, and familiarity with trains.

Three hundred and forty-three railway suicides that occurred in Victoria between 2001 and 2012 were included in this study. The cases were comprised of 71% males and 29% females. A total of 652 living controls (70% males, 30% females) were selected from HILDA. Several factors were found to be associated with railway suicide after controlling for confounding variables. People diagnosed with a mental illness were six times more likely to die by railway suicide than people without a mental illness diagnosis (OR 6.4, 95 % CI 4.5, 9.2). Individuals living near railway tracks were twice as likely to die by railway suicide than those who did not (OR 1.8, 95 % CI 1.2, 2.8). People living in an urban area were also at greater risk of railway suicide compared to those living in regional or remote areas (OR 3.2, 95 % CI 1.9, 5.4). There were also greater odds of railway suicide for people living in an area with a rising general suicide rate (OR 1.02, 95 % CI 1.01, 1.04).

Implications: This was the first Australian study to simultaneously examine individual- and community-level factors associated with railway suicide. The use of a case control method allowed for greater causal inferences to be drawn from the findings. The study did have some limitations. Railway suicide data may have been under-reported due to the frequency of active coronial investigations and the misclassification of suicides as other causes of death (e.g., unintentional)[2]. People missing a residential postcode were also excluded from the analysis, meaning that homeless people, who sometimes have temporary shelter situated near railway tracks and are at an elevated risk of suicide, were excluded. This paper's findings should be used to inform policy, in particular initiatives which seek to reduce railway suicide in vulnerable people. For example, where possible physical barriers which limit people's access to railway tracks should be implemented as they have been shown to significantly reduce railway suicides in other jurisditions[3,4].

Endnote

1. Krysinska K, De Leo D (2008). Suicide on railway networks: Epidemiology, risk factors and prevention. *Australian and New Zealand Journal of Psychiatry* 42, 763–771.
2. Australian Bureau of Statistics (2007). *Information paper: External causes of death, data quality, 2005.* Cat. no. 3317.0.55.001. Australian Bureau of Statistics, Canberra.
3. Ueda M, Sawada Y, Matsubayashi T (2015). The effectiveness of installing physical barriers for preventing railway suicides and accidents: Evidence from Japan. *Journal of Affective Disorders* 178, 1–4.
4. Law CK, Yip PSF, Chan WSC, Fu KW, Wong PWC, Law YW (2009). Evaluating the effectiveness of barrier installation for preventing railway suicides in Hong Kong. *Journal of Affective Disorders* 114, 254–262.

Suicide prevention strategies revisited: 10-year systematic review

Zalsman G, Hawton K, Wasserman D, van Heeringen K, Arensman E, Sarchiapone M, Carli V, Höschl C, Barzilay R, Balazs J, Purebl G, Kahn JP, Sáiz PA, Lipsicas CB, Bobes J, Cozman D, Hegerl U, Zohar J (Israel)

Lancet Psychiatry 3, 646-659, 2016

Background: Many countries are developing suicide prevention strategies for which up-to-date, high-quality evidence is required. We present updated evidence for the effectiveness of suicide prevention interventions since 2005.

Methods: We searched PubMed and the Cochrane Library using multiple terms related to suicide prevention for studies published between Jan 1, 2005, and Dec 31, 2014. We assessed seven interventions: public and physician education, media strategies, screening, restricting access to suicide means, treatments, and internet or hotline support. Data were extracted on primary outcomes of interest, namely suicidal behaviour (suicide, attempt, or ideation), and intermediate or secondary outcomes (treatment-seeking, identification of at-risk individuals, antidepressant prescription or use rates, or referrals). 18 suicide prevention experts from 13 European countries reviewed all articles and rated the strength of evidence using the Oxford criteria. Because the heterogeneity of populations and methodology did not permit formal meta-analysis, we present a narrative analysis.

Findings: We identified 1797 studies, including 23 systematic reviews, 12 meta-analyses, 40 randomised controlled trials (RCTs), 67 cohort trials, and 22 ecological or population-based investigations. Evidence for restricting access to lethal means in prevention of suicide has strengthened since 2005, especially with regard to control of analgesics (overall decrease of 43% since 2005) and hot-spots for suicide by jumping (reduction of 86% since 2005, 79% to 91%). School-based awareness programmes have been shown to reduce suicide attempts (odds ratio [OR] 0.45, 95% CI 0.24-0.85; p=0.014) and suicidal ideation (0.5, 0.27-0.92; p=0.025). The anti-suicidal effects of clozapine and lithium have been substantiated, but might be less specific than previously thought. Effective pharmacological and psychological treatments of depression are important in prevention. Insufficient evidence exists to assess the possible benefits for suicide prevention of screening in primary care, in general public education and media guidelines. Other approaches that need further investigation include gatekeeper training, education of physicians, and internet and helpline support. The paucity of RCTs is a major limitation in the evaluation of preventive interventions.

Interpretation: In the quest for effective suicide prevention initiatives, no single strategy clearly stands above the others. Combinations of evidence-based strategies at the individual level and the population level should be assessed with robust research designs.

Comment

Main findings: Suicide prevention research is complicated by the multifaceted nature of suicide and relatively low base rates of suicide[1]. As a result, it is difficult to draw conclusions regarding the effectiveness of particular interventions. Given that the last systematic review on the effectiveness of approaches to suicide prevention was published in 2005, the authors conducted this systematic review for the purpose of assessing the progress of suicide prevention since the original study. Online databases were searched for all relevant English language studies published between 1 January 2005 and 31 December 2014 utilising specific search terms related to suicide prevention. Papers were included in the review where they examined completed suicides, suicide attempts, suicidal ideation or if they included applicable intermediate outcomes such as help-seeking behaviour or identification of at-risk individuals. Papers were classified based on the suicide intervention they examined, which included means restriction; treatment interventions, including pharmacotherapy and psychotherapy; community and family-based interventions; follow-up and chain-of-care; education and awareness; media, telephone or internet-based interventions; screening; and combined prevention interventions. Papers were ranked by 18 suicide experts according to their quality of research and intervention classification, with those papers deemed to be irrelevant or low in quality excluded. As a result, 224 papers met the initial selection criteria, with 80 of these being excluded due to irrelevance or poor quality evidence. Heterogeneity in study methodology and in populations prevented the authors from conducting a formal meta-analysis, so a narrative synthesis of results in key domains of suicide prevention strategies was presented.

Thirty studies examined suicide prevention by restricting access to means, with 14 of these studies focusing on firearm restrictions. Firearm availability in households was found to increase the risk of firearm suicides by 3.24 times (95% CI 2.41–4.40) compared to non-availability. Other studies supported the use of means restriction for pesticides in countries where this suicide method is prevalent. In the United Kingdom small packet sizes for analgesics were shown to reduce the number of suicides. Three papers strongly supported the use of barriers at popular jumping sites, with an overall reduction of suicide by jumping of 86%. Pharmacological treatments were also shown to prevent suicides. Randomised control trials (RCTs) demonstrated that lithium is an effective treatment for suicide risk in those with mood disorders. Clozapine was shown to reduce suicide risk in those with schizophrenia compared to other drugs. Furthermore, large-scale ecological studies found that antidepressant use is not associated with increased suicide risk, while continued use of pharmacotherapy for depression is associated with a reduced risk of suicide. Cognitive-based therapies were effective in reducing suicidal ideation and behaviours in adolescents compared to treatment as usual or minimal treatment. These therapies were also somewhat effective for adults and for people with schizophrenia and borderline personality disorder. Dialectical behaviour therapy (DBT) was also shown to reduce suicidality in adolescents and women with borderline personality disorders. The evidence concerning the effectiveness of psychosocial treatments is unclear. However, a multi-systemic therapy approach that addresses improving parenting skills, community, school and peer support, and engagement in pro-social activities was associated with a reduction of suicide attempts when compared with hospitalisation in adolescents. The evidence for the efficacy of contact interventions, such as regular telephone or face-to-face contact remains mixed, with different findings for low, middle and high-income countries. Although gatekeeper training has been shown to have a positive effect on people's knowledge, skills and attitudes towards suicidality, no RCTs have demonstrated that gatekeeper training alone reduces suicide rates.

Implications: This systematic review provides an updated assessment of the effectiveness of current suicide interventions. Overall, means restriction and some pharmacological interventions were found to have the strongest evidence base supporting their use. The findings validate the implementation of current means restriction measures in suicide hot spots in Australia such as the suicide prevention initiatives at Sydney's Gap Park[2] and the recent installation of barriers on the Story Bridge in Brisbane[3]. A major limitation of the review was the heterogeneity of the studies included, preventing the use of meta-analyses, and thus restricting conclusions about the effectiveness of different interventions. The authors recommend that future research also examines the use of potential interventions using new social media, mobile technologies and the monitoring of large datasets.

Endnotes

1. Turecki G, Brent DA (2015). Suicide and suicidal behaviour. *Lancet* 387, 1227–1239.
2. Pirkis J, San Too L, Spittal MJ, Krysinska K, Robinson J, Cheung YTD. (2015). Interventions to reduce suicides at suicide hotspots: a systematic review and meta-analysis. *Lancet Psychiatry* 2, 994-1001.
3. Moore T (2015). *Suicide prevention barriers finally go up on Story Bridge*. Retrieved 27 October 2016 from http://www.brisbanetimes.com.au/queensland/suicide-prevention-barriers-finally-go-up-on-story-bridge-20150903-gjepz8.html.

Suicidal behaviours: Prevalence estimates from the second Australian Child and Adolescent Survey of Mental Health and Wellbeing

Zubrick SR, Hafekost J, Johnson SE, Lawrence D, Saw S, Sawyer M, Ainley J, Buckingham WJ (Australia)

Australian and New Zealand Journal of Psychiatry 50, 899-910, 2016

Objective: To (1) estimate the lifetime and 12-month prevalence of suicidal behaviours in Australian young people aged 12-17 years, (2) describe their co-morbidity with mental illness and (3) describe the co-variation of these estimates with social and demographic variables.

Method: A national random sample of children aged 4-17 years was recruited in 2013-2014. The response rate to the survey was 55% with 6310 parents and carers of eligible households participating. In addition, of the 2967 young people aged 11-17 years in these households, 89% (2653) of the 12- to 17-year-olds completed a self-report questionnaire that included questions about suicidal behaviour.

Results: In any 12-month period, about 2.4% or 41,400 young people would have made a suicide attempt. About 7.5% of 12- to 17-year-olds report having suicidal ideation, 5.2% making a plan and less than 1% (0.6%) receiving medical treatment for an attempt. The presence of a mental disorder shows the largest significant association with lifetime and 12-month suicidal behaviour, along with age, gender, sole parent family status and poor family functioning. Of young people with a major depressive disorder, 19.7% reported making a suicide attempt within the previous 12 months. There are also significant elevations in the proportions of young people reporting suicidal behaviour who have anxiety and conduct disorders.

Conclusion: Mental disorders should be a leading intervention point for suicide prevention both in the primary health sector and in the mental health sector specifically. The associations examined here also suggest that efforts to assist sole parent and/or dysfunctional families would be worthy areas in which to target these efforts.

Comment

Main findings: National data on suicidality is vital for determining nation-wide prevalence rates and for tracking suicide. In Australia, estimates of 12-month prevalence rates for suicidal behaviours in 13-17 year olds were last collected in 1998 and reported in 2000[1]. This study sought to update this data, investigating 12-month and lifetime prevalence rates for suicidal behaviour in Australians aged 12-17 years. It also examined the co-morbidity of suicidal behaviours with mental illnesses and their co-variation with key social and demographic variables. Data were collected through the 2013-2014 second Australian and Adolescent Survey of Mental Health and Wellbeing. Participants were randomly sampled based on geographic area and recruited from households where there was at least one child was aged 4-17 years. Where there was more than one eligible child in a household, only one was randomly selected for inclusion. The survey response rate was 55%, with 6,310 parents and carers participating. Out of a possible 2976 eligible young people, 2655 (89.2%) completed the youth questionnaire which contained questions about suicidal behaviour. Young peoples' responses were completed on a tablet computer, were confidential, and not shared with the consenting parent. Mental disorders were measured using seven modules from the Diagnostic Interview Schedule for Children Version IV (DISC-IV). These were social phobia, separation anxiety disorder, generalised anxiety disorder, obsessive-compulsive disorder, major depressive disorder (MDD), attention-deficit/hyperactivity disorder (ADHD) and conduct disorder. Data were collected from both young people and their parents or carers. Young people participating in the survey were given the option of not answering the suicide questions, of which 5.6% did not.

Based on parents and carer reports, 5.0% of 12-17 year olds had MDD, 6.3% ADHD, 2.1% conduct disorder and 7.0% anxiety disorders. Interestingly, 12-17 year olds rated their MDD rates higher at 8.6%. Lifetime prevalence for suicide attempts for 12-17 year olds was 3.2%, with 16-17 year olds reporting a significantly higher proportion of attempts than 12-15 year olds. Twelve month prevalence rates for suicide attempts was 2.4% for 12-17 year olds, with 7.5% also reporting suicidal ideation and 5.2% having made a suicide plan in the past 12 months. Once again, 12-month prevalence for suicidality was higher in 16-17 year olds, with 11.2% having suicidal ideation, 7.8% having a plan and 3.8% having made a suicide attempt. In the last 12 months, significantly more females reported attempting suicide, having suicidal ideation and making a suicide plan compared to males. Suicidal behaviour was also more prevalent amongst young people with psychological disorders, with 11.5% reporting at least one lifetime suicide attempt. These findings were mirrored in 12-month prevalence rates for suicide ideation, suicide plans and attempts. In particular, 19.7% of young people with MDD (based on youth self-report) reported attempting suicide in the past 12 months. Age and gender were significantly associated with suicidal behaviours, with 16-17 year old females being the most suicidal. However, when the authors conducted multivariate analyses controlling for socio-demographic variables they found that only MDD was associated with 12-month prevalence rates for suicidal ideation. Multivariate analyses were also conducted for 12-month suicide attempt prevalence rates with the authors finding that only MDD, sole parent family status and poor family functioning were strongly associated with suicide attempts.

Implications: This study provides a contemporary, community-based estimate of lifetime and 12-month prevalence rates for suicidal behaviours in young Australian people. It also provides an update on suicidal behaviours in young people and current associated factors (MDD, sole parent family status and poor family functioning). MDD in particular stands out as a significant risk factor for suicidality in 12-17 year old Australians. Improved prevention, identification and treatment of mental disorders in young people will be imperative, as are programs that assist sole parent, dysfunctional, and/or disadvantaged families. Gatekeeper training in school settings may also be effective in helping teachers identify suicidality in vulnerable students[2]. The paper was not without some limitations. The study relies on self-reported data, a method of data collection subject to participant bias, incomplete information and uncertain reliability. Furthermore, analyses were unable to be conducted on some suicidal behaviours because of the small proportion of participants engaging in these behaviours.

Endnote

1. Sawyer MG, Arney FM, Baghurst PA Clark JJ, Graetz BW, Kosky RJ, Nurcombe B, Patton GC, Prior MR, Raphael B, Rey J, Whaites LC, Zubrick SR (2000). *The National Survey of Mental Health and Wellbeing: The Mental Health of Young People in Australia*. Canberra, ACT: Commonwealth Department of Health and Aged Care.
2. Tompkins TL, Witt J, Abraibesh N (2010). Does a gatekeeper suicide prevention program work in a school setting? Evaluating training outcome and moderators of effectiveness. *Suicide and Life-Threatening Behavior, 40*, 506-515.

Recommended Readings

Suicide in older men: The health in men cohort study (HIMS)

Almeida OP, McCaul K, Hankey GJ, Yeap BB, Golledge J, Flicker L (Australia)
Preventive Medicine 93, 33-38, 2016

Suicide rates are high in later life, particularly among older men. Mood disorders are known risk factors, but the risk of suicide associated with poor physical health remains unclear. We completed a cohort study of a community representative sample of 38,170 men aged 65-85 in 1996 who were followed for up to 16years. Data on suicide attempts and completion were obtained from the Western Australia Data Linkage System, as was information about medical and mental health diagnoses. 240 (0.6%) participants had a recorded history of past suicide attempt, most commonly by poisoning (85%). Sixty-nine men died by suicide during follow up (0.3% of all deaths), most often by hanging (50.7%). Age-adjusted competing risk regression showed that past suicide attempt was not a robust predictor of future suicide completion (sub-hazard ratio, SHR=1.58, 95%CI=0.39, 6.42), but bipolar (SHR=7.82, 95%CI=3.08, 19.90), depressive disorders (SHR=2.26, 95%CI=1.14, 4.51) and the number of health systems affected by disease (SHR for 3-4 health systems=6.02, 95%CI=2.69, 13.47; SHR for ≥5 health systems=11.18, 95%CI=4.89, 25.53) were. The population fraction of suicides attributable to having 5 or more health systems affected by disease was 79% (95%CI=57%, 90%), and for any mood disorder (bipolar or depression) it was 17% (95%CI=3%, 28%). Older Australian men with multiple health morbidities have the highest risk of death by suicide, even after taking into account the presence of mood disorders. Improving the overall health of the population may be the most effective way of decreasing the rates of suicide in later life.

Direct and indirect forms of childhood maltreatment and nonsuicidal self-injury among clinically-referred children and youth.

Armiento J, Hamza CA, Stewart SL, Leschied A (Canada)
Journal of Affective Disorders 200, 212-217, 2016

Background: Although exposure to direct forms of childhood maltreatment is among the most widely studied risk factors for nonsuicidal self-injury (NSSI), research on NSSI has largely overlooked the role of exposure to indirect forms of child maltreatment (i.e. witnessing domestic violence). To address this gap in the literature, the present study examined associations among both direct and indirect forms of child maltreatment and NSSI among clinically-referred children and youth.

Methods: Data was collected using the interRAI Child and Youth Mental Health Assessment (ChYMH) at ten mental health agencies. The ChYMH is a comprehensive standardized clinical assessment tool completed by trained assessors using multiple sources. The study included a convenience sample of 747 children and youth (68% male) between ages 8-18 with complex mental health histories referred for inpatient or outpatient care in Ontario, Canada.

Results: Univariate chi-square analyses indicated positive associations with NSSI and both direct (i.e. physical, sexual) and indirect child maltreatment (i.e. witnessing domestic violence). In a binary multivariate logistic regression analysis controlling for participant age and sex, only exposure to indirect child maltreatment emerged as multivariate predictor of NSSI.

Limitations: The sample was limited to only 10 mental health agencies and only consenting parents/guardians referred to mental health services suggesting the study may not be generalizable to all clinical samples.

Conclusion: The present study provides evidence that witnessing domestic violence in childhood is an important risk factor for NSSI. Clinical relevance includes implications for clinicians to develop targeted intervention and prevention strategies for NSSI for children who have witnessed domestic violence.

Suicide attempts among alcohol-dependent pain patients before and after an inpatient hospitalization

Ashrafioun L, Kane C, Stephens B, Britton PC, Conner KR (United States)
Drug and Alcohol Dependence 163, 209-215, 2016

Background: This study examined (1) whether pain diagnoses were risk factors for non-fatal suicide attempts before and after inpatient hospitalizations in alcohol-dependent veterans, and (2) the characteristics of pain patients who attempted suicide.

Method: Administrative data from the Veterans Health Administration were used to identify veterans with an alcohol use disorder who had an inpatient hospitalization during fiscal year 2011 (n=13,047). Logistic regression analyses were used to examine the associations of suicide attempts before and after hospitalizations with pain diagnoses, demographics, medical comorbidity, and psychiatric comorbidity.

Results: Bivariate analyses and analyses controlling for demographics and medical comorbidity, indicated that pain diagnoses were significantly associated with suicide attempts in the 365days before hospitalization (Odds Ratio Adjusted [OR]=1.22). This effect was not significant after controlling for psychiatric disorders. Pain diagnoses were not identified as risk factors of suicide attempts in the 365days following discharge. Subgroup analyses among only those with a pain diagnosis revealed that being younger (OR=2.64), being female (OR=2.28), and having an attempt in the year prior to hospitalization (OR=4.11) were risk factors of suicide attempts in the year following hospitalization. Additionally, younger age (OR=2.13) and depression (OR=3.53) were associated with attempts in the year prior to the hospitalization.

Conclusions: This study suggests that psychiatric disorders account for the relationship between pain diagnoses and past suicide attempts among hospitalized alcohol-dependent veterans. Pain-specific suicide prevention efforts may be better targeted at less intensive levels of care.

Rail-suicide prevention: Systematic literature review of evidence-based activities

Barker E, Kõlves K, De Leo D (Australia)
Asia Pacific Psychiatry. Published online: 14 July 2016. doi: 10.1111/appy.12246

Background: Rail-related suicide is a relatively rare but extremely lethal method of suicide that can have far-reaching consequences.

Objective: The aim of the systematic literature review was to analyze the existing literature on the effectiveness of rail-suicide prevention activities.

Data Sources: Databases used were Scopus, Medline, and ProQuest.

Search Terms: The search terms used were "suicid*," "prevent*," "rail*," or "train."

Eligibility Criteria: English-language studies published in peer-reviewed journals between 1 January 1990 and 30 April 2015 that presented an overview of rail-related suicide prevention activities and included an analysis of effectiveness were used.

Results: We retrieved 1,229 results in the original search with nine papers presenting empirical evidence. Three studies in the review analyzed the effectiveness of platform screen doors and another three analyzed the installation of blue lights, two papers analyzed the effectiveness of suicide pits, and one included the influence of media reporting guidelines.

Conclusion: Platform screen doors, suicide pits, blue lights, and improved media guidelines all have the potential to reduce rail-related suicide events and deaths.

Limitations: The review was restricted to English-language peer-reviewed papers published within the chosen time period.

Sluggish cognitive tempo is associated with suicide risk in psychiatrically hospitalized children

Becker SP, Withrow AR, Stoppelbein L, Luebbe AM, Fite PJ, Greening L (United States)
Journal of Child Psychology and Psychiatry. Published online: 1 June 2016. doi: 10.1111/jcpp.12580

Background: Although identified as a significant public health concern, few studies have examined correlates of suicide risk in school-aged children. Recent studies show a relation between sluggish cognitive tempo (SCT) symptoms and a range of adverse outcomes linked to suicidal ideation, including depression, emotion dysregulation, lowered self-esteem, and peer problems/social withdrawal, yet no study to date has examined SCT in relation to suicide risk.

Methods: We tested the hypothesis that SCT would be associated with suicide risk in a sample of 95 psychiatrically hospitalized children (74% male; 62% black) between the ages of 8 and 12 (M = 10.01, SD = 1.50). Parents completed measures of their child's psychiatric symptoms, including SCT and depression, as well as a measure of their own psychopathology. Children completed measures assessing loneliness and depression. Both parents and children completed measures of suicide risk.

Results: White children reported greater suicide risk than nonwhite children. After controlling for demographic characteristics, loneliness, parental psychopathology, and correlated psychiatric symptoms, including both parent- and child self-reported depressive symptoms, SCT remained uniquely associated with children's suicide risk. Results were consistent across both parent and child measures of suicide risk.

Conclusions: This multi-informant study provides strong preliminary support for an association between SCT symptoms and suicide risk in psychiatrically hospitalized children, above and beyond loneliness, depression, and demographic characteristics. Findings are discussed in the context of the interpersonal theory of suicide. Additional studies are needed to replicate and extend these findings, with a particular need for studies that examine the cognitive processes and daydreaming content of individuals displaying elevated SCT symptomatology.

Trauma exposure and risk of suicidal ideation among older adults

Beristianos MH, Maguen S, Neylan TC, Byers AL (United States)
American Journal of Geriatric Psychiatry 24, 639-643, 2016

Objective: To determine if trauma exposure is associated with suicidal ideation in a nationally representative sample of older adults.

Methods: This study included 3,277 participants 55 years and older involved in the Collaborate Psychiatric Epidemiology Surveys (2001-2003).

Results: Of the 84.8% of older adults who were exposed to any trauma, 2.2% endorsed late-life suicidal ideation. Multivariable models fully adjusted for sociodemographics, post-traumatic stress disorder, major depressive disorder, and substance use revealed exposure to serious accidents/illness was associated with suicidal ideation (odds ratio: 2.55; 95% confidence interval: 1.16-5.59; Wald chi(2) = 5.47, df = 1, p = 0.019). Investigation of specific traumas within the category revealed that life-threatening illness was specifically associated with suicidal ideation in older adults (odds ratio: 2.12; 95% confidence interval: 1.34-3.36; Wald chi(2) = 10.33, df = 1, p = 0.001).

Conclusion: These findings highlight the need for monitoring of suicidal ideation among older adults who have been informed of a life-threatening illness diagnosis.

Self-harm emergencies after bariatric surgery: A population-based cohort study

Bhatti JA, Nathens AB, Thiruchelvam D, Grantcharov T, Goldstein BI, Redelmeier DA (Canada)
JAMA Surgery 151, 226-232, 2016

Importance: Self-harm behaviors, including suicidal ideation and past suicide attempts, are frequent in bariatric surgery candidates. It is unclear, however, whether these behaviors are mitigated or aggravated by surgery.

Objective: To compare the risk of self-harm behaviors before and after bariatric surgery.

Design, Setting, and Participants: In this population-based, self-matched, longitudinal cohort analysis, we studied 8815 adults from Ontario, Canada, who underwent bariatric surgery between April 1, 2006, and March 31, 2011. Follow-up for each patient was 3 years prior to surgery and 3 years after surgery.

Main Outcomes and Measures: Self-harm emergencies 3 years before and after surgery.

Results: The cohort included 8815 patients of whom 7176 (81.4%) were women, 7063 (80.1%) were 35 years or older, and 8681 (98.5%) were treated with gastric bypass. A total of 111 patients had 158 self-harm emergencies during follow-up. Overall, self-harm emergencies significantly increased after surgery (3.63 per 1000 patient-years) compared with before surgery (2.33 per 1000 patient-years), equaling a rate ratio (RR) of 1.54 (95%CI, 1.03-2.30; P =.007). Self-harm emergencies after surgery were higher than before surgery among patients older than 35 years (RR, 1.76; 95%CI, 1.05-2.94; P =.03), those with a low-income status (RR, 2.09; 95%CI, 1.20-3.65; P =.01), and those living in rural areas (RR, 6.49; 95% CI, 1.42-29.63; P =.02). The most common self-harm mechanism was an intentional overdose (115 [72.8%]). A total of 147 events (93.0%) occurred in patients diagnosed as having a mental health disorder during the 5 years before the surgery. *Conclusions and Relevance*: In this study, the risk of self-harm emergencies increased after bariatric surgery, underscoring the need for screening for suicide risk during follow-up.

Childhood household dysfunction and risk of self-harm: A cohort study of 107 518 young adults in Stockholm county

Bjorkenstam E, Kosidou K, Bjorkenstam C (Sweden, United States)
International Journal of Epidemiology 45, 501-511, 2016

Background: Childhood household dysfunction (CHD) is a risk indicator for self-harm in young adulthood. However, less is known about the effects of cumulative exposure to CHD and the role of school performance and childhood psychopathology in the relationship.

Methods: We used a Swedish cohort of 107 518 individuals born in 1987-91. Register-based CHD indicators included familial death, parental substance abuse and psychiatric morbidity, parental somatic disease, parental criminality, parental separation/single-parent household, public assistance receipt and residential instability. Estimates of risk of self-harm from age 15 [measured as registered diagnosis of self-harm according to the International Classification of Disease (ICD)] were calculated as hazard ratios (HR) with 95% confidence intervals (CIs).

Results: CHD indicators, with exceptions of familial death and parental somatic disease, were associated with an increased risk of self-harm. Accumulating CHD indicators increased the risk of self-harm in a graded manner, and individuals exposed to five or more indicators had a f5-fold risk [hazard ratio (HR): 4.9, 95% CI 3.8-6.4) after adjustment for school performance, childhood psychopathology and confounders. Exposure to five or more CHD indicators and poor school performance conferred a 20-fold increased risk, compared with non-exposed individuals in the highest grade group. The risk was elevated by 9-fold for those with five or more CHD indicators and a history of childhood psychopathology.

Conclusion: Childhood household dysfunction is associated with the risk of self-harm in young adults, particularly when accumulated. The risk is markedly increased in the subgroup of disadvantaged children that fail in school or develop childhood psychopathology.

The course of suicide risk following traumatic injury

Bryant RA, O'Donnell ML, Forbes D, McFarlane AC, Silove D, Creamer M (Australia)

Journal of Clinical Psychiatry 77, 648-653, 2016

Objective: Although traumatic injuries affect millions of patients each year and increase risk for psychiatric disorder, no evidence currently exists regarding associated suicidal risk. This study reports a longitudinal investigation of suicidal risk in the 2 years after traumatic injury.

Methods: A prospective design cohort study was conducted in 4 major trauma hospitals across Australia. A total of 1,129 traumatically injured patients were assessed during hospital admission between April 2004 and February 2006 and were followed up at 3 months (88%), 12 months (77%), and 24 months (72%). Lifetime psychiatric disorder was assessed in hospital using the Mini-International Neuropsychiatric Interview, version 5.5, which was also used to assess the prevalence of suicidality, psychiatric disorder, and exposure to adverse life events at 3, 12, and 24 months after traumatic injury.

Results: Approximately 6% of patients reported moderate/high suicidal risk at each assessment. At each assessment, half of suicidal patients reported no suicidal risk at the previous assessment. Suicidality at 24 months was predicted by current pain levels (odds ratio [OR] = 1.16; 95% CI, 1.09-1.23), recent life events (OR = 1.30; 95% CI,1.17-1.44), and current psychiatric disorder (OR = 17.07; 95% CI, 7.03-41.42), whereas only 36.6% of suicidal patients had consulted a mental health professional in the previous month, and 66.2% had consulted a primary care physician.

Conclusions: Suicidal risk affects a significant proportion of patients who experience a traumatic injury, and the risk for suicide fluctuates markedly in the initial years following the injury. Primary care physicians need to be trained to assess for suicidal risk in the initial years after a traumatic injury.

Suicide risk characteristics among aborted, interrupted, and actual suicide attempters

Burke TA, Hamilton JL, Ammerman BA, Stange JP, Alloy LB (United States)

Psychiatry Research 242, 357-364, 2016

Few studies have investigated suicide risk characteristics associated with interrupted and aborted suicide attempts. The present study aimed to empirically examine whether assessing a history of interrupted and aborted suicide attempts is valuable when assessing suicide risk, given the relative lack of literature in this area to date. To inform this question, the current study examined differences in risk factors for suicidal behavior among individuals who have carried out a suicide attempt, individuals who report having a history of only interrupted and/or aborted suicide attempts, and non-attempter controls. Approximately 447 undergraduates (M=21.10 years; SD=4.16; 77.6% female) completed measures of carried out suicide attempts, interrupted suicide attempts, aborted suicide attempts, acquired capability for suicide, suicide likelihood, depressive symptoms, suicidal ideation, and non-suicidal self-injury. Results suggest that a faction of individuals endorse interrupted and/or aborted suicide attempts (8.7%), but do not endorse carried out suicide attempts, even in non-clinical samples. Furthermore, results suggest that there are few clinically meaningful differences between those with a history of carried out suicide attempts and interrupted/aborted suicide attempts, suggesting that individuals with a history of these lesser studied suicidal behaviors are an important group to target for suicide risk intervention.

Is psychotherapy effective for reducing suicide attempt and non-suicidal self-injury rates? Meta-analysis and meta-regression of literature data

Calati R, Courtet P (France)

Journal of Psychiatric Research 79, 8-20, 2016

Objective: To determine the efficacy of psychotherapy interventions for reducing suicidal attempts (SA) and non-suicidal self-injury (NSSI).

Methods: Meta-analysis of randomized controlled trials (RCTs) comparing psychotherapy interventions and treatment as usual (TAU; including also enhanced usual care, psychotropic treatment alone, cognitive remediation, short-term problem-oriented approach, supportive relationship treatment, community treatment by non-behavioral psychotherapy experts, emergency care enhanced by provider education, no treatment) for SA/NSSI. RCTs were extracted from MEDLINE, EMBASE, PsycINFO and Cochrane Library and analyzed using the Cochrane Collaboration Review Manager Software and Comprehensive Meta-analysis.

Results: In the 32 included RCTs, 4114 patients were randomly assigned to receive psychotherapy (n = 2106) or TAU (n = 2008). Patients who received psychotherapy were less likely to attempt suicide during the follow-up. The pooled risk difference for SA was -0.08 (95% confidence intervals = -0.04 to -0.11). The absolute risk reduction was 6.59% (psychotherapy: 9.12%; TAU: 15.71%), yielding an estimated number needed to treat of 15. Sensitivity analyses showed that psychotherapy was effective for SA mainly in adults, outpatients, patients with borderline personality disorder, previously and non-previously suicidal patients (heterogeneous variable that included past history of SA, NSSI, deliberate self-harm, imminent suicidal risk or suicidal ideation), long- and short-term therapies, TAU only as a control condition, and mentalization-based treatment (MBT). No evidence of efficacy was found for NSSI, with the exception of MBT. Between-study heterogeneity and publication bias were detected. In the presence of publication bias, the Duval and Tweedie's "trim and fill" method was applied.

Conclusion: Psychotherapy seems to be effective for SA treatment. However, trials with lower risk of bias, more homogeneous outcome measures and longer follow-up are needed.

Diagnoses and prescriptions of antidepressants in suicides: Register findings from the Friuli Venezia Giulia Region, Italy, 2002-2008

Castelpietra G, Bovenzi M, Clagnan E, Barbone F, Balestrieri M, Isacsson G (Sweden, Italy)
International Journal of Psychiatry in Clinical Practice 20, 121-124, 2016

Objective: To explore to what extent and under which diagnoses individuals who committed suicide had received psychiatric in-patient care, and how many had previously committed non-lethal self-harm. To investigate the antidepressant treatment received by these individuals.

Methods: Case-control study based on a health register.

Results: Psychiatric hospitalisation was found in 31.2% of the cases and 2.3% of the controls, and was a strong predictor for suicide with an odds ratio (OR) = 19.5. This did not differ significantly between diagnostic categories (except anxiety disorders with OR = 5.3). Non-lethal self-harm in the study period was committed by 14.3% of the cases and 0.14% of the controls, and was twice as common in female cases than in male cases. Previous self-harm was a very strong independent predictor for suicide with OR = 53.1 when a single episode of self-harm had occurred, and OR = 98.0 for repeated episodes (adjusted for age, gender and hospitalisation). Only 16.1% of the cases were currently on antidepressant medication at the time of suicide.

Conclusions: Few of the suicides had previously been psychiatric in-patients. Even fewer had current prescriptions for antidepressants. This suggests that better diagnosis and treatment of psychiatric patients is an important suicide preventive intervention.

An analysis of depression, self-harm, and suicidal ideation content on Tumblr.

Cavazos-Rehg PA, Krauss MJ, Sowles SJ, Connolly S, Rosas C, Bharadwaj M, Grucza R, Bierut LJ (United States)
Crisis. Published online: 22 July 2016. doi: 10.1027/0227-5910/a000409

Background: Social networking about depression can be indicative of self-reported depression and/or can normalize risk behaviors such as self-harm and suicidal ideation.

Aim: To gain a better understanding of the depression, self-harm, and suicidal content that is being shared on Tumblr.

Method: From April 16 to May 10, 2014, 17 popular depression-related Tumblr accounts were monitored for new posts and engagement with other Tumblr users. A total of 3,360 posts were randomly selected from all historical posts from these accounts and coded based on themes ascertained by the research team.

Results: The 17 Tumblr accounts posted a median number of 185 posts (range = 0-2,954). Content was engaged with (i.e. re-blogged or liked) a median number of 1,677,362 times (range = 0-122,186,504). Of the 3,360 randomly selected posts, 2,739 (82%) were related to depression, suicide, or self-harm. Common themes were self-loathing (412, 15%), loneliness/feeling unloved (405, 15%), self-harm (407, 15%), and suicide (372, 14%).

Conclusion: This study takes an important first step at better understanding the displayed depression-related references on Tumblr. The findings signal a need for suicide prevention efforts to intervene on Tumblr and use this platform in a strategic way, given the depression and suicidal content that was readily observed on Tumblr.

Predicting suicide following self-harm: A systematic review of risk factors and risk scales

Chan MKY, Bhatti H, Meader N, Stockton S, Evans J, O'Connor R, Kapur N, Kendall T (Hong Kong, Canada, United Kingdom)

British Journal of Psychiatry 209, 277-283, 2016

Background: Suicide and self-harm are major public health problems. People with a history of self-harm are at a far greater risk of suicide than the general population. However, the relationship between self-harm and suicide is complex. We have undertaken the first systematic review and meta-analysis of prospective studies of risk factors and risk assessment scales to predict suicide following self-harm, undertaken as part of the development of the National Institute for Health and Care Excellence (NICE) guideline.

Methods: For this systematic review, Embase, MEDLINE, PsycINFO and CINAHL were searched for English-language prospective cohort studies of populations who had selfharmed. For the review of risk scales we also included studies examining the risk of suicide in people under specialist mental health care, in order to broaden the scope of the review and increase the number of studies considered. Differences in predictive accuracy between populations were examined where applicable.

Results: Twelve studies on risk factors and 7 studies on risk scales were included. Four risk factors emerged from the meta-analysis, with robust effect sizes that showed little change when adjusted for important potential confounders. These included: previous episodes of selfharm (HR 1.68, 95% CI 1.38 to 2.05, K=4), suicidal intent (HR 2.7, 95% CI 1.91 to 3.81, K=3), physical health problems (HR 1.99, 95% CI 1.16-3.43, K=3) and male gender (HR 2.05, 95% CI 1.70 to 2.46, K=5). The included studies evaluated only 3 risk scales (Beck Hopelessness Scale [BHS], Suicide Intent Scale [SIS] and Scale for Suicide Ideation [SSI]). Where meta-analyses were possible (BHS, SIS), the analysis was based on sparse data and a high heterogeneity was observed. The positive predictive values ranged from 1.3% to 16.7%.

Interpretation: Four factors indicated an increased risk of suicide following self-harm. Although of interest, these are unlikely to be of much practical use because they are comparatively common in clinical populations. No scales have sufficient evidence to support their use in predicting suicide. The use of these scales, or an over-reliance on the identification of risk factors in clinical practice, may provide false reassurance and are, therefore, potentially dangerous. Comprehensive psychosocial assessments of the risks and needs that are specific to the individual should be central to the management of people who have self-harmed.

A comparison of methods of self-harm without intent to die: Cutting versus self-poisoning

Chartrand H, Kim H, Sareen J, Mahmoudi M, Bolton JM (Canada)
Journal of Affective Disorders 205, 200-206, 2016

Background: Non-suicidal self-injury (NSSI) in DSM-5 Section 3 is restricted to damaging the skin, while self-poisoning is not considered NSSI even if there was no suicidal intent. The objective of this study was to compare correlates of people who self-cut and those who self-poison without suicidal intent, to determine whether people who harm themselves by cutting are a distinct subgroup.

Methods: There were 12,435 presentations to adult psychiatric services in the emergency departments of tertiary care hospitals in Manitoba between January 2009 and December 2013. Chart reviews were conducted for all presentations with self-harm without suicidal intent (n=219; 1.8% of the total sample). People presenting with cutting (n=47) were compared to those presenting with self-poisoning (n=116).

Results: There were no differences between the groups on most demographic measures, except for age, where the people who cut were younger. Mental disorders were common in both groups. 31.9% of the cutting group had an alcohol use disorder, as did 25% of the self-poisoning group. Cluster B personality traits/disorder was diagnosed more frequently in the cutting group (51.1%) than the self-poisoning group (37.9%), but this difference was non-significant. Previous non-suicidal self-harm was more common among people cutting.

Limitations: We were unable to draw conclusions about the risk of suicide.

Conclusions: People who engage in non-suicidal self-harm have high rates of mental disorders. The method that people use to harm themselves does not appear to distinguish these groups; they appear to be similar on most demographic and diagnostic correlates. Further study is required to determine the validity of NSSI, including studies that compare those who self-harm with and without suicidal intent.

Self-harm in nurses: Prevalence and correlates

Cheung T, Yip PS (Hong Kong)
Journal of Advanced Nursing 72, 2124-2137

Aims: The aim of this study was to examine the weighed prevalence of self-harm and its correlates among Hong Kong nurses.

Background: Recent epidemiological data suggest that the weighted prevalence of past-year suicidality among Hong Kong nurses was found to be 14.9%. Deliberate self-harm was a significant correlate of suicidality. Nonetheless, there are few population-based studies exploring the prevalence of self-harm and its correlates among medical occupational groups in Asia.

Design: The study uses a cross-sectional survey design.

Method: Data were collected in Hong Kong over a four-week period from October-November 2013. Statistical methods, including binary and multivariate logistic regression models, were used to examine the weighted prevalence of self-harm and its associated factors in nurses.

Results: A total of 850 nurses participated in the study. Seventy-nine participants (9.3%) reported self-harm in the past year. Nurses aged between 25-44 were at especially high risk of self-harm. Female nurses reported self-harm more than male nurses. The most common forms of self-harm were self-cutting, striking oneself and poisoning oneself. Clinical experience, chronic illness, relationship crises with family members, a family history of self-harm, smoking, symptoms of stress and psychiatric disorder were significantly associated with nurses' self-harm. The positive correlation between psychiatric disorder and self-harm was confirmed.

Conclusions: There is a need for a raft of self-harm prevention strategies, including a continuous monitoring system in the healthcare setting detecting and managing the risks of self-harm in nurses as part of the ordinary provision for their well-being.

Reducing suicidal ideation through evidence-based treatment for posttraumatic stress disorder

Cox KS, Mouilso ER, Venners MR, Defever ME, Duvivier L, Rauch SAM, Strom TQ, Joiner TE, Tuerk PW (United States)
Journal of Psychiatric Research 80, 59-63, 2016

Background: Suicide is a major public health concern in military and civilian contexts. Veteran populations are at increased risk for suicide, especially veterans with mental health disorders such as Posttraumatic Stress Disorder (PTSD). Suicidal ideation (SI) is a primary risk factor for suicide.

Methods: We investigated changes in SI in a multi-site sample of treatment seeking veterans from three separate Veterans Health Administration (VA) medical centers (n = 289) who received Prolonged Exposure (PE) therapy, an evidence-based treatment (EBT) for PTSD. SI and PTSD symptoms were assessed, using self-report instruments, throughout routine clinical care.

Results: Both PTSD and SI symptoms reduced over the course of treatment (d-type effect sizes of 1.47 and 0.27, respectively). While SI was associated with PTSD symptoms at all time points, appropriately specified, time lagged models indicated that changes in PTSD symptoms were predictive of future declines in SI, while the converse was not true.

Conclusions: Results indicate that treating PTSD symptoms with an EBT for PTSD can be an effective way to reduce SI, at least partially, and for some patients. These data are significant in light of the resources and programming devoted to addressing SI in the VA relative to available empirical evidence regarding the effectiveness of developed strategies. The findings demonstrate the importance of facilitating EBT referrals for specific disorders as a component of broad-based suicide outreach and preventions strategies

A comparison of suicides in psychiatric in-patients, after discharge and in not recently hospitalized individuals

Deisenhammer EA, Behrndt E-M, Kemmler G, Haring C, Miller C (Austria)
Comprehensive Psychiatry 69, 100-105, 2016

Objective: Time of in-patient treatment and the first weeks after hospital discharge have repeatedly been described as periods of increased suicide risk. This study compared demographic, clinical and suicide related factors between in-patient, post-discharge and not recently hospitalized suicides.

Methods: Suicide data from the Tyrol Suicide Register were linked with registers of three psychiatric hospitals in the state of Tyrol, Austria. Suicide cases then were categorized as in-patient suicides, post-discharge suicides (suicide within 12 weeks after discharge) or never/not within 12 weeks before death hospitalized suicides. Data were collected between 2004 and 2011.

Results: Of the total of 711 cases, 30 were in-patient, 89 post-discharge and 592 not recently hospitalized suicides. The three groups differed with regard to male-to-female ratio (lower in both hospitalized groups), marital status, suicide method used (jumping in in-patients, hanging in not recently hospitalized suicides), history of attempted suicide and suicide threats (highest in in-patients) and whether suicides had been in psychiatric or general practitioner treatment shortly before death. In most variables with significant differences there was a gradual increase/decrease with post-discharge suicides taking the middle place between the two other groups.

Conclusions: The three suicide populations differed in a number of variables. Varying factors appear to influence suicide risk and choice of method differently in in-patient, post-discharge and not hospitalized suicides.

Suicide risk assessment in hospitals: An expert system-based triage tool

Desjardins I, Cats-Baril W, Maruti S, Freeman K, Althoff R (United States)

Journal of Clinical Psychiatry 77, e874-e882, 2016

Background: The November 2010 Joint Commission Sentinel Event Alert on the prevention of suicides in medical/surgical units and the emergency department (ED) mandates screening every patient treated as an outpatient or admitted to the hospital for suicide risk. Our aim was to develop a suicide risk assessment tool to (1) predict the expert psychiatrist's assessment for risk of committing suicide within 72 hours in the hospital, (2) replicate the recommended intervention by the psychiatrist, and (3) demonstrate acceptable levels of participant satisfaction.

Methods: The 3 phases of tool development took place between October 2012 and February 2014. An expert panel developed key questions for a tablet-based suicide risk questionnaire. We then performed a randomized cross-sectional study comparing the questionnaire to the interview by a psychiatrist, for model derivation. A neural network model was constructed using 255 ED participants. Evaluation was the agreement between the risk/intervention scores using the questionnaire and the risk/intervention scores given by psychiatrists to the same patients. The model was validated using a new population of 124 participants from the ED and 50 participants from medical/surgical units.

Results: The suicide risk assessment tool performed at a remarkably high level. For levels of suicide risk (minimal or low, moderate, or high), areas under the curves were all above 0.938. For levels of intervention (routine, specialized, highly specialized, or secure), areas under the curves were all above 0.914. Participants reported that they liked the tool, and it took less than a minute to use.

Conclusions: An expert-based neural network model predicted psychiatrists' assessments of risk of suicide in the hospital within 72 hours. It replicated psychiatrist-recommended interventions to mitigate risk in EDs and medical/surgical units.

Suicide risk in primary care patients diagnosed with a personality disorder: A nested case control study

Doyle M, While D, Mok PLH, Windfuhr K, Ashcroft DM, Kontopantelis E, Chew-Graham CA, Appleby L, Shaw J, Webb RT (United Kingdom)

BMC Family Practice 17, 106, 2016

Background: Personality disorder (PD) is associated with elevated suicide risk, but the level of risk in primary care settings is unknown. We assessed whether PD among primary care patients is linked with a greater elevation in risk as compared with other psychiatric diagnoses, and whether the association is modified by gender, age, type of PD, and comorbid alcohol misuse.

Methods: Using data from the UK Clinical Practice Research Datalink, 2384 suicides were matched to 46,899 living controls by gender, age, and registered practice.

Prevalence of PD, other mental disorders, and alcohol misuse was calculated for cases and controls separately and conditional logistic regression models were used to estimate exposure odds ratios. We also fitted gender interaction terms and formally tested their significance, and estimated gender age-specific effects.

Results: We found a 20-fold increase in suicide risk for patients with PD versus no recorded psychiatric disorder, and a four-fold increase versus all other psychiatric illnesses combined. Borderline PD and PD with comorbid alcohol misuse were associated with a 37- and 45-fold increased risk, respectively, compared with those with no psychiatric disorders. Relative risks were higher for female than for male patients with PD. Significant risks associated with PD diagnosis were identified across all age ranges, although the greatest elevations were in the younger age ranges, 16-39 years.

Conclusions: The large elevation in suicide risk among patients diagnosed with PD and comorbid alcohol misuse is a particular concern. GPs have a potentially key role to play in intervening with patients diagnosed with PD, particularly in the presence of comorbid alcohol misuse, which may help reduce suicide risk. This would mean working with specialist care, agreed clinical pathways and availability of services for comorbidities such as alcohol misuse, as well as opportunities for GPs to develop specific clinical skills.

The role of schools in children and young people's self-harm and suicide: Systematic review and meta-ethnography of qualitative research

Evans R, Hurrell C (United Kingdom)
BMC Public Health *16*, 401, 2016

Background: Evidence reports that schools influence children and young people's health behaviours across a range of outcomes. However there remains limited understanding of the mechanisms through which institutional features may structure self-harm and suicide. This paper reports on a systematic review and meta-ethnography of qualitative research exploring how schools influence self-harm and suicide in students.

Methods: Systematic searches were conducted of nineteen databases from inception to June 2015. English language, primary research studies, utilising any qualitative research design to report on the influence of primary or secondary educational settings (or international equivalents) on children and young people's self-harm and suicide were included. Two reviewers independently appraised studies against the inclusion criteria, assessed quality, and abstracted data. Data synthesis was conducted in adherence with Noblit and Hare's meta-ethnographic approach. Of 6744 unique articles identified, six articles reporting on five studies were included in the meta-ethnography.

Results: Five meta-themes emerged from the studies. First, self-harm is often rendered invisible within educational settings, meaning it is not prioritised within the curriculum despite students' expressed need. Second, where self-harm transgresses institutional rules it may be treated as 'bad behaviour', meaning adequate support is denied. Third, schools' informal management strategy of escalating incidents of self-harm to external 'experts' serves to contribute to non-help seeking behaviour amongst students who desire confidential support from teachers. Fourth, anxiety and stress associated with school performance may escalate self-harm and suicide. Fifth, bullying within the school context can contribute to self-harm, whilst some young people may engage in these practices as initiation into a social group.

Conclusions: Schools may influence children and young people's self-harm, although evidence of their impact on suicide remains limited. Prevention and intervention needs to acknowledge and accommodate these institutional-level factors. Studies included in this review are limited by their lack of conceptual richness, restricting the process of interpretative synthesis. Further qualitative research should focus on the continued development of theoretical and empirical insight into the relationship between institutional features and students' self-harm and suicide.

Presence of minor and major mental health impairment in adolescence and death from suicide and unintentional injuries/accidents in men: A national longitudinal cohort study

Fadum EA, Fonnebo V, Borud EK (Norway)

Journal of Epidemiology and Community Health. Published online: 14 July 2016. doi:10.1136/jech-2016-207656

Objective: To examine the association between minor and major mental health impairment in late adolescence and death from suicide and unintentional injuries/accidents in men.

Methods: In Norway, all men attend a compulsory military medical and psychological examination. We included 558 949 men aged 17-19 years at the time of military examination in 1980-1999 and followed them up for death from suicide and unintentional injuries/accidents until the end of 2013. We used Cox proportional hazard models to examine the association between the presence of minor and major mental health impairments at examination and death from suicide and unintentional injuries/accidents.

Results: Compared to men with no mental health impairment, those with minor mental health impairment was associated with an increased risk of death from suicide (adjusted HR (HRadj)=1.63, 95% CI 1.39 to 1.92), transport accidents (HRadj=1.33, 95% CI 1.09 to 1.63), accidental poisoning (HRadj=2.27, 95% CI 1.79 to 2.88) and other unintentional injuries/accidents (HRadj=1.54, 95% CI 1.17 to 2.02). In men with major mental health impairment, the risk of death from suicide and accidental poisoning was elevated two times (HRadj=2.29, 95% CI 1.85 to 2.85) and three times (HRadj=3.53, 95% CI 2.61 to 4.79), respectively.

Conclusions: We found an increased risk of death from suicide and unintentional injuries/accidents in men who had minor and major mental health impairment at age 17-19 years.

The impact of suicidality on health-related quality of life: A latent growth curve analysis of community-based data

Fairweather-Schmidt AK, Batterham PJ, Butterworth P, Nada-Raja S (Australia, New Zealand)
Journal of Affective Disorders 203, 14-21, 2016

Objective: The subjective burden of suicidality on mental and physical health-related quality of life (HRQoL) remains to be examined. Eight-year trajectories of mental and physical components of HRQoL were compared for suicidal and non-suicidal participants at baseline. The effect of poor mental and/or physical HRQoL on subsequent suicidality was also investigated.

Method: Randomly-selected community data (W1=7485; W2=6715; W3=6133) were analysed with multivariate latent growth curve (LGC) and logistic regression models.

Results: Adjusted LGC modelling identified that baseline ideation was associated with poorer mental, but better physical HRQoL at baseline (b=-3.93, 95% CI=-4.75 to -3.12; b=1.38, 95% CI=0.53-2.23, respectively). However, ideation was associated with a declining physical HRQoL trajectory over 8 subsequent years (b=-0.88, 95% CI=-1.42 to -0.35). Poorer mental HRQoL was associated with higher odds of ideation onset (OR=0.98, 95% Cl=0.96-0.99).

Limitations: Frequency of data collection was four-yearly, while suicidality was reported for the previous 12-months; analyses did not control for physical health problems at baseline, baseline depression may have influenced physical QoL; suicidality was assessed with binary measures; and, prior analyses of attrition over time showed those with poorer health were less likely to continue participating in the study.

Conclusions: Suicidality has differential longitudinal effects on mental and physical HRQoL. Findings emphasise the considerable subjective HRQoL burden upon suicidal individuals. HRQoL may be useful to compare relative social and economical impacts.

Benefits of a secondary prevention program in suicide

Farré A, Portella MJ, De Angel L, Díaz A, de Diego-Adeliño J, Vegué J, Duran-Sindreu S, Faus G, Tejedor C, Álvarez E, Perez V (Spain)
Crisis. Published online: 1 June 2016. doi: 10.1027/0227-5910/a000388

Background: The effectiveness of suicide intervention programs has not been assessed with experimental designs.

Aim: To determine the risk of suicide reattempts in patients engaged in a secondary prevention program.

Method: We included 154 patients with suicidal behavior in a quasi-experimental study with a nontreatment concurrent control group. In all, 77 patients with suicidal behavior underwent the Suicide Behavior Prevention Program (SBPP), which includes specialized early assistance during a period of 3-6 months. A matched sample of patients with suicidal behavior (n = 77) was selected without undergoing any specific suicide prevention program. Data on sociodemographics, clinical characteristics, and suicidal behavior were collected at baseline (before SBPP) and at 12 months.

Results: After 12 months, SBPP patients showed a 67% lower relative risk of reattempt ($\chi(2)$ = 11.75, p =.001, RR = 0.33 95% CI = 0.17-0.66). Cox proportional hazards models revealed that patients under SBPP made a new suicidal attempt significantly much later than control patients did (Cox regression = 0.293, 95% CI = 0.138-0.624, p =.001). The effect was even stronger among first attempters.

Limitations: Sampling was naturalistic and patients were not randomized.

Conclusion: The SBPP was effective in delaying and preventing suicide reattempts at least within the first year after the suicide behavior. In light of our results, implementation of suicide prevention programs is strongly advisable.

Repeated suicide attempts and suicide among individuals with a first emergency department contact for attempted suicide: A prospective, nationwide, Danish register-based study

Fedyszyn IE, Erlangsen A, Hjorthøj C, Madsen T, Nordentoft M (Denmark, United States)
Journal of Clinical Psychiatry 77, 832-840, 2016

Objective: Emergency departments are important, albeit underutilized, sites for suicide prevention. Preventive strategies and interventions could benefit from a greater understanding of factors influencing the course of suicide risk after emergency department contact due to attempted suicide. The aim of our study was 2-fold: to identify predictors of repeated suicide attempts and suicide and to investigate the timing of these events.

Methods: Data from Danish nationwide, longitudinal registers were used in this prospective, population-based study of all individuals first presenting to an emergency department after attempted suicide (index attempt) between January 1, 1996, and December 31, 2011 (N = 11,802). Cox regression analysis identified predictors, and Kaplan-Meier survival analysis modeled the time to repeated suicide attempts and suicide.

Results: Sixteen percent of the sample repeated suicide attempt, and 1.4% died by suicide. Repetition was less likely among men than women (adjusted hazard ratio [AHR] = 0.70; 95% CI, 0.63-0.79), whereas those most prone to repeated attempts were individuals with recent psychiatric treatment (AHR = 2.19; 95% CI, 1.97-2.43) and those with recent psychiatric treatment (AHR = 2.19; 95% CI, 1.97-2.43). Predictors of suicide included age over 35 years (AHR = 5.56; 95% CI, 2.89-10.69); hanging, strangling, or suffocation as the method of the index attempt (AHR = 2.55; 95% CI, 1.29-5.01); and receiving psychiatric hospitalization for the index attempt (AHR = 1.74; 95% CI, 1.22-2.49). The cumulative rates of repeated attempts and suicide deaths in the total sample were particularly high within the first week of the index attempt, reaching 3.6% and 0.1%, respectively.

Conclusions: Preventive efforts need to target the period close to discharge from emergency departments.

Suicide in obsessive-compulsive disorder: A population-based study of 36 788 Swedish patients

Fernandez de la Cruz L, Rydell M, Runeson B, D'Onofrio BM, Brander G, Ruck C, Lichtenstein P, Larsson H, Mataix-Cols D (Sweden, United States)

Molecular Psychiatry. Published online: 19 July 2016. doi: 10.1038/mp.2016.115

The risk of death by suicide in individuals with obsessive-compulsive disorder (OCD) is largely unknown. Previous studies have been small and methodologically flawed. We analyzed data from the Swedish national registers to estimate the risk of suicide in OCD and identify the risk and protective factors associated with suicidal behavior in this group. We used a matched case-cohort design to estimate the risk of deaths by suicide and attempted suicide in individuals diagnosed with OCD, compared with matched general population controls (1:10). Cox regression models were used to study predictors of suicidal behavior. We identified 36 788 OCD patients in the Swedish National Patient Register between 1969 and 2013. Of these, 545 had died by suicide and 4297 had attempted suicide. In unadjusted models, individuals with OCD had an increased risk of both dying by suicide (odds ratio (OR)=9.83 (95% confidence interval (CI), 8.72-11.08)) and attempting suicide (OR=5.45 (95% CI, 5.24-5.67)), compared with matched controls. After adjusting for psychiatric comorbidities, the risk was reduced but remained substantial for both death by suicide and attempted suicide. Within the OCD cohort, a previous suicide attempt was the strongest predictor of death by suicide. Having a comorbid personality or substance use disorder also increased the risk of suicide. Being a woman, higher parental education and having a comorbid anxiety disorder were protective factors. We conclude that patients with OCD are at a substantial risk of suicide. Importantly, this risk remains substantial after adjusting for psychiatric comorbidities. Suicide risk should be carefully monitored in patients with OCD.

Changes in parenting strategies after a young person's self-harm: A qualitative study

Ferrey AE, Hughes ND, Simkin S, Locock L, Stewart A, Kapur N, Gunnell D, Hawton K (United Kingdom)

Child and Adolescent Psychiatry and Mental Health 10, 20, 2016

Background: When faced with the discovery of their child's self-harm, mothers and fathers may re-evaluate their parenting strategies. This can include changes to the amount of support they provide their child and changes to the degree to which they control and monitor their child.

Methods: We conducted an in-depth qualitative study with 37 parents of young people who had self-harmed in which we explored how and why their parenting changed after the discovery of self-harm.

Results: Early on, parents often found themselves "walking on eggshells" so as not to upset their child, but later they felt more able to take some control. Parents' reactions to the self-harm often depended on how they conceptualised it: as part of adolescence, as a mental health issue or as "naughty behaviour". Parenting of other children in the family could also be affected, with parents worrying about less of their time being available for siblings. Many parents developed specific strategies they felt helped them to be more effective parents, such as learning to avoid blaming themselves or their child for the self-harm and developing new ways to communicate with their child. Parents were generally eager to pass their knowledge on to other people in the same situation.

Conclusions: Parents reported changes in their parenting behaviours after the discovery of a child's self-harm. Professionals involved in the care of young people who self-harm might use this information in supporting and advising parents.

Impact of client suicide on psychologists in Australia

Finlayson M, Graetz Simmonds J (Australia)

Australian Psychologist. Published online: 11 August 2016. doi: 10.1111/ap.12240

Objective: This research aimed to assess the frequency and impact of client suicides on psychologists in Australia.

Method: Participants were 178 psychologists who completed an online self-report questionnaire concerning the frequency of occurrence and impact of client suicide.

Result: Fifty six (31.5%) participants reported one or more client suicides. Psychologists with more years of experience reported more client suicides. Participants who had experienced a client suicide reported a range of emotional, cognitive and behavioural reactions as well as professional impacts. Ratings of responsibility, preventability and predictability of a client suicide were associated with emotional and/or professional impacts. Beneficial coping responses included talking to supervisors and colleagues, recognising the psychologist is not responsible and having increased acceptance of a client suicide.

Conclusions: The findings have important implications for training, workplace practices and research.

Overview evidence on interventions for population suicide with an eye to identifying best-supported strategies for LMICs

Fleischmann A, Arensman E, Berman A, Carli V, De Leo D, Hadlaczky G, Howlader S, Vijayakumar L, Wasserman D, Saxena S (Switzerland, Ireland, USA, Sweden, Australia, India)

Global Mental Health 3, e5, 2016

Globally, over 800 000 people died by suicide in 2012 and there are indications that for each adult who died of suicide there were likely to be many more attempting suicide. There are many millions of people every year who are affected by suicide and suicide attempts, taking into consideration the family members, friends, work colleagues and communities, who are bereaved by suicide. In the WHO Mental Health Action Plan 2013-2020, Member States committed themselves to work towards the global target of reducing the suicide rate in countries by 10% by 2020. Hence, the first-ever WHO report on suicide prevention, Preventing suicide: a global imperative, published in September 2014, is a timely call to take action using effective evidence-based interventions. Their relevance for low- and middle-income countries is discussed in this paper, highlighting restricting access to means, responsible media reporting, introducing mental health and alcohol policies, early identification and treatment, training of health workers, and follow-up care and community support following a suicide attempt.

GPs' experiences of dealing with parents bereaved by suicide: A qualitative study

Foggin E, McDonnell S, Cordingley L, Kapur N, Shaw J, Chew-Graham CA (United Kingdom)

British Journal of General Practice 66, e737-e746, 2016

Background: Suicide prevention is an NHS priority in England. Bereavement by suicide is a risk factor for suicide, but the needs of those bereaved by suicide have not been addressed, and little is known about how GPs support these patients, and how they deal with this aspect of their work.

Aim: This study explores the experiences of GPs dealing with parents bereaved by suicide.

Design and Setting: Qualitative study using interviews with 13 GPs in the UK.

Method: Parents, whose adult offspring had died by suicide between 2002 and 2012, were recruited and gave the name of their GP to be invited for interview. Semi-structured interviews were conducted. The topic guide explored experiences of dealing with suicide and bereavement. Data were analysed thematically using constant comparison techniques.

Results: GPs described mental health as 'part and parcel' of primary care, but disclosed low confidence in dealing with suicide and an unpreparedness to face parents bereaved by suicide. Some GPs described guilt surrounding the suicide, and a reluctance to initiate contact with the bereaved parents. GPs talked of their duty to care for the bereaved patients, but admitted difficulties in knowing what to do, particularly in the perceived absence of other services. GPs reflected on the impact of the suicide on themselves and described a lack of support or supervision.

Conclusion: GPs need to feel confident and competent to support parents bereaved by suicide. Although this may be facilitated through training initiatives, and accessible services to refer parents to, GPs also require formal support and supervision, particularly around significant events such as suicide. Results from this qualitative study have informed the development of evidence-based suicide bereavement training for health professionals.

Relationship of suicide rates with climate and economic variables in Europe during 2000-2012

Fountoulakis KN, Chatzikosta I, Pastiadis K, Zanis P, Kawohl W, Kerkhof AJFM, Navickas A, Höschl C, Lecic-Tosevski D, Sorel E, Rancans E, Palova E, Juckel G, Isacsson G, Jagodic HK, Botezat-Antonescu I, Rybakowski J, Azorin JM, Cookson J, Waddington J, Pregelj P, Demyttenaere K, Hranov LG, Stevović LI, Pezawas L, Adida M, Figuera ML, Jakovljević M, Vichi M, Perugi G, Andreassen OA, Vuković O, Mavrogiorgou P, Värnik P, Döme P, Winkler P, Salokangas RKR, From T, Danileviciute V, Gonda X, Rihmer Z, Forsman J, Grady A, Hyphantis T, Dieset I, Soendergaard S, Pompili M, Bech P (Greece, Switzerland, The Netherlands, Lithuania, Czech Republic, Serbia, United States, Latvia, Slovakia, Germany, Sweden, Slovenia, Romania, Poland, France, United Kingdom, Ireland, Belgium, Bulgaria, Montenegro, Austria, Portugal, Croatia, Italy, Norway, Estonia, Hungary, Denmark)

Annals of General Psychiatry 15, 19, 2016

Background: It is well known that suicidal rates vary considerably among European countries and the reasons for this are unknown, although several theories have been proposed. The effect of economic variables has been extensively studied but not that of climate.

Methods: Data from 29 European countries covering the years 2000-2012 and concerning male and female standardized suicidal rates (according to WHO), economic variables (according World Bank) and climate variables were gathered. The statistical analysis included cluster and principal component analysis and categorical regression.

Results: The derived models explained 62.4 % of the variability of male suicidal rates. Economic variables alone explained 26.9 % and climate variables 37.6 %. For females, the respective figures were 41.7, 11.5 and 28.1 %. Male suicides correlated with high unemployment rate in the frame of high growth rate and high inflation and low GDP per capita, while female suicides correlated negatively with inflation. Both male and female suicides correlated with low temperature.

Discussion: The current study reports that the climatic effect (cold climate) is stronger than the economic one, but both are present. It seems that in Europe suicidality follows the climate/temperature cline which interestingly is not from south to north but from south to north-east. This raises concerns that climate change could lead to an increase in suicide rates. The current study is essentially the first successful attempt to explain the differences across countries in Europe; however, it is an observational analysis based on aggregate data and thus there is a lack of control for confounders.

A brief mobile app reduces nonsuicidal and suicidal self-injury: Evidence from three randomized controlled trials

Franklin JC, Fox KR, Franklin CR, Kleiman EM, Ribeiro JD, Jaroszewski AC, Hooley JM, Nock MK (United States)

Journal of Consulting and Clinical Psychology 84, 544-557, 2016

Objective: Self-injurious thoughts and behaviors (SITBs) are a major public health problem that traditional interventions have been unable to address on a large scale. The goal of this series of studies was to take initial steps toward developing an effective SITB treatment that can be easily delivered on a very large scale.

Method: We created a brief (1-2 min), game-like app called Therapeutic Evaluative Conditioning (TEC), designed to increase aversion to SITBs and decrease aversion to the self. In 3 separate studies, we recruited participants with recent and severe histories of SITBs from web forums focused on self-injury and psychopathology (Ns = 114, 131, and 163) and randomly assigned them to receive access to the mobile treatment TEC app or a control app for 1 month. We tested the effect of TEC on the frequency of self-cutting, nonsuicidal self-injury more generally, suicide ideation, suicide plans, and suicidal behaviors.

Results: Analyses showed that, compared with the control app, TEC produced moderate reductions for all SITBs except suicide ideation. Across studies, the largest and most consistent reductions were for self-cutting episodes (32%-40%), suicide plans (21%-59%), and suicidal behaviors (33%-77%). Two of the 3 studies showed that TEC impacted its intended treatment targets and that greater change in these targets was associated with greater SITB reductions. TEC effects were not maintained at the 1-month posttreatment follow-up.

Conclusions: Future versions of brief, mobile interventions like that tested here may have the potential to reduce SITBs and related behaviors on a large scale.

Arthritis and suicide attempts: Findings from a large nationally representative Canadian survey

Fuller-Thomson E, Ramzan N, Baird SL (Canada)
Rheumatology International 36, 1237-1248, 2016

The objectives of this study were (1) to determine the odds of suicide attempts among those with arthritis compared with those without and to see what factors attenuate this association and (2) to identify which factors are associated with suicide attempts among adults with arthritis. Secondary data analysis of the nationally representative 2012 Canadian Community Health Survey-Mental Health (CCHS-MH) was performed. For objective 1, those with and without arthritis were included (n = 21,744). For objective 2, only individuals who had arthritis (n = 4885) were included. A series of binary logistic regression analyses of suicide attempts were conducted for each objective, with adjustments for socio-demographics, childhood adversities, lifetime mental health and chronic pain. After full adjustment for the above listed variables, the odds of suicide attempts among adults with arthritis were 1.46. Among those with arthritis, early adversities alone explained 24 % of the variability in suicide attempts. After full adjustment, the odds of suicide attempts among those with arthritis were significantly higher among those who had experienced childhood sexual abuse (OR = 3.77), chronic parental domestic violence (OR = 3.97) or childhood physical abuse (1.82), those who had ever been addicted to drugs or alcohol (OR = 1.76) and ever had a depressive disorder (OR = 3.22) or an anxiety disorder (OR = 2.34) and those who were currently in chronic pain (OR = 1.50). Younger adults with arthritis were more likely to report having attempted suicide. Future prospective research is needed to uncover plausible mechanisms through which arthritis and suicide attempts are linked.

Epidemiology and trends in non-fatal self-harm in three centres in England, 2000-2012: Findings from the multicentre study of self-harm in England.

Geulayov G, Kapur N, Turnbull P, Clements C, Waters K, Ness J, Townsend E, Hawton K (United Kingdom)

BMJ Open 6, e010538, 2016

Objectives: Self-harm is a major health problem in many countries, with potential adverse outcomes including suicide and other causes of premature death. It is important to monitor national trends in this behaviour. We examined trends in non-fatal self-harm and its management in England during the 13-year period, 2000-2012.

Design and Setting: This observational study was undertaken in the three centres of the Multicentre Study of Self-harm in England. Information on all episodes of self-harm by individuals aged 15 years and over presenting to five general hospitals in three cities (Oxford, Manchester and Derby) was collected through face-to-face assessment or scrutiny of emergency department electronic databases. We used negative binomial regression models to assess trends in rates of self-harm and logistic regression models for binary outcomes (eg, assessed vs non-assessed patients).

Participants: During 2000-2012, there were 84 378 self-harm episodes (58.6% by females), involving 47 048 persons.

Results: Rates of self-harm declined in females (incidence rate ratio (IRR) 0.98; 95% CI 0.97 to 0.99, p<0.0001). In males, rates of self-harm declined until 2008 (IRR 0.96; 95% CI 0.95 to 0.98, p<0.0001) and then increased (IRR 1.05; 95% CI 1.02 to 1.09, p=0.002). Rates of self-harm were strongly correlated with suicide rates in England in males (r=0.82, p=0.0006) and females (r=0.74, p=0.004). Over 75% of self-harm episodes were due to self-poisoning, mainly with analgesics (45.7%), antidepressants (24.7%) and benzodiazepines (13.8%). A substantial increase in self-injury occurred in the latter part of the study period. This was especially marked for self-cutting/stabbing and hanging/asphyxiation. Psychosocial assessment by specialist mental health staff occurred in 53.2% of episodes.

Conclusions: Trends in rates of self-harm and suicide may be closely related; therefore, self-harm can be a useful mental health indicator. Despite national guidance, many patients still do not receive psychosocial assessment, especially those who self-injure.

Adolescents' viewing of suicide-related web content and psychological problems: Differentiating the roles of cyberbullying involvement

Görzig A (United Kingdom)

Cyberpsychology, Behavior and Social Networking 19, 502-509, 2016

Possible links of cyberbullying with suicide and psychological problems have recently received considerable attention. Suicide-related behaviors have also been linked with viewing of associated web content. Studies on traditional bullying indicate that the roles of bullying involvement (bullies, victims, and bully-victims) matter in terms of associations with specific suicide-related behaviors and psychological problems. Yet, related research in the area of cyberbullying is lacking. The current study investigates the association of cyberbullying roles with viewing of specific suicide-related web content and psychological problems. Data from N=19,406 (50 percent girls) 11-16-year-olds (M=13.54, SD=1.68) of a representative sample of Internet-using children in Europe were analyzed. Self-reports were obtained for cyberbullying role, viewing of web content related to self-harm, and suicide, as well as the emotional, peer, and conduct problem subscales of the Strengths and Difficulties Questionnaire (SDQ). Multinomial logistic regression analyses revealed that compared with those not involved in cyberbullying, viewing of web content related to suicide was higher for cybervictims and cyberbully-victims, but not for cyberbullies. Viewing of web content related to self-harm was higher for all cyberbullying roles, especially for cyberbully-victims. Rates of emotional problems were higher among cybervictims and cyberbully-victims, rates of peer problems were higher for cybervictims, and rates of conduct problems were higher for all cyberbullying roles. Moreover, the links between cyberbullying role and viewing of suicide-related web content were independent of psychological problems. The results can be useful to more precisely target efforts toward the specific problems of each cyberbullying role. The outcomes on viewing of web content also indicate an opportunity to enhance the presence of health service providers on Internet platforms.

Association between nonmedical use of prescription drugs and suicidal behavior among adolescents

Guo L, Xu Y, Deng J, Huang J, Huang G, Gao X, Wu H, Pan S, Zhang WH, Lu C (Taiwan, Belgium)

JAMA Pediatrics 170, 971-978, 2016

Importance: Suicidal behavior is a leading cause of injury and death worldwide, and previous cross-sectional studies have demonstrated that nonmedical use of prescription drugs (NMUPD) was associated with suicidality. However, there is not any study in China having examined the longitudinal relationships between NMUPD, suicidal ideation, and suicidal attempts, as well as explored the potential mediating effects of depressive symptoms.

Objective: To determine whether baseline NMUPD was associated with subsequent suicidal ideation and attempts while controlling for depressive symptoms and to determine whether the increased risks were mediated by depressive symptoms.

Design, Setting, and Participants: In this longitudinal study, a total of 3273 students in randomly selected schools in Guangzhou were surveyed from 2009 to 2010 (response rate, 96.8%) and followed up at 1 year (2011-2012; retention rate, 96.1%). The dates of data analysis were October 9, 2015, to October 15, 2015; additional data analysis occurred March 23, 2016, to March 29, 2016.

Main Outcomes and Measures: Suicidal ideation, suicidal attempts, NMUPD, depressive symptoms, and alcohol-related problems.

Results: Overall, 3273 adolescents (mean [SD] age, 13.7 [1.0] years) were recruited for this study. The final results showed that after controlling for sociodemographic information (including sex, age, household socioeconomic status, and living arrangements), baseline depressive symptoms, baseline alcohol-related problems, baseline suicidal ideation, and baseline suicidal attempts, baseline opioids misuse (adjusted odds ratio [AOR], 2.31; 95% CI, 1.30-4.11), sedatives misuse (AOR, 4.46; 95% CI, 1.54-7.94), and nonmedical use of any prescription drug (AOR, 1.97; 95% CI, 1.21-3.23) were positively associated with suicidal ideation at follow-up. Additionally, baseline opioid misuse (AOR, 3.39; 95% CI, 1.33-5.63) and nonmedical use of any prescription drug (AOR, 2.91; 95% CI, 1.26-3.71) were also associated with subsequent suicidal attempts after controlling for sex, age, household socioeconomic status, living arrangements, depressive symptoms, alcohol-related problems, suicidal ideation, and suicidal attempts at baseline. There were significant standardized indirect effects of baseline opioids misuse on subsequent suicidal ideation (standardized beta estimate = 0.020; 95% CI, 0.010-0.030) and suicidal attempts (standardized beta estimate = 0.009; 95% CI, 0.004-0.015) through depressive symptoms; the standardized indirect effect of baseline sedatives misuse on subsequent suicidal ideation through depressive symptoms was also significant (standardized beta estimate = 0.016; 95% CI, 0.005-0.026).

Conclusions and Relevance: In this study, NMUPD at baseline was associated with subsequent suicidal ideation and attempts. These findings support that proper surveillance systems with the potential to reduce adolescent suicidality should be established to control and supervise suicidality and NMUPD among Chinese adolescents.

Abyss or shelter? On the relevance of web search engines' search results when people google for suicide

Haim M, Arendt F, Scherr S (Germany)
Health Communication.
Published online: 19 May 2016. doi: 10.1080/10410236.2015.1113484

Despite evidence that suicide rates can increase after suicides are widely reported in the media, appropriate depictions of suicide in the media can help people to overcome suicidal crises and can thus elicit preventive effects. We argue on the level of individual media users that a similar ambivalence can be postulated for search results on online suicide-related search queries. Importantly, the filter bubble hypothesis (Pariser, 2011) states that search results are biased by algorithms based on a person's previous search behavior. In this study, we investigated whether suicide-related search queries, including either potentially suicide-preventive or -facilitative terms, influence subsequent search results. This might thus protect or harm suicidal Internet users. We utilized a 3 (search history: suicide-related harmful, suicide-related helpful, and suicide-unrelated) × 2 (reactive: clicking the top-most result link and no clicking) experimental design applying agent-based testing. While findings show no influences either of search histories or of reactivity on search results in a subsequent situation, the presentation of a helpline offer raises concerns about possible detrimental algorithmic decision-making: Algorithms "decided" whether or not to present a helpline, and this automated decision, then, followed the agent throughout the rest of the observation period. Implications for policy-making and search providers are discussed.

Suicidal ideation, suicide attempt, and occupations among employed adults aged 18-64years in the United States

Han B, Crosby AE, Ortega LAG, Parks SE, Compton WM, Gfroerer J (United States)
Comprehensive Psychiatry 66, 176-186, 2016

Objective: Approximately 70% of all US suicides are among working-age adults. This study was to determine whether and how 12-month suicidal ideation and suicide attempt were associated with specific occupations among currently employed adults aged 18-64 in the U.S.

Methods: Data were from 184,300 currently employed adults who participated in the 2008-2013 National Surveys on Drug Use and Health (NSDUH). NSDUH provides nationally representative data on suicidal ideation and suicide attempt. Descriptive analyses and multivariable logistic regressions were conducted.

Results: Among currently employed adults aged 18-64 in the U.S. 3.5% had suicidal ideation in the past 12months (3.1% had suicidal ideation only, and 0.4% had suicidal ideation and attempted suicide). Compared with adults in farming, fishing, and forestry occupations (model adjusted prevalence (MAP)=1.6%), adults in the following occupations were 3.0-3.6 times more likely to have suicidal ideation in the past year (model adjusted relative risks (MARRs)=3.0-3.6): lawyers, judges, and legal support workers (MAP=4.8%), social scientists and related workers (MAP=5.4%), and media and communication workers (MAP=5.8%).

Conclusions: Among employed adults aged 18-64 in the U.S. the 12-month prevalence of suicidal ideation varies by occupations. Adults in occupations that are at elevated risk for suicidal ideation may warrant focused suicide prevention.

Psychosocial interventions following self-harm in adults: A systematic review and meta-analysis

Hawton K, Witt KG, Salisbury TL, Arensman E, Gunnell D, Hazell P, Townsend E, van Heeringen K (United Kingdom, Belgium)
Lancet Psychiatry 3, 740-750, 2016

Background: Self-harm (intentional acts of non-fatal self-poisoning or self-injury) is common, particularly in young adults aged 15-35 years, often repeated, and strongly associated with suicide. Effective aftercare of individuals who self-harm is therefore important. We have undertaken a Cochrane systematic review and meta-analysis of the effectiveness of psychosocial interventions for self-harm in adults.

Methods: We searched five electronic databases (CCDANCTR-Studies and References, CENTRAL, MEDLINE, Embase, and PsycINFO) between Jan 1, 1998, and April 29, 2015, for randomised controlled trials of psychosocial interventions for adults after a recent (within 6 months) episode of self-harm. Most interventions were assessed in single trials. We report results for interventions for which at least three randomised controlled trials comparing interventions with treatment as usual have been published and hence might contribute to clinical guidance. The primary outcome was repetition of self-harm at the conclusion of treatment and at 6, 12, and 24 months' follow-up analysed, when available, with the intention-to-treat method; if this was not possible, we analysed with all available case data.

Findings: We identified 29 non-overlapping randomised controlled trials with three independent trials of the same intervention. Cognitive-behavioural-based psychotherapy (CBT; comprising cognitive-behavioural and problem-solving therapy) was associated with fewer participants repeating self-harm at 6 months' (odds ratio 0.54, 95% CI 0.34-0.85; 12 trials; n=1317) and at 12 months' follow-up (0.80, 0.65-0.98; ten trials; n=2232). There were also significant improvements in the secondary outcomes of depression, hopelessness, suicidal ideation, and problem solving. Patients receiving dialectical behaviour therapy (in three trials) were not less likely to repeat self-harm compared with those provided with treatment as usual at 6 months (odds ratio [OR] 0.59, 95% CI 0.16-2.15; n=267, three trials) or at 12 months (0.36, 0.05-2.47; n=172, two trials). However, the secondary endpoint of frequency of self-harm was associated with a significant reduction with use of dialectical behaviour therapy (mean difference -18.82, 95% CI -36.68 to -0.95). Four trials each of case management (OR 0.78, 95% CI 0.47-1.30; n=1608) and sending regular postcards (OR 0.87, 95% CI 0.62-1.23; n=3277) did not reduce repetition of self-harm.

Interpretation: CBT seems to be effective in patients after self-harm. Dialectical behaviour therapy did not reduce the proportion of patients repeating self-harm but did reduce the frequency of self-harm. However, aside from CBT, there were few trials of other promising interventions, precluding firm conclusions as to their effectiveness.

Self-harm, unintentional injury, and suicide in bipolar disorder during maintenance mood stabilizer treatment: A UK population-based electronic health records study

Hayes JF, Pitman A, Marston L, Walters K, Geddes JR, King M, Osborn DP (United Kingdom)

JAMA Psychiatry 73, 630-637, 2016

Importance: Self-harm is a prominent cause of morbidity in patients with bipolar disorder and is strongly associated with suicide. There is evolving evidence that lithium use may reduce suicidal behavior, in addition to concerns that the use of anticonvulsants may increase self-harm. Information is limited about the effects of antipsychotics when used as mood stabilizer treatment. Rates of unintentional injury are poorly defined in bipolar disorder, and understanding drug associations with this outcome may shed light on mechanisms for lithium's potential antisuicidal properties through reduction in impulsive aggression.

Objective: To compare rates of self-harm, unintentional injury, and suicide in patients with bipolar disorder who were prescribed lithium, valproate sodium, olanzapine, or quetiapine fumarate.

Design, Setting, and Participants: This investigation was a propensity score (PS)-adjusted and PS-matched longitudinal cohort study in a nationally representative UK sample using electronic health records data collected between January 1, 1995, and December 31, 2013. Participants included all patients diagnosed as having bipolar disorder who were prescribed lithium, valproate, olanzapine, or quetiapine as maintenance mood stabilizer treatment.

Main Outcomes and Measures: The primary outcome was any form of self-harm. Secondary outcomes were unintentional injury and suicide.

Results: Of the 14396 individuals with a diagnosis of BPD, 6671 were included in the cohort, with 2148 prescribed lithium, 1670 prescribed valproate, 1477 prescribed olanzapine, and 1376 prescribed quetiapine as maintenance mood stabilizer treatment. Self-harm rates were lower in patients prescribed lithium (205; 95% CI, 175-241 per 10000 person-years at risk [PYAR]) compared with those prescribed valproate (392; 95% CI, 334-460 per 10000 PYAR), olanzapine (409; 95% CI, 345-483 per 10000 PYAR), or quetiapine (582; 95% CI, 489-692 per 10000 PYAR). This association was maintained after PS adjustment (hazard ratio [HR], 1.40; 95% CI, 1.12-1.74 for valproate, olanzapine, or quetiapine vs lithium) and PS matching (HR, 1.51; 95% CI, 1.21-1.88). After PS adjustment, unintentional injury rates were lower for lithium compared with valproate (HR, 1.32; 95% CI, 1.10-1.58) and quetiapine (HR, 1.34; 95% CI, 1.07-1.69) but not olanzapine. The suicide rate in the cohort was 14 (95% CI, 9-21) per 10000 PYAR. Although this rate was lower in the lithium group than for other treatments, there were too few events to allow accurate estimates.

Conclusions and Relevance: Patients taking lithium had reduced self-harm and unintentional injury rates. This finding augments limited trial and smaller observational study results. It supports the hypothesis that lithium use reduces impulsive aggression in addition to stabilizing mood.

Effective psychological and psychosocial approaches to reduce repetition of self-harm: A systematic review, meta-analysis and meta-regression

Hetrick SE, Robinson J, Spittal MJ, Carter G (Australia)

BMJ Open 6, e011024, 2016

Objective: To examine the efficacy of psychological and psychosocial interventions for reductions in repeated self-harm.

Design: We conducted a systematic review, meta-analysis and meta-regression to examine the efficacy of psychological and psychosocial interventions to reduce repeat self-harm in adults. We included a sensitivity analysis of studies with a low risk of bias for the meta-analysis. For the meta-regression, we examined whether the type, intensity (primary analyses) and other components of intervention or methodology (secondary analyses) modified the overall intervention effect.

Data Sources: A comprehensive search of Medline, PsycInfo and Embase (from 1999 to June 2016) was performed.

Eligibility Criteria for Selecting Studies: Randomised controlled trials of psychological and psychosocial interventions for adult self-harm patients.

Results: Forty-five trials were included with data available from 36 (7354 participants) for the primary analysis. Meta-analysis showed a significant benefit of all psychological and psychosocial interventions combined (risk ratio 0.84; 95% CI 0.74 to 0.96; number needed to treat=33); however, sensitivity analyses showed that this benefit was non-significant when restricted to a limited number of high-quality studies. Meta-regression showed that the type of intervention did not modify the treatment effects.

Conclusions: Consideration of a psychological or psychosocial intervention over and above treatment as usual is worthwhile; with the public health benefits of ensuring that this practice is widely adopted potentially worth the investment. However, the specific type and nature of the intervention that should be delivered is not yet clear. Cognitive-behavioural therapy or interventions with an interpersonal focus and targeted on the precipitants to self-harm may be the best candidates on the current evidence. Further research is required.

The impact of telephone crisis services on suicidal users: A systematic review of the past 45 years

Hvidt EA, Ploug T, Holm S (Denmark, United Kingdom)

Mental Health Review Journal 21, 141-160, 2016

Purpose: Telephone crisis services are increasingly subject to a requirement to "prove their worth" as a suicide prevention strategy. The purpose of this paper is to: first, provide a detailed overview of the evidence on the impact of telephone crisis services on suicidal users; second, determine the limitations of the outcome measures used in this evidence; and third, suggest directions for future research. *Design/Methodology/Approach*: MEDLINE via Pubmed (from 1966), PsycINFO APA (from 1967) and ProQuest Dissertation and Theses (all to 4 June 2015) were searched. Papers were systematically extracted by title then abstract according to predefined inclusion and exclusion criteria.

Findings: In total, 18 articles met inclusion criteria representing a range of outcome measures: changes during calls, reutilization of service, compliance with advice, caller satisfaction and counsellor satisfaction. The majority of studies showed beneficial impact on an immediate and intermediate degree of suicidal urgency, depressive mental states as well as positive feedback from users and counsellors.

Research Limitations/Implications: A major limitation pertains to differences in the use of the term "suicidal". Other limitations include the lack of long-term follow-up and of controlled research designs. Future research should include a focus on long-term follow-up designs, involving strict data protection. Furthermore, more qualitative research is needed in order to capture the essential nature of the intervention.

Originality/Value: This paper attempts to broaden the study and the concept of "effectiveness" as hitherto used in the literature about telephone crisis services and offers suggestions for future research.

Rapid and sustained reductions in current suicidal ideation following repeated doses of intravenous ketamine: Secondary analysis of an open-label study

Ionescu DF, Swee MB, Pavone KJ, Taylor N, Akeju O, Baer L, Nyer M, Cassano P, Mischoulon D, Alpert JE, Brown EN, Nock MK, Fava M, Cusin C (United States)

Journal of Clinical Psychiatry 77, e719-e725, 2016

Background: Ketamine rapidly reduces thoughts of suicide in patients with treatment-resistant depression who are at low risk for suicide. However, the extent to which ketamine reduces thoughts of suicide in depressed patients with current suicidal ideation remains unknown.

Methods: Between April 2012 and October 2013, 14 outpatients with DSM-IV-diagnosed major depressive disorder were recruited for the presence of current, stable ($\geq$ 3 months) suicidal thoughts. They received open-label ketamine infusions over 3 weeks (0.5 mg/kg over 45 minutes for the first 3 infusions; 0.75 mg/kg over 45 minutes for the last 3). In this secondary analysis, the primary outcome measures of suicidal ideation (Columbia-Suicide Severity Rating Scale [C-SSRS] and the Suicide Item of the 28-item Hamilton Depression Rating Scale [HDRS28-SI]) were assessed at 240 minutes postinfusion and for 3 months thereafter in a naturalistic follow-up.

Results: Over the course of the infusions (acute treatment phase), 7 of 14 patients (50%) showed remission of suicidal ideation on the C-SSRS Ideation scale (even among patients whose depression did not remit). There was a significant linear decrease in this score over time (P <.001), which approached significance even after controlling for severity of 6-item Hamilton Depression Rating Scale (HDRS6) core depression items (P =.05). Similarly, there were significant decreases in the C-SSRS Intensity (P <.01) and HDRS28-SI (P <.001) scores during the acute treatment phase. Two of the 7 patients who achieved remission during the acute treatment phase (29%) maintained their remission throughout a 3-month naturalistic follow-up.

Conclusions: In this preliminary study, repeated doses of open-label ketamine rapidly and robustly decreased suicidal ideation in pharmacologically treated outpatients with treatment-resistant depression with stable suicidal thoughts; this decrease was maintained for at least 3 months following the final ketamine infusion in 2 patients.

An aboriginal youth suicide prevention project in rural Victoria

Isaacs A, Sutton K (Australia)
Advances in Mental Health 14, 118-125, 2016

Objective: To describe an Aboriginal youth suicide prevention project developed by Njernda Aboriginal Corporation.

Method: This is a descriptive study of an Aboriginal youth suicide prevention project developed by Njernda Aboriginal Corporation based in Echuca, Victoria. Information about the program was obtained from interviewing the project worker and the social and emotional wellbeing worker. Further information was obtained about the program by examining activity registers, program flyers and posters.

Results: The Aboriginal youth suicide prevention project was designed and implemented by Njernda Aboriginal Corporation over a period of three years. The main components of the project were building resilience, early intervention response and immediate postvention support. Resilience was built through the Bullroarer program, the Red Dust Healing program and community awareness programs. Another program, the Jekkora group was developed and implemented as an early intervention response. A postvention service is in the planning stage.

Conclusions: During a three-year period Njernda Aboriginal Corporation established community resilience building and early intervention programs. Developing and implementing a comprehensive suicide prevention plan at the community level requires adequate time as well as support from mainstream services. These findings therefore have implications for future planning of Aboriginal suicide prevention projects.

Staring down death: Is abnormally slow blink rate a clinically useful indicator of acute suicide risk?

Joiner TE, Hom MA, Rogers ML, Chu C, Stanley IH, Wynn GH, Gutierrez PM (United States)
Crisis 37, 212-217, 2016

Background: Lowered eye blink rate may be a clinically useful indicator of acute, imminent, and severe suicide risk. Diminished eye blink rates are often seen among individuals engaged in heightened concentration on a specific task that requires careful planning and attention. Indeed, overcoming one's biological instinct for survival through suicide necessitates premeditation and concentration; thus, a diminished eye blink rate may signal imminent suicidality.

Aims: This article aims to spur research and clinical inquiry into the role of eye blinks as an indicator of acute suicide risk.

Method: Literature relevant to the potential connection between eye blink rate and suicidality was reviewed and synthesized.

Results: Anecdotal, cognitive, neurological, and conceptual support for the relationship between decreased blink rate and suicide risk is outlined.

Conclusion: Given that eye blinks are a highly observable behavior, the potential clinical utility of using eye blink rate as a marker of suicide risk is immense. Research is warranted to explore the association between eye blink rate and acute suicide risk.

Newspaper reporting on a cluster of suicides in the UK

John A, Hawton K, Gunnell D, Lloyd K, Scourfield J, Jones PA, Luce A, Marchant A, Platt S, Price S, Dennis MS (United Kingdom)

Crisis. Published online: 22 July 2016. doi: 10.1027/0227-5910/a000410

Background: Media reporting may influence suicide clusters through imitation or contagion. In 2008 there was extensive national and international newspaper coverage of a cluster of suicides in young people in the Bridgend area of South Wales, UK.

Aims: To explore the quantity and quality of newspaper reporting during the identified cluster.

Method: Searches were conducted for articles on suicide in Bridgend for 6 months before and after the defined cluster (June 26, 2007, to September 16, 2008). Frequency, quality (using the PRINTQUAL instrument), and sensationalism were examined.

Results: In all, 577 newspaper articles were identified. One in seven articles included the suicide method in the headline, 47.3% referred to earlier suicides, and 44% used phrases that guidelines suggest should be avoided. Only 13% included sources of information or advice.

Conclusion: A high level of poor-quality and sensationalist reporting was found during an ongoing suicide cluster at the very time when good-quality reporting could be considered important. A broad awareness of media guidelines and expansion and adherence to press codes of practice are required by journalists to ensure ethical reporting.

Predicting risk of suicide attempt using history of physical illnesses from electronic medical records

Karmakar C, Luo W, Tran T, Berk M, Venkatesh S (Australia)
JMIR Mental Health 3, e19, 2016

Background: Although physical illnesses, routinely documented in electronic medical records (EMR), have been found to be a contributing factor to suicides, no automated systems use this information to predict suicide risk.

Objective: The aim of this study is to quantify the impact of physical illnesses on suicide risk, and develop a predictive model that captures this relationship using EMR data.

Methods: We used history of physical illnesses (except chapter V: Mental and behavioral disorders) from EMR data over different time-periods to build a lookup table that contains the probability of suicide risk for each chapter of the International Statistical Classification of Diseases and Related Health Problems, 10th Revision (ICD-10) codes. The lookup table was then used to predict the probability of suicide risk for any new assessment. Based on the different lengths of history of physical illnesses, we developed six different models to predict suicide risk. We tested the performance of developed models to predict 90-day risk using historical data over differing time-periods ranging from 3 to 48 months. A total of 16,858 assessments from 7399 mental health patients with at least one risk assessment was used for the validation of the developed model. The performance was measured using area under the receiver operating characteristic curve (AUC).

Results: The best predictive results were derived (AUC=0.71) using combined data across all time-periods, which significantly outperformed the clinical baseline derived from routine risk assessment (AUC=0.56). The proposed approach thus shows potential to be incorporated in the broader risk assessment processes used by clinicians.

Conclusions: This study provides a novel approach to exploit the history of physical illnesses extracted from EMR (ICD-10 codes without chapter V-mental and behavioral disorders) to predict suicide risk, and this model outperforms existing clinical assessments of suicide risk.

Heavy alcohol use among suicide decedents relative to a nonsuicide comparison group: Gender-specific effects of economic contraction

Kaplan MS, Huguet N, Caetano R, Giesbrecht N, Kerr WC, McFarland BH (United States)
Alcoholism 40, 1501-1506, 2016

Background: The primary objective of this gender-stratified study was to assess the rate of heavy alcohol use among suicide decedents relative to a nonsuicide comparison group during the 2008 to 2009 economic crisis.

Methods: The National Violent Death Reporting System and the Behavioral Risk Factor Surveillance System were analyzed by gender-stratified multiple logistic regression to test whether change in acute intoxication (blood alcohol content ≥ 0.08 g/dl) before (2005 to 2007), during (2008 to 2009), and after (2010 to 2011) the Great Recession mirrored change in heavy alcohol use in a living sample.

Results: Among men, suicide decedents experienced a significantly greater increase (+8%) in heavy alcohol use at the onset of the recession (adjusted ratio of odds ratio = 1.15, 95% confidence interval = 1.10 to 1.20) (relative to the prerecession period) than did men in a nonsuicide comparison group (-2%). Among women, changes in rates of heavy alcohol use were similar in the suicide and nonsuicide comparison groups at the onset and after the recession.

Conclusions: Acute alcohol use contributed to suicide among men during the recent economic downturn. Among women who died by suicide, acute alcohol use mirrored consumption in the general population. Women may show resilience (or men, vulnerability) to deleterious interaction of alcohol with financial distress.

Mental health services, suicide and 7-day working

Kapur N, Ibrahim S, Hunt IM, Turnbull P, Shaw J, Appleby L (United Kingdom)
British Journal of Psychiatry 209, 334-339, 2016

Background: Patients admitted to hospital at the weekend appear to be at increased risk of death compared with those admitted at other times. However, a 'weekend effect' has rarely been explored in mental health and there may also be other times of year when patients are vulnerable.

Aims: To investigate the timing of suicide in high-risk mental health patients.

Method: We compared the incidence of suicide at the weekend v. during the week, and also in August (the month of junior doctor changeover) v. other months in in-patients, patients within 3 months of discharge and patients under the care of crisis resolution home treatment (CRHT) teams (2001-2013).

Results: The incidence of suicide was lower at the weekends for each group (incidence rate ratio (IRR) = 0.88 (95% CI 0.79-0.99) for in-patients, IRR = 0.85 (95% CI 0.78-0.92) for post-discharge patients, IRR = 0.87 (95% CI 0.78-0.97) for

CRHT patients). Patients who died by suicide were also less likely to have been admitted at weekends than during the week (IRR = 0.52 (95% CI 0.45-0.60)). The incidence of suicide in August was not significantly different from other months.

Conclusions: We found evidence of a weekend effect for suicide risk among high-risk mental health patients, but with a 12-15% lower incidence at weekends. Our study does not support the claim that safety is compromised at weekends, at least in mental health services.

Mental health service changes, organisational factors, and patient suicide in England in 1997-2012: A before-and-after study

Kapur N, Ibrahim S, While D, Baird A, Rodway C, Hunt IM, Windfuhr K, Moreton A, Shaw J, Appleby L (United Kingdom)

Lancet Psychiatry 3, 526-534, 2016

Background: Research into which aspects of service provision in mental health are most effective in preventing suicide is sparse. We examined the association between service changes, organisational factors, and suicide rates in a national sample.

Methods: We did a before-and-after analysis of service delivery data and an ecological analysis of organisational characteristics, in relation to suicide rates, in providers of mental health care in England. We also investigated whether the effect of service changes varied according to markers of organisational functioning.

Findings: Overall, 19 248 individuals who died by suicide within 12 months of contact with mental health services were included (1997-2012). Various service changes related to ward safety, improved community services, staff training, and implementation of policy and guidance were associated with a lower suicide rate after the introduction of these changes (incidence rate ratios ranged from 0.71 to 0.79, p<0.0001). Some wider organisational factors, such as non-medical staff turnover (Spearman's r=0.34, p=0.01) and incident reporting (0.46, 0.0004), were also related to suicide rates but others, such as staff sickness (-0.12, 0.37) and patient satisfaction (-0.06, 0.64), were not. Service changes had more effect in organisations that had low rates of staff turnover but high rates of overall event reporting.

Interpretation: Aspects of mental health service provision might have an effect on suicide rates in clinical populations but the wider organisational context in which service changes are made are likely to be important too. System-wide change implemented across the patient care pathway could be a key strategy for improving patient safety in mental health care.

Parents' experiences of nonsuicidal self-injury among adolescents and young adults

Kelada L, Whitlock J, Hasking P, Melvin G (Australia)
Journal of Child and Family Studies. Published online: 23 August 2016. doi: 10.1007/s10826-016-0496-4

We assessed the impact of adolescent nonsuicidal self-injury (NSSI) on parents in two studies. In Study 1, 16 Australian parents of adolescents with a history of non-suicidal self-injury responded to open-ended questions about their child's non-suicidal self-injury. Data from 10 of the adolescents were matched with parents' responses regarding the nature and extent of nonsuicidal self-injury, revealing that parents underestimated the frequency of nonsuicidal self-injury, the age of onset, and the likelihood their child would continue to self-injure. In Study 2, 22 American parents of adolescents with a history of nonsuicidal self-injury partici-pated in interviews about their experiences. Parents in both studies reported changes in the parent–adolescent relationship after self-injury, which posed chal-lenges to the family unit. When professional help had been sought, experiences were largely negative. Results support further investigation into family-based interventions to equip parents with tools to better relate to, and communicate with, their adolescent following self-injury. Results also suggest that mental-health professionals and general practitioners may require further training for nonsuicidal self-injury.

Pain and self-harm: A systematic review

Kirtley OJ, O'Carroll RE, O'Connor RC (United Kingdom)
Journal of Affective Disorders 203, 347-363, 2016

Background: A growing body of research has explored altered physical pain threshold and tolerance in non-suicidal self-injury (NSSI) and suicidal self-harm. The evidence, however, is inconsistent such that the nature of the relationship is unclear, and whether or not this effect is also present in suicidal self-harm is equivocal.

Methods: A keyword search of three major psychological and medical databases (PsycINFO, Medline and Web of Knowledge) was conducted, yielding 1,873 records. Following duplicate removal and screening, 25 articles were quality assessed, and included in the final systematic review.

Results: There is strong evidence for increased pain tolerance in NSSI, and some evidence for this in suicidal individuals, but notably, there were no prospective studies. The review found a lack of substantive focus on psychological correlates of altered pain tolerance in this population. Several candidate explanatory mech-anisms were proposed within the reviewed studies.

Limitations: The current review was a narrative systematic review; methods used to assess pain were considered too heterogeneous to conduct a meta-analysis.

Conclusions: The evidence suggests that there is elevated pain tolerance among those who engage in NSSI. Future prospective research should determine if altered pain tolerance is a cause or a consequence of the behaviour. The identification of psychological correlates of increased pain tolerance is a neglected area of research. It could provide opportunities for treatment/intervention development, if mediating or moderating pathways can be identified. Too few studies have directly investigated candidate explanatory mechanisms to draw definitive conclusions.

Suicide prevention public service announcements impact help seeking attitudes: The message makes a difference

Klimes-Dougan B, Wright N, Klingbeil DA (United States)

Frontiers in Psychiatry 7, 124, 2016

Suicide continues to be one of the most serious public health challenges. Public service announcements (PSAs) are frequently used to address this challenge, but are rarely sufficiently evaluated to determine if they meet the intended goals, or are associated with potential iatrogenic effects. Although it is challenging to assess the relative impact of different PSA modalities, our group previously noted that one billboard message failed to show the same benefits as one TV ad [e.g. Klimes-Dougan and Lee (1)]. The purpose of this study was to extend these findings to test critical aspects of suicide prevention billboard messaging. Although both simulated billboard messages presented had identical supporting messages, we predicted that the more personal billboard message, focused on saving one's life, would cause more favorable help-seeking attitudes than the message focused on suicide. Young adult university students (N = 785) were randomly assigned to one of three conditions; one of two billboard simulations or a TV ad simulation. Help-seeking attitudes, maladaptive coping, and reports of concern and distress were evaluated. The results of this study suggest some relative benefits in endorsement of favorable help-seeking attitudes for one of the billboard conditions stop depression from taking another life. Although further research is needed to determine what methods will alter the risk for suicide in the population, the results of this study provide a useful first step showing that some billboard messaging may favorably influence help-seeking attitudes.

Technology-enhanced suicide prevention interventions: A systematic review of the current state of the science

Kreuze E, Jenkins C, Gregoski M, York J, Mueller M, Lamis DA, Ruggiero KJ (United States)

Journal of Telemedicine and Telecare. Published online: 3 July 2016. doi: 10.1177/1357633X16657928

Objective: Suicide prevention is a high priority. Scalable and sustainable interventions for suicide prevention are needed to set the stage for population-level impact. This systematic review explores how technology-enhanced interventions target suicide risk and protective factors, using the Centers for Disease Control and Prevention (CDC, 2015) Risk and Protective Factors Ecological Model.

Methods: Information databases (PsycINFO, PubMed and CINAHL) were systematically searched and records including technology-enhanced interventions for suicide prevention (n=3764) were reviewed. Records with varying technologies and diverse methodologies were integrated into the search.

Results: Review of the records resulted in the inclusion of 16 studies that utilized technology-enhanced interventions to address determinants of suicidal behaviour. This includes the use of standalone or, in most cases, adjunct technology-enhanced interventions for suicide prevention delivered by mobile phone application, text message, telephone, computer, web, CD-ROM and video.

Conclusion: Intervention effectiveness was variable, but several technology-enhanced interventions have demonstrated effectiveness in reducing suicidal ideation and mental health co-morbidities. Large-scale research and evaluation initiatives are needed to evaluate the costs and long-term population-level impact of these interventions.

A systematic assessment of smartphone tools for suicide prevention

Larsen ME, Nicholas J, Christensen H (Australia)

PLoS One 11, e0152285, 2016

Background: Suicide is a leading cause of death globally, and there has been a rapid growth in the use of new technologies such as mobile health applications (apps) to help identify and support those at risk. However, it is not known whether these apps are evidence-based, or indeed contain potentially harmful content. This review examines the concordance of features in publicly available apps with current scientific evidence of effective suicide prevention strategies.

Methods: Apps referring to suicide or deliberate self-harm (DSH) were identified on the Android and iOS app stores. Systematic review methodology was employed to screen and review app content. App features were labelled using a coding scheme that reflected the broad range of evidence-based medical and population-based suicide prevention interventions. Best-practice for suicide prevention was based upon a World Health Organization report and supplemented by other reviews of the literature.

Results: One hundred and twenty-three apps referring to suicide were identified and downloaded for full review, 49 of which were found to contain at least one interactive suicide prevention feature. Most apps focused on obtaining support from friends and family (n = 27) and safety planning (n = 14). Of the different suicide prevention strategies contained within the apps, the strongest evidence in the literature was found for facilitating access to crisis support (n = 13). All reviewed apps contained at least one strategy that was broadly consistent with the evidence base or best-practice guidelines. Apps tended to focus on a single suicide prevention strategy (mean = 1.1), although safety plan apps provided the opportunity to provide a greater number of techniques (mean = 3.9). Potentially harmful content, such as listing lethal access to means or encouraging risky behaviour in a crisis, was also identified.

Discussion: Many suicide prevention apps are available, some of which provide elements of best practice, but none that provide comprehensive evidence-based support. Apps with potentially harmful content were also identified. Despite the number of apps available, and their varied purposes, there is a clear need to develop useful, pragmatic, and multifaceted mobile resources for this population. Clinicians should be wary in recommending apps, especially as potentially harmful content can be presented as helpful. Currently safety plan apps are the most comprehensive and evidence-informed, for example, "Safety Net" and "MoodTools-Depression Aid".

A pilot study on the efficacy of volunteer mentorship for young adults with self-harm behaviors using a quasi-experimental design

Law YW, Yip PS, Lai CC, Kwok CL, Wong PW, Liu KS, Ng PW, Liao CW, Wong TW (Hong Kong)
Crisis. Published online: 9 June 2016. doi: 10.1027/0227-5910/a000393

Background: Studies have shown that postdischarge care for self-harm patients is effective in reducing repeated suicidal behaviors. Little is known about whether volunteer support can help reduce self-harm repetition and improve psychosocial well-being.

Aim: This study investigated the efficacy of volunteer support in preventing repetition of self-harm.

Method: This study used a quasi-experimental design by assigning self-harm patients admitted to the emergency departments to an intervention group with volunteer support and treatment as usual (TAU) for 9 months and to a control group of TAU. Outcome measures include repetition of self-harm, suicidal ideation, hopelessness, and level of depressive and anxiety symptoms.

Results: A total of 74 cases were recruited (38 participants; 36 controls). There were no significant differences in age, gender, and clinical condition between the two groups at the baseline. The intervention group showed significant improvements in hopelessness and depressive symptoms. However, the number of cases of suicide ideation and of repetition of self-harm episodes was similar for both groups at the postintervention period.

Conclusion: Postdischarge care provided by volunteers showed significant improvement in hopelessness and depression. Volunteers have been commonly involved in suicide prevention services. Further research using rigorous methods is recommended for improving service quality in the long term.

Serious suicide attempts: Toward an Integration of Terms and Definitions

Levi-Belz Y, Beautrais A (Israel)
Crisis. Published online: 1 June 2016. doi: 10.1027/0227-5910/a000386

Background: Suicidal behavior comprises a diverse set of behaviors with significant differences among several behavioral categories. One noteworthy category includes individuals who have made serious suicide attempts, epidemiologically very similar to those completing suicide. This behavioral category is important, since interviewing survivors of a potentially lethal incident of self-harm enables a detailed investigation of the psychological process leading to the suicidal act.

Aim: To achieve a consensus definition and operational criteria of serious suicide attempts.

Method: We reviewed studies that included the term serious suicide attempt or related terms (e.g. highly lethal), with a focus on the variety of operational criteria employed across studies.

Results: More than 60 papers addressing various types of serious suicide attempt were explored. We found a large variety of operational definitions, reflecting the lack of consensus regarding terminology and criteria related to the term.

Conclusion: We undertook the challenge of developing an integrative and comprehensive set of criteria of serious suicide attempt and suggest a definition comprising three key dimensions: medical lethality, potential lethality of the method used, and severity of the objective circumstances of the suicide intent. Clinicians and researchers are strongly encouraged to consider using the term serious suicide attempt with its attendant components.

Front-line worker perspectives on indigenous youth suicide in central Australia: Contributors and prevention strategies

Lindeman MA, Kuipers P, Grant L (Australia)

International Journal of Emergency Mental Health 17, 191-196, 2015

This paper presents the perspectives of Central Australian workers in relation to Aboriginal youth suicide. Interviews were conducted as part of a project to develop a data collection system and referral pathway for Indigenous youth suicide and suicide attempts. Twenty-two in-depth interviews were conducted with a range of practitioners who have front-line contact in suicide related issues (such as police, primary health, community support, youth services). The interview schedule reflected the project aims, but the transcripts revealed a much broader consideration of the issue. This paper reports on a secondary analysis of the data. The two major themes of salient contributing factors and service prevention strategies provide insights into these workers' attempts to understand and respond to this issue. There is a need to ensure workers develop and maintain strong networks, are well informed about local socio-cultural factors and skilled to work with local elders, traditional healers and community members, and are well supported in their roles to ensure longevity and relationships. The results contribute to the Aboriginal and Torres Strait Islander suicide prevention sector with particular relevance for remote Australia.

Psychological resilience provides no independent protection from suicidal risk

Liu DWY, Fairweather-Schmidt AK, Burns R, Roberts RM, Anstey KJ (Australia)

Crisis 37, 130-139, 2016

Background: Little is known about the role of resilience in the likelihood of suicidal ideation (SI) over time.

Aims: We examined the association between resilience and SI in a young-adult cohort over 4 years. Our objectives were to determine whether resilience was associated with SI at follow-up or, conversely, whether SI was associated with lowered resilience at follow-up.

Method: Participants were selected from the Personality and Total Health (PATH) Through Life Project from Canberra and Queanbeyan, Australia, aged 28-32 years at the first time point and 32-36 at the second. Multinomial, linear, and binary regression analyses explored the association between resilience and SI over two time points. Models were adjusted for suicidality risk factors.

Results: While unadjusted analyses identified associations between resilience and SI, these effects were fully explained by the inclusion of other suicidality risk factors.

Conclusion: Despite strong cross-sectional associations, resilience and SI appear to be unrelated in a longitudinal context, once risk/resilience factors are controlled for. As independent indicators of psychological well-being, suicidality and resilience are essential if current status is to be captured. However, the addition of other factors (e.g. support, mastery) makes this association tenuous. Consequently, resilience per se may not be protective of SI.

Trajectories of suicidal ideation in people seeking web-based help for suicidality: Secondary analysis of a Dutch randomized controlled trial

Madsen T, van Spijker B, Karstoft KI, Nordentoft M, Kerkhof AJ (Netherlands)
Journal of Medical Internet Research 18, e178, 2016

Background: Suicidal ideation (SI) is a common mental health problem. Variability in intensity of SI over time has been linked to suicidal behavior, yet little is known about the temporal course of SI.

Objective: The primary aim was to identify prototypical trajectories of SI in the general population and, secondarily, to examine whether receiving Web-based self-help for SI, psychiatric symptoms, or sociodemographics predicted membership in the identified SI trajectories.

Methods: We enrolled 236 people, from the general Dutch population seeking Web-based help for SI, in a randomized controlled trial comparing a Web-based self-help for SI group with a control group. We assessed participants at inclusion and at 2, 4, and 6 weeks. The Beck Scale for Suicide Ideation was applied at all assessments and was included in latent growth mixture modeling analysis to empirically identify trajectories.

Results: We identified 4 SI trajectories. The high stable trajectory represented 51.7% (122/236) of participants and was characterized by constant high level of SI. The high decreasing trajectory (50/236, 21.2%) consisted of people with a high baseline SI score followed by a gradual decrease to a very low score. The third trajectory, high increasing (12/236, 5.1%), also had high initial SI score, followed by an increase to the highest level of SI at 6 weeks. The fourth trajectory, low stable (52/236, 22.0%) had a constant low level of SI. Previous attempted suicide and having received Web-based self-help for SI predicted membership in the high decreasing trajectory.

Conclusions: Many adults experience high persisting levels of SI, though results encouragingly indicate that receiving Web-based self-help for SI increased membership in a decreasing trajectory of SI.

Prevention of firearm suicide in the United States: What works and what is possible

Mann JJ, Michel CA (United States)

American Journal of Psychiatry 173, 969-979, 2016

Objective: About 21,000 suicides in the United States in 2014 involved a firearm. The authors reviewed evidence from around the world regarding the relationship between firearm ownership rates and firearm suicide rates and the potential effectiveness of policy-based strategies for preventing firearm suicides in the United States.

Method: Relevant publications were identified by searches of PubMed, PsycINFO, MEDLINE, and Google Scholar from 1980 to September 2015, using the search terms suicide AND firearms OR guns. Excluding duplicates, 1,687 results were found, 60 of which were selected for inclusion; these sources yielded an additional 10 studies, for a total of 70 studies.

Results: Case-control and ecological studies investigating geographic and temporal variations in firearm ownership and firearm suicide rates indicate that greater firearm availability is associated with higher firearm suicide rates. Time-series analyses, mostly from other countries, show that legislation reducing firearm ownership lowers firearm suicide rates. Because the Second Amendment curtails legislation broadly restricting firearm access in the United States, the emphasis is shifted to restricting access for those at risk of harming themselves or others. Most suicides involve guns purchased years earlier. Targeted initiatives like gun violence restraining orders, smart gun technology, and gun safety education campaigns potentially reduce access to already purchased firearms by suicidal individuals. Such measures are too new to have evidence of effectiveness.

Conclusions: Broadly reducing availability and access to firearms has lowered firearm suicide rates in other countries but does not appear feasible in the United States. Approaches restricting access of at-risk individuals to already purchased firearms by engaging the public and major stakeholders require urgent implementation and outcome evaluation for firearm suicide prevention.

Prevention of suicidal behavior in prisons: An Overview of Initiatives Based on a Systematic Review of Research on Near-Lethal Suicide Attempts

Marzano L, Hawton K, Rivlin A, Smith EN, Piper M, Fazel S (United Kingdom)

Crisis. Published online: 9 June 2016. doi: 10.1027/0227-5910/a000394

Background: Worldwide, prisoners are at high risk of suicide. Research on near-lethal suicide attempts can provide important insights into risk and protective factors, and inform suicide prevention initiatives in prison.

Aims: To synthesize findings of research on near-lethal attempts in prisons, and consider their implications for suicide prevention policies and practice, in the context of other research in custody and other settings.

Method: We searched two bibliographic indexes for studies in any language on near-lethal and severe self-harm in prisoners, supplemented by targeted searches over the period 2000-2014. We extracted information on risk factors descriptively. Data were not meta-analyzed owing to heterogeneity of samples and methods.

Results: We identified eight studies reporting associations between prisoner near-lethal attempts and specific factors. The latter included historical, prison-related, and clinical factors, including psychiatric morbidity and comorbidity, trauma, social isolation, and bullying. These factors were also identified as important in prisoners' own accounts of what may have contributed to their attempts (presented in four studies).

Conclusion: Factors associated with prisoners' severe suicide attempts include a range of potentially modifiable clinical, psychosocial, and environmental factors. We make recommendations to address these factors in order to improve detection, management, and prevention of suicide risk in prisoners.

Childhood emotional maltreatment as a robust predictor of suicidal ideation: A 3-year multi-wave, prospective investigation

Miller AB, Jenness JL, Oppenheimer CW, Gottleib AL, Young JF, Hankin BL (United States)
Journal of Abnormal Child Psychology. Published online: 31 March 2016. doi: 10.1007/s10802-016-0150-z

Despite literature suggesting a relationship between child maltreatment and suicidal ideation, few studies have examined the prospective course of this relationship. The current study examined this relationship in a sample of 682 community youth who were followed over the course of 3 years. Repeated measures of suicidal ideation, emotional maltreatment, and depressive symptom severity were examined in multi-wave path analysis models. Overall, results suggest that emotional maltreatment over time contributes uniquely to the prospective prediction of suicidal ideation, even when controlling for age, previous suicidal ideation, biological sex, and depression symptom severity. Unlike previous studies that have only measured emotional maltreatment at one-time point, the current study demonstrates that emotional maltreatment contributes unique risk to suicidal ideation prospectively among youth. Results speak to the importance of examining emotional maltreatment and suicidal ideation within prospective models of risk and suggest that emotional maltreatment is a robust predictor of suicidal ideation, over and above history of suicidal ideation and depression.

Mechanisms of brief contact interventions in clinical populations: A systematic review

Milner A, Spittal MJ, Kapur N, Witt K, Pirkis J, Carter G (Australia)

BMC Psychiatry 16, 194, 2016

Background: Brief Contact Interventions (BCIs) have been of increasing interest to suicide prevention clinicians, researchers and policy makers. However, there has been no systematic assessment into the mechanisms underpinning BCIs. The aim of the current paper is to provide a systematic review of the proposed mechanisms underpinning BCIs across trial studies.

Method: A systematic review was conducted of trials using BCIs (post-discharge telephone contacts; emergency or crisis cards; and postcard or letter contacts) for suicide or self-harm. Following PRISMA guidelines, we searched CENTRAL, MEDLINE, EMBASE, and the reference lists of all past reviews in the area. Secondary searches of reference lists were undertaken.

Results: Sixteen papers provided a description of possible mechanisms which we grouped into three main areas: social support; suicide prevention literacy, and; learning alternative coping behaviours. After assessment of the studies and considering the plausibility of mechanisms, we suggest social support and improved suicide prevention literacy are the most likely mechanisms underpinning BCIs.

Conclusion: Researchers need to better articulate and measure the mechanisms they believe underpin BCIs in trial studies. Understanding more about the mechanisms of BCIs' will inform the development of future interventions for self-harm and suicide.

Evaluation of the 113Online suicide prevention crisis chat service: Outcomes, helper behaviors and comparison to telephone hotlines

Mokkenstorm JK, Eikelenboom M, Huisman A, Wiebenga J, Gilissen R, Kerkhof AJ, Smit JH (Netherlands)

Suicide and Life-Threatening Behavior. Published online: 19 August 2016. doi: 10.1111/sltb.12286

Recognizing the importance of digital communication, major suicide prevention helplines have started offering crisis intervention by chat. To date there is little evidence supporting the effectiveness of crisis chat services. To evaluate the reach and outcomes of the 113Online volunteer-operated crisis chat service, 526 crisis chat logs were studied, replicating the use of measures that were developed to study telephone crisis calls. Reaching a relatively young population of predominantly females with severe suicidality and (mental) health problems, chat outcomes for this group were found to be comparable to those found for crisis calls to U.S. Lifeline Centers in 2003-2004, with similar but not identical associations with specific helpers' styles and attitudes. Our findings support a positive effect of the 113Online chat service, to be enhanced by practice standards addressing an apparent lack of focus on the central issue of suicidality during chats, as well as by the development of best practices specific for online crisis intervention.

Reconsidering criterion A for the diagnosis of non-suicidal self-injury disorder

Muehlenkamp JJ, Brausch AM (United States)

Journal of Psychopathology and Behavioral Assessment. Published online: 21 March 2016. doi: 10.1007/s10862-016-9543-0

Empirical research is needed to verify that the DSM-5 proposed diagnostic criteria for non-suicidal self-injury (NSSI) disorder provide a valid and clinically meaningful symptom set. The current study used data-driven methods to examine the diagnostic validity of the frequency and recency thresholds (i.e. Criterion A) for NSSI disorder. Data were collected from a random sample (n = 2206) of undergraduates. Participants completed counter-balanced questionnaires assessing the frequency, recency, and functions of NSSI, psychopathology symptoms, and indicators of distress and functional impairment. Discriminant functional analyses identified a significant differentiation for frequency between 10 or more acts of NSSI and 1–9 acts. Groups were also differentiated with a split on recency between less than 12-months ago and more than 12-months ago. After re-grouping the sample into categories based on the new frequency and 12-month recency threshold, the 10+ NSSI group reported significantly more functions for NSSI, including higher scores on affect regulation, self-punishment, and sensation seeking, than the subthreshold NSSI group. The 10+ NSSI group also reported significantly worse psychopathology, greater distress, and more impairment than both the subthreshold group and controls (no NSSI history). These findings indicate the current DSM-5 diagnostic criteria for NSSI disorder may be too liberal, and offer support for increasing the frequency thresholds for the diagnosis to ensure clinical validity and utility.

Developmental trajectories of self-injurious behavior, suicidal behavior and substance misuse and their association with adolescent borderline personality pathology

Nakar O, Brunner R, Schilling O, Chanen A, Fischer G, Parzer P, Carli V, Wasserman D, Sarchiapone M, Wasserman C, Hoven CW, Resch F, Kaess M (Germany)

Journal of Affective Disorders 197, 231-238, 2016

Objective: Adolescent risk-taking and self-harm behaviors are associated with affect dysregulation and impulsivity, both core features of borderline personality disorder (BPD). We hypothesized that the developmental courses of these behaviors i) tend to cluster rather than appear individually, and ii) might indicate adolescent BPD pathology. Therefore, we explored the developmental trajectories of self-injurious behavior (SIB), suicidal behavior (SB) and substance misuse (SM) in a community sample of adolescents; and we investigated the trajectories' overlap and its associations with BPD traits.

Method: 513 adolescents, aged 15-17 years, were followed for two years as part of the Saving and Empowering Young Lives in Europe study and its subsequent follow-up. Distinct developmental trajectories were explored using general growth mixture modeling.

Results: Three distinct classes were identified within each of the harmful behaviors SIB, SB and SM. Both the high-risk SIB trajectory and the high-risk SB trajectory demonstrated elevated initial degree of engagement, followed by a gradual decrease. The SM high-risk trajectory had a medium initial degree of engagement, which increased over time. There was a high degree of overlap (80-90%) among the high-risk trajectories for the three behaviors (SIB, SB and SM), and this overlap was significantly associated with elevated levels of BPD pathology.

Limitations: The data collection was based on participants' self-report.

Conclusion: The findings indicate a similar pattern of reduction over time between SIB and SB for the high-risk trajectories, whereas the high-risk trajectories for SM show a pattern of increase over time. The observed symptom shift is associated with borderline personality pathology in adolescents. Therefore these behaviors might represent early indicators of risk supporting potential early detection.

Exploring the relationship between experiential avoidance, coping functions and the recency and frequency of self-harm

Nielsen E, Sayal K, Townsend E (United Kingdom)

PLoS One 11, e0159854, 2016

This study investigated the relationship between experiential avoidance, coping and the recency and frequency of self-harm, in a community sample (N = 1332, aged 16-69 years). Participants completed online, self-report measures assessing self-harm, momentary affect, experiential avoidance and coping in response to a recent stressor. Participants who had self-harmed reported significantly higher levels of experiential avoidance and avoidance coping, as well as lower levels of approach, reappraisal and emotional regulation coping, than those with no self-harm history. Moreover, more recent self-harm was associated with lower endorsement of approach, reappraisal and emotion regulation coping, and also higher levels of both avoidance coping and experiential avoidance. Higher experiential avoidance and avoidance coping also predicted increased lifetime frequency of self-harm. Conversely, increased approach and reappraisal coping were associated with a decreased likelihood of high frequency self-harm. Although some of the effects were small, particularly in relation to lifetime frequency of self-harm, overall our results suggest that experiential avoidance tendency may be an important psychological factor underpinning self-harm, regardless of suicidal intent (e.g. including mixed intent, suicidal intent, ambivalence), which is not accounted for in existing models of self-harm.

The area level association between suicide, deprivation, social fragmentation and population density in the Republic of Ireland: A national study

O'Farrell IB, Corcoran P, Perry IJ (Ireland)

Social Psychiatry and Psychiatric Epidemiology 51, 839-847, 2016

Purpose: Numerous studies have examined the ecological relationship between suicide and area level determinants such as deprivation and social fragmentation. In Ireland, there is considerable geographic variation in the rates of suicide. However, there is a dearth of Irish studies investigating the geographic variability of suicide.

Methods: The Irish Central Statistics Office (CSO) provided data relating to all deaths by suicide and deaths of undetermined intent that occurred from 2009 to 2011. Negative binomial regression was used to examine the relationship between area level suicide rates and measures of deprivation, social fragmentation and population density that were taken from the 2011 National Census.

Results: Overall deprivation had the strongest independent effect on small-area rates of suicide, with the most deprived areas showing the greatest risk of suicide (risk ratio = 2.1; 95 % CI 1.70-2.52). Low population density (rurality) was associated with an increased risk suicide in males across both age groups and among females in the older 40-64-year age group. Conversely, a weak association between high population density (urbanicity) and increased suicide risk was found among females in the 15-39-year age group. Associations with social fragmentation only became apparent in the sub group analysis. Social fragmentation was associated with an elevated risk of suicide in the older 40-64 age group, with this effect being most pronounced among females.

Conclusion: The findings of this study demonstrate marked geographical inequalities in the distribution of suicide in Ireland and highlight the importance of targeting suicide prevention resources in the most deprived areas.

Encountering the body at the site of the suicide: A population-based survey in Sweden

Omerov P, Pettersén R, Titelman D, Nyberg T, Steineck G, Dyregrov A, Nyberg U (Sweden)
Suicide and Life-Threatening Behavior. Published online: 25 April 2016. doi: 10.1111/sltb.12260

Encountering the body of a child who died by suicide at the site of death is believed to be especially harmful for bereaved parents. We investigated the association between encountering the body at the site of the suicide and psychological distress in 666 suicide-bereaved parents. Parents who had encountered their child's body at the site of the suicide (n = 147) did not have a higher risk of nightmares (relative risk [RR] 0.95, 95% confidence interval [CI] 0.67-1.35), intrusive memories (RR 0.97, 95% CI 0.84-1.13), avoidance of thoughts (RR 0.97, 95% CI 0.74-1.27), avoidance of places or things (RR 0.91, 95% CI 0.66-1.25), anxiety (RR 0.93, 95% CI 0.64-1.33), or depression (RR 0.94, 95% CI 0.63-1.42) compared with parents who had not encountered the body (n = 512). Our results suggest that losing a child by suicide is sufficiently disastrous by itself to elicit posttraumatic responses or psychiatric morbidity whether or not the parent has encountered the deceased child at the site of death.

Positron emission tomographic imaging of the serotonergic system and prediction of risk and lethality of future suicidal behavior

Oquendo MA, Galfalvy H, Sullivan GM, Miller JM, Milak MM, Sublette ME, Cisneros-Trujillo S, Burke AK, Parsey RV, Mann JJ (United States)
JAMA Psychiatry 73, 1048-1055, 2016

Importance: Biomarkers that predict suicidal behavior, especially highly lethal behavior, are urgently needed. In cross-sectional studies, individuals with depression who attempt suicide have lower midbrain serotonin transporter binding potential compared with those who do not attempt suicide, and higher serotonin1A binding potential in the raphe nuclei (RN) is associated with greater lethality of past suicide attempts and suicidal intent and ideation.

Objectives: To determine whether serotonin transporter binding potential in the lower midbrain predicts future suicide attempts and whether higher RN serotonin1A binding potential predicts future suicidal ideation and intent and lethality of future suicide attempts.

Design, Setting, and Participants: In this prospective 2-year observational study, a well-characterized cohort of 100 patients presenting for treatment of a major depressive episode of at least moderate severity underwent positron emission tomography using carbon 11-labeled N-(2-(1-(4-(2-methoxyphenyl)-1-piperazinyl)ethyl))-N-(2-pyridyl)-cyclohexanecarbo xamide ([11C]WAY-100635), a serotonin1A antagonist; a subset of 50 patients also underwent imaging with carbon 11-labeled 3-amino-4-(2-dimethylaminomethyl-phenylsulfanyl)- benzonitrile ([11C]DASB), a serotonin transporter radioligand. Imaging was performed at Columbia University Medical Center from May 3, 1999, to March 11, 2008. Follow-up was completed on May 28, 2010, and data were analyzed from August 1, 2013, to March 1, 2016.

Exposures: Patients were treated naturalistically in the community and followed up for 2 years with documentation of suicidal behavior, its lethality, and suicidal ideation and intent.

Main Outcomes and Measures: Suicide attempt or suicide.

Results: Of the 100 patients undergoing follow-up for more than 2 years (39 men; 61 women; mean [SD] age, 40.2 [11.2] years), 15 made suicide attempts, including 2 who died by suicide. Higher RN serotonin1A binding potential predicted more suicidal ideation at 3 (b = 0.02; t = 3.45; P = .001) and 12 (b = 0.02; t = 3.63; P = .001) months and greater lethality of subsequent suicidal behavior (b = 0.08; t = 2.89; P = .01). Exploratory analyses suggest that the serotonin1A binding potential of the insula (t = 2.41; P = .04), anterior cingulate (t = 2.27; P = .04), and dorsolateral prefrontal cortex (t = 2.44; P = .03) were also predictive of lethality. Contrary to our hypotheses, suicidal intent was not predicted by serotonin1A binding potential in any brain region (F1,10 = 0.83; P = .38), and midbrain serotonin transporter binding potential did not predict future attempts (log-rank chi21 = 0.4; P = .54), possibly owing to low power.

Conclusions and Relevance: Greater RN serotonin1A binding potential predicted higher suicidal ideation and more lethal suicidal behavior during a 2-year period. This effect may be mediated through less serotonin neuron firing and release, which affects mood and suicidal ideation and thereby decision making.

Body mass index is an important predictor for suicide: Results from a systematic review and meta-analysis

Perera S, Eisen RB, Dennis BB, Bawor M, Bhatt M, Bhatnagar N, Thabane L, de Souza R, Samaan Z (Canada)
Suicide and Life-Threatening Behavior. Published online: 20 April 2016. doi: 10.1111/sltb.12244

Public health concerns for the independent management of obesity and suicidal behavior are rising. Emerging evidence suggests body weight plays an important role in quantifying the risk of suicide. In light of these findings, we aimed to clarify the association between body mass index (BMI) and suicidal behavior by systematically reviewing and evaluating the literature. Studies were identified by searching MEDLINE, EMBASE, PsycINFO, and CINAHL from inception to January 2015, supplemented by hand and grey literature searches. Study screening, data extraction, and risk of bias assessment were conducted in duplicate. We included 38 observational studies. Meta-analyses supported an inverse association between BMI and completed suicide. Pooled summary estimates demonstrated that underweight was significantly associated with an increased risk of completed suicide (HR = 1.21, 95% CI 1.07 to 1.36, p = .002), and obesity (HR = 0.71, 95% CI 0.56

to 0.89, p = .003) and overweight (HR = 0.78, 95% CI 0.75 to 0.82, p < .0001) were significantly associated with a decreased risk of completed suicide relative to normal weight. A qualitative summary of the literature demonstrated conflicting evidence regarding the association between BMI and attempted suicide and revealed no association between BMI and suicidal ideation. BMI may be used to aid the assessment of suicide risk, especially that of completed suicide. However, unmeasured confounders and systematic biases of individual studies limit the quality of evidence.

The stigma perceived by people bereaved by suicide and other sudden deaths: A cross-sectional UK study of 3432 bereaved adults

Pitman AL, Osborn DPJ, Rantell K, King MB (United Kingdom)
Journal of Psychosomatic Research 87, 22-29, 2016

Objective: To test the hypothesis that perceived stigma scores in young adults bereaved by suicide are significantly higher than in young adults bereaved by other sudden deaths, whether blood-related to the deceased or not.

Methods: We conducted a cross-sectional study of all staff and students aged 18-40 at 37 UK higher educational institutions in 2010, and identified 3432 respondents who had experienced a sudden bereavement of a close contact since reaching the age of 10, either due to sudden natural causes, sudden unnatural causes, or suicide. We used multivariable regression to compare scores on the stigma, shame, responsibility and guilt subscales of the Grief Experience Questionnaire, adjusting for socio-demographic factors and pre-bereavement psychopathology.

Results: People bereaved by suicide (n = 614) had higher stigma scores than people bereaved by sudden natural death (n = 2106; adjusted coefficient = 2.52; 95% CI = 2.13-2.90; p = <. 0.001) and people bereaved by sudden unnatural death (n = 712; adjusted coefficient = 1.69; 95% CI = 1.25-2.13; p = <. 0.001). Shame, responsibility and guilt scores were also significantly higher in people bereaved by suicide, whether compared with bereavement by sudden natural death or sudden unnatural death. Associations were not modified by whether the bereaved was blood-related to the deceased or not.

Conclusions: Stigma was perceived more acutely by the relatives and friends of those who died by suicide than those bereaved by other causes of sudden natural or sudden unnatural death. Their high levels of perceived stigma, shame, responsibility and guilt require qualitative investigation to identify whether these grief dimensions limit social functioning, help-seeking behaviour and/or support offered.

Neuropsychological markers of suicidal risk in the context of medical rehabilitation

Pustilnik A, Elkana O, Vatine J-J, Franko M, Hamdan S (Israel)
Archives of Suicide Research. Published online: 6 April 2016.doi: 10.1080/13811118.2016.1171815

Objective: While great strides have been made to advance the understanding of the neurobiology of suicidal behavior (SB), the neural and neuropsychological mechanisms associated with SB are not well understood. The purpose of the current study is to identify neurocognitive markers of SB in the context of medical rehabilitation.

Method: The performances of 39 patients at a medical rehabilitation center, aged 21-78, were examined on a series of neurocognitive executive tasks- decision-making (Iowa Gambling Task - IGT), mental flexibility (WCST), response inhibition (SST) and working memory (digit span). Self-report questionnaires were administered, for Suicidal behaviors, depression, Anxiety and PTSD as well as perceived social support.

Results: Suicidal participants performed more poorly on the IGT. A mediation analysis presented a significant direct effect of decision making on suicidal risk ($p < 0.14$) as well as significant indirect effect of decision making on suicidal risk that was mediated by the depressive symptoms (95% BCa CI [-0.15, -0.018]) with a medium effect size ($\kappa(2) = 0.20$, 95% BCa CI [0.067, 0.381]).

Conclusions: Despite the complexity of relationship between decision-making and suicidal risk, these results suggest that clinicians should routinely assess decision-making abilities in adults at risk for suicide due the fact that impaired decision- making may increase suicidal risk above and beyond that conferred by depression.

Disability pension due to common mental disorders and subsequent suicidal behaviour: A population-based prospective cohort study

Rahman SG, Alexanderson K, Jokinen J, Mittendorfer-Rutz E (Sweden)
BMJ Open 6, 1-9, 2016

Objective: Adverse health outcomes, including suicide, in individuals on disability pension (DP) due to mental diagnoses have been reported. However, scientific knowledge on possible risk factors for suicidal behaviour (suicide attempt and suicide) in this group, such as age, gender, underlying DP diagnoses, comorbidity and DP duration and grade, is surprisingly sparse. This study aimed to investigate associations of different measures (main and secondary diagnoses, duration and grade) of DP due to common mental disorders (CMD) with subsequent suicidal behaviour, considering gender and age differences.

Design: Population-based prospective cohort study based on Swedish nationwide registers.

Methods: A cohort of 46 515 individuals aged 19-64 years on DP due to CMD throughout 2005 was followed-up for 5 years. In relation to different measures of DP, univariate and multivariate HRs and 95% CIs for suicidal behaviour were estimated by Cox regression. All analyses were stratified by gender and age.

Results: During 2006-2010, 1036 (2.2%) individuals attempted and 207 (0.5%) completed suicide. Multivariate analyses showed that a main DP diagnosis of 'stress-related mental disorders' was associated with a lower risk of subsequent suicidal behaviour than 'depressive disorders' (HR range 0.4-0.7). Substance abuse or personality disorders as a secondary DP diagnosis predicted suicide attempt in all subgroups (HR range 1.4-2.3) and suicide in women and younger individuals (HR range 2.6-3.3). Full-time DP was associated with a higher risk of suicide attempt compared with part-time DP in women and both age groups (HR range 1.4-1.7).

Conclusions: Depressive disorders as the main DP diagnosis and substance abuse or personality disorders as the secondary DP diagnosis were risk markers for subsequent suicidal behaviour in individuals on DP due to CMD. Particular attention should be paid to younger individuals on DP due to anxiety disorders because of the higher suicide risk.

Timelines for difficult times: Use of visual timelines in interviewing suicide attempters

Rimkeviciene J, O'Gorman J, Hawgood J, De Leo D (Australia)
Qualitative Research in Psychology 13, 231-245, 2016

The stories of people who attempt suicide are insufficiently reflected in suicide research in psychology. This article outlines a method using a visual timeline during the interviews to explore the narratives of suicide attempts. The method was successfully employed in two studies to collect data on the suicidal process from people with prior experience of suicide attempts. The advantages of the method in collecting comprehensive data, building rapport, and fostering participants' insight are outlined. Strategies that were used to ensure safety of participants are described in addition to the requirements for interviewers seeking to apply this method.

The effects of the family bereavement program to reduce suicide ideation and/or attempts of parentally bereaved children six and fifteen years later

Sandler I, Tein J-Y, Wolchik S, Ayers TS (United States)
Suicide and Life-Threatening Behavior 46, S32-S38, 2016

Findings concerning the long-term effects of the Family Bereavement Program (FBP) to reduce suicide ideation and/or attempts of parentally bereaved children and adolescents are presented. Parental death is a significant risk factor for suicide among offspring (Guldin et al. 2015). This study is a long-term follow-up of 244 children and adolescents who had participated in a randomized trial of the FBP, examining the intervention effects on suicide ideation and/or attempts as assessed through multiple sources. Results indicate a significant effect of the FBP to reduce suicide ideation and/or attempts at the 6- and 15-year follow-up evaluation. The findings support the potential benefits of further research on "upstream" suicide prevention.

Successful treatment of suicidal risk: What helped and what was internalized?

Schembari BC, Jobes DA, Horgan RJ (United States)
Crisis 37, 218-223, 2016

Background: In this article we focused on analyzing surveyed patient-generated responses based on two outcome questions derived from a suicide-specific framework called the Collaborative Assessment and Management of Suicidality (CAMS): Q1 - "Were there any aspects of your treatment that were particularly helpful to you? If so, please describe these. Be as specific as possible." Q2 - "What have you learned from your clinical care that could help you if you became suicidal in the future?"

Aims: To develop a reliable coding system based on formerly suicidal patients' responses to two open-ended prompts and examine most frequently identified themes.

Method: The present study utilized a consensual qualitative research process to examine responses of clinically resolved suicidal patients, based on the CAMS resolution criteria (i.e. three consecutive CAMS sessions reporting the effective management of suicidal risk), to two Suicide Status Form (SSF) outcome questions (n = 49 for Q1, and n = 52 for Q2).

Results: Reliable coding systems were developed and used to determine major themes of successful patient responses.

Conclusion: The results of this study provide insight into patients' experiences of a successful treatment for suicidal risk with larger implications for suicide-specific treatments in general.

Acute Suicidal Affective Disturbance (ASAD): A confirmatory factor analysis with 1442 psychiatric inpatients

Stanley IH, Rufino KA, Rogers ML, Ellis TE, Joiner TE (United States)

Journal of Psychiatric Research 80, 97-104, 2016

Acute Suicidal Affective Disturbance (ASAD) is a newly proposed diagnostic entity that characterizes rapid onset suicidal intent. This study aims to confirm the factor structure of ASAD among psychiatric inpatients, and to determine the clinical utility of ASAD in predicting suicide attempt status. Overall, 1442 psychiatric inpatients completed a battery of self-report questionnaires assessing symptoms theorized to comprise the ASAD construct. Utilizing these data, a confirmatory factor analysis with a one-factor solution was performed. Regression analyses were employed to determine if the ASAD construct predicted past suicide attempts, and analyses of variance (ANOVAs) were employed to determine if ASAD symptoms differed by the presence and number of past suicide attempts. The one-factor solution indicated good fit: $\chi(2)(77) = 309.1$, $p < 0.001$, Tucker-Lewis Index (TLI) = 0.96, comparative fit index (CFI) = 0.97, root-mean-square error of approximation (RMSEA) = 0.05. Controlling for depressive disorders and current symptoms, the ASAD construct significantly predicted the presence of a past suicide attempt. Moreover, ASAD differentiated in the expected directions between individuals with a history of multiple suicide attempts, individuals with a single suicide attempt, and individuals with no history of a suicide attempt. Acute Suicidal Affective Disturbance (ASAD) appears to be a unified construct that predicts suicidal behavior and is distinct from an already-defined mood disorder.

Suicide in Canada: Is poisoning misclassification an issue?

Skinner R, McFaull S, Rhodes AE, Bowes M, Rockett IRH (Canada)

Canadian Journal of Psychiatry. Published online: 23 March 2016. doi: 10.1177/0706743716639918

Objective: The aim of this study is to compare Canadian suicide rates with other external causes of death to examine potential poisoning misclassifications as a contributor to suicide underreporting.

Method: The study used Statistics Canada mortality data from 2000 to 2011 to calculate sex-and age-specific ratios by external cause of injury codes.

Results: The overall Canadian suicide rate, as well as the poisoning suicide rate, declined over the study timeframe by an average annual percentage change (AAPC) of 1.0% each year. However, unintentional and undetermined poisonings increased significantly during the timeframe. Unintentional poisoning mortality (primarily narcotics and hallucinogens, including opioids) increased in proportion to suicides for both sexes, although females were consistently higher. The undetermined death to suicide ratio was higher and increasing for females. Poisonings of undetermined intent increased over time to comprise 47% to 80% of the undetermined death category for males and females combined.

Conclusions: Canadian poisoning suicide rates declined, in contrast to rising unintentional and undetermined poisoning mortality rates. This trend is similar to that of the United States, supporting the hypothesis that misclassification of poisoning deaths may also be an issue in Canada.

Discussing firearm ownership and access as part of suicide risk assessment and prevention: "Means safety" versus "means restriction"

Stanley IH, Hom MA, Rogers ML, Anestis MD, Joiner TE (United States)

Archives of Suicide Research. Published online: 13 April 2016. doi: 10.1080/13811118.2016.1175395

Objectives: To describe the relative utility of the terms "means safety" versus "means restriction" in counseling individuals to limit their access to firearms in the context of a mock suicide risk assessment.

Method: Overall, 370 participants were randomized to read a vignette depicting a clinical scenario in which managing firearm ownership and access was discussed either using the term "means safety" or "means restriction."

Results: Participants rated the term "means safety" as significantly more acceptable and preferable than "means restriction." Participants randomized to the "means safety" condition reported greater intentions to adhere to clinicians' recommendations to limit access to a firearm for safety purposes ($F[1,367] = 7.393$, $p = .007$, etap2 = .020).

Conclusions: The term "means safety" may be more advantageous than "means restriction" when discussing firearm ownership and access in clinical settings and public health-oriented suicide prevention efforts.

Trajectories of self-rated health in the last 15 years of life by cause of death

Stenholm S, Kivimaki M, Jylha M, Kawachi I, Westerlund H, Pentti J, Goldberg M, Zins M, Vahtera J (France)

European Journal of Epidemiology 31, 177-185, 2016

Poor self-rated health is associated with increased risk of mortality, but no previous study has examined how long-term trajectories of self-rated health differ among people at risk of subsequent death compared to those who survive. Data were drawn from French occupational cohort (the GAZEL study, 1989-2010). This nested case-control study included 915 deceased men and women and 2578 controls matched for sex, baseline age, occupational grade and marital status. Self-rated health was measured annually and dichotomized into good versus poor health. Trajectories of poor self-rated health up to 15 years were compared among people who subsequently died to those who survived. Participants contributed to an average 10.3 repeated assessments of self-rated health. Repeated-measures log-binomial regression analysis with generalized estimating equations showed an increased prevalence of poor self-rated health in cases 13-15 years prior to death from ischemic and other cardiovascular disease [multivariable-adjusted risk ratio 2.06, 95 % confidence interval (CI) 1.55-2.75], non-smoking-related cancers (1.57, 95 % CI 1.30-1.89), and suicide (1.78, 95 % CI 1.00-3.16). Prior to death from ischemic and other cardiovascular disease, increased rates of poor self-rated health were evident even among persons who were free of cardiovascular diseases (2.05, 95 % CI 1.50-2.78). In conclusion, perceptions of health diverged between the surviving controls and the deceased already 15 years prior to death. For cardiovascular mortality, decline in self-rated health started before diagnosis of the disease leading to death. The findings suggest that declining self-rated health might capture pathological changes before and beyond the disease diagnosis.

Passive suicide ideation among older adults in Europe: A multilevel regression analysis of individual and societal determinants in 12 countries (SHARE)

Stolz E, Fux B, Mayerl H, Rasky E, Freidl W (Austria)

Journal of Gerontology: Psychological Sciences & Social Sciences. Published online: 5 April 2016. doi: 10.1093/geronb/gbw041

Objectives: Passive suicide ideation (PSI) is common among older adults, but prevalences have been reported to vary considerably across European countries. The goal of this study was to assess the role of individual-level risk factors and societal contextual factors associated with PSI in old age.

Method: We analyzed longitudinal data from the Survey of Health, Ageing, and Retirement in Europe (SHARE) on 6,791 community-dwelling respondents (75+) from 12 countries. Bayesian logistic multilevel regression models were used to assess variance components, individual-level and country-level risk factors.

Results: About 4% of the total variance of PSI was located at the country level, a third of which was attributable to compositional effects of individual-level predictors. Predictors for the development of PSI at the individual level were female gender, depression, older age, poor health, smaller social network size, loneliness, nonreligiosity, and low perceived control (R 2 = 25.8%). At the country level, cultural acceptance of suicide, religiosity, and intergenerational cohabitation were associated with the rates of PSI.

Discussion: Cross-national variation in old-age PSI is mostly attributable to individual-level determinants and compositional differences, but there is also evidence for contextual effects of country-level characteristics. Suicide prevention programs should be intensified in high-risk countries and attitudes toward suicide should be addressed in information campaigns.

A population study of the association between sleep disturbance and suicidal behaviour in people with mental illness

Stubbs B, Wu Y-T, Prina AM, Leng Y, Cosco TD (United States)
Journal of Psychiatric Research 82, 149-154, 2016

Limited representative research has considered the relationship between sleep disturbance and suicidal behaviour among people with mental illness. We investigated the relationship between sleep disturbance and suicidal behaviour across Part II interview of the National Comorbidity Survey Replication (NCSR). The associations between sleep disturbance and suicidal behaviour (thoughts, plans and attempts) were investigated using logistic and multinomial logistic regressions and stratified across six mental disorder groups (depression, anxiety, substance use disorders (SUD), eating disorders (ED), bipolar disorders (BD) and early life disorders). From 5701 participants (mean age 43.4 years 58% women), people with any mental disorder experiencing sleep disturbance were at increased odds of suicidal thoughts (odds ratio (OR): 2.5; 95% CI: 1.7, 3.6) and suicidal plans and attempts (OR: 5.7; 95% CI: 2.7, 11.9) adjusting for age, sex and income. People with BD (OR: 8.9; 95 CI: 2.1, 38.1), early life disorders (OR 6.98, 95% ci 2.48, 19.67), depression (OR 1.88, 95% CI 1.14, 3.11), anxiety (OR 1.90, 95% CI 1.28, 2.85) and SUD (2.60, 95% CI 1.23, 5.49) but not ED, were at increased odds of suicidal thoughts in the presence of sleep disturbance. Adjusting for antidepressant intake attenuated the effect sizes by up to 20% but the associations remained significant. In conclusion, sleep disturbance is a potential risk factor for suicidal behaviours in people with mental illness. Monitoring and management of sleep disturbance in clinical practice might be an important strategy to mitigate suicidal behaviours in people with mental illness.

The continuing implications of the "crime' of suicide: A brief history of the present

Tait G, Carpenter B (Australia)
International Journal of Law in Context 12, 210-224, 2016

The long history of suicide as a criminal offence still has a significant contemporary effect on how it is perceived, conceptualised and adjudged. This is particularly the case within countries where suicide is largely determined within a coronial system, such as Australia, the UK and the US. This paper details the outcomes of a study involving semi-structured interviews with coroners both in England and Australia, as well as observations at inquests. It focuses around the widely held contention that the suicide rates produced within these coronial systems are underestimations of anywhere between 15 to 50 per cent. The results of these interviews suggest that there are three main reasons for this systemic underestimation. The first reflects the legacy of suicide as a criminal offence, resulting in the highest standard of proof for findings of suicide in the UK, and a continuing stigma attached to families of the deceased. The second is the considerable pressure brought to bear upon coroners by the family of the deceased, who, because of that stigma, commonly agitate for any finding other than that of suicide. The third involves the rise of therapeutic jurisprudence', wherein coroners take on the responsibility of the emotional well-being of the grieving families, which in turn affects the likelihood of reaching a finding of suicide. The conclusions drawn by the paper are also twofold: first - with respect to the stigma of suicide - it will take a lot more than simple decriminalisation to change deeply held social perceptions within the community. Second, given that suicide prevention programmes and policies are based on such deeply questionable statistics, targeted changes to coronial legislation and practice would appear to be required.

Risk and protective factors for suicidal behaviors among pacific youth in New Zealand

Teevale T, Lee AC, Tiatia-Seath J, Clark TC, Denny S, Bullen P, Fleming T, Peiris-John RJ (New Zealand)

Crisis. Published online: 9 June 2016. doi: 10.1027/0227-5910/a000396

Background: New Zealand has the second highest youth suicide rate in the OECD and particularly among Pacific New Zealanders, who have a threefold higher risk of suicide attempt compared with the general population.

Aims: Protective and risk factors for suicide attempts among New Zealand Pacific adolescents were assessed using data from Youth'12, an adolescent health and well-being survey.

Method: This randomly selected nationally representative sample of New Zealand secondary school students included 1,445 Pacific high school students aged 12-17 years.

Results: One in 10 (11.6%) Pacific adolescents reported attempting suicide. Risk factors for suicide included: being female, household food insecurity, low levels of family connections and family monitoring, life dissatisfaction, having a religious affiliation, and previous suicide by a family member or friend. Of those who had made a suicide attempt, 71% also experienced both suicide ideation and self-harm.

Conclusion: This study suggests that given the high rates of suicide ideation and attempts among Pacific young people, targeted trials for new ways of support should be prioritized for this high-risk group. The Pacific family environment, which continues to be the critical space for intervening, and the school environment, as a provider of health services, were both protective of suicide attempt.

Relationship satisfaction and risk factors for suicide

Till B, Tran US, Niederkrotenthaler T (Austria)
Crisis. Published online: 22 July 2016. doi: 10.1027/0227-5910/a000407

Background: Previous studies suggest that troubled romantic relationships are associated with higher risk factors for mental health. However, studies examining the role of relationship satisfaction in suicide risk factors are scarce.

Aims: We investigated differences in risk factors for suicide between individuals with high relationship satisfaction, individuals with low relationship satisfaction, and singles. Furthermore, we explored patterns of experiencing, and dealing with, conflicts in the relationship and examined associations with suicide risk factors.

Method: In this cross-sectional study, we assessed relationship status, relationship satisfaction, specific types of relationship conflicts, and suicide risk factors (i.e. suicidal ideation, hopelessness, depression) with questionnaires among 382 individuals in Austria.

Results: Risk factors for suicide were higher among singles than among individuals in happy relationships, but lower among those with low relationship satisfaction. Participants reporting a high number of unsolved conflicts in their relationship had higher levels of suicidal ideation, hopelessness, and depression than individuals who tend to solve issues with their partner amicably or report no conflicts.

Conclusion: Relationship satisfaction and relationship conflicts reflect risk factors for suicide, with higher levels of suicidal ideation, hopelessness, and depression reported by individuals who mentioned unsolved conflicts with their partner and experienced low satisfaction with their relationship.

The influences of parental divorce and maternal-versus-paternal alcohol abuse on offspring lifetime suicide attempt

Thompson RG, Jr. Alonzo D, Hu MC, Hasin DS (United States)
Drug and Alcohol Review. Published online: 19 August 2016. doi: 10.1111/dar.12441

Introduction and Aims: Research indicates that parental divorce and parental alcohol abuse independently increase likelihood of offspring lifetime suicide attempt. However, when experienced together, only parental alcohol abuse significantly increased odds of suicide attempt. It is unclear to what extent differences in the effect of maternal versus paternal alcohol use exist on adult offspring lifetime suicide attempt risk. This study examined the influences of parental divorce and maternal-paternal histories of alcohol problems on adult offspring lifetime suicide attempt.

Design and Methods: The sample consisted of participants from the 2001-2002 National Epidemiological Survey on Alcohol and Related Conditions. The simultaneous effect of childhood or adolescent parental divorce and maternal and paternal history of alcohol problems on offspring lifetime suicide attempt was estimated using a logistic regression model with an interaction term for demographics and parental history of other emotional and behavioural problems.

Results: Parental divorce and maternal-paternal alcohol problems interacted to differentially influence the likelihood of offspring lifetime suicide attempt. Experiencing parental divorce and either maternal or paternal alcohol problems nearly doubled the likelihood of suicide attempt. Divorce and history of alcohol problems for both parents tripled the likelihood.

Discussion and Conclusion: Individuals who experienced parental divorce as children or adolescents and who have a parent who abuses alcohol are at elevated risk for lifetime suicide attempt. These problem areas should become a routine part of assessment to better identify those at risk for lifetime suicide attempt and to implement early and targeted intervention to decrease such risk.

Suicidal behavior in mood disorders: Response to pharmacological treatment

Tondo L, Baldessarini RJ (United States)

Current Psychiatry Reports 18, 88, 2016

Suicidal behavior is strongly associated with depression, especially if accompanied by behavioral activation, dysphoria, or agitation. It may respond to some treatments, but the design of scientifically sound, ethical trials to test for therapeutic effects on suicidal behavior is highly challenging. In bipolar disorder, and possibly also unipolar major depression, an underprescribed medical intervention with substantial evidence of preventive effects on suicidal behavior is long-term treatment with lithium. It is unclear whether this effect is specifically antisuicidal or reflects beneficial effects of lithium on depression, mood instability, and perhaps aggression and impulsivity. Antisuicidal effects of anticonvulsant mood stabilizers (carbamazepine, lamotrigine, valproate) appear to be less than with lithium. Further evaluation is needed for potential antisuicidal effects of atypical antipsychotics with growing evidence of efficacy in depression, particularly acute bipolar depression, while generally lacking risk of inducing agitation, mania, or mood instability. Short-term and long-term value and safety of antidepressants are relatively secure for unipolar depression but uncertain and poorly tested for bipolar depression; their effects on suicidal risk in unipolar depression may be age-dependent. Sedative anxiolytics are virtually unstudied as regards suicidal risks. Adequate management of suicidal risks in mood disorder patients requires comprehensive, clinically skillful monitoring and timely interventions.

Clusters of suicides and suicide attempts: Detection, proximity and correlates

Too LS, Pirkis J, Milner A, Spittal MJ (Australia)

Epidemiology Psychiatric Sciences. Published online: 9 June 2016. doi: 10.1017/S2045796016000391

Background: A suicide cluster is defined as a higher number of observed cases occurring in space and/or time than would typically be expected. Previous research has largely focused on identifying clusters of suicides, while there has been comparatively limited research on clusters of suicide attempts. We sought to identify clusters of both types of behaviour, and having done that, identify the factors that distinguish suicide attempts inside a cluster from those that were outside a cluster.

Methods: We used data from Western Australia from 2000 to 2011. We defined suicide attempts as admissions to hospital for deliberate self-harm and suicides as deaths due to deliberate self-harm. Using an analytic strategy that accounted for the repetition of attempted suicide within a cluster, we performed spatial-temporal analysis using Poisson discrete scan statistics to detect clusters of suicide attempts and clusters of suicides. Logistic regression was then used to compare clustered attempts with non-clustered attempts to identify risk factors for an attempt being in a cluster.

Results: We detected 350 (1%) suicide attempts occurring within seven spatial-temporal clusters and 12 (0.6%) suicides occurring within two spatial-temporal clusters. Both of the suicide clusters were located within a larger but later suicide attempt cluster. In multivariate analysis, suicide attempts by individuals who lived in areas of low socioeconomic status had higher odds of being in a cluster than those living in areas of high socioeconomic status [odds ratio (OR) = 29.1, 95% confidence interval (CI) = 6.3-135.5]. A one percentage-point increase in the proportion of people who had changed address in the last year was associated with a 60% increase in the odds of the attempt being within a cluster (OR = 1.60, 95% CI = 1.29-1.98) and a one percentage-point increase in the proportion of Indigenous people in the area was associated with a 7% increase in the suicide being within a cluster (OR = 1.07, 95% CI = 1.00-1.13). Age, sex, marital status, employment status, method of harm, remoteness, percentage of people in rented accommodation and percentage of unmarried people were not associated with the odds of being in a suicide attempt cluster.

Conclusions: Early identification of and responding to suicide clusters may reduce the likelihood of subsequent clusters forming. The mechanisms, however, that underlie clusters forming is poorly understood.

Risk factors, methods, and timing of suicide attempts among US Army soldiers

Ursano RJ, Kessler RC, Stein MB, Naifeh JA, Aliaga PA, Fullerton CS, Wynn GH, Vegella PL, Ng TH, Zhang BG, Wryter CL, Sampson NA, Kao TC, Colpe LJ, Schoenbaum M, McCarroll JE, Cox KL, Heeringa SG (United States)
JAMA Psychiatry 73, 741-749, 2016

Importance: Suicide attempts in the US Army have risen in the past decade. Understanding the association between suicide attempts and deployment, as well as method and timing of suicide attempts, can assist in developing interventions.

Objective: To examine suicide attempt risk factors, methods, and timing among soldiers currently deployed, previously deployed, and never deployed at the time this study was conducted.

Design, Setting, and Participants: This longitudinal, retrospective cohort study of Regular Army-enlisted soldiers on active duty from 2004 through 2009 used individual-level person-month records to examine risk factors (sociodemographic, service related, and mental health), method, and time of suicide attempt by deployment status (never, currently, and previously deployed). Administrative data for the month before each of 9650 incident suicide attempts and an equal-probability sample of 153528 control person-months for other soldiers were analyzed using a discrete-time survival framework.

Main Outcomes and Measures: Suicide attempts and career, mental health, and demographic predictors were obtained from administrative and medical records.

Results: Of the 9650 enlisted soldiers who attempted suicide, 86.3% were male, 68.4% were younger than 30 years, 59.8% were non-Hispanic white, 76.5% were high school educated, and 54.7% were currently married. The 40.4% of enlisted soldiers who had never been deployed (n = 12421294 person-months) accounted for 61.1% of enlisted soldiers who attempted suicide (n = 5894 cases). Risk among those never deployed was highest in the second month of service (103 per 100000 person-months). Risk among soldiers on their first deployment was highest in the sixth month of deployment (25 per 100000 person-months). For those previously deployed, risk was highest at 5 months after return (40 per 100000 person-months). Currently and previously deployed soldiers were more likely to attempt suicide with a firearm than those never deployed (currently deployed: OR, 4.0; 95% CI, 2.9-5.6; previously deployed: OR, 2.7; 95% CI, 1.8-3.9). Across deployment status, suicide attempts were more likely among soldiers who were women (currently deployed: OR, 3.4; 95% CI, 3.0-4.0; previously deployed: OR, 1.5; 95% CI, 1.4-1.7; and never deployed: OR, 2.4; 95% CI, 2.3-2.6), in their first 2 years of service (currently deployed: OR, 1.9; 95% CI, 1.5-2.3; previously deployed: OR, 2.2; 95% CI, 1.9-2.7; and never deployed: OR, 3.1; 95% CI, 2.7-3.6), and had a recently received a mental health diagnosis in the previous month (currently deployed: OR, 29.8; 95% CI, 25.0-35.5; previously deployed: OR, 22.2; 95% CI, 20.1-24.4; and never deployed: OR, 15.0; 95% CI, 14.2-16.0). Among soldiers with

1 previous deployment, odds of a suicide attempt were higher for those who screened positive for depression or posttraumatic stress disorder after return from deployment and particularly at follow-up screening, about 4 to 6 months after deployment (depression: OR, 1.4; 95% CI, 1.1-1.9; posttraumatic stress disorder: OR, 2.4; 95% CI, 2.1-2.8).

Conclusions and Relevance: Identifying the timing and risk factors for suicide attempt in soldiers requires consideration of environmental context, individual characteristics, and mental health. These factors can inform prevention efforts.

Predictors of suicide ideation in a random digit dial study: Exposure to suicide matters

van de Venne J, Cerel J, Moore M, Maple M (United States)
Archives of Suicide Research. Published online: 20 July 2016. doi: 10.1080/13811118.2016.1211044

Suicide is an important public health concern requiring ongoing research to understand risk factors for suicide ideation. A dual-frame, random digit dial survey was utilized to identify demographic and suicide-related factors associated with suicide ideation in a statewide sample of 1,736 adults. The PH-Q 9 Depression scale suicide ideation question was used to assess current suicide ideation in both the full sample and suicide exposed sub-sample. Being non-married and having previous suicide exposure were separately associated with higher risks of suicide ideation in the full sample. Being male, having increased suicide exposures, and having increased perceptions of closeness to the decedent increased risks, while older age decreased risks for the suicide exposed. Implications for future screening and research are discussed.

Association between religious service attendance and lower suicide rates among US women

VanderWeele TJ, Li S, Tsai AC, Kawachi I (United States)
JAMA Psychiatry 73, 845-851, 2016

Importance: Previous studies have linked suicide risk with religious participation, but the majority have used ecologic, cross-sectional, or case-control data.

Objective: To examine the longitudinal association between religious service attendance and suicide and the joint associations of suicide with service attendance and religious affiliation.

Design, Setting, and Participants: We evaluated associations between religious service attendance and suicide from 1996 through June 2010 in a large, long-term prospective cohort, the Nurses' Health Study, in an analysis that included 89708 women. Religious service attendance was self-reported in 1992 and 1996. Data analysis was conducted from 1996 through 2010.

Main Outcomes and Measures: Cox proportional hazards regression models were used to examine the association between religious service attendance and suicide, adjusting for demographic covariates, lifestyle factors, medical history, depressive symptoms, and social integration measures. We performed sensitivity analyses to examine the influence of unmeasured confounding.

Results: Among 89708 women aged 30 to 55 years who participated in the Nurses' Health Study, attendance at religious services once per week or more was associated with an approximately 5-fold lower rate of suicide compared with never attending religious services (hazard ratio, 0.16; 95% CI, 0.06-0.46). Service attendance once or more per week vs less frequent attendance was associated with a hazard ratio of 0.05 (95% CI, 0.006-0.48) for Catholics but only 0.34 (95% CI, 0.10-1.10) for Protestants (P = .05 for heterogeneity). Results were robust in sensitivity analysis and to exclusions of persons who were previously depressed or had a history of cancer or cardiovascular disease. There was evidence that social integration, depressive symptoms, and alcohol consumption partially mediated the association among those occasionally attending services, but not for those attending frequently.

Conclusions and Relevance: In this cohort of US women, frequent religious service attendance was associated with a significantly lower rate of suicide.

Gender and age group differences in suicide risk associated with co-morbid physical and psychiatric disorders in older adults

Vasiliadis HM, Lamoureux-Lamarche C, Gontijo Guerra S (Canada)
International Psychogeriatrics. Published online: 8 September 2016. doi: 10.1017/S1041610216001290

Background: It is unclear whether health service use influences the association between psychiatric and physical co-morbidity and suicide risk in older adults.

Methods: Controls were older adults (n = 2,494) participating in a longitudinal study on the health of the elderly carried out between 2004 and 2007, in Quebec. The cases were all suicide decedents (n = 493) between 2004 and 2007, confirmed by the Quebec Coroner's office. Multivariate analyses were carried out to test the association between suicide and the presence of psychiatric and physical illnesses controlling for health service use and socio-demographic factors by gender and age group. Interaction terms were also tested between suicide and co-morbidity on outpatient service use.

Results: The presence of physical illnesses only, was associated with a reduced risk of suicide across all sex and age groups. The presence of a mental disorder only was associated with an increased risk of suicide overall and specifically in females and those aged 70 to 84 years of age. Suicide risk was lower in those with a psychiatric and physical co-morbidity and consulting mental health services.

Conclusions: Increased mental health follow-up in older adults with psychiatric illnesses is needed for the detection of suicidal behavior and reducing suicide risk in males. Further research should focus on the mitigating effect of the presence of physical illnesses on stigma and health service use and the presence of social support in the elderly.

Clinician prediction of future suicide attempts: A longitudinal study

Wang Y, Bhaskaran J, Sareen J, Bolton SL, Chateau D, Bolton JM (Canada)
Canadian Journal of Psychiatry 61, 428-432, 2016

Objective: Established risk assessment tools are often inaccurate at predicting future suicide risk. We therefore investigated whether clinicians are able to predict individuals' suicide risk with greater accuracy.

Method: We used the SAFE Database, which included consecutive adult (age ≥18 years) presentations (N = 3818) over a 22- month period to the 2 tertiary care hospitals in Manitoba, Canada. Medical professionals assessed each individual and recorded his or her predicted risk for future suicide attempt (SA) on a 0-10 scale - the clinician prediction scale. The SAD PERSONS scale was completed as a comparison. SAs within 6 months, assessed using the Columbia Classification Algorithm for Suicide Assessment, were the primary outcome measure. Receiver operating characteristic curve and logistic regression analyses were conducted to determine the accuracy of both scales to predict SAs, and the scales were compared with z scores. Clinician prediction scale performance was stratified based on level of training.

Results: Clinicians were able to predict future SAs with significantly greater accuracy (area under the curve [AUC] = 0.73; 95% CI, 0.68 to 0.77; P < 0.001) compared with the SAD PERSONS scale (z = 3.79, P < 0.001). Both scales nonetheless showed positive predictive value of less than 7%. Analyses by level of training showed that junior psychiatric residents and non-psychiatric residents did not accurately predict SAs, whereas senior psychiatric residents and staff psychiatrists demonstrated greater accuracy (AUC = 0.76 and 0.78, respectively).

Conclusions: Clinicians are able to predict future attempts with fewer false positives than a conventional risk assessment scale, and this skill appears related to training level. Predicting future suicidal behaviour remains very challenging.

Association between diabetes and risk of suicide death: A meta-analysis of 3 million participants

Wang Y, Tang S, Xu S, Weng S, Liu Z (China)

Comprehensive Psychiatry 71, 11-16, 2016

Background: Results of the relationships between diabetes and the risk of suicide death are inconclusive. This meta-analysis was conducted to assess this association.

Methods: We systematically searched PubMed, EMBASE, Web of Science and the Cochrane Library up to February 29, 2016 for relevant observational studies regarding the association between diabetes and risk of suicide. Random-effects models were used to calculate summary relative risk (RR) and 95% confidence interval (CI).

Results: 6 observational studies (8 independent reports) with a total of 3,075,214 participants and 3038 suicide deaths events were included in the meta-analysis. Overall, diabetes was not associated with risk of suicide deaths, with significant heterogeneity among studies observed (Summary RR=1.61, 95% CI: 0.91-2.83, Pheterogeneity<0.001, $I(2)$=97.2%). No publication bias was detected across studies, and both the subgroup analysis and sensitivity analysis suggested that the general result was robust.

Conclusion: Our meta-analysis based on more than 3 million participants indicates that diabetes is not associated with increased risk of suicide death. Further well-designed prospective cohort studies are needed to confirm the findings of this meta-analysis.

Psychological autopsy of seventy high school suicides: Combined qualitative/quantitative approach

Zalsman G, Siman Tov Y, Tzuriel D, Shoval G, Barzilay R, Tiech Fire N, Sherf M, John Mann J
(Israel)

European Psychiatry 38, 8-14, 2016

Objective: Suicide is the leading cause of death among Israeli youths but data on causes are scarce. This study used psychological autopsies of 70 Israeli school students who committed suicide during 2004-2011, attempting to determine the causes.

Methods: Four narratives of the self were identified (qualitative analysis) and compared (quantitative analysis): (1) regressive: functioning and mood deteriorated continuously (45%); (2) tragic: doing well until rapid decline around suicidal crisis (20%); (3) unstable: peaks and crises throughout life (20%); and (4) stable: long lasting state of adverse living circumstances (15%). Functioning, mental disorders, stressful life events and substance abuse were examined.

Results: A representative profile of the suicide-completer emerged. Suicidality in the tragic narrative involved shorter crisis, fewer risk factors and less psychopathology than the other narratives, also better general functioning and better school performance. Though decrease in functioning was evident in all groups, in the tragic group it tended to be disregarded.

Conclusion: This study presents an in-depth analysis of a unique suicide population of high school students. A combined methodology of qualitative and quantitative analyses reveals a distinct subpopulation of suicidal adolescents with little or no overt psychopathology that poses a challenge to suicide prevention strategies.

Citation List

FATAL SUICIDAL BEHAVIOR

Epidemiology

Agrawaal KK, Karki P (2015). Clinico-epidemiological study on pesticide poisoning in a tertiary care hospital in Eastern Nepal. *Journal of the Nepal Medical Association* 52, 972-976.

Anglemyer A, Miller ML, Buttrey S, Whitaker L (2016). Suicide rates and methods in active duty military personnel, 2005 to 2011: A cohort study. *Annals of Internal Medicine* 165, 167-174.

Antonakakis N, Gupta R (2016). Is economic policy uncertainty related to suicide rates? Evidence from the United States. *Social Indicators Research* 201573, 1-14.

Auerswald CL, Lin JS, Parriott A (2016). Six-year mortality in a street-recruited cohort of homeless youth in San Francisco, California. *Peerj* 4, e1909.

Azizpour Y, Asadollahi K, Sayehmiri K, Kaikhavani S, Abangah G (2016). Epidemiological survey of intentional poisoning suicide during 1993-2013 in Ilam province, Iran. *BMC Public Health* 16, 902.

Badiadka KK, Dsouza DH, Vasu S (2016). Varying pattern of injuries in different types of railway fatalities. *Medico-Legal Update* 16, 142-145.

Balica E, Stockl H (2016). Homicide-suicides in Romania and the role of migration. *European Journal of Criminology* 13, 517-534.

Basu D, Das D, Misra K (2016). Farmer suicides in India. *Economic and Political Weekly* 51, 61-65.

Ben Khelil M, Gharbaoui M, Farhani F, Zaafrane M, Harzallah H, Allouche M, Zhioua M, Hamdoun M (2016). Impact of the Tunisian revolution on homicide and suicide rates in Tunisia. *International Journal of Public Health*. Published online: 18 May 2016. doi: 10.1007/s00038-016-0834-8.

Ben Khelil M, Zgarni A, Zaafrane M, Chkribane Y, Gharbaoui M, Harzallah H, Banasr A, Hamdoun M (2016). Suicide by self-immolation in Tunisia: A 10 year study (2005-2014). *Burns: Journal of the International Society for Burn Injuries*. Published online: 19 May 2016. doi:10.1016/j.burns.2016.04.019.

Bronson J, Reviere R (2016). Pregnancy-associated deaths in Virginia due to homicides, suicides, and accidental overdoses compared with natural causes. *Violence Against Women*. Published online: 1 September 2016. doi: 10.1177/1077801216663658.

Brunstein Klomek A, Nakash O, Goldberger N, Haklai Z, Geraisy N, Yatzkar U, Birnai A, Levav I (2016). Completed suicide and suicide attempts in the Arab population in Israel. *Social Psychiatry and Psychiatric Epidemiology* 51, 869.

Burns RA (2016). Sex and age trends in Australia's suicide rate over the last decade: Something is still seriously wrong with men in middle and late life. *Psychiatry Research* 245, 224-229.

Byard RW (2016). Further observations on plastic bag asphyxia using helium gas. *Australian Journal of Forensic Sciences*. Published online: 10 May 2016. doi: 10.1080/00450618.2016.1177594.

Ceccato V, Uittenbogaard A (2016). Suicides in commuting railway systems: The case of Stockholm County, Sweden. *Journal of Affective Disorders* 198, 206-221.

Chaitanya R, Patil D (2016). A retrospective study of profile of unnatural deaths. *Indian Journal of Forensic Medicine and Toxicology* 10, 261-263.

Chapman S, Alpers P, Jones M (2016). Association between gun law reforms and intentional firearm deaths in Australia, 1979-2013. *JAMA* 316, 291-299.

Corona-Miranda B, Hernandez-Sanchez M, Lomba-Acevedo P (2016). Epidemiology of suicide in Cuba, 1987-2014. *MEDICC Review* 18, 15-20.

Curtin SC, Warner M, Hedegaard H (2016). Increase in suicide in the United States, 1999-2014. *NCHS Data Brief* 241, 1-8.

Dandona R, Bertozzi-Villa A, Kumar GA, Dandona L (2016). Lessons from a decade of suicide surveillance in India: Who, why and how? *International Journal of Epidemiology*. Published online: 2 June 2016 doi: 10.1093/ije/dyw113.

de Beurs DP, Hooiveld M, Kerkhof AJ, Korevaar JC, Donker GA (2016). Trends in suicidal behaviour in Dutch general practice 1983-2013: A retrospective observational study. *British Medical Journal Open* 6, e010868.

Dhoble SV, Dhawane SG, Tumram NK, Dere RC, Kukde HG (2016). Burn deaths in females of reproductive age: An autopsy study. *Indian Journal of Forensic Medicine and Toxicology* 10, 83-88.

Dogan H, Adigüzel L, Uysal E, Sarikaya S, Ozucelik DN, Okuturlar Y, Giray TA, Kayipmaz AE, Yazicioglu M, Sisek C (2016). Differences between adolescent and adult cases of suicidal drug intoxication. *Medical Journal of Bakirkoy* 12, 20-23.

Gogoi NK (2015). A study of the pattern of agricultural poisoning cases in medico-legal autopsies in Guwahati, Assam. *Medico-Legal Update* 15, 113-119.

Hampson NB (2016). US mortality from carbon monoxide poisoning 1999-2014: Accidental and intentional deaths. *Annals of the American Thoracic Society*. Published online: 28 July 2016. doi: 10.1513/AnnalsATS.201604-318OC.

Han B, Kott PS, Hughes A, McKeon R, Blanco C, Compton WM (2016). Estimating the rates of deaths by suicide among adults who attempt suicide in the United States. *Journal of Psychiatric Research* 77, 125-133.

Hawes AM, Chancellor KE, Rogers WR, Ledford JA (2016). Fatal firearm injuries in Tennessee: A comparison study of Tennessee's two most populous counties 2009-2012. *Journal of Forensic Sciences* 61, 666-670.

Herman J, Peiris-John R, Wainiqolo I, Kafoa B, Laginikoro P, McCaig E, Ameratunga S (2016). Epidemiology of fatal and hospitalised injuries among youth in Fiji (TRIP 15). *Journal of Paediatrics and Child Health*. Published online: 27 August 2016. doi: 10.1111/jpc.13250.

Hoye A, Nesvag R, Reichborn-Kjennerud T, Jacobsen BK (2016). Sex differences in mortality among patients admitted with affective disorders in North Norway: A 33-year prospective register study. *Bipolar Disorders* 18, 272-281.

Imtiaz F, Ali M, Ali L (2016). Prevalence of chemical poisoning for suicidal attempts in Karachi, Pakistan. *Emergency Medicine: Open Access* 5, e1000247.

Issa SY, El Dossary M, Abdel Salam M, Al Madani O, AlMazroua MK, Alsowayigh K, Hamd MA, AboZayed AH, Kharoshah M (2016). Suicidal deaths in depth-Eastern Province-Saudi Arabia. *Egyptian Journal of Forensic Sciences* 6, 240-247.

Jayachandran M, Chief T, Richard GM, Askar SI, Gope R (2016). A study on contemporary trends of acute fatal poisoning of pediatric age group in rural tertiary care hospital. *Medico-Legal Update* 16, 86-90.

Jiang F-F, Xu H-l, Liao H-Y, Zhang T (2016). Analysis of internet suicide pacts reported by the media in mainland China. *Crisis*. Published online: 9 June 2016. doi: 10.1027/0227-5910/a000402.

Jiang Y, Perez B, Viner-Brown S (2015). Rhode Island violent death reporting system, 2004-2013. *Rhode Island Medical Journal* 98, 36-39.

Joo Y (2016). Spatiotemporal study of elderly suicide in Korea by age cohort. *Public Health*. Published online: 6 September 2016. doi: 10.1016/j.puhe.2016.07.016.

Kamalakar MV (2015). An epidemiological study of organophosphorus poisoning at tertiary hospital, Andhra Pradesh. *Medico-Legal Update* 15, 14-16.

Kaplan MS, Huguet N, Caetano R, Giesbrecht N, Kerr WC, McFarland BH (2016). Heavy alcohol use among suicide decedents relative to a nonsuicide comparison group: Gender-specific effects of economic contraction. *Alcoholism: Clinical and Experimental Research*. Published online: 17 May 2016. doi: 10.1111/acer.13100.

Kõlves K, De Leo D (2016). Suicide methods in children and adolescents. *European Child and Adolescent Psychiatry*. Published online: 18 May 2016. doi: 10.1007/s00787-016-0865-y.

Kouyoumdjian FG, Kiefer L, Wobeser W, Gonzalez A, Hwang SW (2016). Mortality over 12 years of follow-up in people admitted to provincial custody in Ontario: A retrospective cohort study. *Canadian Medical Association Journal Open* 4, E153-161.

Kumar S, Patil R, Dad GL (2016). A retrospective study of poisoning cases at a tertiary care teaching hospital of Southern Rajasthan. *Medico-Legal Update* 16, 235-239.

Lamb T, Selvarajah LR, Mohamed F, Jayamanne S, Gawarammana I, Mostafa A, Buckley NA, Roberts MS, Eddleston M (2016). High lethality and minimal variation after acute self-poisoning with carbamate insecticides in Sri Lanka - implications for global suicide prevention. *Clinical Toxicology* 54, 624-631.

Lang FU, Hubel N, Kosters M, Messer T, Dinse-Lambracht A, Jager M (2016). Suicidality in emergency medicine: Results from a retrospective analysis of emergency documentation forms. *Neuropsychiatrie* 30, 69-73.

Lazzarini T, Rohrbaugh RM, Croda J, Gonçalves C, Ko A, Benites W, Silva LD (2015). Adolescent suicide among the Guarani-Kaiowá in Dourados, Mato Grosso do Sul, Brazil. *Annals of Global Health* 81, e114.

Lee D, Delcher C, Maldonado-Molina MM, Thogmartin JR, Goldberger BA (2016). Manners of death in drug-related fatalities in Florida. *Journal of Forensic Sciences* 61, 735-742.

Lopez-Munoz F, Cuerda-Galindo E, Krischel M (2016). Study of deaths by suicide in the Soviet Special Camp Number 7 (Sachsenhausen), 1945-1950. *Psychiatric Quarterly*. Published online: 9 May 2016. doi: 10.1007/s11126-016-9435-1.

Lucas N, Cook M, Wallace J, Kirkbride KP, Kobus H (2016). Quantifying gunshot residues in cases of suicide: Implications for evaluation of suicides and criminal shootings. *Forensic Science International* 266, 289-298.

Lyons BH, Fowler KA, Jack SP, Betz CJ, Blair JM (2016). Surveillance for violent deaths — National Violent Death Reporting System, 17 states, 2013. *MMRW: Surveillance Summaries* 65, 1-42.

Ma J, Jing H, Zeng Y, Tao L, Yang Y, Ma K, Chen L (2016). Retrospective analysis of 319 hanging and strangulation cases between 2001 and 2014 in Shanghai. *Journal of Forensic and Legal Medicine* 42, 19-24.

Mackenzie DW, Lester D, Manson R, Yeh C (2016). Do suicides from the Golden Gate Bridge cluster? *Psychological Reports* 118, 70-73.

Manoj TM, Raveendran R, Balaram NA (2016). Socio-demographic pattern of burn deaths-an autopsy based study. *Medico-Legal Update* 16, 115-119.

Matsuyama T, Kitamura T, Kiyohara K, Hayashida S, Kawamura T, Iwami T, Ohta B (2016). Characteristics and outcomes of emergency patients with self-inflicted injuries: A report from ambulance records in Osaka city, Japan. *Scandinavian Journal of Trauma, Resuscitation and Emergency Medicine* 24, 68.

McHugh C, Campbell A, Chapman M, Balaratnasingam S (2016). Increasing indigenous self-harm and suicide in the Kimberley: An audit of the 2005–2014 data. *Medical Journal of Australia* 205, 33.

McIntosh WL, Spies E, Stone DM, Lokey CN, Trudeau A-RT, Bartholow B (2016). Suicide rates by occupational group - 17 states, 2012. *MMWR: Morbidity and Mortality Weekly Report* 65, 641-645.

McLone SG, Loharikar A, Sheehan K, Mason M (2016). Suicide in Illinois, 2005-2010: A reflection of patterns and risks by age groups and opportunities for targeted prevention. *Journal of Trauma and Acute Care Surgery* 4, s30-s35.

Memchoubi P, Sangma MM, Das NG, Nabachandra H (2015). A 5-yr study of adolescent deaths from 2009-2013 in Imphal. *Medico-Legal Update* 15, 10-13.

Milner AJ, Maheen H, Bismark MM, Spittal MJ (2016). Suicide by health professionals: A retrospective mortality study in Australia, 2001-2012. *Medical Journal of Australia* 205, 260-265.

Mishra A, Sahoo PC, Lepcha C (2016). Trends of intentional self harm in a tertiary care hospital in Sikkim – an autopsy based study. *Indian Journal of Forensic Medicine and Toxicology* 10, 183-187.

Mohammadi AA, Tohidinik HR, Zardosht M, Seyed Jafari SM (2016). Self-burns in Fars province, Southern Iran. *World Journal of Plastic Surgery* 5, 32-36.

Mohiddin SK, Rao BVN, Raju B (2016). A comprehensive study of deaths due to fire arm injuries. *Indian Journal of Forensic Medicine and Toxicology* 10, 34-37.

Naghshvarian M, Kaveh MH, Hesampour M, Rezaee F, Mirahmadizadeh AR (2016). Epidemiologic study of suicidal attempt cases in Fars Province, south of Iran, 2010-2011. *Journal of Health Sciences and Surveillance Systems* 4, 32-39.

Naresh K, Lavanya Kowsil G (2016). A study of violent asphyxial deaths. *Indian Journal of Forensic Medicine and Toxicology* 10, 126-129.

Nayak GH, Biradar SS, Ravindra Kumar CN, Madhu Sudhan S, Karlawad M, Selvan M (2016). Deaths due to hanging in and around Hubballi. *Journal of South India Medicolegal Association* 8, 90-93.

Papaslanis T, Kontaxakis V, Christodoulou C, Konstantakopoulos G, Kontaxaki MI, Papadimitriou GN (2016). Suicide in Greece 1992-2012: A time-series analysis. *International Journal of Social Psychiatry.* Published online: 9 May 2016. doi: 10.1177/0020764016647753.

Park S, Lee HB, Lee SY, Lee GE, Ahn MH, Yi KK, Hong JP (2016). Trends in suicide methods and rates among older adults in South Korea: A comparison with Japan. *Psychiatry Investigation* 13, 184-189

Pollock NJ, Mulay S, Valcour J, Jong M (2016). Suicide rates in aboriginal communities in Labrador, Canada. *American Journal of Public Health* 106, 1309-1315.

Prajapati P, Jhaveri S, Zanzrukhiya K, Govekar G (2016). A medico-legal study of hanging – a way of suicide. *Indian Journal of Forensic Medicine and Toxicology* 10, 295-300.

Prajapati P, Patel R, Patel U (2016). Epidemiological profile of suicidal cases in Surat city: An autopsy based study. *Medico-Legal Update* 16, 101-105.

Preti A, Lentini G (2016). Forecast models for suicide: Time-series analysis with data from Italy. *Chronobiology International.* Published online: 2 August 2016. doi: 10.1080/07420528.2016.1211669.

Quintiliano DC, de Moura Ferreira MC (2016). Characterization of self-extermination attempt cases in an emergency department in a university hospital. *Bioscience Journal* 32, 524-533.

Rajavelu K, Selvaraj T (2016). Detailed analysis of ante-mortem burns in relevant to carboxy haemoglobin. *Medico-Legal Update* 16, 193-196.

Rao D (2015). An autopsy study of 74 cases of cut throat injuries. *Egyptian Journal of Forensic Sciences* 5, 144-149.

Redmore J, Kipping R, Trickey A, May MT, Gunnell D (2016). Analysis of trends in adolescent suicides and accidental deaths in England and Wales, 1972-2011. *British Journal of Psychiatry.* Published online: June 2016. doi: 10.1192/bjp.bp.114.162347.

Rockett IR, Lilly CL, Jia H, Larkin GL, Miller TR, Nelson LS, Nolte KB, Putnam SL, Smith GS, Caine ED (2016). Self-injury mortality in the United States in the early 21st century: A comparison with proximally ranked diseases. *JAMA Psychiatry.* Published online: 24 August 2016. doi:10.1001/jamapsychiatry.2016.1870.

Rocos B, Chesser TJ (2016). Injuries in jumpers - are there any patterns? *World Journal of Orthopedics* 7, 182-187.

Roxburgh A, Hall WD, Burns L, Pilgrim J, Saar E, Nielsen S, Degenhardt L (2015). Trends and characteristics of accidental and intentional codeine overdose deaths in Australia. *Medical Journal of Australia* 203, 299.

Russo MC, Verzeletti A, Piras M, De Ferrari F (2016). Hanging deaths: A retrospective study regarding 260 cases. *American Journal of Forensic Medicine and Pathology* 37, 141-145.

Saeheim A, Hestetun I, Mork E, Nrugham L, Mehlum L (2016). A 12-year national study of suicide by jumping from bridges in Norway. *Archives of Suicide Research.* Published online: 16 June 2016. doi: 10.1080/13811118.2016.1199988.

Schofield L, Walsh D, Munoz-Arroyo R, McCartney G, Buchanan D, Lawder R, Armstrong M, Dundas R, Leyland AH (2016). Dying younger in Scotland: Trends in mortality and deprivation relative to England and Wales, 1981-2011. *Health Place* 40, 106-115.

Selvaraj T, Rajavelu K (2016). Trends of suicidal death in and around Madurai city during the period between January 2015 to December 2015-a retrospective study. *Medico-Legal Update* 16, 120-124.

Selvaraj T, Saravanan S, Manigandan G (2016). A retrospective study about the pattern of suicides among students' population. *Indian Journal of Forensic Medicine and Toxicology* 10, 200-203.

Sha F, Yip PS, Law YW (2016). Decomposing change in China's suicide rate, 1990-2010: Ageing and urbanisation. *Injury Prevention.* Published online: 16 June 2016. doi: 10.1136/injuryprev-2016-042006.

Shah A, Sava-Shah S, Wijeratne C, Draper B (2016). Are elite cricketers more prone to suicide? A psychological autopsy study of test cricketer suicides. *Australasia Psychiatry* 24, 295-299.

Shankar R, Master PB, Obulesu LC (2015). A medicolegal study of asphyxial deaths with special reference to hanging. *Journal of Evolution of Medical and Dental Sciences* 4, 14124-14128.

Shao Y, Zhu C, Zhang Y, Yu H, Peng H, Jin Y, Shi G, Wang N, Chen Z, Chen Y, Jiang Q (2016). Epidemiology and temporal trend of suicide mortality in the elderly in Jiading, Shanghai, 2003-2013: A descriptive, observational study. *British Medical Journal Open* 6, e012227.

Sharma MK, Punia RK, Dutta S, Pathak D (2016). Descriptive analysis of pattern of unnatural female deaths at SMS hospital, Jaipur (an autopsy based study during the year 2014-15). *Medico-Legal Update* 16, 95-100.

Siddiqui ARO, Hussain IB (2016). A study on fatal organo-phosphorous poisoning cases with respect to age and sex. *Indian Journal of Forensic Medicine and Toxicology* 10, 188-192.

Silveira ML, Wexler L, Chamberlain J, Money K, Spencer RMC, Reich NG, Bertone-Johnson ER (2016). Seasonality of suicide behavior in northwest Alaska: 1990-2009. *Public Health* 137, 35-42.

Singh TK, Venkata Naga Mohan Rao B, Raju B (2016). Study of violent asphyxial deaths in and around Warangal region. *Medico-Legal Update* 16, 208-211.

Skinner R, McFaull S, Rhodes AE, Bowes M, Rockett IRH (2016). Suicide in Canada: Is poisoning misclassification an issue? *Canadian Journal of Psychiatry.* Published online: 23 March 2016. doi: 10.1177/0706743716639918.

Stanley IH, Hom MA, Joiner TE (2016). Suicide mortality among firefighters: Results from a large, urban fire department. *American Journal of Industrial Medicine.* Published online: 24 May 2016. doi: 10.1002/ajim.22587.

Subba Reddy K, Sukanya P, Abdul Khalid M (2016). Murder-suicide cases. *Indian Journal of Forensic Medicine and Toxicology* 10, 291-294.

Sugawara A, Kunieda E (2016). Suicide in patients with gastric cancer: A population-based study. *Japanese Journal of Clinical Oncology.* Published online: 15 June 2016. doi: 10.1093/jjco/hyw075.

Tandle Ranjit M, Kadu Sandeep S, Deshpande VL, Waje Dilip R (2016). Study of acute poisoning cases at rural tertiary care hospital in Ahmednagar, Maharashtra. *Medico-Legal Update* 16, 42-45.

Taromsari MR, Karkan MF, Sadrmomtaz F, Keihanian F, Saeidinia A (2016). Frequency and associated factors of mortality rate due to rice tablet consumption in Razi hospital, Rasht, 2012-13. *Journal of Chemical and Pharmaceutical Research* 8, 628-633.

Tugaleva E, Gorassini DR, Shkrum MJ (2016). Retrospective analysis of hanging deaths in Ontario. *Journal of Forensic Sciences.* Published online: 12 August 2016. doi: 10.1111/1556-4029.13179.

Tyrrell EG, Orton E, Sayal K, Baker R, Kendrick D (2016). Differing patterns in intentional and unintentional poisonings among young people in England, 1998-2014: A population-based cohort study. *Journal of Public Health.* Published online: 13 August 2016. doi: 10.1093/pubmed/fdw075.

Tyrrell EG, Orton E, Tata LJ (2016). Changes in poisonings among adolescents in the UK between 1992 and 2012: A population based cohort study. *Injury Prevention.* Published online: 16 May 2016. doi: 10.1136/injuryprev-2015-041901.

van den Hondel KE, Buster M, Reijnders UJL (2016). Suicide by asphyxiation with or without helium inhalation in the region of Amsterdam (2005–2014). *Journal of Forensic and Legal Medicine* 44, 24-26.

Vancayseele N, Portzky G, van Heeringen K (2016). Increase in self-injury as a method of self-harm in Ghent, Belgium: 1987-2013. *PLoS One* 11, e0156711.

Vigo D, Thornicroft G, Atun R (2016). Estimating the true global burden of mental illness. *Lancet Psychiatry* 3, 171-178.

Wagenaar BH, Raunig-Berhó M, Cumbe V, Rao D, Napúa M, Sherr K (2016). Suicide attempts and deaths in Sofala, Mozambique, from 2011 to 2014. *Crisis.* Published online: 1 June 2016. doi: 10.1027/0227-5910/a000383.

Wang Z, Wang J, Bao J, Gao X, Yu C, Xiang H (2016). Temporal trends of suicide mortality in mainland China: Results from the age-period-cohort framework. *International Journal of Environmental Research and Public Health* 13, e13080784.

Wang Z, Yu C, Wang J, Bao J, Gao X, Xiang H (2016). Age-period-cohort analysis of suicide mortality by gender among white and black Americans, 1983-2012. *International Journal for Equity in Health* 15, e107.

Wasnik RN, Choudhary UK, Zine KU (2016). A sixteen year retrospective study of custodial deaths in Marathwada region of Maharashtra, India. *Medico-Legal Update* 16, 63-68.

Wigen Skjerdal J, Andrew E, Gjertsen F (2016). Deaths by poisoning in Norway 2003-2012. *Clinical Toxicology* 54, 495-500.

Zhong B-L, Chiu HFK, Conwell Y (2016). Rates and characteristics of elderly suicide in China, 2013-14. *Journal of Affective Disorders* 206, 273-279.

Risk and protective factors

Anonymous (2015). Suicide study of Korean entertainers: A report on causation of Korean entertainer suicides presented by media. *Suicidology Online* 6, 63-73.

Anonymous (2016). A nationwide cohort study of the association between hospitalization with infection and risk of death by suicide. *JAMA Psychiatry* 73, 912-919.

Almeida OP, McCaul K, Hankey GJ, Yeap BB, Golledge J, Flicker L (2016). Risk of dementia and death in community-dwelling older men with bipolar disorder. *British Journal of Psychiatry* 209, 121-126.

Almeida OP, McCaul K, Hankey GJ, Yeap BB, Golledge J, Flicker L (2016). Suicide in older men: The health in men cohort study (HIMS). *Preventative Medicine.* Published online: 20 September 2016. doi: 10.1016/j.ypmed.2016.09.022.

Ballard ED, Vande Voort JL, Luckenbaugh DA, Machado-Vieira R, Tohen M, Zarate CA (2016). Acute risk factors for suicide attempts and death: Prospective findings from the STEP-BD study. *Bipolar Disorders.* Published online: 27 May 2016. doi: 10.1111/bdi.12397.

Bardon C, Cote LP, Mishara BL (2016). Cluster analysis of characteristics of persons who died by suicide in the Montreal metro transit. *Crisis.* Published online: 9 June 2016. doi: 10.1027/0227-5910/a000398.

Beckman K, Mittendorfer-Rutz E, Lichtenstein P, Larsson H, Almqvist C, Runeson B, Dahlin M (2016). Mental illness and suicide after self-harm among young adults: Long-term follow-up of self-harm patients, admitted to hospital care, in a national cohort. *Psychological Medicine.* Published online: 20 September 2016. doi: 10.1017/S0033291716002282.

Björkenstam C, Andersson G, Dalman C, Cochran S, Kosidou K (2016). Suicide in married couples in Sweden: Is the risk greater in same-sex couples? *European Journal of Epidemiology* 31, 685-690.

Björkenstam C, Ekselius L, Berlin M, Gerdin B, Björkenstam E (2016). Suicide risk and suicide method in patients with personality disorders. *Journal of Psychiatric Research.* Published online: 12 August 2016. doi: 10.1016/j.jpsychires.2016.08.008.

Bossard C, Santin G, Canu IG (2016). Suicide among farmers in France: Occupational factors and recent trends. *Journal of Agromedicine* 21, 310-315.

Bostwick JM, Pabbati C, Geske JR, McKean AJ (2016). Suicide attempt as a risk factor for completed suicide: Even more lethal than we knew. *American Journal of Psychiatry.* Published online: 13 August 2016. doi: 10.1176/appi.ajp.2016.15070854.

Brenner P, Burkill S, Jokinen J, Hillert J, Bahmanyar S, Montgomery S (2016). Multiple sclerosis and risk of attempted and completed suicide – a cohort study. *European Journal of Neurology* 23, 1329-1336.

Bucic M, Pregelj P, Zupanc T, Videtic Paska A (2016). Completed suicide, depression, and RELN polymorphisms. *Psychiatric Genetics* 26, 218-222.

Campbell A, Chapman M, McHugh C, Sng A, Balaratnasingam S (2016). Rising Indigenous suicide rates in Kimberley and implications for suicide prevention. *Australasia Psychiatry.* Published online: 15 September 2016. doi: 10.1177/1039856216665281.

Castellanos D, Kosoy JE, Ayllon KD, Acuna J (2016). Presence of alcohol and drugs in Hispanic versus non-Hispanic youth suicide victims in Miami-Dade County, Florida. *Journal of Immigrant and Minority Health* 18, 1024-1031.

Castelpietra G, Bovenzi M, Clagnan E, Barbone F, Balestrieri M, Isacsson G (2016). Diagnoses and prescriptions of antidepressants in suicides: Register findings from the Friuli Venezia Giulia Region, Italy, 2002-2008. *International Journal of Psychiatry in Clinical Practice* 20, 121-124.

Cederlof M, Larsson H, Lichtenstein P, Almqvist C, Serlachius E, Ludvigsson JF (2016). Nationwide population-based cohort study of psychiatric disorders in individuals with Ehlers-Danlos syndrome or hypermobility syndrome and their siblings. *BMC Psychiatry* 16, 207.

Chauvel L, Leist AK, Ponomarenko V (2016). Testing persistence of cohort effects in the epidemiology of suicide: An age-period-cohort hysteresis model. *PLoS One* 11, e0158538.

Chen C-M, Chung Y-C, Tsai L-H, Tung Y-C, Lee H-M, Lin M-L, Liu H-L, Tang W-R (2016). A nationwide population-based study of corrosive ingestion in Taiwan: Incidence, gender differences, and mortality. *Gastroenterology Research and Practice* 2016, 7905425.

Chen HM, Hung TH, Chou SY, Tsai CS, Su JA (2016). Three-year mortality rate of suicide attempters in consultation-liaison service. *International Journal of Psychiatry in Clinical Practice* 20, 254-259.

Chen SLS, Lee CS, Yen AMF, Chen HH, Chan CC, Chiu SYH, Fann JCY, Chang JC (2016). A 10-year follow-up study on suicidal mortality after 1999 Taiwan earthquake. *Journal of Psychiatric Research* 79, 42-49.

Chen YC, Tseng YC, Huang WH, Hsu CW, Weng CH, Liu SH, Yang HY, Chen KH, Chen HL, Fu JF, Lin WR, Wang IK, Yen TH (2016). Acute kidney injury predicts mortality after charcoal burning suicide. *Scientific Reports* 6, 29656.

Chetankumar R, Kokatanur CM (2016). A study of relationship between menstrual cycle and hanging. *Medico-Legal Update* 16, 23-25.

Choi S (2016). Stock market returns and suicide rates: Evidence from the United States. *Social Behavior and Personality* 44, 89-102.

Chon DS (2015). Religiosity and regional variation of lethal violence: Integrated model. *Homicide Studies* 20, 129-149.

Chon DS (2016). National religious affiliation and integrated model of homicide and suicide. *Homicide Studies*. Published online: 29 February 2016. doi: 10.1177/1088767916634407.

Colson KE, Galin J, Ahern J (2016). Spatial proximity to incidents of community violence is associated with fewer suicides in urban California. *Journal of Urban Health*. Published online: 19 August 2016. doi: 10.1007/s11524-016-0072-7.

Comiford AL, Sanderson WT, Chesnut L, Brown S (2016). Predictors of intimate partner problem-related suicides among suicide decedents in Kentucky. *Journal of Injury and Violence Research* 8, e776.

Conejero I, Lopez-Castroman J, Giner L, Baca-Garcia E (2016). Sociodemographic antecedent validators of suicidal behavior: A review of recent literature. *Current Psychiatry Reports* 18, e94.

Datir S, Petkar M, Farooqui J, Chavan K, Bangal R (2016). Causes of suicide in acute poisoning cases in different age groups: A study. *Journal of Indian Academy of Forensic Medicine* 38, 63.

Deisenhammer EA, Behrndt E-M, Kemmler G, Haring C, Miller C (2016). A comparison of suicides in psychiatric in-patients, after discharge and in not recently hospitalized individuals. *Comprehensive Psychiatry* 69, 100-105.

Densley JA, Hilal SM, Li SD, Tang W (2016). Homicide–suicide in China: An exploratory study of characteristics and types. *Asian Journal of Criminology*. Published online: 16 June 2016. doi: 10.1007/s11417-016-9238-1.

Deshpande G, Baxi M, Witte T, Robinson JL (2016). A neural basis for the acquired capability for suicide. *Frontiers in Psychiatry* 7, 125.

Dogan KH, Unaldi M, Demirci S (2016). Evaluation of postmortem cerebrospinal fluid s100b protein and serotonin levels: Comparison of suicidal versus nonsuicidal deaths in Konya, Turkey. *Journal of Forensic Sciences* 61, 1285-1291.

Economou M, Angelopoulos E, Peppou LE, Souliotis K, Tzavara C, Kontoangelos K, Madianos M, Stefanis C (2016). Enduring financial crisis in Greece: Prevalence and correlates of major depression and suicidality. *Social Psychiatry and Psychiatric Epidemiology* 51, 1015-1024.

Fadum EA, Fonnebo V, Borud EK (2016). Presence of minor and major mental health impairment in adolescence and death from suicide and unintentional injuries/accidents in men: A national longitudinal cohort study. *Journal of Epidemiology and Community Health*. Published online: 14 July 2016. doi: 10.1136/jech-2016-207656.

Fairthorne J, Walker R, de Klerk N, Shepherd C (2016). Early mortality from external causes in Aboriginal mothers: A retrospective cohort study. *BMC Public Health* 16, 461.

Farrell S, Kapur N, While D, Appleby L, Windfuhr K (2016). Suicide in a national student mental health patient population, 1997-2012. *Crisis*. Published online: 22 July 2016. doi: 10.1027/0227-5910/a000412.

Fedyszyn IE, Erlangsen A, Hjorthøj C, Madsen T, Nordentoft M (2016). Repeated suicide attempts and suicide among individuals with a first emergency department contact for attempted suicide: A prospective, nationwide, Danish register-based study. *Journal of Clinical Psychiatry* 77, 832-840.

Fernández-Arteaga V, Tovilla-Zárate CA, Fresán A, González-Castro TB, Juárez-Rojop IE, López-Narváez L, Hernández-Díaz Y (2016). Association between completed suicide and environmental temperature in a Mexican population, using the knowledge discovery in database approach. *Computer Methods and Programs in Biomedicine* 135, 219-224.

Fernandez de la Cruz L, Rydell M, Runeson B, D'Onofrio BM, Brander G, Ruck C, Lichtenstein P, Larsson H, Mataix-Cols D (2016). Suicide in obsessive-compulsive disorder: A population-based study of 36 788 Swedish patients. *Molecular Psychiatry*. Published online: 19 July 2016. doi: 10.1038/mp.2016.115. doi: 10.1038/npp.2016.124.

Fitzgerald ML, Kassir SA, Underwood MD, Bakalian MJ, Mann JJ, Arango V (2016). Dysregulation of striatal dopamine receptor binding in suicide. *Neuropsychopharmacology*. Published online: 10 August 2016. doi: 10.1038/npp.2016.124.

Flynn S, Gask L, Appleby L, Shaw J (2016). Homicide-suicide and the role of mental disorder: A national consecutive case series. *Social Psychiatry and Psychiatric Epidemiology* 51, 877-884.

Fontanella CA, Campo JV, Phillips GS, Hiance-Steelesmith DL, Sweeney HA, Tam K, Lehrer D, Klein R, Hurst M (2016). Benzodiazepine use and risk of mortality among patients with schizophrenia: A retrospective longitudinal study. *Journal of Clinical Psychiatry* 77, E661-E667.

Fountoulakis KN, Chatzikosta I, Pastiadis K, Zanis P, Kawohl W, Kerkhof AJFM, Navickas A, Höschl C, Lecic-Tosevski D, Sorel E, Rancans E, Palova E, Juckel G, Isacsson G, Jagodic HK, Botezat-Antonescu I, Rybakowski J, Azorin JM, Cookson J, Waddington J, Pregelj P, Demyttenaere K, Hranov LG, Stevovi LI, Pezawas L, Adida M, Figuera ML, Jakovljevi M, Vichi M, Perugi G, Andreassen OA, Vukovi O, Mavrogiorgou P, Värnik P, Döme P, Winkler P, Salokangas RKR, From T, Danileviciute V, Gonda X, Rihmer Z, Forsman J, Grady A, Hyphantis T, Dieset I, Soendergaard S, Pompili M, Bech P (2016). Relationship of suicide rates with climate and economic variables in Europe during 2000-2012. *Annals of General Psychiatry* 15, e19.

Gjelsvik B, Heyerdahl F, Holmes J, Lunn D, Hawton K (2016). Is there a relationship between suicidal intent and lethality in deliberate self-poisoning? *Suicide and Life-Threatening Behavior*. Published online: 15 July 2016. doi: 10.1111/sltb.12277.

Griffith J (2016). A description of suicides in the army national guard during 2007-2014 and associated risk factors. *Suicide and Life-Threatening Behavior*. Published online: 7 July 2016. doi: 10.1111/sltb.12275.

Hayes JF, Pitman A, Marston L, Walters K, Geddes JR, King M, Osborn DP (2016). Self-harm, unintentional injury, and suicide in bipolar disorder during maintenance mood stabilizer treatment: A UK population-based electronic health records study. *JAMA Psychiatry* 73, 630-637.

Hekimoglu Y, Esen Melez I, Canturk N, Erkol ZZ, Dizdar MG, Canturk G, Melez DO, Kir Z (2016). A descriptive study of female suicide deaths from 2005 to 2011 in Van City, Turkey. *BMC Womens Health* 16, 20.

Huber CG, Schneeberger AR, Kowalinski E, Fröhlich D, von Felten S, Walter M, Zinkler M, Beine K, Heinz A, Borgwardt S, Lang UE (2016). Suicide risk and absconding in psychiatric hospitals with and without open door policies: A 15 year, observational study. *Lancet Psychiatry* 3, 842-849.

Hunt S (2016). Case 18: Infected self-harm injury on the left ankle. *Journal of Wound Care* 25, S27.

Huvinen M, Pukkala E (2016). Cause-specific mortality in Finnish ferrochromium and stainless steel production workers. *Occupational Medicine* 66, 241-246.

Ikeda SS, Zhang Y (2016). A dynamic panel analysis of suicide in Japanese municipalities. *Economics Bulletin* 36, 640-664.

Jayakrishnan TT, Sekigami Y, Rajeev R, Gamblin TC, Turaga KK (2016). Morbidity of curative cancer surgery and suicide risk. *Psycho-Oncology*. Published online: 16 July 2016. doi: 10.1002/pon.4221.

Jeon SY, Reither EN, Masters RK (2016). A population-based analysis of increasing rates of suicide mortality in Japan and South Korea, 1985-2010. *BMC Public Health* 16, 356.

Jiang Y, Ciano MA, Hill J, Viner-Brown S (2016). Characteristics of suicide attempts and deaths among those aged 60 years and older in Rhode Island. *Rhode Island Medical Journal* 99, 42-45.

Kapur N, Ibrahim S, Hunt IM, Turnbull P, Shaw J, Appleby L (2016). Mental health services, suicide and 7-day working. *British Journal of Psychiatry*. Published online: 7 July 2016. doi: 10.1192/bjp.bp.116.184788.

Kapur N, Ibrahim S, While D, Baird A, Rodway C, Hunt IM, Windfuhr K, Moreton A, Shaw J, Appleby L (2016). Mental health service changes, organisational factors, and patient suicide in England in 1997-2012: A before-and-after study. *Lancet Psychiatry* 6, 526-534.

Karanikolos M, Heino P, McKee M, Stuckler D, Legido-Quigley H (2016). Effects of the global financial crisis on health in high-income OECD countries: A narrative review. *International Journal of Health Services* 46, 208-240.

Katrnak T, Tyrychtrova L (2016). Social determinants of suicides in the Czech Republic between 1995 and 2010. *Sociologicky Casopis-Czech Sociological Review* 52, 293-319.

Khang YH, Bahk J, Yi N, Yun SC (2016). Age- and cause-specific contributions to income difference in life expectancy at birth: Findings from nationally representative data on one million South Koreans. *European Journal of Public Health* 26, 242-248.

Kimura T, Iso H, Honjo K, Ikehara S, Sawada N, Iwasaki M, Tsugane S (2016). Educational levels and risk of suicide in Japan: The Japan Public Health Center Study (JPHC) cohort I. *Journal of Epidemiology* 26, 315-321.

Kriikku P, Ojanperä I (2016). The relationship between bupropion and suicide in post-mortem investigations. *Forensic Science International* 266, 343-348.

Lagerros YT, Brandt L, Hedberg J, Sundbom M, Boden R (2016). Suicide, self-harm, and depression after gastric bypass surgery: A nationwide cohort study. *Annals of Surgery*. Published online: 5 July 2016. doi: 10.1097/SLA.0000000000001884.

Larsen JK (2016). Neurotoxicity and LSD treatment: A follow-up study of 151 patients in Denmark. *History of Psychiatry* 27, 172-189.

Leavey G, Rosato M, Galway K, Hughes L, Mallon S, Rondón J (2016). Patterns and predictors of help-seeking contacts with health services and general practitioner detection of suicidality prior to suicide: A cohort analysis of suicides occurring over a two-year period. *BMC Psychiatry* 16, e120.

Lee T, Lee HB, Ahn MH, Kim J, Kim MS, Chung SJ, Hong JP (2016). Increased suicide risk and clinical correlates of suicide among patients with Parkinson's disease. *Parkinsonism and Related Disorders*. Published online: 6 September 2016. doi: 10.1016/j.parkreldis.2016.09.006.

Lenz B, Thiem D, Bouna-Pyrrou P, Muhle C, Stoessel C, Betz P, Kornhuber J (2016). Low digit ratio (2D:4D) in male suicide victims. *Journal of Neural Transmission*. Published Online: 26 August 2016. doi: 10.1007/s00702-016-1608-4.

Levey DF, Niculescu EM, Le-Niculescu H, Dainton HL, Phalen PL, Ladd TB, Weber H, Belanger E, Graham DL, Khan FN, Vanipenta NP, Stage EC, Ballew A, Yard M, Gelbart T, Shekhar A, Schork NJ, Kurian SM, Sandusky GE, Salomon DR, Niculescu AB (2016). Towards understanding and predicting suicidality in women: Biomarkers and clinical risk assessment. *Molecular Psychiatry* 21, 768-785.

Li LW, Xu H, Zhang Z, Liu J (2016). An ecological study of social fragmentation, socioeconomic deprivation, and suicide in rural China: 2008-2010. *SSM - Population Health* 2, 365-372.

Linsley KR, Schapira MA, Schapira K, Lister C (2016). Changes in risk factors for young male suicide in Newcastle upon Tyne, 1961-2009. *BJPsych Bulletin* 40, 136-141.

Liu BP, Liu X, Jia CX (2016). Characteristics of suicide completers and attempters in rural Chinese population. *Comprehensive Psychiatry* 70, 134-140.

Liu CH, Yeh MK, Weng SC, Bai MY, Chang JC (2016). Suicide and chronic kidney disease: A case-control study. *Nephrology Dialysis Transplantation*. Published online: 16 September 2016. doi: 10.1093/ndt/gfw244.

Liu D-C (2016). The discouraged worker and suicide in the United States. *Social Indicators Research*. Published online: 30 August 2016. doi: 10.1007/s11205-016-1437-8.

Mackay-Smith M, Ahmadi J, Pridmore S (2015). Suicide in shooting galleries. *ASEAN Journal of Psychiatry* 16, 50-56.

Matsubayashi T, Ueda M (2016). Suicides and accidents on birthdays: Evidence from Japan. *Social Science and Medicine* 159, 61-72.

Matsubayashi T, Ueda M, Yoshikawa K (2016). School and seasonality in youth suicide: Evidence from Japan. *Journal of Epidemiology and Community Health*. Published online: 25 May 2016. doi: 10.1136/jech-2016-207583.

McCoy TH, Jr., Castro VM, Roberson AM, Snapper LA, Perlis RH (2016). Improving prediction of suicide and accidental death after discharge from general hospitals with natural language processing. *JAMA Psychiatry*. Published online: 14 September 2016. doi:10.1001/jamapsychiatry.2016.2172.

McGlade E, Bakian A, Coon H, Yurgelun-Todd D, Callor WB, Byrd J, Gray D (2016). Male suspected suicide decedents in Utah: A comparison of Veterans and nonveterans. *Comprehensive Psychiatry* 69, 1-10.

McLone SG, Kouvelis A, Mason M, Sheehan K (2016). Factors associated with suicide among adolescents and young adults not in mental health treatment at time of death. *Journal of Trauma and Acute Care Surgery* 81, s25-s29.

Milner A, Spittal MJ, Pirkis J, Chastang J-F, Niedhammer I, Lamontagne AD (2016). Low control and high demands at work as risk factors for suicide: An Australian national population-level case-control study. *Psychosomatic Medicine*. Published online: 31 August 2016. doi: 10.1097/PSY.0000000000000389.

Mishara BL, Bardon C (2017). Characteristics of railway suicides in Canada and comparison with accidental railway fatalities: Implications for prevention. *Safety Science* 91, 251-259.

Nagy C, Torres-Platas SG, Mechawar N, Turecki G (2016). Repression of astrocytic connexins in cortical and subcortical brain regions and prefrontal enrichment of H3K9me3 in depression and suicide. *International Journal of Neuropsychopharmacology*. Published online: 8 September 2016. doi: 10.1093/ijnp/pyw071.

Naz F (2016). Risk factors of successful suicide attempts in Punjab. *Journal of Postgraduate Medical Institute* 30, 277-281.

Nazarzadeh M, Bidel Z, Ranjbaran M, Hemmati R, Pejhan A, Asadollahi K, Sayehmiri K (2016). Fatal suicide and modelling its risk factors in a prevalent area of Iran. *Archives of Iranian Medicine* 19, 571-576.

Neider D, Lindstrom LH, Boden R (2016). Risk factors for suicide among patients with schizophrenia: A cohort study focused on cerebrospinal fluid levels of homovanillic acid and 5-hydroxyindoleacetic acid. *Neuropsychiatric Disease and Treatment* 12, 1711-1714.

Ng CFS, Stickley A, Konishi S, Watanabe C (2016). Ambient air pollution and suicide in Tokyo, 2001-2011. *Journal of Affective Disorders* 201, 194-202.

O'Farrell IB, Corcoran P, Perry IJ (2016). The area level association between suicide, deprivation, social fragmentation and population density in the republic of Ireland: A national study. *Social Psychiatry and Psychiatric Epidemiology* 51, 839-847.

Odafe MO, Talavera DC, Cheref S, Hong JH, Walker RL (2016). Suicide in racial and ethnic minority adults: A review of the last decade. *Current Psychiatry Reviews* 12, 181-198.

Olfson M, Wall M, Wang S, Crystal S, Liu SM, Gerhard T, Blanco C (2016). Short-term suicide risk after psychiatric hospital discharge. *JAMA Psychiatry*. Published online: 21 September 2016. doi:10.1001/jamapsychiatry.2016.2035.

Olsson MO, Bradvik L, Ojehagen A, Håkansson A (2016). Risk factors for unnatural death: Fatal accidental intoxication, undetermined intent and suicide: Register follow-up in a criminal justice population with substance use problems. *Drug and Alcohol Dependence* 162, 176-181.

Osman M, Parnell AC, Haley C (2016). "Suicide shall cease to be a crime": Suicide and undetermined death trends 1970–2000 before and after the decriminalization of suicide in Ireland 1993. *Irish Journal of Medical Science*. Published online: 17 May 2016. doi: 10.1007/s11845-016-1468-9.

Paraschakis A, Michopoulos I, Christodoulou C, Koutsaftis F, Douzenis A (2016). Psychiatric medication intake in suicide victims: Gender disparities and implications for suicide prevention. *Journal of Forensic Sciences*. Published online: 19 September 2016. doi: 10.1111/1556-4029.13195.

Park J, Choi N, Kim SJ, Kim S, An H, Lee HJ, Lee YJ (2016). The impact of celebrity suicide on subsequent suicide rates in the general population of Korea from 1990 to 2010. *Journal of Korean Medical Science* 31, 598-603.

Park S, Hong JP, Lee J-K, Park Y-M, Park Y, Jeon J, Ahn MH, Yoon SC (2016). Associations between the neuron-specific glucocorticoid receptor (NR3C1) Bcl-1 polymorphisms and suicide in cancer patients within the first year of diagnosis. *Behavioral and Brain Functions* 12, 22.

Parkinson J, Minton J, Lewsey J, Bouttell J, McCartney G (2016). Recent cohort effects in suicide in Scotland: A legacy of the 1980s? *Journal of Epidemiology and Community Health*. Published online: 18 July 2016. doi:10.1136/jech-2016-207296.

Perera S, Eisen RB, Dennis BB, Bawor M, Bhatt M, Bhatnagar N, Thabane L, de Souza R, Samaan Z (2016). Body mass index is an important predictor for suicide: Results from a systematic review and meta-analysis. *Suicide and Life-Threatening Behavior*. Published online: 20 April 2016. doi: 10.1111/sltb.12244.

Perlis ML, Grandner MA, Brown GK, Basner M, Chakravorty S, Morales KH, Gehrman PR, Chaudhary NS, Thase ME, Dinges DF (2016). Nocturnal wakefulness as a previously unrecognized risk factor for suicide. *Journal of Clinical Psychiatry* 77, e726-e733.

Pigeon WR, Bishop TM, Titus CE (2016). The relationship between sleep disturbance, suicidal ideation, suicide attempts, and suicide among adults: A systematic review. *Psychiatric Annals* 46, 177-186.

Pompili M, Belvederi Murri M, Patti S, Innamorati M, Lester D, Girardi P, Amore M (2016). The communication of suicidal intentions: A meta-analysis. *Psychological Medicine* 46, 2239-2253.

Pridmore S, Auchincloss S, Ahmadi J (2016). Suicide triggers described by Herodotus. *Iranian Journal of Psychiatry* 11, 128-132.

Reger MA, Smolenski DJ, Skopp NA, Metzger-Abamukong MJ, Kang HK, Bullman TA, Gahm GA (2016). Suicide risk among wounded U.S. Service members. *Suicide and Life-Threatening Behavior*. Published online: 5 August 2016. doi: 10.1111/sltb.12282.

Rodway C, Tham S-G, Ibrahim S, Turnbull P, Windfuhr K, Shaw J, Kapur N, Appleby L (2016). Suicide in children and young people in England: A consecutive case series. *Lancet Psychiatry* 3, 751-759.

Rojas Y, Stenberg SA (2016). Evictions and suicide: A follow-up study of almost 22 000 Swedish households in the wake of the global financial crisis. *Journal of Epidemiology and Community Health* 70, 409-413.

Rostami M, Jalilian A, Rezaei-Zangeneh R, Salari A (2016). Factors associated with the choice of suicide method in Kermanshah province, Iran. *Annals of Saudi Medicine* 36, 7-16.

Saarela J, Cederstrom A, Rostila M (2016). Birth order and mortality in two ethno-linguistic groups: Register-based evidence from Finland. *Social Science & Medicine* 158, 8-13.

Saitzyk A, Vorm E (2016). Self-directed violence aboard US navy aircraft carriers: An examination of general and shipboard-specific risk and protective factors. *Military Medicine* 181, 343-349

Schuerch M, Gasse C, Robinson NJ, Alvarez Y, Walls R, Mors O, Christensen J, Hesse U, de Groot M, Schlienger R, Reynolds R, Klungel O, de Vries F (2016). Impact of varying outcomes and definitions of suicidality on the associations of antiepileptic drugs and suicidality: Comparisons from UK Clinical Practice Research Datalink (CPRD) and Danish National Registries (DNR). *Pharmacoepidemiology and Drug Safety* 25, 142-155.

Sheftall AH, Asti L, Horowitz LM, Felts A, Fontanella CA, Campo JV, Bridge JA (2016). Suicide in elementary school-aged children and early adolescents. *Pediatrics*. Published online: September 2016. doi: 10.1542/peds.2016-0436.

Shiner B, Riblet N, Westgate CL, Young-Xu Y, Watts BV (2016). Suicidal ideation is associated with all-cause mortality. *Military Medicine* 181, 1040-1045.

Siegel M, Rothman EF (2016). Firearm ownership and suicide rates among US men and women, 1981-2013. *American Journal of Public Health* 106, 1316-1322.

Skerrett DM, Kõlves K, De Leo D (2016). Factors related to suicide in LGBT populations. *Crisis*. Published online: 23 September 2016. doi: 10.1027/0227-5910/a000423.

Skerrett DM, Kõlves K, De Leo D (2016). Pathways to suicide in lesbian and gay populations in Australia: A life chart analysis. *Archives of Sexual Behavior*. Published online: 29 August 2016. doi: 10.1007/s10508-016-0827-y.

Smaira G, Mehdi JM, Sara S, Reza M (2016). Comparison between big five personality traits, brain-behavioral systems and cognitive emotion regulation strategies in women who committed suicide by poisoning and normal women. *International Journal of Advanced Biotechnology and Research* 7, 487-496.

Sohn K (2016). Suicides around major public holidays in South Korea. *Suicide and Life Threatening Behavior*. Published online: 23 July 2016. doi: 10.1111/sltb.12281.

Solje E, Riipinen P, Helisalmi S, Sarkioja T, Laitinen M, Hiltunen M, Hakko H, Remes AM (2016). The role of the FTD-ALS associated C9ORF72 expansion in suicide victims. *Amyotrophic Lateral Sclerosis and Frontotemporal Degeneration*. Published online: 8 July 2014. doi: 10.1080/21678421.2016.1203337.

Stack S, Laubepin F, Vichi M, Minelli G, Lester D, Ferracuti S, Girardi P, Pompili M (2016). Economic deprivation as a predictor of the direction of lethal violence: An analysis of Italian provinces. *Archives of Suicide Research* 20, 483-487.

Stefansson J, Chatzittofis A, Nordström P, Arver S, Åsberg M, Jokinen J (2016). CSF and plasma testosterone in attempted suicide. *Psychoneuroendocrinology* 74, 1-6.

Stefenson A, Titelman D (2016). Psychosis and suicide: Suicidal communication and critical life events before suicide in a 1-year psychiatric cohort. *Crisis* 37, 224-231.

Stickley A, Sheng Ng CF, Inoue Y, Yazawa A, Koyanagi A, Kodaka M, Devylder JE, Watanabe C (2016). Birthdays are associated with an increased risk of suicide in Japan: Evidence from 27,007 deaths in Tokyo in 2001-2010. *Journal of Affective Disorders* 200, 259-265.

Strale M, Krysinska K, Overmeiren GV, Andriessen K (2016). Geographic distribution of suicide and railway suicide in Belgium, 2008-2013: A principal component analysis. *International Journal of Injury Control and Safety Promotion*. Published online: 20 April 2016. doi: 10.1080/17457300.2016.1166140.

Strand LB, Mukamal KJ, Halasz J, Vatten LJ, Janszky I (2016). Short-term public health impact of the July 22, 2011, terrorist attacks in Norway: A nationwide register-based study. *Psychosomatic Medicine* 78, 525-531.

Sumarokov YA, Brenn T, Kudryavtsev AV, Sidorenkov O, Nilssen O (2016). Alcohol and suicide in the Nenets Autonomous Okrug and Arkhangelsk Oblast, Russia. *International Journal of Circumpolar Health* 75, e30965.

Takeuchi T, Takenoshita S, Taka F, Nakao M, Nomura K (2016). The relationship between psychotropic drug use and suicidal behavior in Japan: Japanese adverse drug event report. *Pharmacopsychiatry*. Published online: 5 September 2016. doi: 10.1055/s-0042-113468.

Talukder N, Karim KA, Chowdhury T, Habib A, Chowdhury AM, Perveen K (2014). Study of autopsy based suicidal hanging. *Bangladesh Journal of Physiology and Pharmacology* 30, 14-17.

Tian N, Cui W, Zack M, Kobau R, Fowler KA, Hesdorffer DC (2016). Suicide among people with epilepsy: A population-based analysis of data from the U.S. National Violent Death Reporting System, 17 states, 2003-2011. *Epilepsy and Behavior* 61, 210-217.

Too LS, Spittal MJ, Bugeja L, McClure R, Milner A (2016). Individual and community factors for railway suicide: A matched case-control study in Victoria, Australia. *Social Psychiatry and Psychiatric Epidemiology* 51, 849-856.

van Ginneken EFJC, Sutherland A, Molleman T (2016). An ecological analysis of prison overcrowding and suicide rates in England and Wales, 2000-2014. *International Journal of Law and Psychiatry*. Published online: 14 May 2016. doi: 10.1016/j.ijlp.2016.05.005.

VanderWeele TJ, Li S, Tsai AC, Kawachi I (2016). Association between religious service attendance and lower suicide rates among US women. *JAMA Psychiatry* 73, 845-851.

Veisani Y, Delpisheh A, Sayehmiri K, Moradi G, Hassanzadeh J (2016). Suicide attempts in Ilam Province, Western Iran, 2010-2014: A time trend study. *Journal of Research in Health Sciences* 16, 64-67.

Wallace ME, Hoyert D, Williams C, Mendola P (2016). Pregnancy-associated homicide and suicide in 37 US states with enhanced pregnancy surveillance. *American Journal of Obstetrics and Gynecology* 215, 364.e1–364.e10.

Wang M, Alexanderson K, Runeson B, Mittendorfer-Rutz E (2016). Morbidity and suicide mortality following sick leave in relation to changes of social insurance regulations in Sweden. *European Journal of Public Health*. Published online: 14 July 2016. doi: 10.1093/eurpub/ckw101.

Wang Y, Tang S, Xu S, Weng S, Liu Z (2016). Association between diabetes and risk of suicide death: A meta-analysis of 3 million participants. *Comprehensive Psychiatry* 71, 11-16.

Weng SC, Chang JC, Yeh MK, Wang SM, Chen YH (2016). Factors influencing attempted and completed suicide in postnatal women: A population-based study in Taiwan. *Scientific Reports* 6, 25770.

Wingren CJ, Ottosson A (2016). Body mass index and suicide methods. *Journal of Forensic and Legal Medicine* 42, 45-50.

Yi S-W (2016). Depressive symptoms on the geriatric depression scale and suicide deaths in older middle-aged men: A prospective cohort study. *Journal of Preventive Medicine and Public Health* 49, 176-182.

Yin H, Galfalvy H, Pantazatos SP, Huang YY, Rosoklija GB, Dwork AJ, Burke A, Arango V, Oquendo MA, Mann JJ (2016). Glucocorticoid receptor-related genes: Genotype and brain gene expression relationships to suicide and major depressive disorder. *Depression and Anxiety*. Published online: 31 March 2016. doi: 10.1002/da.22499.

Zalsman G, Siman Tov Y, Tzuriel D, Shoval G, Barzilay R, Tiech Fire N, Sherf M, John Mann J (2016). Psychological autopsy of seventy high school suicides: Combined qualitative/quantitative approach. *European Psychiatry* 38, 8-14.

Zhao J, Verwer RWH, van Wamelen DJ, Qi XR, Gao SF, Lucassen PJ, Swaab DF (2016). Prefrontal changes in the glutamate-glutamine cycle and neuronal/glial glutamate transporters in depression with and without suicide. *Journal of Psychiatric Research* 82, 8-15.

Zonda T, Bozsonyi K, Kmetty Z, Veres E, Lester D (2016). The birthday blues: A study of a large Hungarian sample (1970-2002). *Omega* 73, 87-9.

Prevention

Bal AS, Weidner K, Leeds C, Raaka B (2016). Getting real about suicide prevention in the classroom and beyond: Using a classroom simulation to create communications for at-risk individuals. *Journal of Marketing Education* 38, 90-97.

Baran A, Kropiwnicki P (2015). Advantages and pitfalls of the Swedish national program for suicide prevention 2008. *Psychiatria I Psychologia Kliniczna* 15, 175-181.

Brennan PL, Del Re AC, Henderson PT, Trafton JA (2016). Healthcare system-wide implementation of opioid-safety guideline recommendations: The case of urine drug screening and opioid-patient suicide- and overdose-related events in the Veterans Health Administration. *Translational Behavioral Medicine*. Published online: 6 July 2016. doi: 10.1007/s13142-016-0423-7.

Burrage RL, Gone JP, Momper SL (2016). Urban American Indian community perspectives on resources and challenges for youth suicide prevention. *American Journal of Community Psychology*. Published online: 31 August 2016. doi: 10.1002/ajcp.12080.

Chauliac N, Brochard N, Payet C, Margue Y, Bordin P, Depraz P, Dumont A, Kroupa E, Pacaut-Troncin M, Polo P, Straub S, Boissin J, Burtin C, Montoya G, Rivière A, Didier C, Fournel C, Durand C, Barrellon M, Amigues O, Brosson A, Mahé E, Haxaire O, Bonnot C, Defaux M, Rougier D, Gaultier A, Gutierrez A, Pozo M, Lefèvre V, Nier A, Bolzan S, Liautaud M, Barbosa S, Garcia S, Anfreville A, Mazille S, Durantet C, Morlon M, Gaboriau C, Halbert C, Cholvy M, Milinkovich P, Martin L, Maury-Abello L, Toulier B, Kerleguer V, Gabriel S, Duclos A, Terra JL (2016). How does gatekeeper training improve suicide prevention for elderly people in nursing homes? A controlled study in 24 centres. *European Psychiatry* 37, 56-62.

Connell AM, McKillop HN, Dishion TJ (2016). Long-term effects of the family check-up in early adolescence on risk of suicide in early adulthood. *Suicide and Life Threatening Behavior* 46, S15-S22.

De Silva SA, Colucci E, Mendis J, Kelly CM, Jorm AF, Minas H (2016). Suicide first aid guidelines for Sri Lanka: A Delphi consensus study. *International Journal of Mental Health Systems* 10, 53.

Dillman Carpentier FR, Parrott MS (2016). Young adults' information seeking following celebrity suicide: Considering involvement with the celebrity and emotional distress in health communication strategies. *Health Communication* 33, 1334-1344.

Havârneanu GM, Bonneau MH, Colliard J (2016). Lessons learned from the collaborative European project RESTRAIL: Reduction of suicides and trespasses on railway property. *European Transport Research Review* 8, 16.

Isaacs A, Sutton K (2016). An Aboriginal youth suicide prevention project in rural Victoria. *Advances in Mental Health* 14, 118-125.

Kelly J, Sammon N, Byrne M (2014). APSI: A proposed integrative model for suicide prevention. *Irish Journal of Psychological Medicine* 31, 203-212.

Kim J-P, Yang J (2016). Effectiveness of a community-based program for suicide prevention among elders with early-stage dementia: A controlled observational study. *Geriatric Nursing*. Published online: 1 September 2016. doi: 10.1016/j.gerinurse.2016.08.002.

Klimes-Dougan B, Wright N, Klingbeil DA (2016). Suicide prevention public service announcements impact help seeking attitudes: The message makes a difference. *Frontiers in Psychiatry* 7, 124.

Lamis DA, Underwood M, D'Amore N (2016). Outcomes of a suicide prevention gatekeeper training program among school personnel. *Crisis*. Published online: 26 August 2016. doi: 10.1027/0227-5910/a000414.

Large M, Kaneson M, Myles N, Myles H, Gunaratne P, Ryan C (2016). Meta-analysis of longitudinal cohort studies of suicide risk assessment among psychiatric patients: Heterogeneity in results and lack of improvement over time. *PLoS One* 11, e0156322.

Lees D, Procter N, Fassett D, Handley C (2016). Involving mental health service users in suicide-related research: A qualitative inquiry model. *Nurse Researcher* 23, 30-34.

Mok K, Donovan R, Hocking B, Maher B, Lewis R, Pirkis J (2016). Stimulating community action for suicide prevention: Findings on the effectiveness of the Australian R U OK? Campaign. *International Journal of Mental Health Promotion* 18, 213-221.

Mokkenstorm JK, Eikelenboom M, Huisman A, Wiebenga J, Gilissen R, Kerkhof AJ, Smit JH (2016). Evaluation of the 113 online suicide prevention crisis chat service: Outcomes, helper behaviors and comparison to telephone hotlines. *Suicide and Life-Threatening Behavior*. Published online: 19 August 2016. doi: 10.1111/sltb.12286.

Mullaney C (2016). Reshaping time: Recommendations for suicide prevention in LBGT populations. *Journal of Homosexuality* 63, 461-465.

Ranahan P (2016). Protocols or principles? Reimagining suicide risk assessment as an embedded, principle-based ongoing conversation in youth work practice. *Child and Youth Services*. Published online 4 May 2016. doi: 10.1080/0145935X.2016.1158095.

Robinson G, Leckning B, Midford R, Harper H, Silburn S, Gannaway J, Dolan K, Delphine T, Hayes C (2016). Developing a school-based preventive life skills program for youth in a remote Indigenous community in North Australia. *Health Education* 116, 510-523.

Robinson WL, Case MH, Whipple CR, Gooden AS, Lopez-Tamayo R, Lambert SF, Jason LA (2016). Culturally grounded stress reduction and suicide prevention for African American adolescents. *Practice Innovations* 1, 117-128.

Rosenberg K (2016). ED screening may detect patients at risk for suicide. *American Journal of Nursing* 116, 54.

Ross V, Kõlves K, De Leo D (2016). Teachers' perspectives on preventing suicide in children and adolescents in schools: A qualitative study. *Archives of Suicide Research*. Published online: 31 August 2016. doi: 10.1080/13811118.2016.1227005.

Snyder DJ, Ballard ED, Stanley IH, Ludi E, Kohn-Godbout J, Pao M, Horowitz LM (2016). Patient opinions about screening for suicide risk in the adult medical inpatient unit. *The Journal of Behavioral Health Services & Research*. Published online: 12 April 2016. doi: 10.1007/s11414-016-9498-7.

Stanley IH, Hom MA, Rogers ML, Anestis MD, Joiner TE (2016). Discussing firearm ownership and access as part of suicide risk assessment and prevention: "Means safety" versus "means restriction". *Archives of Suicide Research*. Published online: 13 April 2016. doi: 10.1080/13811118.2016.1175395.

Teo AR, Andrea SB, Sakakibara R, Motohara S, Matthieu MM, Fetters MD (2016). Brief gatekeeper training for suicide prevention in an ethnic minority population: A controlled intervention. *BMC Psychiatry* 16, 211.

Torcasso G, Hilt LM (2016). Suicide prevention among high school students: Evaluation of a nonrandomized trial of a multi-stage suicide screening program. *Child and Youth Care Forum*. Published online: 28 June 2016. doi: 10.1007/s10566-016-9366-x.

Tyson P, Law C, Reed S, Johnsey E, Aruna O, Hall S (2016). Preventing suicide and self-harm. *Crisis*. Published online: 9 June 2016. doi: 10.1027/0227-5910/a000390.

Postvention and Bereavement

Appel CW, Johansen C, Christensen J, Frederiksen K, Hjalgrim H, Dalton SO, Dencker A, Dige J, Boge P, Dyregrov A, Mikkelsen OA, Lund LW, Hoybye MT, Bidstrup PE (2016). Risk of use of antidepressants among children and young adults exposed to the death of a parent. *Epidemiology* 27, 578-585.

Boelen PA, Reijntjes A, J. Djelantik AAAM, Smid GE (2016). Prolonged grief and depression after unnatural loss: Latent class analyses and cognitive correlates. *Psychiatry Research* 240, 358-363.

Castelli Dransart DA (2016). Reclaiming and reshaping life: Patterns of reconstruction after the suicide of a loved one. *Qualitative Health Research*. Published online: 6 April 2016. doi: 10.1177/1049732316637590.

Foggin E, McDonnell S, Cordingley L, Kapur N, Shaw J, Chew-Graham CA (2016). GPs' experiences of dealing with parents bereaved by suicide: A qualitative study. *British Journal of General Practice*. Published online: 16 August 2016. doi: 10.3399/bjgp16X686605.

Matthews LR, Fitzpatrick SJ, Quinlan MG, Ngo M, Bohle P (2016). Bereaved families and the coronial response to traumatic workplace fatalities: Organizational perspectives. *Death Studies* 40, 191-200.

Moore H, Donohue G (2016). The impact of suicide prevention on experienced Irish clinicians. *Counselling and Psychotherapy Research* 16, 24-34.

Omerov P, Pettersen R, Titelman D, Nyberg T, Steineck G, Dyregrov A, Nyberg U (2016). Encountering the body at the site of the suicide: A population-based survey in Sweden. *Suicide and Life-Threatening Behavior*. Published online: 25 April 2016. doi: 10.1111/sltb.12260.

Peters K, Cunningham C, Murphy G, Jackson D (2016). Helpful and unhelpful responses after suicide: Experiences of bereaved family members. *International Journal of Mental Health Nursing* 25, 418-425.

Peters K, Cunningham C, Murphy G, Jackson D (2016). "People look down on you when you tell them how he died': Qualitative insights into stigma as experienced by suicide survivors. *International Journal of Mental Health Nursing* 25, 251-257.

Pitman AL, Osborn DPJ, Rantell K, King MB (2016). The stigma perceived by people bereaved by suicide and other sudden deaths: A cross-sectional UK study of 3432 bereaved adults. *Journal of Psychosomatic Research* 87, 22-29.

Schaffer A, Sinyor M, Kurdyak P, Vigod S, Sareen J, Reis C, Green D, Bolton J, Rhodes A, Grigoriadis S, Cairney J, Cheung A (2016). Population-based analysis of health care contacts among suicide decedents: Identifying opportunities for more targeted suicide prevention strategies. *World Psychiatry* 15, 135-145.

Van Der Pol S, Pehrsson DE (2016). Examination of the grieving processes of suicide survivors. *Qualitative Research Journal* 16, 159-168.

NON-FATAL SUICIDAL BEHAVIOR

Epidemiology

Ahmed SA, Omar QH, Abo Elamaim AA (2016). Forensic analysis of suicidal ideation among medical students of Egypt: A crosssectional study. *Journal of Forensic and Legal Medicine* 44, 1-4.

Alshawi A, Lafta R, Al-Nuaimi A (2015). Prevalence of suicidal thoughts among a sample from Baghdad. *Journal of Community Medicine and Health Education* 5, e1000334.

Asgeirsdottir HG, Asgeirsdottir TL, Nyberg U, Thorsteinsdottir TK, Mogensen B, Matthiasson P, Lund SH, Valdimarsdottir UA, Hauksdottir A (2016). Suicide attempts and self-harm during a dramatic national economic transition: A population-based study in Iceland. *European Journal of Public Health*. Published online: 31 August 2016. doi: 10.1093/eurpub/ckw137.

Badr HE (2016). Suicidal behaviors among adolescents - the role of school and home environment. *Crisis*. Published online: 23 September 2016. doi: 10.1027/0227-5910/a000426.

Barratt H, Rojas-Garcia A, Clarke K, Moore A, Whittington C, Stockton S, Thomas J, Pilling S, Raine R (2016). Epidemiology of mental health attendances at emergency departments: Systematic review and meta-analysis. *PLoS One* 11, e0154449.

Betz ME, Arias SA, Segal DL, Miller I, Camargo CA, Boudreaux ED (2016). Screening for suicidal thoughts and behaviors in older adults in the emergency department. *Journal of the American Geriatrics Society*. Published online: 6 September 2016. doi: 10.1111/jgs.14529.

Beutel ME, Jünger C, Klein EM, Wild P, Lackner KJ, Blettner M, Banerjee M, Michal M, Wiltink J, Brähler E (2016). Depression, anxiety and suicidal ideation among 1st and 2nd generation migrants - results from the Gutenberg Health Study. *BMC Psychiatry* 16, 288.

Bhatti JA, Nathens AB, Thiruchelvam D, Grantcharov T, Goldstein BI, Redelmeier DA (2016). Self-harm emergencies after bariatric surgery a population-based cohort study. *Journal of the American Medical Association Surgery* 151, 226-232.

Borges G, Benjet C, Orozco R, Medina-Mora Me (2016). The growth of suicide ideation, plan and attempt among young adults in the Mexico City metropolitan area. *Epidemiology and Psychiatric Sciences*. Published online: 15 August 2016. doi: 10.1017/S2045796016000603.

Bosak A, Brooks DE, Welch S, Padilla-Jones A, Gerkin RD (2015). A retrospective review of 911 calls to a regional poison control center. *Journal of Family Medicine and Primary Care* 4, 546-550.

Farrugia LA, Rhyee SH, Campleman SL, Ruha AM, Weigand T, Wax PM, Brent J (2016). The toxicology investigators consortium case registry-the 2015 experience. *Journal of Medical Toxicology* 12, 224-247.

Fisher LB, Pedrelli P, Iverson GL, Bergquist TF, Bombardier CH, Hammond FM, Hart T, Ketchum JM, Giacino J, Zafonte R (2016). Prevalence of suicidal behaviour following traumatic brain injury: Longitudinal follow-up data from the NIDRR traumatic brain injury model systems. *Brain Injury*. Published online: 19 August 2016. doi: 10.1080/02699052.2016.1195517.

Gesink D, Brennan DJ, Rhodes AE, Bogaert L, Hottes TS (2016). Lifetime prevalence of suicide attempts among sexual minority adults by study sampling strategies: A systematic review and meta-analysis. *American Journal of Public Health* 106, e1-e12.

Geulayov G, Kapur N, Turnbull P, Clements C, Waters K, Ness J, Townsend E, Hawton K (2016). Epidemiology and trends in non-fatal self-harm in three centres in England, 2000-2012: Findings from the multicentre study of self-harm in England. *British Medical Journal Open* 6, e010538.

Han B, Compton WM, Eisenberg D, Milazzo-Sayre L, McKeon R, Hughes A (2016). Prevalence and mental health treatment of suicidal ideation and behavior among college students aged 18-25 years and their non-college-attending peers in the United States. *Journal of Clinical Psychiatry* 77, 815-824.

Herbert A, Gonzalez-Izquierdo A, McGhee J, Li L, Gilbert R (2016). Time-trends in rates of hospital admission of adolescents for violent, self-inflicted or drug/alcohol-related injury in England and Scotland, 2005-11: Population-based analysis. *Journal of Public Health*. Published online: 21 March 2016. doi: 10.1093/pubmed/fdw020.

Kalkan EA, Yıldırım A, Akdur O (2016). Trauma and intentional injury characteristics of pediatric forensic cases applying to emergency room. *Journal of Clinical and Analytical Medicine* 7, 668-671.

Kamijo Y, Takai M, Fujita Y, Sakamoto T (2016). A multicenter retrospective survey of poisoning after consumption of products containing novel psychoactive substances from 2013 to 2014 in Japan. *American Journal of Drug and Alcohol Abuse* 42, 513-519.

Kann L, McManus T, Harris WA, Shanklin SL, Flint KH, Hawkins J, Queen B, Lowry R, Olsen EO, Chyen D, Whittle L, Thornton J, Lim C, Yamakawa Y, Brener N, Zaza S (2016). Youth risk behavior surveillance - United States, 2015. *MMWR: Surveillance Summaries* 65, 1-174.

Kim H, Kim B, Kang SG, Kim MD, Kim MH, Kim SI, Kim JM, Moon E, Ahn JH, Lee KU, Lee SH, Lee SJ, Jeong SH, Chung YC, Jung HY, Ju G, Cha B, Ha TH, Ahn YM (2015). Attempted suicides in South Korea: A multi-center analysis of causes, methods, and psychiatric diagnoses of suicidal attempters in 2013. *Korean Journal of Biological Psychiatry* 22, 187-194.

Krishnaram VD, Aravind VK, Vimala AR (2016). Deliberate self-harm seen in a government licensed private psychiatric hospital and institute. *Indian Journal of Psychological Medicine* 38, 137-141.

Lopez-Castroman J, Nogue E, Guillaume S, Picot MC, Courtet P (2016). Clustering suicide attempters: Impulsive-ambivalent, well-planned, or frequent. *Journal of Clinical Psychiatry* 77, e711-e718.

Martins Junior DF, Felzemburgh RM, Dias AB, Caribe AC, Bezerra-Filho S, Miranda-Scippa A (2016). Suicide attempts in Brazil, 1998-2014: An ecological study. *BMC Public Health* 16, 990.

Matsuyama T, Kitamura T, Kiyohara K, Hayashida S, Nitta M, Kawamura T, Iwami T, Ohta B (2016). Incidence and outcomes of emergency self-harm among adolescents: A descriptive epidemiological study in Osaka city, Japan. *British Medical Journal Open* 6, e011419.

Mekaoui N, Karboubi L, Ouadghiri FZ, Dakhama BSB (2016). Epidemiological aspects of suicide attempts among Moroccan children. *Pan African Medical Journal* 24, 112.

Newton AS, Rosychuk RJ, Carlisle CE, Zhang X, Bethell J, Rhodes AE (2016). Time trends in emergency department visits for suicide-related behaviours by girls and boys in Alberta a population-based retrospective cohort study. *Canadian Journal of Psychiatry* 61, 422-427.

Ohtaki Y, Oi Y, Doki S, Kaneko H, Usami K, Sasahara S, Matsuzaki I (2016). Characteristics of telephone crisis hotline callers with suicidal ideation in Japan. *Suicide and Life Threatening Behavior*. Published online: 1 June 2016. doi: 10.1027/0227-5910/a000384.

Oneib B, Sabir M, Otheman Y, Abda N, Ouanass A (2016). Suicidal ideations, plans and attempts in primary care in Morocco: Cross-sectional study of consultants at primary health care system in Morocco. *Pan African Medical Journal* 24, e274.

Pawłowska B, Potembska E, Zygo M, Olajossy M, Dziurzy ska E (2016). Prevalence of self-injury performed by adolescents aged 16-19 years. *Psychiatria Polska* 50, 29-42.

Peterson CM, Matthews A, Copps-Smith E, Conard LA (2016). Suicidality, self-harm, and body dissatisfaction in transgender adolescents and emerging adults with gender dysphoria. *Suicide and Life-Threatening Behavior*. Published online: 19 August 2016. doi: 10.1111/sltb.12289.

Price JH, Khubchandani J (2016). Latina adolescents health risk behaviors and suicidal ideation and suicide attempts: Results from the National Youth Risk Behavior Survey 2001-2013. *Journal of Immigrant and Minority Health.* Published online: 10 June 2016. doi: 10.1007/s10903-016-0445-8.

Qiao N, Bell TM (2016). Indigenous adolescents' suicidal behaviors and risk factors: Evidence from the National Youth Risk Behavior Survey. *Journal of Immigrant and Minority Health.* Published online: 6 June 2015. doi: 10.1007/s10903-016-0443-x.

Rahme E, Low NCP, Lamarre S, Daneau D, Habel Y, Turecki G, Bonin J-P, Morin S, Szkrumelak N, Singh S, Lesage A (2016). Correlates of attempted suicide from the emergency room of 2 general hospitals in Montreal, Canada. *Canadian Journal of Psychiatry* 61, 382-393.

Rochon-Terry G, Gruneir A, Seeman MV, Ray JG, Rochon P, Dennis CL, Grigoriadis S, Fung K, Kurdyak PA, Vigod SN (2016). Hospitalizations and emergency department visits for psychiatric illness during and after pregnancy among women with schizophrenia. *Journal of Clinical Psychiatry* 77, 541-547.

Rosychuk RJ, Johnson DW, Urichuk L, Dong K, Newton AS (2016). Does emergency department use and post-visit physician care cluster geographically and temporally for adolescents who self-harm? A population-based 9-year retrospective cohort study from Alberta, Canada. *BMC Psychiatry* 16, 229.

Saeed S, Shuaib M (2016). An epidemiological study of suicidal attempt victims at J.N Medical College, Aligarh. *Indian Journal of Forensic Medicine and Toxicology* 10, 117-122.

Segu S, Tataria R (2016). Paediatric suicidal burns: A growing concern. *Burns* 42, 825-829.

Shin HY, Lee H, Park SM (2016). Mental health and its associated factors among North Korean defectors living in South Korea: A case-control study. *Asia-Pacific Journal of Public Health.* Published online: 25 July 2016. doi: 10.1177/1010539516660192.

Shrinivasan K (2016). A profile of acute self drug poisoning: Our experience in a tertiary care medical college teaching hospital. *International Journal of Biomedical and Advance Research* 7, 369-372.

Stahlman S, Grosso A, Ketende S, Pitche V, Kouanda S, Ceesay N, Ouedraogo HG, Ky-Zerbo O, Lougue M, Diouf D, Anato S, Tchalla J, Baral S (2016). Suicidal ideation among MSM in three West African countries: Associations with stigma and social capital. *International Journal of Social Psychiatry* 62, 522-531.

Tong HY, Medrano N, Borobia AM, Ruiz JA, Martínez AM, Martín J, Quintana M, García S, Carcas AJ, Ramírez E (2016). Hepatotoxicity induced by acute and chronic paracetamol overdose in children: Where do we stand? *World Journal of Pediatrics* 72, 370-378.

Vancayseele N, Portzky G, van Heeringen K (2016). Increase in self-injury as a method of self-harm in Ghent, Belgium: 1987-2013. *PLoS One* 11, e0156711.

Zubrick SR, Hafekost J, Johnson SE, Lawrence D, Saw S, Sawyer M, Ainley J, Buckingham J (2016). Suicidal behaviours: Prevalence estimates from the second Australian Child and Adolescent Survey of Mental Health and Wellbeing. *Australian and New Zealand Journal of Psychiatry* 50, 899-891.

Risk and protective factors

Aday RH, Dye MH, Kaiser AK (2014). Examining the traumatic effects of sexual victimization on the health of incarcerated women. *Women and Criminal Justice* 24, 341-361.

Agnew-Blais J, Danese A (2016). Childhood maltreatment and unfavourable clinical outcomes in bipolar disorder: A systematic review and meta-analysis. *Lancet Psychiatry* 3, 342-349.

Aitken M, VanderLaan DP, Wasserman L, Stojanovski S, Zucker KJ (2016). Self-harm and suicidality in children referred for gender dysphoria. *Journal of the American Academy of Child and Adolescent Psychiatry* 55, 513-520.

Alves CAS, Jr., Nunes HEG, De Andrade Gonçalves EC, Silva DAS (2016). Suicidal behaviour in adolescents: Characteristics and prevalence. *Journal of Human Growth and Development* 26, 88-94.

Alves VdM, Francisco LCFdL, Belo FMP, de-Melo-Neto VL, Barros VG, Nardi AE (2016). Evaluation of the quality of life and risk of suicide. *Clinics* 71, 135-139.

Alves VdM, Santos MBdF, Nascimento LMS, Ferro GC, Silva LKBd, Tenório FE, Nardi AE (2015). Suicidal ideation and chronotype assessment in nurses and police officers. *Medical Express* 2, M150305.

Ambrus L, Lindqvist D, Träskman-Bendz L, Westrin A (2016). Hypothalamic-pituitary-adrenal axis hyperactivity is associated with decreased brain-derived neurotrophic factor in female suicide attempters. *Nordic Journal of Psychiatry* 70, 575-581.

Ambrus L, Sunnqvist C, Ekman R, Traskman-Bendz L, Westrin A (2016). Plasma brain-derived neurotrophic factor and psychopathology in attempted suicide. *Neuropsychobiology* 73, 241-248.

Anderberg J, Bogren M, Mattisson C, Bråkvik L (2016). Long-term suicide risk in anxiety—the Lundby study 1947–2011. *Archives of Suicide Research* 20, 463-475.

Andrewes HE, Hulbert C, Cotton SM, Betts J, Chanen AM (2016). Ecological momentary assessment of nonsuicidal self-injury in youth with borderline personality disorder. *Personality Disorders*. Published online: 8 August 2016. doi: 10.1037/per0000205.

Angelakis I, Gooding PA, Panagioti M (2016). Suicidality in body dysmorphic disorder (BDD): A systematic review with meta-analysis. *Clinical Psychology Review* 49, 55-66.

Ara S, Ahad R (2016). Depression and suicidal ideation among older adults of Kashmir. *International Journal of Indian Psychology* 3, 137-145.

Arango A, Opperman KJ, Gipson PY, King CA (2016). Suicidal ideation and suicide attempts among youth who report bully victimization, bully perpetration and/or low social connectedness. *Journal of Adolescence* 51, 19-29.

Arias SA, Orianne D, Sullivan AF, Boudreaux ED, Miller I, Camargo CA (2016). Substance use as a mediator of the association between demographics, suicide attempt history, and future suicide attempts in emergency department patients. *Crisis*. Published online: 4 April 2016. doi: 10.1027/0227-5910/a000380.

Armiento J, Hamza CA, Stewart SL, Leschied A (2016). Direct and indirect forms of childhood maltreatment and nonsuicidal self-injury among clinically-referred children and youth. *Journal of Affective Disorders* 200, 212-217.

Ashrafioun L, Kane C, Stephens B, Britton PC, Conner KR (2016). Suicide attempts among alcohol-dependent pain patients before and after an inpatient hospitalization. *Drug and Alcohol Dependence* 163, 209-215.,

Auerbach RP, Stewart JG, Johnson SL (2016). Impulsivity and suicidality in adolescent inpatients. *Journal of Abnormal Child Psychology*. Published online: 30 March 2016. doi: 10.1007/s10802-016-0146-8.

Avci D, Selcuk KT, Do an S (2016). Suicide risk in the hospitalized elderly in Turkey and affecting factors. *Archives of Psychiatric Nursing*. Published online: 10 August 2016. doi: 10.1016/j.apnu.2016.08.002.

Aviad-Wilchek Y, Ne'eman-Haviv V, Malka M (2016). Connection between suicidal ideation, life meaning, and leisure time activities. *Deviant Behavior*. Published online: 8 September 2016. doi:10.1080/01639625.2016.1197590.

Backman O, Stockeld D, Rasmussen F, Näslund E, Marsk R (2016). Alcohol and substance abuse, depression and suicide attempts after Roux-en-Y gastric bypass surgery. *British Journal of Surgery* 103, 1336-1342.

Baker AW, Goetter EM, Bui E, Shah R, Charney ME, Mauro C, Shear MK, Simon NM (2016). The influence of anxiety sensitivity on a wish to die in complicated grief. *Journal of Nervous and Mental Disease* 204, 314-316.

Baldessarini RJ, Vazquez GH, Tondo L (2016). Affective temperaments and suicidal ideation and behavior in mood and anxiety disorder patients. *Journal of Affective Disorders* 198, 78-82.

Ballard ED, Vande Voort JL, Bernert RA, Luckenbaugh DA, Richards EM, Niciu MJ, Furey ML, Duncan WC, Zarate CA (2016). Nocturnal wakefulness is associated with next-day suicidal ideation in major depressive disorder and bipolar disorder. *Journal of Clinical Psychiatry* 77, 825-831.

Bantjes JR, Kagee A, McGowan T, Steel H (2016). Symptoms of posttraumatic stress, depression and anxiety as predictors of suicidal ideation among South African university students. *Journal of American College Health* 64, 429-437.

Barak-Corren Y, Castro VM, Javitt S, Hoffnagle AG, Dai Y, Perlis RH, Nock MK, Smoller JW, Reis BY (2016). Predicting suicidal behavior from longitudinal electronic health records. *American Journal of Psychiatry*. Published online: 9 September 2016. doi: 10.1176/appi.ajp.2016.16010077.

Barboza GE, Dominguez S, Chance E (2016). Physical victimization, gender identity and suicide risk among transgender men and women. *Preventive Medicine Reports* 4, 385-390.

Barr N, Fulginiti A, Rhoades H, Rice E (2016). Can better emotion regulation protect against suicidality in traumatized homeless youth? *Archives of Suicide Research*. Published online: 23 August 2016. doi: 10.1080/13811118.2016.1224989.

Barr NU, Sullivan K, Kintzle S, Castro CA (2016). PTSD symptoms, suicidality and non-suicidal risk to life behavior in a mixed sample of pre- and post-9/11 veterans. *Social Work in Mental Health* 14, 465-473.

Barrett JR, Shetty H, Broadbent M, Cross S, Hotopf M, Stewart R, Lee W (2016). 'He left me a message on Facebook': Comparing the risk profiles of self-harming patients who leave paper suicide notes with those who leave messages on new media. *BJPsych Open* 2, 217-220.

Barry LC, Wakefield DB, Trestman RL, Conwell Y (2016). Disability in prison activities of daily living and likelihood of depression and suicidal ideation in older prisoners. *International Journal of Geriatric Psychiatry*. Published online: 21 September 2016. doi: 10.1002/gps.4578.

Basharpoor S, Daneshvar S, Noori H (2016). The relation of self-compassion and anger control dimensions with suicide ideation in university students. *International Journal of High Risk Behaviors and Addiction*. Published online: 30 August 2016. doi: 10.5812/ijhrba.26165.

Baytunca MB, Ata E, Ozbaran B, Kaya A, Kose S, Aktas EO, Aydın R, Guney S, Yuncu Z, Erermis S, Bildik T, Aydin C (2016). Childhood sexual abuse and supportive factors. *Pediatrics International*. Published online: 11 June 2016. doi: 10.1111/ped.13065.

Becker SP, Withrow AR, Stoppelbein L, Luebbe AM, Fite PJ, Greening L (2016). Sluggish cognitive tempo is associated with suicide risk in psychiatrically hospitalized children. *Journal of Child Psychology and Psychiatry*. Published online: 1 June 2016. doi: 10.1111/jcpp.12580.

Beden O, Senol E, Atay S, Ak H, Altintoprak AE, Kiyan GS, Petin B, Yaman U, Aydin HH (2016). TPH1 A218 allele is associated with suicidal behavior in Turkish population. *Legal Medicine* 21, 15-18.

Benau EM, Jenkins AL, Conner BT (2016). Perceived parental monitoring and sexual orientation moderate lifetime acts of non-suicidal self-injury. *Archives of Suicide Research*. Published online: 2 May 2016. doi: 10.1080/13811118.2016.1182092.

Benute GRG, Bordini DCN, Juhas TR, Cabar FR, Pereira PP, Lucia MCSd, Francisco RPV (2016). Depression, stress and guilt are linked to the risk of suicide associated to ectopic pregnancy. *Medical Express* 3, M160307.

Beristianos MH, Maguen S, Neylan TC, Byers AL (2016). Trauma exposure and risk of suicidal ideation among older adults. *American Journal of Geriatric Psychiatry* 24, 639-643.

Berkol TD, İslam S, Kırlı E, Pınarbaşı R, Ozyildirim I (2016). Suicide attempts and clinical features of bipolar patients. *Saudi Medical Journal* 37, 662-667.

Besteher B, Wagner G, Koch K, Schachtzabel C, Reichenbach JR, Schlosser R, Sauer H, Schultz CC (2016). Pronounced prefronto-temporal cortical thinning in schizophrenia: Neuroanatomical correlate of suicidal behavior? *Schizophrenia Research* 173, 151-157.

Bethune A, da Costa L, van Niftrik CH, Feinstein A (2016). Suicidal ideation after mild traumatic brain injury: A consecutive Canadian sample. *Archives of Suicide Research*. Published online: 16 June 2016. doi: 10.1080/13811118.2016.1199990.

Beydoun HA, Williams M, Beydoun MA, Eid SM, Zonderman AB (2016). Relationship of physical intimate partner violence with mental health diagnoses in the nationwide emergency department sample. *Journal of Womens Health*. Published online: 10 August 2016. doi: 10.1089/jwh.2016.5840.

Bhatt-Poulose K, James K, Reid M, Harrison A, Asnani M (2016). Increased rates of body dissatisfaction, depressive symptoms, and suicide attempts in Jamaican teens with sickle cell disease. *Pediatric Blood & Cancer*. Published online: 9 July 2016. doi: 10.1002/pbc.26091.

Bhise MC, Behere PB (2016). A case-control study of psychological distress in survivors of farmers' suicides in Wardha district in Central India. *Indian Journal of Psychiatry* 58, 147-151.

Bjorkenstam E, Kosidou K, Bjorkenstam C (2016). Childhood household dysfunction and risk of self-harm: A cohort study of 107 518 young adults in Stockholm county. *International Journal of Epidemiology* 45, 501-511.

Black EB, Mildred H (2016). Characteristics of non-suicidal self-injury in women accessing internet help sites. *Clinical Psychologist*. Published online: 15 April 2016. doi: 10.1111/cp.12094.

Blasco-Fontecilla H, Rodrigo-Yanguas M, Giner L, Lobato-Rodriguez MJ, De Leon J (2016). Patterns of comorbidity of suicide attempters: An update. *Current Psychiatry Reports* 18, 93.

Blosnich JR, Brenner LA, Bossarte RM (2016). Population mental health among U.S. military veterans: Results of the veterans health module of the Behavioral Risk Factor Surveillance System, 2011-2012. *Annals of Epidemiology* 26, 592-596.

Blosnich JR, Marsiglio MC, Gao S, Gordon AJ, Shipherd JC, Kauth M, Brown GR, Fine MJ (2016). Mental health of transgender veterans in US states with and without discrimination and hate crime legal protection. *American Journal of Public Health* 106, 534-540.

Bodnar-Deren S, Klipstein K, Fersh M, Shemesh E, Howell EA (2016). Suicidal ideation during the postpartum period. *Journal of Womens Health*. Published online: 26 May 2016. doi: 10.1089/jwh.2015.5346.

Bogers ICHM, Zuidersma M, Boshuisen ML, Comijs HC, Oude Voshaar RC (2016). The influence of thoughts of death and suicidal ideation on the course of depression in older depressed patients. *International Journal of Geriatric Psychiatry*. Published online: 5 July 2016. doi: 10.1002/gps.4541.

Borges G, Cherpitel CJ, Orozco R, Ye Y, Monteiro M, Hao W, Benegal V (2016). A dose-response estimate for acute alcohol use and risk of suicide attempt. *Addiction Biology*. Published online: 10 August 2016. doi: 10.1111/adb.12439.

Bornheimer LA (2016). Moderating effects of positive symptoms of psychosis in suicidal ideation among adults diagnosed with schizophrenia. *Schizophrenia Research* 176, 364-370.

Bornheimer LA, Jaccard J (2016). Symptoms of depression, positive symptoms of psychosis, and suicidal ideation among adults diagnosed with schizophrenia within the clinical antipsychotic trials of intervention effectiveness (CATIE). *Archives of Suicide Research*. Published online: 23 August 2016. doi: 10.1080/13811118.2016.1224990.

Bozzay ML, Karver MS, Verona E (2016). Linking insomnia and suicide ideation in college females: The role of socio-cognitive variables and depressive symptoms in suicide risk. *Journal of Affective Disorders* 199, 106-113.

Brandt CP, Bakhshaie J, Jardin C, Lemaire C, Kauffman BY, Sharp C, Zvolensky MJ (2016). The moderating effect of smoking status on the relation between anxiety sensitivity, sexual compulsivity, and suicidality among people with HIV/AIDS. *International Journal of Behavioral Medicine*. Published online: 11 May 2016. doi: 10.1007/s12529-016-9568-5.

Brausch AM, Williams AG, Cox EM (2016). Examining intent to die and methods for nonsuicidal self-injury and suicide attempts. *Suicide and Life-Threatening Behavior*. Published online: 25 April 2016. doi: 10.1111/sltb.12262.

Breton JJ, Labelle R, Berthiaume C, Royer C, St-Georges M, Ricard D, Abadie P, Gérardin P, Cohen D, Guilé JM (2015). Protective factors against depression and suicidal behaviour in adolescence. *Canadian Journal of Psychiatry* 60, S5-S15.

Briere J, Eadie EM (2016). Compensatory self-injury: Posttraumatic stress, depression, and the role of dissociation. *Psychological Trauma* 8, 618-625.

Brodsky BS (2016). Early childhood environment and genetic interactions: The diathesis for suicidal behavior. *Current Psychiatry Reports* 18, e86.

Brown LA, Armey MA, Sejourne C, Miller IW, Weinstock LM (2016). Trauma history is associated with prior suicide attempt history in hospitalized patients with major depressive disorder. *Psychiatry Research* 243, 191-197.

Brundin L, Sellgren CM, Lim CK, Grit J, Palsson E, Landen M, Samuelsson M, Lundgren K, Brundin P, Fuchs D, Postolache TT, Traskman-Bendz L, Guillemin GJ, Erhardt S (2016). An enzyme in the kynurenine pathway that governs vulnerability to suicidal behavior by regulating excitotoxicity and neuroinflammation. *Translational Psychiatry* 6, e865.

Bryan ABO, Bryan CJ, Morrow CE, Etienne N, Sannerud BR (2014). Moral injury, suicidal ideation, and suicide attempts in a military sample. *Traumatology* 20, 154-160.

Bryan CJ (2016). Treating PTSD within the context of heightened suicide risk. *Current Psychiatry Reports* 18, 73.

Bryan CJ, Garland EL, Rudd MD (2016). From impulse to action among military personnel hospitalized for suicide risk: Alcohol consumption and the reported transition from suicidal thought to behavior. *General Hospital Psychiatry* 41, 13-19.

Bryan CJ, Rudd MD (2015). Demographic and diagnostic differences among suicide ideators, single attempters, and multiple attempters among military personnel and veterans receiving outpatient mental health care. *Military Behavioral Health* 3, 289-295.

Bryan CJ, Rudd MD, Peterson AL, Young-McCaughan S, Wertenberger EG (2016). The ebb and flow of the wish to live and the wish to die among suicidal military personnel. *Journal of Affective Disorders* 202, 58-66.

Bryan CJ, Rudd MD, Wertenberger E (2016). Individual and environmental contingencies associated with multiple suicide attempts among U.S. Military personnel. *Psychiatry Research* 242, 88-93.

Bryan CJ, Sinclair S, Heron EA (2016). Do military personnel "acquire" the capability for suicide from combat? A test of the interpersonal-psychological theory of suicide. *Clinical Psychological Science* 4, 376-385.

Bryant RA, O'Donnell ML, Forbes D, McFarlane AC, Silove D, Creamer M (2016). The course of suicide risk following traumatic injury. *Journal of Clinical Psychiatry* 77, 648-653.

Burk T, Sampilo ML, Wendling T, Nguyen C, Piatt J (2016). Prescription drug misuse and associated risk behaviors among public high school students in Oklahoma: Data from the 2013 Oklahoma Youth Risk Behavior Survey. *The Journal of the Oklahoma State Medical Association* 109, 103-110.

Burke TA, Hamilton JL, Ammerman BA, Stange JP, Alloy LB (2016). Suicide risk characteristics among aborted, interrupted, and actual suicide attempters. *Psychiatry Research* 242, 357-364.

Byun J, Kim H-R, Lee H-E, Kim S-E, Lee J (2016). Factors associated with suicide ideation among subway drivers in Korea. *Annals of Occupational and Environmental Medicine* 28, e31.

Campos RC, Holden RR, Costa F, Oliveira AR, Abreu M, Fresca N (2016). The moderating effect of gender on the relationship between coping and suicide risk in a Portuguese community sample of adults. *Journal of Mental Health*. Published online: 20 September 2016. doi: 10.1080/09638237.2016.1222066.

Canal-Rivero M, Barrigón ML, Perona-Garcelán S, Rodriguez-Testal JF, Giner L, Obiols-Llandrich JE, Ruiz-Veguilla M (2016). One-year follow-up study of first suicide attempts in first episode psychosis: Personality traits and temporal pattern. *Comprehensive Psychiatry* 71, 121-129.

Cao J, Chen X, Chen J, Ai M, Gan Y, Wang W, Lv Z, Zhang S, Zhang S, Wang S, Kuang L, Fang W (2016). Resting-state functional MRI of abnormal baseline brain activity in young depressed patients with and without suicidal behavior. *Journal of Affective Disorders* 205, 252-263.

Carroll R, Corcoran P, Griffin E, Perry I, Arensman E, Gunnell D, Metcalfe C (2016). Variation between hospitals in inpatient admission practices for self-harm patients and its impact on repeat presentation. *Social Psychiatry and Psychiatric Epidemiology*. Published online: 14 June 2016. doi: 10.1007/s00127-016-1247-y.

Carter JM, Arentsen TJ, Cordova MJ, Ruzek J, Reiser R, Suppes T, Ostacher MJ (2016). Increased suicidal ideation in patients with co-occurring bipolar disorder and posttraumatic stress disorder. *Archives of Suicide Research*. Published online: 16 June 2016. doi: 10.1080/13811118.2016.1199986.

Catchpole REH, Brownlie EB (2016). Characteristics of youth presenting to a Canadian youth concurrent disorders program: Clinical complexity, trauma, adaptive functioning and treatment priorities. *Journal of the Canadian Academy of Child and Adolescent Psychiatry* 25, 106-115.

Cerel J, Frey LM, Maple M, Kinner DG (2016). Parents with suicidal behavior: Parenting is not always protective. *Journal of Child and Family Studies* 25, 2327-2336.

Cha C, Nam SJ (2016). Premenstrual symptom clusters and women's coping style in Korea: Happy healthy 20s application study. *Journal of Psychosomatic Obstetrics and Gynaecology* 37, 91-100.

Chan LF, Mohamad Adam B, Norazlin KN, Siti Haida MI, Lee VY, Norazura AW, Ek Zakuan K, Tan SMK (2016). Suicidal ideation among single, pregnant adolescents: The role of sexual and religious knowledge, attitudes and practices. *Journal of Adolescence* 52, 162-169.

Chan YY, Lim KH, Teh CH, Kee CC, Ghazali SM, Lim KK, Khoo YY, Tee EO, Ahmad NA, Ibrahim N (2016). Prevalence and risk factors associated with suicidal ideation among adolescents in Malaysia. *International Journal of Adolescence Medicine and Health*. Published online: 5 August 2016. doi: 10.1515/ijamh-2016-0053.

Chang BP, Franklin JC, Ribeiro JD, Fox KR, Bentley KH, Kleiman EM, Nock MK (2016). Biological risk factors for suicidal behaviors: A meta-analysis. *Translational Psychiatry* 6, e887.

Chang BP, Sano ED, Suh EH, Tichter A (2016). Demographic characteristics of individuals admitted to the hospital for suicidal ideation in the emergency department. *American Journal of Emergency Medicine* 34, 1174-1175.

Chang EC, Yu EA, Yu T, Kahle ER, Hernandez V, Kim JM, Jeglic EL, Hirsch JK (2016). Ethnic variables and negative life events as predictors of depressive symptoms and suicidal behaviors in latino college students: On the centrality of Receptivo a los Demas. *Hispanic Journal of Behavioral Sciences* 38, 206-221.

Chartrand H, Kim H, Sareen J, Mahmoudi M, Bolton JM (2016). A comparison of methods of self-harm without intent to die: Cutting versus self-poisoning. *Journal of Affective Disorders* 205, 200-206.

Chaudhury SR, Singh T, Burke A, Stanley B, Mann JJ, Grunebaum M, Sublette ME, Oquendo MA (2016). Clinical correlates of planned and unplanned suicide attempts. *Journal of Nervous and Mental Disease.* Published online: 22 April 2016. doi: 10.1097/NMD.0000000000000502.

Cheung T, Yip PSF (2016). Self-harm in nurses: Prevalence and correlates. *Journal of Advanced Nursing.* Published online: 28 April 2016. doi: 10.1111/jan.12987.

Ching TH, Williams M, Siev J (2016). Violent obsessions are associated with suicidality in an OCD analog sample of college students. *Cognitive Behaviour Therapy.* Published online: 23 Sep 2016. doi: 10.1080/16506073.2016.1228084.

Chisholm A, Pearce CJ, Chinoy H, Warren RB, Bundy C (2016). Distress, misperceptions, poor coping and suicidal ideation in psoriatic arthritis: A qualitative study. *Rheumatology* 55, 1047-1052.

Chiurliza B, Michaels MS, Joiner TE (2016). Acquired capability for suicide among individuals with American Indian/Alaska Native backgrounds within the military. *American Indian and Alaska Native Mental Health Research* 23, 1-15.

Christodoulou C, Efstathiou V, Ferentinos P, Poulios A, Papadopoulou A, Douzenis A (2016). Comparative study of hostility in depressive patients with and without a suicide attempt history. *Psychology, Health and Medicine.* Published online: 22 September 2016. doi: 10.1080/13548506.2016.1238491.

Chu C, Hom MA, Rogers ML, Ringer FB, Hames JL, Suh S, Joiner TE (2016). Is insomnia lonely? Exploring thwarted belongingness as an explanatory link between insomnia and suicidal ideation in a sample of South Korean university students. *Journal of Clinical Sleep Medicine* 12, 647-652.

Chung JH, Kim JB, Kim JH (2016). Suicidal ideation and attempts in patients with stroke: A population-based study. *Journal of Neurology* 263, 2032-2038.

Claes L, De Raedt R, Van de Walle M, Bosmans G (2016). Attentional bias moderates the link between attachment-related expectations and non-suicidal self-injury. *Cognitive Therapy and Research* 40, 540-548.

Clark CB, Li Y, Cropsey KL (2016). Family dysfunction and suicide risk in a community corrections sample. *Crisis.* Published online: 22 July 2016. doi: 10.1027/0227-5910/a000406.

Coelho BM, Andrade LH, Borges G, Santana GL, Viana MC, Wang YP (2016). Do childhood adversities predict suicidality? Findings from the general population of the metropolitan area of Sao Paulo, Brazil. *PLoS One* 11, e0155639.

Collins PY, Kondos L, Pillai A, Joestl SS, Frohlich J (2016). Passive suicidal ideation and community mental health resources in South Africa. *Community Mental Health Journal* 52, 541-550.

Collins SE, Taylor EM, King VL, Hatsukami AS, Jones MB, Lee C-Y, Lenert J, Jing JM, Barker CR, Goldstein SC, Hardy RV, Kaese G, Nelson LA (2016). Suicidality among chronically homeless people with alcohol problems attenuates following exposure to housing first. *Suicide and Life-Threatening Behavior*. Published online: 8 April 2016. doi: 10.1111/sltb.12250.

Comtois KA, Chalker SA, Kerbrat AH (2016). Pre- versus postenlistment timing of first suicide attempt as a predictor of suicide risk factors in an active duty military population with suicidal thoughts. *Military Behavioral Health*. Published online: 16 March 2016. doi: 10.1080/21635781.2015.1133344.

Conlin S, Littlechild J, Aditya H, Bahia H (2016). Surgical and psychiatric profile of patients who self-harm by burning in a regional burn unit over an 11-year period. *Scottish Medical Journal* 61, 17-25.

Connell M, Betts K, McGrath JJ, Alati R, Najman J, Clavarino A, Mamun A, Williams G, Scott JG (2016). Hallucinations in adolescents and risk for mental disorders and suicidal behaviour in adulthood: Prospective evidence from the MUSP birth cohort study. *Schizophrenia Research* 176, 546-551.

Coryell W, Yolken R, Butcher B, Burns T, Dindo L, Schlechte J, Calarge C (2016). Toxoplasmosis titers and past suicide attempts among older adolescents initiating SSRI treatment. *Archives of Suicide Research* 20, 605-613.

Coulter RW, Kessel Schneider S, Beadnell B, O'Donnell L (2016). Associations of outside- and within-school adult support on suicidality: Moderating effects of sexual orientation. *American Journal of Orthopsychiatry*. Published online: 5 September 2016. doi: 10.1037/ort0000209.

Courtemanche AB, Black WR, Reese RM (2016). The relationship between pain, self-injury, and other problem behaviors in young children with autism and other developmental disabilities. *American Journal on Intellectual and Developmental Disabilities* 121, 194-203.

Crane MF, Phillips JK, Karin E (2016). "I've been a long time leaving": The role of limited skill transferability in increasing suicide-related cognitions and behavior in veterinarians. *Suicide and Life-Threatening Behavior*. Published online: 12 July 2016. doi: 10.1111/sltb.12279.

Cristancho P, O'Connor B, Lenze EJ, Blumberger DM, Reynolds CF, 3rd, Dixon D, Mulsant BH (2016). Treatment emergent suicidal ideation in depressed older adults. *International Journal of Geriatric Psychiatry*. Published online: 9 May 2016. doi: 10.1002/gps.4498.

Curtis C (2016). Young women's experiences of self-harm commonalities, distinctions and complexities. *Young* 24, 17-35.

Cyprien F, de Champfleur NM, Deverdun J, Olié E, Le Bars E, Bonafé A, Mura T, Jollant F, Courtet P, Artero S (2016). Corpus callosum integrity is affected by mood disorders and also by the suicide attempt history: A diffusion tensor imaging study. *Journal of Affective Disorders* 206, 115-124.

Czyz EK, Horwitz AG, King CA (2016). Self-rated expectations of suicidal behavior predict future suicide attempts among adolescent and young adult psychiatric emergency patients. *Depression and Anxiety* 33, 512-519.

Daray FM, Rojas SM, Bridges AJ, Badour CL, Grendas L, Rodante D, Puppo S, Rebok F (2016). The independent effects of child sexual abuse and impulsivity on lifetime suicide attempts among female patients. *Child Abuse and Neglect* 58, 91-98.

Davidson M, Werbeloff N, Levav I, Dohrenwend BP, Burshtein S, Weiser M (2016). Religiosity as a protective factor against suicidal behaviour. *Acta Psychiatrica Scandinavica* 133, 481-488.

de Almeida SM, Barbosa FJ, Kamat R, de Pereira AP, Raboni SM, Rotta I, Ribeiro CE, Cherner M, Ellis RJ, Atkinson JH (2016). Suicide risk and prevalence of major depressive disorder (MDD) among individuals infected with HIV-1 subtype C versus B in Southern Brazil. *Journal of Neurovirology*. Published online: 18 July 2016. doi: 10.1007/s13365-016-0454-3.

de Araujo RM, Lara DR (2016). More than words: The association of childhood emotional abuse and suicidal behavior. *European Psychiatry* 37, 14-21.

Decou CR, Lynch SM, Dehart DD, Belknap J (2016). Evaluating the association between childhood sexual abuse and attempted suicide across the lifespan: Findings from a nationwide study of women in jail. *Psychological Services* 13, 254-260.

DeVylder JE, Kelleher I (2016). Clinical significance of psychotic experiences in the context of sleep disturbance or substance use. *Psychological Medicine* 46, 1761-1767.

Diaz-Caneja CM, Pina-Camacho L, Rodriguez-Quiroga A, Fraguas D, Parellada M, Arango C (2015). Predictors of outcome in early-onset psychosis: A systematic review. *Npj Schizophrenia* 1, 14005.

Diaz-Frutos D, Baca-Garcia E, Garcia-Foncillas J, Lopez-Castroman J (2016). Predictors of psychological distress in advanced cancer patients under palliative treatments. *European Journal of Cancer Care* 25, 608-615.

Dillard DA, Avey JP, Robinson RF, Smith JJ, Beals J, Manson SM, Comtois KA (2016). Demographic, clinical, and service utilization factors associated with suicide-related visits among Alaska Native and American Indian adults. *Suicide and Life-Threatening Behavior.* Published online: 25 April 2016. doi: 10.1111/sltb.12259.

Dirkes J, Hughes T, Ramirez-Valles J, Johnson T, Bostwick W (2016). Sexual identity development: Relationship with lifetime suicidal ideation in sexual minority women. *Journal of Clinical Nursing.* Published online: 1 August 2016. doi: 10.1111/jocn.13313.

Distel MA, Smit JH, Spinhoven P, Penninx BWJH (2016). Borderline personality features in depressed or anxious patients. *Psychiatry Research* 241, 224-231.

Dogan B, Canturk G, Canturk N, Guney S, Özcan E (2016). Assessment of private security guards by suicide probability scale and brief symptom inventory. *Rivista Di Psichiatria* 51, 72-78.

Doki S, Kaneko H, Oi Y, Usami K, Sasahara S, Matsuzaki I (2016). Risk factors for suicidal ideation among telephone crisis hotline callers in Japan. *Crisis.* Published online: 1 June 2016. doi: 10.1027/0227-5910/a000384.

Doorley J, Williams C, Mallard T, Esposito-Smythers C, McGeary J (2016). Sexual trauma, the dopamine D4 receptor, and suicidal ideation among hospitalized adolescents: A preliminary investigation. *Archives of Suicide Research.* Published online: 7 June 2016. doi: 10.1080/13811118.2016.1166089.

Doyle M, While D, Mok PLH, Windfuhr K, Ashcroft DM, Kontopantelis E, Chew-Graham CA, Appleby L, Shaw J, Webb RT (2016). Suicide risk in primary care patients diagnosed with a personality disorder: A nested case control study. *BMC Family Practice* 17, e106.

Drennan V (2016). How parents react when their children self-harm. *Primary Health Care* 26, 13.

Drum DJ, Brownson C, Hess EA, Burton Denmark A, Talley AE (2016). College students' sense of coherence and connectedness as predictors of suicidal thoughts and behaviors. *Archives of Suicide Research.* Published online: 6 April 2016. doi: 10.1080/13811118.2016.1166088.

Dudeck M, Sosic-Vasic Z, Otte S, Rasche K, Leichauer K, Tippelt S, Shenar R, Klingner S, Vasic N, Streb J (2016). The association of adverse childhood experiences and appetitive aggression with suicide attempts and violent crimes in male forensic psychiatry inpatients. *Psychiatry Research* 240, 352-357.

Eberhard J, Weiller E (2016). Suicidality and symptoms of anxiety, irritability, and agitation in patients experiencing manic episodes with depressive symptoms: A naturalistic study. *Neuropsychiatric Disease and Treatment* 12, 2265-2271.

Egeberg A, Hansen PR, Gislason GH, Skov L, Mallbris L (2016). Risk of self-harm and non-fatal suicide attempts, and completed suicide in patients with psoriasis - a population-based cohort study. *British Journal of Dermatology* 175, 493-500.

Eisen RB, Perera S, Bawor M, Dennis BB, El-Sheikh W, Dejesus J, Rangarajan S, Vair J, Sholer H, Hutchinson N, Iordan E, Mackie P, Islam S, Dehghan M, Brasch J, Anglin R, Minuzzi L, Thabane L, Samaan Z (2016). Exploring the association between serum BDNF and attempted suicide. *Scientific Reports* 6, 25229.

Eisenberg ME, McMorris BJ, Gower AL, Chatterjee D (2016). Bullying victimization and emotional distress: Is there strength in numbers for vulnerable youth? *Journal of Psychosomatic Research* 86, 13-19.

Elkins RL, King K, Nabors L, Vidourek R (2016). Steroid use and school violence, school violent victimization, and suicidal ideation among adolescents. *Journal of School Violence*. Published online: 15 March 2016. doi: 10.1080/15388220.2016.1159574.

Ellis TE, Rufino KA (2016). Change in experiential avoidance is associated with reduced suicidal ideation over the course of psychiatric hospitalization. *Archives of Suicide Research* 20, 426-437.

Emery AA, Heath NL, Mills DJ (2016). The role of basic need satisfaction in the onset, maintenance, and cessation of non-suicidal self-injury: An application of self-determination theory. *Archives of Suicide Research*. Published online: 20 July 2016. doi: 10.1080/13811118.2016.1211043.

Fairweather-Schmidt AK, Batterham PJ, Butterworth P, Nada-Raja S (2016). The impact of suicidality on health-related quality of life: A latent growth curve analysis of community-based data. *Journal of Affective Disorders* 203, 14-21.

Fanning JR, Lee R, Coccaro EF (2016). Comorbid intermittent explosive disorder and posttraumatic stress disorder: Clinical correlates and relationship to suicidal behavior. *Comprehensive Psychiatry* 70, 125-133.

Fatemi AB, Graff A, Zai C, Strauss J, De Luca V (2016). GWAS analysis of suicide attempt in schizophrenia: Main genetic effect and interaction with early life trauma. *Neuroscience Letters* 27, 102-106.

Feng CX, Waldner C, Cushon J, Davy K, Neudorf C (2016). Suicidal ideation in a community-based sample of elementary school children: A multilevel and spatial analysis. *Canadian Journal of Public Health* 107, e100-e105.

Finkelstein Y, Macdonald EM, Hollands S, Sivilotti ML, Hutson JR, Mamdani MM, Koren G, Juurlink DN (2016). Repetition of intentional drug overdose: A population-based study. *Clinical Toxicology* 54, 585-589.

Fisher K, Houtsma C, Assavedo BL, Green BA, Anestis MD (2016). Agitation as a moderator of the relationship between insomnia and current suicidal ideation in the military. *Archives of Suicide Research*. Published online: 19 July 2016. doi: 10.1080/13811118.2016.1193077.

Forrest LN, Zuromski KL, Dodd DR, Smith AR (2016). Suicidality in adolescents and adults with binge-eating disorder: Results from the national comorbidity survey replication and adolescent supplement. *International Journal of Eating Disorders*. Published online: 20 July 2016. doi: 0.1002/eat.22582.

Fortuna LR, Alvarez K, Ramos Ortiz Z, Wang Y, Mozo Alegria X, Cook BL, Alegria M (2016). Mental health, migration stressors and suicidal ideation among Latino immigrants in Spain and the United States. *European Psychiatry* 36, 15-22.

Foster KT, Li N, McClure EA, Sonne SC, Gray KM (2016). Gender differences in internalizing symptoms and suicide risk among men and women seeking treatment for cannabis use disorder from late adolescence to middle adulthood. *Journal of Substance Abuse Treatment* 66, 16-22.

Fox-Thomas LG (2016). Suicidal ideation among patients with chronic tinnitus. *Hearing Journal* 69, 10-11.

Fox C (2016). A preliminary investigation into counselling student attitudes towards self-harming behaviour. *Counselling and Psychotherapy Research* 16, 119-122.

Freitas-Rosa M, Gonçalves S, Antunes H (2016). Is being overweight associated with engagement in self-injurious behaviours in adolescence, or do psychological factors have more "weight"? *Eating and Weight Disorders* 21, 493-500.

Fresan N, Camarena B, Gonzalez-Castro TB, Tovilla-Zarate CA, Juarez-Rojop IE, Lopez-Narvaez L, Gonzalez-Ramon AE, Hernandez-Diaz Y (2016). Risk-factor differences for nonsuicidal self-injury and suicide attempts in Mexican psychiatric patients. *Neuropsychiatric Disease and Treatment* 12, 1631-1637.

Fulginiti A, Brekke JS (2016). Suicide attempt status and quality of life disparity among individuals with schizophrenia: A longitudinal analysis. *Journal of the Society for Social Work and Research* 7, 269-288.

Fulginiti A, Rice E, Hsu HT, Rhoades H, Winetrobe H (2016). Risky integration. *Crisis* 37, 184-193.

Fuller-Thomson E, Baird SL, Dhrodia R, Brennenstuhl S (2016). The association between adverse childhood experiences (ACEs) and suicide attempts in a population-based study. *Child: Care, Health and Development* 42, 725-734.

Fuller-Thomson E, Hollister B (2016). Schizophrenia and suicide attempts: Findings from a representative community-based Canadian sample. *Schizophrenia Research and Treatment* 2016, 3165243.

Fuller-Thomson E, Ramzan N, Baird SL (2016). Arthritis and suicide attempts: Findings from a large nationally representative Canadian survey. *Rheumatology International* 36, 1237-1248.

Gandhi A, Luyckx K, Goossens L, Maitra S, Claes L (2016). Sociotropy, autonomy, and non-suicidal self-injury: The mediating role of identity confusion. *Personality and Individual Differences* 99, 272-277.

Gandhi A, Luyckx K, Maitra S, Kiekens G, Claes L (2016). Reactive and regulative temperament and non-suicidal self-injury in Flemish adolescents: The intervening role of identity formation. *Personality and Individual Differences* 99, 254-259.

Ganocy SJ, Goto T, Chan PK, Cohen GH, Sampson L, Galea S, Liberzon I, Fine T, Shirley E, Sizemore J, Calabrese JR, Tamburrino MB (2016). Association of spirituality with mental health conditions in Ohio National Guard Soldiers. *Journal of Nervous and Mental Disease* 204, 524-529.

Gaskin-Wasson AL, Walker KL, Shin LJ, Kaslow NJ (2016). Spiritual well-being and psychological adjustment: Mediated by interpersonal needs? *Journal of Religion and Health*. Published online: 4 July 2016. doi: 10.1007/s10943-016-0275-y.

Gauthier JM, Witte TK, Correia CJ (2016). Suicide ideation, alcohol consumption, motives, and related problems: Exploring the association in college students. *Suicide and Life-Threatening Behavior*. Published online: 13 June 2016. doi: 10.1111/sltb.12269.

Gaynor SC, Breen ME, Monson ET, de Klerk K, Parsons M, DeLuca AP, Scheetz TE, Zandi PP, Potash JB, Willour VL (2016). A targeted sequencing study of glutamatergic candidate genes in suicide attempters with bipolar disorder. *American Journal of Medical Genetics B: Neuropsychiatric Genetics*. Published online: 2 August 2016. doi: 10.1002/ajmg.b.32479.

Gesi C, Carmassi C, Miniati M, Benvenuti A, Massimetti G, Dell'osso L (2016). Psychotic spectrum symptoms across the lifespan are related to lifetime suicidality among 147 patients with bipolar I or major depressive disorder. *Annals of General Psychiatry* 15, e15.

Geulayov G, Metcalfe C, Gunnell D (2016). Parental suicide attempt and offspring educational attainment during adolescence in the Avon Longitudinal Study of Parents and Children (ALSPAC) birth cohort. *Psychological Medicine* 46, 2097-2107.

Ghanem M, El-Serafi D, Sabry W, El Rasheed AH, Razek GA, Soliman A, Amar W (2016). Executive dysfunctions in borderline personality disorder: Correlation with suicidality and impulsivity. *Middle East Current Psychiatry* 23, 85-92.

Gibbs HM, Davis L, Han X, Clothier J, Eads LA, Caceda R (2016). Association between C-reactive protein and suicidal behavior in an adult inpatient population. *Journal of Psychiatric Research* 79, 28-33.

Gili M, Peake C, Castro A, Homar C, Roca M (2016). Suicidal ideation in depressive patients: Rates and predictors before and during economic crisis in Spain. *Medicina Balear* 31, 30-36.

Gilreath TD (2016). Perceived support, substance use, suicidal ideation, and psychological distress among military-connected adolescents. *Military Behavioral Health* 4, 1-7.

Gim W, Yoo J-H, Shin J-Y, Goo A-J (2016). Relationship between secondhand smoking with depressive symptom and suicidal ideation in Korean non-smoker adults: The Korean National Health and Nutrition Examination Survey 2010-2012. *Korean Journal of Family Medicine* 37, 97-104.

Gjelsvik B, Heyerdahl F, Holmes J, Lunn D, Hawton K (2016). Looking back on self-poisoning: The relationship between depressed mood and reporting of suicidal intent in people who deliberately self-poison. *Suicide and Life-Threatening Behavior.* Published online: 15 July 2016. doi: 10.1111/sltb.12278.

Goldmann E, Roberts ET, Parikh NS, Boden-Albala B (2016). Chronic physical illness burden and suicidal ideation among Dominicans in New York City. *Journal of Immigrant and Minority Health.* Published online: 9 August 2016. doi: 10.1007/s10903-016-0477-0.

Goldston DB, Erkanli A, Daniel SS, Heilbron N, Weller B, Doyle O (2016). Developmental trajectories of suicidal thoughts and behaviors from adolescence through adulthood. *Journal of the American Academy of Child and Adolescent Psychiatry* 55, 400-407.

Gómez-Expósito A, Wolz I, Fagundo AB, Granero R, Steward T, Jimenez-Murcia S, Agüera Z, Fernández-Aranda F (2016). Correlates of non-suicidal self-injury and suicide attempts in bulimic spectrum disorders. *Frontiers in Psychology* 7, 1244.

Goncalves S, Machado BC, Martins C, Hoek HW, Machado PPP (2016). Retrospective correlates for bulimia nervosa: A matched case-control study. *European Eating Disorders Review* 24, 197-205.

Gooding PA, Tarrier N, Dunn G, Awenat Y, Shaw J, Ulph F, Pratt D (2016). Psychological characteristics and predictors of suicide probability in high-risk prisoners. *Criminal Justice and Behavior.* Published online: 19 May 2016. doi: 10.1177/0093854816650478.

Gorodetsky E, Carli V, Sarchiapone M, Roy A, Goldman D, Enoch MA (2016). Predictors for self-directed aggression in Italian prisoners include externalizing behaviors, childhood trauma and the serotonin transporter gene polymorphism 5-httlpr. *Genes, Brain and Behavior* 15, 465-473.

Gramaglia C, Feggi A, Bergamasco P, Bert F, Gattoni E, Marangon D, Siliquini R, Torre E, Zeppegno P (2016). Clinical characteristics associated with suicide attempts in clinical settings: A comparison of suicidal and non-suicidal depressed inpatients. *Frontiers in Psychiatry* 7, e109.

Groschwitz RC, Plener PL, Groen G, Bonenberger M, Abler B (2016). Differential neural processing of social exclusion in adolescents with non-suicidal self-injury: An fMRI study. *Psychiatry Research* 255, 43-49.

Grover S, Sarkar S, Bhalla A, Chakrabarti S, Avasthi A (2016). Demographic, clinical and psychological characteristics of patients with self-harm behaviours attending an emergency department of a tertiary care hospital. *Asian Journal of Psychiatry* 20, 3-10.

Grover S, Sarkar S, Bhalla A, Chakrabarti S, Avasthi A (2016). Religious coping among self-harm attempters brought to emergency setting in India. *Asian Journal of Psychiatry* 23, 78-86.

Guillou-Landreat M, Guilleux A, Sauvaget A, Brisson L, Leboucher J, Remaud M, Challet-Bouju G, Grall-Bronnec M (2016). Factors associated with suicidal risk among a French cohort of problem gamblers seeking treatment. *Psychiatry Research* 240, 11-18.

Guo L, Xu Y, Deng J, Huang J, Huang G, Gao X, Wu H, Pan S, Zhang WH, Lu C (2016). Association between nonmedical use of prescription drugs and suicidal behavior among adolescents. *JAMA Pediatrics*. Published online: 15 August 2016. doi: 10.1001/jamapediatrics.2016.1802.

Gyorffy Z, Dweik D, Girasek E (2016). Workload, mental health and burnout indicators among female physicians. *Human Resources for Health* 14, 12.

Haberstick BC, Boardman JD, Wagner B, Smolen A, Hewitt JK, Killeya-Jones LA, Tabor J, Halpern CT, Brummett BH, Williams RB, Siegler IC, Hopfer CJ, Mullan Harris K (2016). Depression, stressful life events, and the impact of variation in the serotonin transporter: Findings from the National Longitudinal Study of Adolescent to Adult Health (ADD Health). *PLoS One* 11, e0148373.

Hackett C, Feeny D, Tompa E (2016). Canada's residential school system: Measuring the intergenerational impact of familial attendance on health and mental health outcomes. *Journal of Epidemiology and Community Health*. Published online: 11 May 2016. doi: 10.1136/jech-2016-207380.

Hagan CR, Joiner TE (2016). The indirect effect of perceived criticism on suicide ideation and attempts. *Archives of Suicide Research*. Published online: 3 August 2016. doi: 10.1080/13811118.2016.1218398.

Hamza CA, Willoughby T (2016). Nonsuicidal self-injury and suicidal risk among emerging adults. *Journal of Adolescent Health* 59, 411-415.

Han B, Compton WM, Blanco C (2016). Tobacco use and 12-month suicidality among adults in the United States. *Nicotine & Tobacco Research*. Published online: 17 May 2016. doi: 10.1093/ntr/ntw136.

Han B, Crosby AE, Ortega LAG, Parks SE, Compton WM, Gfroerer J (2016). Suicidal ideation, suicide attempt, and occupations among employed adults aged 18-64years in the United States. *Comprehensive Psychiatry* 66, 176-186.

Harford TC, Chen CM, Grant BF (2016). Other- and self-directed forms of violence and their relationship with number of substance use disorder criteria among youth ages 12–17: Results from the National Survey on Drug Use and Health. *Journal of Studies on Alcohol and Drugs* 77, 277-286.

Harolds JA, Parikh JR, Bluth EI, Dutton SC, Recht MP (2016). Burnout of radiologists: Frequency, risk factors, and remedies: A report of the ACR commission on human resources. *Journal of the American College of Radiology* 13, 411-416.

Harris KM, Goh MT (2016). Is suicide assessment harmful to participants? Findings from a randomized controlled trial. *International Journal of Mental Health Nursing*. Published online: 16 April 2016. doi: 10.1111/inm.12223.

Hassan AN, Stuart EA, De Luca V (2016). Childhood maltreatment increases the risk of suicide attempt in schizophrenia. *Schizophrenia Research* 176, 572-577.

Hazlett EA, Blair NJ, Fernandez N, Mascitelli K, Perez-Rodriguez MM, New AS, Goetz RR, Goodman M (2016). Startle amplitude during unpleasant pictures is greater in veterans with a history of multiple-suicide attempts and predicts a future suicide attempt. *Psychophysiology* 53, 1524-1534.

He T, Wan Y, Zhang C (2016). Mediating effect of psychological symptoms on the relationship between childhood abuses and non-suicidal self-injuries among medical college students. *Wei Sheng Yan Jiu* 45, 200-204.

Heath NL, Joly M, Carsley D (2016). Coping self-efficacy and mindfulness in non-suicidal self-injury. *Mindfulness* 7, 1132-1141.

Hedeland RL, Teilmann G, Jorgensen MH, Thiesen LR, Andersen J (2016). Risk factors and characteristics of suicide attempts among 381 suicidal adolescents. *Acta Paediatrica*. Published online: 31 May 2016. doi: 10.1111/apa.13458.

Heisel MJ, Flett GL (2016). Does recognition of meaning in life confer resiliency to suicide ideation among community-residing older adults? A longitudinal investigation. *American Journal of Geriatric Psychiatry* 24, 455-466.

Herberman Mash HB, Fullerton CS, Ng TH, Nock MK, Wynn GH, Ursano RJ (2016). Alcohol use and reasons for drinking as risk factors for suicidal behavior in the U.S. Army. *Military Medicine* 181, 811-820.

Hernández Blázquez M, Cruzado JA (2016). A longitudinal study on anxiety, depressive and adjustment disorder, suicide ideation and symptoms of emotional distress in patients with cancer undergoing radiotherapy. *Journal of Psychosomatic Research* 87, 14-21.

Heslin M, Lappin JM, Donoghue K, Lomas B, Reininghaus U, Onyejiaka A, Croudace T, Jones PB, Murray RM, Fearon P, Doody GA, Dazzan P, Craig TJ, Morgan C (2016). Ten-year outcomes in first episode psychotic major depression patients compared with schizophrenia and bipolar patients. *Schizophrenia Research* 176, 417-422.

Hickmann AK, Nadji-Ohl M, Haug M, Hopf NJ, Ganslandt O, Giese A, Renovanz M (2016). Suicidal ideation, depression, and health-related quality of life in patients with benign and malignant brain tumors: A prospective observational study in 83 patients. *Acta Neurochirurgica* 158, 1669-1682.

Higgins A, Doyle L, Downes C, Morrissey J, Costello P, Brennan M, Nash M (2016). There is more to risk and safety planning than dramatic risks: Mental health nurses' risk assessment and safety-management practice. *International Journal of Mental Health Nursing* 25, 159-170.

Hollingshaus MS, Coon H, Crowell SE, Gray DD, Hanson HA, Pimentel R, Smith KR (2016). Differential vulnerability to early-life parental death: The moderating effects of family suicide history on risks for major depression and substance abuse in later life. *Biodemography and Social Biology* 62, 105-125.

Hom MA, Lim IC, Stanley IH, Chiurliza B, Podlogar MC, Michaels MS, Buchman-Schmitt JM, Silva C, Ribeiro JD, Joiner TE, Jr. (2016). Insomnia brings soldiers into mental health treatment, predicts treatment engagement, and outperforms other suicide-related symptoms as a predictor of major depressive episodes. *Journal of Psychiatric Research* 79, 108-115.

Honings S, Drukker M, van Nierop M, van Winkel R, Wittchen HU, Lieb R, ten Have M, de Graaf R, van Dorsselaer S, van Os J (2016). Psychotic experiences and incident suicidal ideation and behaviour: Disentangling the longitudinal associations from connected psychopathology. *Psychiatry Research* 245, 267-275.

Horwitz AG, Berona J, Czyz EK, Yeguez CE, King CA (2016). Positive and negative expectations of hopelessness as longitudinal predictors of depression, suicidal ideation, and suicidal behavior in high-risk adolescents. *Suicide and Life-Threatening Behavior.* Published online: 2 July 2016. doi: 10.1111/sltb.12273.

Huang L-B, Tsai Y-F, Liu C-Y, Chen Y-J (2016). Influencing and protective factors of suicidal ideation among older adults. *International Journal of Mental Health Nursing.* Published online: 25 June 2016. doi: 10.1111/inm.12247.

HyunMyoungHo, Sung K, Kwon YS (2015). The associations between aggression, acquired capability for suicide and suicidal behavior in male alcohol use disorders. *Korean Journal of Health Psychology* 20, 253-265.

Ibiloglu AO, Atli A, Kaya MC, Demir S, Bulut M, Sir A (2016). A case of skin picking disorder of a patient with a history of childhood abuse. *Noropsikiyatri Arsivi-Archives of Neuropsychiatry* 53, 181-183.

Iliceto P, D'Antuono L, Cassarà L, Giacolini T, Sabatello U, Candilera G (2016). Obsessive-compulsive tendencies, self/other perception, personality, and suicidal ideation in a non-clinical sample. *Psychiatric Quarterly.* Published online: 22 July 2016. doi: 10.1007/s11126-016-9457-8.

Inoue K, Kaiya H, Hara N, Okazaki Y (2016). Clear trends in panic disorder with a possibility of suicide risk. *International Journal of Emergency Mental Health* 18, 753-755.

Jahn DR, DeVylder JE, Drapalski AL, Medoff D, Dixon LB (2016). Personal recovery as a protective factor against suicide ideation in individuals with schizophrenia. *Journal of Nervous and Mental Disease.* Published online: 22 April 2016. doi: 10.1097/NMD.0000000000000521.

Jaiswal SV, Faye AD, Gore SP, Shah HR, Kamath RM (2016). Stressful life events, hopelessness, and suicidal intent in patients admitted with attempted suicide in a tertiary care general hospital. *Journal of Postgraduate Medicine* 62, 102-104.

Jakubczyk A, Ashrafioun L, Ilgen M, Kopera M, Klimkiewicz A, Krasowska A, Solowiej M, Brower KJ, Wojnar M (2016). Physical pain and history of suicidal behaviors in alcohol-dependent patients entering treatment in Poland. *Substance Use & Misuse* 51, 1307-1317.

Jalenques I, Rondepierre F, Massoubre C, Haffen E, Grand JP, Labeille B, Perrot JL, Aubin F, Skowron F, Mulliez A, D'Incan M (2016). High prevalence of psychiatric disorders in patients with skin-restricted lupus: A case-control study. *British Journal of Dermatology* 174, 1051-1060.

Järvholm K, Karlsson J, Olbers T, Peltonen M, Marcus C, Dahlgren J, Gronowitz E, Johnsson P, Flodmark CE (2016). Characteristics of adolescents with poor mental health after bariatric surgery. *Surgery for Obesity and Related Diseases* 12, 882-890.

Jarvi SM, Hearon BA, Batejan KL, Gironde S, Bjorgvinsson T (2016). Relations between past-week physical activity and recent nonsuicidal self-injury in treatment-seeking psychiatric adults. *Journal of Clinical Psychology.* Published online: 26 August 2016. doi: 10.1002/jclp.22342.

Jarvi SM, Swenson LP (2016). The role of positive expectancies in risk behavior. *Crisis.* Published online: 8 July 2016. doi: 10.1027/0227-5910/a000417.

Jeon-Slaughter H, Claassen CA, Khan DA, Mihalakos P, Lee KB, Brown ES (2016). Temporal association between nonfatal self-directed violence and tree and grass pollen counts. *Journal of Clinical Psychiatry.* Published online: 7 June 2016. doi: 10.4088/JCP.15m09864.

Jeong JH, Kim JS (2015). The effect of abuse experience and coping styles on suicidal ideation in the elderly. *Journal of Korean Academy of Community Health Nursing* 26, 42.

Jeong KC, Koo KM, Kim CJ (2016). An analysis on relationships among exercise participation, depression experience, and suicidal ideation of people with visual impairment. *Indian Journal of Science and Technology* 9, 1-5.

Jia CX, Li SB, Han M, Bo QG (2016). Health-related factors and suicidal ideation in high school students in rural China. *Omega* 73, 263-274.

Jo HK, Kim HK (2016). Factors affecting suicidal ideation among middle-aged Korean women in an urban-rural province. *Archives of Psychiatric Nursing* 30, 539-543

Jo SJ, Ko JA, Park JS, Yim HW, Lee KM, Lee MS (2016). Psychosocial factors associated with suicide re-attempts in persons with chronic mental disabilities in Korea. *Community Mental Health Journal* 30, 539-543.

Joe S, Banks A, BeLue R (2016). Suicide risk among urban children. *Children and Youth Services Review* 68, 73-79.

Mann J, Ellis SP, Currier D, Zelazny J, Birmaher B, Oquendo MA, Kolko DJ, Stanley B, Melhem N, Burke AK, Brent DA (2016). Self-rated depression severity relative to clinician-rated depression severity: Trait stability and potential role in familial transmission of suicidal behavior. *Archives of Suicide Research* 20, 412-425.

Johnco C, McGuire JF, McBride NM, Murphy TK, Lewin AB, Storch EA (2016). Suicidal ideation in youth with tic disorders. *Journal of Affective Disorders* 200, 204-211.

Johnson SL, Carver CS, Tharp JA (2016). Suicidality in bipolar disorder: The role of emotion-triggered impulsivity. *Suicide and Life-Threatening Behavior.* Published online: 13 July 2016. doi: 10.1111/sltb.12274.

Joo J, Hwang S, Gallo JJ (2016). Death ideation and suicidal ideation in a community sample who do not meet criteria for major depression. *Crisis* 37, 161-165.

Joo Y (2016). Spatiotemporal study of elderly suicide in Korea by age cohort. *Public Health*. Published online: 6 September 2016. doi: 10.1016/j.puhe.2016.07.016.

Ju YJ, Park E-C, Han K-T, Choi JW, Kim JL, Cho KH, Park S (2016). Low socioeconomic status and suicidal ideation among elderly individuals. *International Psychogeriatrics*. Published online: 26 July 2016. doi: 10.1017/S1041610216001149.

Jung KI, Park CK (2016). Mental health status and quality of life in undiagnosed glaucoma patients: A nationwide population-based study. *Medicine* 95, e3523.

Kaess M, Brunner R, Parzer P, Edanackaparampil M, Schmidt J, Kirisgil M, Fischer G, Wewetzer C, Lehmkuhl G, Resch F (2016). Association of adolescent dimensional borderline personality pathology with past and current nonsuicidal self-injury and lifetime suicidal behavior: A clinical multicenter study. *Psychopathology*. Published online: 10 September 2016. doi: 10.1159/000448481.

Kaplan C, Tarlow N, Stewart JG, Aguirre B, Galen G, Auerbach RP (2016). Borderline personality disorder in youth: The prospective impact of child abuse on non-suicidal self-injury and suicidality. *Comprehensive Psychiatry* 71, 86-94.

Kaplan RL, Nehme S, Aunon F, de Vries D, Wagner G (2016). Suicide risk factors among trans feminine individuals in Lebanon. *International Journal of Transgenderism* 17, 23-30.

Karanovic J, Ivkovic M, Jovanovic VM, Pantovic M, Pavlovic-Jankovic N, Damjanovic A, Brajuskovic G, Romac S, Savic-Pavicevic D (2016). Tryptophan hydroxylase 1 variant rs1800532 is associated with suicide attempt in Serbian psychiatric patients but does not moderate the effect of recent stressful life events. *Suicide and Life-Threatening Behavior*. Published online: 2 April 2016. doi: 10.1111/sltb.12246.

Karmakar C, Luo W, Tran T, Berk M, Venkatesh S (2016). Predicting risk of suicide attempt using history of physical illnesses from electronic medical records. *JMIR Mental Health* 3, e19.

Kattari SK, Walls NE, Speer SR, Kattari L (2016). Exploring the relationship between transgender-inclusive providers and mental health outcomes among transgender/gender variant people. *Social Work in Health Care* 55, 635-650.

Kawabe K, Horiuchi F, Ochi M, Oka Y, Ueno S (2016). Suicidal ideation in adolescents and their caregivers: A cross sectional survey in Japan. *BMC Psychiatry* 16, 231.

Kemp K, Tolou-Shams M, Conrad S, Dauria E, Neel K, Brown L (2016). Suicidal ideation and attempts among court-involved, nonincarcerated youth. *Journal of Forensic Psychology Practice* 16, 169-181.

Kene P (2016). Self-injury implicit association test: Comparison of suicide attempters and non-attempters. *Psychiatric Quarterly*. Published online: 13 May 2016. doi: 10.1007/s11126-016-9438-y.

Kerbrat AH, Comtois KA, Stiles BJ, Huh D, Chalker SA, Luxton DD (2015). Gender differences in acquired capability among active-duty service members at high risk for suicide. *Military Behavioral Health* 3, 306-315.

Kessler RC, Stein MB, Petukhova MV, Bliese P, Bossarte RM, Bromet EJ, Fullerton CS, Gilman SE, Ivany C, Lewandowski-Romps L, Millikan Bell A, Naifeh JA, Nock MK, Reis BY, Rosellini AJ, Sampson NA, Zaslavsky AM, Ursano RJ (2016). Predicting suicides after outpatient mental health visits in the Army Study to Assess Risk and Resilience in Servicemembers (Army STARRS). *Molecular Psychiatry*. Published online: 19 July 2016. doi: 10.1038/mp.2016.110.

Khandoker AH, Luthra V, Abouallaban Y, Saha S, Ahmed KI, Mostafa R, Chowdhury N, Jelinek HF (2016). Predicting depressed patients with suicidal ideation from ECG recordings. *Medical & Biological Engineering & Computing*. Published online: 18 August 2016. doi:10.1007/s11517-016-1557-y.

Khanipour H, Hakim Shooshtari M, Bidaki R (2016). Suicide probability in adolescents with a history of childhood maltreatment: The role of non-suicidal self-injury, emotion regulation difficulties, and forms of self-criticism. *International Journal of High Risk Behaviors and Addiction* 5, e23675.

Khazem LR, Anestis MD (2016). Thinking or doing? An examination of well-established suicide risk factors within the ideation to action framework. *Psychiatry Research* 245, 321-326.

Kim BS, Chang SM, Park JE, Seong SJ, Won SH, Cho MJ (2016). Prevalence, correlates, psychiatric comorbidities, and suicidality in a community population with problematic internet use. *Psychiatry Research* 244, 249-256.

Kim DK, Song HJ, Lee EK, Kwon JW (2016). Effect of sex and age on the association between suicidal behaviour and obesity in Korean adults: A cross-sectional nationwide study. *British Medical Journal Open* 6, e010183.

Kim JH, Kim DH, Park YS (2016). Body composition, sarcopenia, and suicidal ideation in elderly Koreans: Hallym Aging Study. *Journal of Korean Medical Science* 31, 604-610.

Kim SM, Jung J-W, Park I-W, Ahn CM, Kim Y-I, Yoo K-H, Chun EM, Jung JY, Park YS, Park J-H, Kim JY, Korean Smoking Cessation Study G (2016). Gender differences in relations of smoking status, depression, and suicidality in Korea: Findings from the Korea National Health and Nutrition Examination Survey 2008-2012. *Psychiatry Investigation* 13, 239-246.

Kim Y, Kim K, Kwon HJ, Kim JS (2016). Associations between adolescents' sleep duration, sleep satisfaction, and suicidal ideation. *Salud Mental* 39, 213-219.

Kimbrel NA, Debeer BB, Meyer EC, Gulliver SB, Morissette SB (2016). Nonsuicidal self-injury and suicide attempts in Iraq/Afghanistan war veterans. *Psychiatry Research* 243, 232-237.

Kimbrel NA, Meyer EC, Debeer BB, Gulliver SB, Morissette SB (2016). A 12-month prospective study of the effects of PTSD-depression comorbidity on suicidal behavior in Iraq/Afghanistan-era veterans. *Psychiatry Research* 243, 97-99.

Kimbrel NA, Pennington ML, Cammarata CM, Leto F, Ostiguy WJ, Gulliver SB (2016). Is cumulative exposure to suicide attempts and deaths a risk factor for suicidal behavior among firefighters? A preliminary study. *Suicide and Life-Threatening Behavior*. Published online: 2 July 2016. doi: 10.1111/sltb.12248.

Kittel JA, DeBeer BB, Kimbrel NA, Matthieu MM, Meyer EC, Gulliver SB, Morissette SB (2016). Does body mass index moderate the association between posttraumatic stress disorder symptoms and suicidal ideation in Iraq/Afghanistan veterans? *Psychiatry Research* 244, 123-129.

Klein A, Golub SA (2016). Family rejection as a predictor of suicide attempts and substance misuse among transgender and gender nonconforming adults. *LGBT Health* 3, 193-199.

Klemera E, Brooks FM, Chester KL, Magnusson J, Spencer N (2016). Self-harm in adolescence: Protective health assets in the family, school and community. *International Journal of Public Health*. Published online: 22 September 2016. doi: 10.1007/s00038-016-0900-2.

Kline A, Weiner MD, Interian A, Shcherbakov A, Hill LS (2016). Morbid thoughts and suicidal ideation in Iraq war veterans: The role of direct and indirect killing in combat. *Depression and Anxiety* 33, 473-482.

Kodish T, Herres J, Shearer A, Atte T, Fein J, Diamond G (2016). Bullying, depression, and suicide risk in a pediatric primary care sample. *Crisis* 37, 241-246.

Koenig J, Brunner R, Fischer-Waldschmidt G, Parzer P, Plener PL, Park J, Wasserman C, Carli V, Hoven CW, Sarchiapone M, Wasserman D, Resch F, Kaess M (2016). Prospective risk for suicidal thoughts and behaviour in adolescents with onset, maintenance or cessation of direct self-injurious behaviour. *European Child and Adolescent Psychiatry*. Published online: 24 August 2016. doi: 10.1007/s00787-016-0896-4.

Kohlbrenner V, Deuba K, Karki DK, Marrone G (2016). Perceived discrimination is an independent risk factor for suicidal ideation among sexual and gender minorities in Nepal. *PLoS One* 11, e0159359.

Kohlmann S, Gierk B, Murray AM, Scholl A, Lehmann M, Lowe B (2016). Base rates of depressive symptoms in patients with coronary heart disease: An individual symptom analysis. *PLoS One* 11, e0156167.

Kok JK, Schalkwyk GJv, Chan AHW (2015). Perceived stressors of suicide and potential prevention strategies for suicide among youths in Malaysia. *International Journal of School and Educational Psychology* 3, 55-63.

Kopacz MS, Morley SW, Wozniak BM, Simons KV, Bishop TM, Vance CG (2016). Religious well-being and suicide ideation in veterans - an exploratory study. *Pastoral Psychology* 65, 481-491.

Koutek J, Kocourková J, Dudova I (2016). Suicidal behavior and self-harm in girls with eating disorders. *Neuropsychiatric Disease and Treatment* 12, 787-793.

Kremer I, Orbach I, Rosenbloom T (2016). Mental pain and suicidal tendencies in sexual and physical abuse victims. *Archives of Suicide Research.* Published online: 13 April 2016. doi: 10.1080/13811118.2016.1175394.

Krzyzanowska M, Steiner J, Brisch R, Mawrin C, Busse S, Karnecki K, Jankowski Z, Gos T (2016). Decreased ribosomal DNA transcription in dorsal raphe nucleus neurons is specific for suicide regardless of psychiatric diagnosis. *Psychiatry Research* 241, 43-46.

Kubiak A, Sakson-Obada O (2016). Repetetive self-injury and the body self. *Psychiatria Polska* 50, 43-54.

Kuipers GS, van Loenhout Z, van der Ark LA, Bekker MH (2016). Attachment insecurity, mentalization and their relation to symptoms in eating disorder patients. *Attachment & Human Development* 18, 250-272.

Laghi F, Terrinoni A, Cerutti R, Fantini F, Galosi S, Ferrara M, Bosco FM (2016). Theory of mind in non-suicidal self-injury (NSSI) adolescents. *Consciousness and Cognition* 43, 38-47.

Lai DWL, Li L, Daoust GD (2016). Factors influencing suicide behaviours in immigrant and ethno-cultural minority groups: A systematic review. *Journal of Immigrant and Minority Health.* Published online: 17 September 2016. doi: 10.1007/s10903-016-0490-3.

Lane R, Cheref S, Miranda R (2016). Ethnic differences in suicidal ideation and its correlates among South Asian American emerging adults. *Asian American Journal of Psychology* 7, 120-128.

Lasrado RA, Chantler K, Jasani R, Young A (2016). Structuring roles and gender identities within families explaining suicidal behavior in South India. *Crisis* 37, 205-211.

Latakiene J, Skruibis P, Dadašev S, Grižas A, Dapševi iute I, Gailiene D (2016). "They don't take it seriously": Perceived reactions of surrounding people to suicide communication. *Illness Crisis and Loss* 24, 123-136.

LaVome Robinson W, Droege JR, Hipwell AE, Stepp SD, Keenan K (2016). Brief report: Suicidal ideation in adolescent girls: Impact of race. *Journal of Adolescence* 53, 16-20.

Leach LS, Poyser C, Butterworth P (2016). Workplace bullying and the association with suicidal ideation/thoughts and behaviour: A systematic review. *Occupational & Environmental Medicine.* Published online: 23 September 2016. doi: 10.1136/oemed-2016-103726.

LeCloux M, Maramaldi P, Thomas K, Wharff E (2016). Family support and mental health service use among suicidal adolescents. *Journal of Child and Family Studies* 25, 2597-2606.

Lee BH, Park YM (2016). How childhood maltreatment is related to suicidality, bipolarity and central serotonergic activity in patients with major depressive disorder: A cross-sectional pilot study. *Psychiatry Investigation* 13, 190-195.

Lee S-U, Roh S, Kim Y-E, Park J-I, Jeon B, Oh I-H (2016). Impact of disability status on suicide risks in South Korea: Analysis of national health insurance cohort data from 2003 to 2013. *Disability and Health Journal.* Published online: 29 June 2016. doi:10.1016/j.dhjo.2016.06.008.

Lee SA, Jang SY, Shin J, Ju YJ, Nam JY, Park EC (2016). The association between inappropriate weight control behaviors and suicide ideation and attempt among Korean adolescents. *Journal of Korean Medical Science* 31, 1529-1537.

Lee SY, Park E-C, Han K-T, Kim SJ, Chun S-Y, Park S (2016). The association of level of internet use with suicidal ideation and suicide attempts in South Korean adolescents: A focus on family structure and household economic status. *Canadian Journal of Psychiatry* 61, 243-251.

Lehman EJ, Hein MJ, Gersic CM (2016). Suicide mortality among retired national football league players who played 5 or more seasons. *American Journal of Sports Medicine.* Published online: 5 May 2016. doi: 10.1177/0363546516645093.

Lehmann M, Hilimire MR, Yang LH, Link BG, DeVylder JE (2016). Investigating the relationship between self-esteem and stigma among young adults with history of suicide attempts. *Crisis.* Published online: 24 June 2016. doi: 10.1027/0227-5910/a000399.

Lemsalu L, Ruutel K, Laisaar KT, Lohmus L, Raidvee A, Uuskula A (2016). Suicidal behavior among people living with HIV (PLHIV) in medical care in Estonia and factors associated with receiving psychological treatment. *AIDS and Behavior.* Published online: 24 September 2016. doi: 10.1007/s10461-016-1561-0.

Lengel GJ, DeShong HL, Mullins-Sweatt SN (2016). Impulsivity and nonsuicidal self-injury: Examining the role of affect manipulation. *Journal of Psychopathology and Behavioral Assessment* 38, 101-112.

Levesque C, Lafontaine M-F, Bureau J-F (2016). The mediating effects of emotion regulation and dyadic coping on the relationship between romantic attachment and non-suicidal self-injury. *Journal of Youth and Adolescence.* Published online: 22 July 2016. doi: 10.1007/s10964-016-0547-6.

Levinger S, Holden RR, Ben-Dor DH (2015). Examining the importance of mental pain and physical dissociation and the fluid nature of suicidality in young suicide attempters. *Omega.* Published online: 12 March 2016. doi: 10.1177/0030222815575899.

Lewitzka U, Denzin S, Sauer C, Bauer M, Jabs B (2016). Personality differences in early versus late suicide attempters. *BMC Psychiatry* 16, 282.

Lheureux F, Truchot D, Borteyrou X (2016). Suicidal tendency, physical health problems and addictive behaviours among general practitioners: Their relationship with burnout. *Work and Stress* 30, 173-192.

Lim M, Lee S, Park J-I (2016). Differences between impulsive and non-impulsive suicide attempts among individuals treated in emergency rooms of South Korea. *Psychiatry Investigation* 13, 389-396.

Linden S, Bussing R, Kubilis P, Gerhard T, Segal R, Shuster JJ, Winterstein AG (2016). Risk of suicidal events with atomoxetine compared to stimulant treatment: A cohort study. *Pediatrics* 137, 53199.

Littlewood DL, Gooding P, Kyle SD, Pratt D, Peters S (2016). Understanding the role of sleep in suicide risk: Qualitative interview study. *British Medical Journal Open* 6, e012113.

Littlewood DL, Gooding PA, Panagioti M, Kyle SD (2016). Investigating psychological mechanisms in relation to sleep problems and suicide. *Journal of Clinical Sleep Medicine* 12, 931.

Liu DWY, Fairweather-Schmidt AK, Burns R, Roberts RM, Anstey KJ (2016). Psychological resilience provides no independent protection from suicidal risk. *Crisis* 37, 130-139.

Liu HC, Liu SI, Tjung JJ, Sun FJ, Huang HC, Fang CK (2016). Self-harm and its association with internet addiction and internet exposure to suicidal thought in adolescents. *Journal of the Formosan Medical Association.* Published online: 1 May 2016. doi: 10.1016/j.jfma.2016.03.010.

Liu M, Ming Q, Yi J, Wang X, Yao S (2016). Screen time on school days and risks for psychiatric symptoms and self-harm in mainland Chinese adolescents. *Frontiers in Psychology* 7, 574.

Liu X, Chen H, Bo QG, Fan F, Jia CX (2016). Poor sleep quality and nightmares are associated with non-suicidal self-injury in adolescents. *European Child and Adolescent Psychiatry*. Published online: 6 July 2016. doi: 10.1007/s00787-016-0885-7.

Lloyd J, Hawton K, Dutton WH, Geddes JR, Goodwin GM, Rogers RD (2016). Thoughts and acts of self-harm, and suicidal ideation, in online gamblers. *International Gambling Studies*. Published online: 5 Aug 2016. doi: 10.1080/14459795.2016.1214166.

Logan J, Bohnert A, Spies E, Jannausch M (2016). Suicidal ideation among young Afghanistan/Iraq war veterans and civilians: Individual, social, and environmental risk factors and perception of unmet mental healthcare needs, United States, 2013. *Psychiatry Research* 245, 398-405.

Logan JE, Vagi KJ, Gorman-Smith D (2016). Characteristics of youth with combined histories of violent behavior, suicidal ideation or behavior, and gun-carrying. *Crisis*. Published online: 1 June 2016. doi: 10.1027/0227-5910/a000389.

Lopes MC, Boronat AC, Wang YP, Fu IL (2016). Sleep complaints as risk factor for suicidal behavior in severely depressed children and adolescents. *CNS Neuroscience & Therapeutics*. Published online: 18 August 2016. doi: 10.1111/cns.12597.

Lopuszanska U, Derewianka-Polak M, Balicka G, Sawicki M, Makara-Studzinska M (2015). Depression and suicidal thoughts in lung cancer patients awaiting surgery. *Psychiatria I Psychologia Kliniczna-Journal of Psychiatry and Clinical Psychology* 15, 122-125.

Lu W, Bian Q, Song Y-y, Ren J-y, Xu X-y, Zhao M (2015). Prevalence and related risk factors of anxiety and depression among Chinese college freshmen. *Journal of Huazhong University of Science and Technology-Medical Sciences* 35, 815-822.

Lüdtke J, In-Albon T, Michel C, Schmid M (2016). Predictors for DSM-5 nonsuicidal self-injury in female adolescent inpatients: The role of childhood maltreatment, alexithymia, and dissociation. *Psychiatry Research* 239, 346-352.

Lund EM, Nadorff MR, Seader K (2016). Relationship between suicidality and disability when accounting for depressive symptomology. *Rehabilitation Counseling Bulletin* 59, 185-188.

Luo X, Wang Q, Wang X, Cai T (2016). Reasons for living and hope as the protective factors against suicidality in Chinese patients with depression: A cross sectional study. *BMC Psychiatry* 16, 252.

Lysell H, Dahlin M, Langstrom N, Lichtenstein P, Runeson B (2016). Killing the mother of one's child: Psychiatric risk factors among male perpetrators and offspring health consequences. *Journal of Clinical Psychiatry* 77, 342-347.

Ma-Kellams C, Baek JH, Or F (2016). Suicide contagion in response to widely publicized celebrity deaths: The roles of depressed affect, death-thought accessibility, and attitudes. *Psychology of Popular Media Culture*. Published online: 21 April 2016. doi: 10.1037/ppm0000115.

Machell KA, Rallis BA, Esposito-Smythers C (2016). Family environment as a moderator of the association between anxiety and suicidal ideation. *Journal of Anxiety Disorders* 40, 1-7.

Maciejewski DF, Renteria ME, Abdellaoui A, Medland SE, Few LR, Gordon SD, Madden PA, Montgomery G, Trull TJ, Heath AC, Statham DJ, Martin NG, Zietsch BP, Verweij KJ (2016). The association of genetic predisposition to depressive symptoms with non-suicidal and suicidal self-injuries. *Behaviour Genetics*. Published online: 2 September 2016. doi: 10.1007/s10519-016-9809-z.

Maciukiewicz M, Dmitrzak-W glarz M, Pawlak J, Kapelski P, Czerski P, Leszczy ska-Rodziewicz A, Zaremba D, Hauser J (2016). Personality traits as an endophenotype in genetic studies on suicidality in bipolar disorder. *Acta Neuropsychiatrica*. Published online: 30 August 2016. doi: 10.1017/neu.2016.43.

MacKinnon N, Colman I (2016). Factors associated with suicidal thought and help-seeking behaviour in transition-aged youth versus adults. *Canadian Journal of Psychiatry*. Published online: 30 August 2016. doi: 10.1177/070674371666741.

Major J, Brackenbury F, Gibbon K, Tomson N (2016). The impact of vulval disease on patients' quality of life. *Journal of Community Nursing* 30, 40-44.

Marín-Navarrete R, Medina-Mora ME, Horigian VE, Salloum IM, Villalobos-Gallegos L, Fernández-Mondragón J (2016). Co-occurring disorders: A challenge for Mexican community-based residential care facilities for substance use. *Journal of Dual Diagnosis*. Published online: 5 August 2016. doi: 10.1080/15504263.2016.1220207.

Martin J, Bureau JF, Yurkowski K, Fournier TR, Lafontaine MF, Cloutier P (2016). Family-based risk factors for non-suicidal self-injury: Considering influences of maltreatment, adverse family-life experiences, and parent-child relational risk. *Journal of Adolescence* 49, 170-180.

Martin MS, Dykxhoorn J, Afifi TO, Colman I (2016). Child abuse and the prevalence of suicide attempts among those reporting suicide ideation. *Social Psychiatry and Psychiatric Epidemiology*. Published online: 11 June 2016. doi: 10.1007/s00127-016-1250-3.

Marzano L, Hawton K, Rivlin A, Smith EN, Piper M, Fazel S (2016). Prevention of suicidal behavior in prisons. *Crisis*. Published online: 9 June 2016. doi: 10.1027/0227-5910/a000394.

Mathews EM, Woodward CJ, Musso MW, Jones GN (2016). Suicide attempts presenting to trauma centers: Trends across age groups using the National Trauma Data Bank. *American Journal of Emergency Medicine* 34, 1620-1624.

Mazur-Mosiewicz A, Carlson HL, Hartwick C, Laliberte C, Tam E, Sherman EMS, Brooks BL (2015). Rates of reporting suicidal ideation and symptoms of depression on children's depression inventory in a paediatric neurology sample. *Journal of Pediatric Neuropsychology* 1, 3-13.

McCall WV, Benca RM, Rosenquist PB, Riley MA, McCloud L, Newman JC, Case D, Rumble M, Krystal AD (2016). Hypnotic medications and suicide: Risk, mechanisms, mitigation, and the FDA. *American Journal of Psychiatry*. Published online: 9 September 2016. doi: 10.1176/appi.ajp.2016.16030336.

McGlinchey EL, Courtney-Seidler EA, Germán M, Miller AL (2016). The role of sleep disturbance in suicidal and nonsuicidal self-injurious behavior among adolescents. *Suicide and Life-Threatening Behavior*. Published online: 7 June 2016. doi: 10.1111/sltb.12268.

McIntyre RS, Woldeyohannes HO, Soczynska JK, Vinberg M, Cha DS, Lee Y, Gallaugher LA, Dale RS, Alsuwaidan MT, Mansur RB, Muzina DJ, Carvalho A, Kennedy S (2016). The prevalence and clinical characteristics associated with Diagnostic and Statistical Manual Version-5-defined anxious distress specifier in adults with major depressive disorder: Results from the International Mood Disorders Collaborative Project. *Therapeutic Advances in Chronic Disease* 7, 153-159.

McKinnon B, Gariepy G, Sentenac M, Elgar FJ (2016). Adolescent suicidal behaviours in 32 low- and middle-income countries. *Bulletin of the World Health Organization* 94, 340F-350F.

McLafferty M, Armour C, O'Neill S, Murphy S, Ferry F, Bunting B (2016). Suicidality and profiles of childhood adversities, conflict related trauma and psychopathology in the Northern Ireland population. *Journal of Affective Disorders* 200, 97-102.

McQuaid RJ, McInnis OA, Matheson K, Anisman H (2016). Oxytocin and social sensitivity: Gene polymorphisms in relation to depressive symptoms and suicidal ideation. *Frontiers in Human Neuroscience*. Published online: 19 July 2016. doi: 10.3389/fnhum.2016.00358.

Melnyk BM, Slevin C, Militello L, Hoying J, Teall A, McGovern C (2016). Physical health, lifestyle beliefs and behaviors, and mental health of entering graduate health professional students: Evidence to support screening and early intervention. *Journal of the American Association of Nurse Practitioners* 28, 204-211.

Miller AB, Jenness JL, Oppenheimer CW, Gottleib AL, Young JF, Hankin BL (2016). Childhood emotional maltreatment as a robust predictor of suicidal ideation: A 3-year multi-wave, prospective investigation. *Journal of Abnormal Child Psychology*. Published online: 31 March 2016. doi: 10.1007/s10802-016-0150-z.

Miller KA, Hitschfeld MJ, Lineberry TW, Palmer BA (2016). How does active substance use at psychiatric admission impact suicide risk and hospital length of stay? *Journal of Addictive Diseases*. Published online: 18 April 2016. doi: 10.1080/10550887.2016.1177808.

Millner AJ, Lee MD, Nock MK (2016). Describing and measuring the pathway to suicide attempts: A preliminary study. *Suicide and Life-Threatening Behavior*. Published online: 1 August 2016. doi: 10.1111/sltb.12284.

Milner A, Page K, Witt K, LaMontagne A (2016). Psychosocial working conditions and suicide ideation: Evidence from a cross-sectional survey of working Australians. *Journal of Occupational and Environmental Medicine* 58, 584-587.

Minkkinen J, Oksanen A, Kaakinen M, Keipi T, Rasanen P (2016). Victimization and exposure to pro-self-harm and pro-suicide websites: A cross-national study. *Suicide and Life-Threatening Behavior*. Published online: 20 April 2016. doi: 10.1111/sltb.12258.

Minor T, Ali MM, Rizzo JA (2016). Body weight and suicidal behavior in adolescent females: The role of self-perceptions. *Journal of Mental Health Policy and Economics* 19, 21-31.

Minzenberg MJ, Lesh TA, Niendam TA, Cheng Y, Carter CS (2016). Conflict-related anterior cingulate functional connectivity is associated with past suicidal ideation and behavior in recent-onset psychotic major mood disorders. *Journal of Neuropsychiatry and Clinical Neurosciences*. Published online: 8 April 2016. doi: 10.1176/appi.neuropsych.15120422.

Mishra KK, Gupta N, Bhabulkar S (2015). Sociodemographic profile of suicide attempters among the rural agrarian community of central India. *Industrial Psychiatry Journal* 24, 185-188.

Mok K, Jorm AF, Pirkis J (2016). Who goes online for suicide-related reasons? *Crisis* 37, 112-120.

Mok PL, Pedersen CB, Springate D, Astrup A, Kapur N, Antonsen S, Mors O, Webb RT (2016). Parental psychiatric disease and risks of attempted suicide and violent criminal offending in offspring: A population-based cohort study. *JAMA Psychiatry* Published online: 31 August 2016. doi: 10.1001/jamapsychiatry.2016.1728.

Monson ET, de Klerk K, Gaynor SC, Wagner AH, Breen ME, Parsons M, Casavant TL, Zandi PP, Potash JB, Willour VL (2016). Whole-gene sequencing investigation of SAT1 in attempted suicide. *American Journal of Medical Genetics Part B: Neuropsychiatric Genetics* 171, 888-895.

Monteith LL, Bahraini NH, Matarazzo BB, Gerber HR, Soberay KA, Forster JE (2016). The influence of gender on suicidal ideation following military sexual trauma among Veterans in the Veterans Health Administration. *Psychiatry Research* 244, 257-265.

Monteith LL, Bahraini NH, Matarazzo BB, Soberay KA, Smith CP (2016). Perceptions of institutional betrayal predict suicidal self-directed violence among Veterans exposed to military sexual trauma. *Journal of Clinical Psychology* 72, 743-755.

Moreno-Kustner B, Jones R, Svab I, Maaroos H, Xavier M, Geerlings M, Torres-Gonzalez F, Nazareth I, Motrico-Martinez E, Monton-Franco C, Gil-de-Gomez MJ, Sanchez-Celaya M, Diaz-Barreiros MA, Vicens-Caldentey C, King M (2016). Suicidality in primary care patients who present with sadness and anhedonia: A prospective European study. *BMC Psychiatry* 16, 94.

Morgan DJ, Ho KM (2016). Incidence and risk factors for deliberate self-harm, mental illness, and suicide following bariatric surgery: A state-wide population-based linked-data cohort study. *Annals of Surgery*. Published online: 18 July 2016. doi: 10.1097/SLA.0000000000001891.

Mozhdehi Fard M, Hakim Shooshtari M, Najarzadegan MR, Khosravi T, Bidaki R, Moradi M, Pourshams M, Mohammadi Farsani H, Ghiasi Z, Mostafavi SA (2016). Adult attention deficit hyperactivity disorder and suicide attempters: A case control study from Iran, West Asia. *International Journal of High Risk Behaviors and Addiction*. Published online: April 2016. doi: 10.5812/ijhrba.29537.

Mu H, Li Y, Liu L, Na J, Yu L, Bi X, An X, Gu Y, Zhou Y, Li S, Zhang R, Jiang C, Pan G (2016). Prevalence and risk factors for lifetime suicide ideation, plan and attempt in Chinese men who have sex with men. *BMC Psychiatry* 16, e117.

Müller A, Claes L, Smits D, Brahler E, de Zwaan M (2016). Prevalence and correlates of self-harm in the German general population. *PLoS One* 11, e0157928.

Muller E, Kempes M (2016). Gender differences in a Dutch forensic sample of severe violent offenders. *International Journal of Forensic Mental Health* 15, 164-173.

Myslimaj F, Dervishi E (2016). Suicide attempts and self-inflicting on prison custody and prisons. *Academic Journal of Interdisciplinary Studies* 5, 175-180.

Myung W, Han CE, Fava M, Mischoulon D, Papakostas GI, Heo JY, Kim KW, Kim ST, Kim DJ, Kim DK, Seo SW, Seong JK, Jeon HJ (2016). Reduced frontal-subcortical white matter connectivity in association with suicidal ideation in major depressive disorder. *Translational Psychiatry* 6, e835.

Nagra GS, Lin A, Upthegrove R (2016). What bridges the gap between self-harm and suicidality? The role of forgiveness, resilience and attachment. *Psychiatry Research* 241, 78-82.

Nakar O, Brunner R, Schilling O, Chanen A, Fischer G, Parzer P, Carli V, Wasserman D, Sarchiapone M, Wasserman C, Hoven CW, Resch F, Kaess M (2016). Developmental trajectories of self-injurious behavior, suicidal behavior and substance misuse and their association with adolescent borderline personality pathology. *Journal of Affective Disorders* 197, 231-238.

Nguyen TQ, Simpson PM, Gabbe BJ (2016). The prevalence of pre-existing mental health, drug and alcohol conditions in major trauma patients. *Australian Health Review*. Published online: 15 July 2016. doi: 10.1071/AH16050.

Niederkrotenthaler T, Gould M, Sonneck G, Stack S, Till B (2016). Predictors of psychological improvement on non-professional suicide message boards: Content analysis. *Psychological Medicine*. Published online: 22 September 2016. doi: 10.1017/S003329171600221X.

Nielsen E, Sayal K, Townsend E (2016). Exploring the relationship between experiential avoidance, coping functions and the recency and frequency of self-harm. *PLoS One* 11, e0159854.

Nielsen MB, Einarsen S, Notelaers G, Nielsen GH (2016). Does exposure to bullying behaviors at the workplace contribute to later suicidal ideation? A three-wave longitudinal study. *Scandinavian Journal of Work, Environment and Health* 42, 246-250.

Ntountoulaki E, Guthrie E, Kotsis K, Paika V, Tatsioni A, Tomenson B, Fountoulakis KN, Carvalho AF, Hyphantis T (2016). Double RASS cutpoint accurately diagnosed suicidal risk in females with long-term conditions attending the emergency department compared to their male counterparts. *Comprehensive Psychiatry* 69, 193-201.

O'Hare T, Shen C, Sherrer MV (2016). Race, trauma, and suicide attempts: Comparing African American, white, and Hispanic people with severe mental illness. *Best Practices in Mental Health* 12, 96-108.

O'Connor SS, Comtois KA, Atkins DC, Kerbrat AH (2016). Examining the impact of suicide attempt function and perceived effectiveness in predicting re-attempt for emergency medicine patients. *Behavior Therapy*. Published online: 25 May 2016. doi: 10.1016/j.beth.2016.05.004.

Oexle N, Rusch N, Viering S, Wyss C, Seifritz E, Xu Z, Kawohl W (2016). Self-stigma and suicidality: A longitudinal study. *European Archives of Psychiatry and Clinical Neuroscience.* Published online: 12 May 2016. doi: 10.1007/s00406-016-0698-1.

Oquendo MA, Galfalvy H, Sullivan GM, Miller JM, Milak MM, Sublette ME, Cisneros-Trujillo S, Burke AK, Parsey RV, Mann JJ (2016). Positron emission tomographic imaging of the serotonergic system and prediction of risk and lethality of future suicidal behavior. *JAMA Psychiatry.* Published online: 27 July 2016. doi: 10.1001/jamapsychiatry.2016.1478.

Ozcan H, Yucel A, Atis O, Yucel N, Bilen A, Emet M, Gur STA (2016). Thyroxin levels associated with current suicide attempts: A case control and follow-up study. *Klinik Psikofarmakoloji Bulteni* 26, 278-286.

Ozsoy S, Kara K, Teke HY, Turker T, Congologlu MA, Sezigen S, Renklidag T, Karapirli M, Javan GT (2016). Relationship between self-injurious behaviors and levels of aggression in children and adolescents who were subject to medicolegal examination. *Journal of Forensic Sciences* 61, 382-387.

Pantazatos SP, Huang YY, Rosoklija GB, Dwork AJ, Arango V, Mann JJ (2016). Whole-transcriptome brain expression and exon-usage profiling in major depression and suicide: Evidence for altered glial, endothelial and ATPase activity. *Molecular Psychiatry.* Published online: 16 August 2016. doi: 10.1038/mp.2016.130.

Paradiso S, Beadle JN, Raymont V, Grafman J (2016). Suicidal thoughts and emotion competence. *Journal of Clinical and Experimental Neuropsychology* 38, 887-899.

Park S-M, Moon S-S (2016). Elderly Koreans who consider suicide: Role of healthcare use and financial status. *Psychiatry Research* 244, 345-350.

Park S, Song H (2016). Factors that affect adolescent drug users' suicide attempts. *Psychiatry Investigation* 13, 360-363.

Park SC, Lee MS, Hahn SW, Si TM, Kanba S, Chong MY, Yoon CK, Udomratn P, Tripathi A, Sartorius N, Shinfuku N, Maramis MM, Park YC (2016). Suicidal thoughts/acts and clinical correlates in patients with depressive disorders in Asians: Results from the REAP-AD study. *Acta Neuropsychiatrica.* Published online: 16 June 2016. doi: 10.1017/neu.2016.27.

Pauwels E, Dierckx E, Schoevaerts K, Claes L (2016). Early maladaptive schemas in eating disordered patients with or without non-suicidal self-injury. *European Eating Disorders Review.* Published online: 28 June 2016. doi: 10.1002/erv.2460.

Pawlak J, Dmitrzak-Weglarz M, Wilkosc M, Szczepankiewicz A, Leszczy ska-Rodziewicz A, Zaremba D, Kapelski P, Rajewska-Rager A, Hauser J (2016). Suicide behavior as a quantitative trait and its genetic background. *Journal of Affective Disorders* 206, 241-250.

Pearson CM, Pisetsky EM, Goldschmidt AB, Lavender JM, Wonderlich SA, Crosby RD, Engel SG, Mitchell JE, Crow SJ, Peterson CB (2016). Personality psychopathology differentiates risky behaviors among women with bulimia nervosa. *The International Journal of Eating Disorders* 49, 681-688.

Perez NM, Jennings WG, Piquero AR, Baglivio MT (2016). Adverse childhood experiences and suicide attempts: The mediating influence of personality development and problem behaviors. *Journal of Youth and Adolescence.* Published online: 11 June 2016. doi: 10.1007/s10964-016-0519-x.

Peter T, Taylor C, Campbell C (2016). "You can't break...when you're already broken": The importance of school climate to suicidality among LGBTQ youth. *Journal of Gay and Lesbian Mental Health.* Published online: 30 March 2016. doi: 10.1080/19359705.2016.1171188.

Petering R (2016). Sexual risk, substance use, mental health, and trauma experiences of gang-involved homeless youth. *Journal of Adolescence* 48, 73-81.

Philip J, Ford T, Henry D, Rasmus S, Allen J (2016). Relationship of social network to protective factors in suicide and alcohol use disorder intervention for rural Yup'ik Alaska native youth. *Psychosocial Intervention* 25, 45-54.

Pina-Watson B, Abraido-Lanza AF (2016). The intersection of fatalismo and pessimism on depressive symptoms and suicidality of Mexican descent adolescents: An attribution perspective. *Cultural Diversity and Ethnic Minority Psychology*. Published online: 27 June 2016. doi: 10.1037/cdp0000115.

Podlogar T, Ziberna J, Postuvan V, D CRK (2016). Belongingness and burdensomeness in adolescents: Slovene translation and validation of the interpersonal needs questionnaire. *Suicide and Life-Threatening Behavior*. Published online: 15 July 2016. doi: 10.1111/sltb.12276.

Polanco-Roman L, Gomez J, Miranda R, Jeglic E (2016). Stress-related symptoms and suicidal ideation: The roles of rumination and depressive symptoms vary by gender. *Cognitive Therapy and Research*. Published online: 3 May 2016. doi: 10.1007/s10608-016-9782-0.

Poorolajal J, Darvishi N (2016). Smoking and suicide: A meta-analysis. *PLoS One* 11, e0156348.

Power J, Gobeil R, Beaudette JN, Ritchie MB, Brown SL, Smith HP (2016). Childhood abuse, nonsuicidal self-injury, and suicide attempts: An exploration of gender differences in incarcerated adults. *Suicide and Life-Threatening Behavior*. Published online: 13 June 2016. doi: 10.1111/sltb.12263.

Price SD, Callahan JL (2016). Religious attendance serves as a protective variable against suicidal ideation during treatment. *Pastoral Psychology*. Published online: 13 July 2016. doi: 10.1007/s11089-016-0725-1.

Priya PK, Rajappa M, Kattimani S, Raj PSM, Revathy G (2016). Association of neurotrophins, inflammation and stress with suicide risk in young adults. *Clinica Chimica Acta*. Published online: 1 June 2016. doi: 10.1016/j.cca.2016.03.019.

Pryor L, Lioret S, van der Waerden J, Fombonne E, Falissard B, Melchior M (2016). Food insecurity and mental health problems among a community sample of young adults. *Social Psychiatry and Psychiatric Epidemiology*. Published online: 13 June 2016. doi: 10.1007/s00127-016-1249-9.

Puckett JA, Horne SG, Surace F, Carter A, Noffsinger-Frazier N, Shulman J, Detrie P, Ervin A, Mosher C (2016). Predictors of sexual minority youth's reported suicide attempts and mental health. *Journal of Homosexuality*. Published online: 7 June 2016. doi: 10.1080/00918369.2016.1196999.

Pustilnik A, Elkana O, Vatine J-J, Franko M, Hamdan S (2016). Neuropsychological markers of suicidal risk in the context of medical rehabilitation. *Archives of Suicide Research*. Published online: 6 April 2016. doi: 10.1080/13811118.2016.1171815.

Quevedo K, Martin J, Scott H, Smyda G, Pfeifer JH (2016). The neurobiology of self-knowledge in depressed and self-injurious youth. *Psychiatry Research - Neuroimaging* 254, 145-155.

Quevedo K, Ng R, Scott H, Martin J, Smyda G, Keener M, Oppenheimer CW (2016). The neurobiology of self-face recognition in depressed adolescents with low or high suicidality. *Journal of Abnormal Psychology*. Published online: 12 September 2016. doi: 10.1037/abn0000200.

Quinlivan EB, Gaynes BN, Lee JS, Heine AD, Shirey K, Edwards M, Modi R, Willig J, Pence BW (2016). Suicidal ideation is associated with limited engagement in HIV care. *Aids and Behavior*. Published online: 5 July 2016. doi: 10.1007/s10461-016-1469-8.

Racine M, Sanchez-Rodriguez E, Galan S, Tome-Pires C, Sole E, Jensen MP, Nielson WR, Miro J, Moulin DE, Choiniere M (2016). Factors associated with suicidal ideation in patients with chronic non-cancer pain. *Pain Medicine*. Published online: 10 June 2016. doi: 10.1093/pm/pnw115.

Rafi Bazrafshan M, Sharif F, Molazem Z, Mani A (2016). The effect of paternal addiction on adolescent suicide attempts: A qualitative study. *International Journal of High Risk Behaviors and Addiction*. Published online: 17 July 2016. doi: 10.5812/ijhrba.22588.

Rahgozar S, Motahari AA, Zolali A (2011). Assessing Bar-On's emotional intelligence components among normal subjects and those of having suicide trial record. *Indian Journal of Science and Technology* 4, 1391-1395.

Rahman SG, Alexanderson K, Jokinen J, Mittendorfer-Rutz E (2016). Disability pension due to common mental disorders and subsequent suicidal behaviour: A population-based prospective cohort study. *British Medical Journal Open* 6, e010152.

Ramalingam SJ, James AGDW, Annamalai AK (2016). Psychosocial factors associated with adolescent suicide attempts- a case control study. *Journal of Evolution of Medical and Dental Sciences* 5, 534-539.

Ramchand R, Ayer L, Kotzias V, Engel C, Predmore Z, Ebener P, Kemp JE, Karras E, Haas G (2016). Suicide risk among women veterans in distress: Perspectives of responders on the Veterans Crisis Line. *Women's Health Issues*. Published online: 27 August 2016. doi: 10.1016/j.whi.2016.07.005.

Rao S, Lam MHB, Yeung VSY, Wing YK, Waye MMY (2016). Association of HOMERr1 rs2290639 with suicide attempts in Hong Kong Chinese and the potentially functional role of this polymorphism. *Springerplus* 5, 767.

Rasmussen S, Hawton K, Philpott-Morgan S, O'Connor RC (2016). Why do adolescents self-harm? An investigation of motives in a community sample. *Crisis* 37, 176-183.

Reisner SL, White JM, Bradford JB, Mimiaga MJ (2014). Transgender health disparities: Comparing full cohort and nested matched-pair study designs in a community health center. *LGBT Health* 1, 177-184.

Reutfors J, Clapham E, Bahmanyar S, Brandt L, Jonsson EG, Ekbom A, Bodén R, Osby U (2016). Suicide risk and antipsychotic side effects in schizophrenia: Nested case-control study. *Human Psychopharmacology*. Published online: 25 April 2016. doi: 10.1002/hup.2536.

Ribeiro DB, Terra MG, Soccol KL, Schneider JF, Camillo LA, Plein FA (2016). Reasons for attempting suicide among men who use alcohol and other drugs. *Revista Gaucha de Enfermagem* 37, e54896.

Rigler T, Gosar D, Modic D (2016). Decision-making in adolescent females who deliberately self-harm. *Psihologija* 49, 87-103.

Roberts N, Booij L, Axas N, Repetti L (2016). Two-year prospective study of characteristics and outcome of adolescents referred to an adolescent urgent psychiatric clinic. *International Journal of Adolescence Medicine and Health*. Published online: 12 March 2016. doi: 10.1515/ijamh-2016-0006.

Robertson HA, Chaudhary Nagaraj N, Vyas AN (2016). Family violence and child sexual abuse among south Asians in the US. *Journal of Immigrant and Minority Health* 18, 921-927.

Rodante D, Rojas SM, Feldner MT, Dutton C, Rebok F, Teti GL, Grendas L, Fógola A, Daray FM (2016). Differences between female suicidal patients with family history of suicide attempt and family history of completed suicide. *Comprehensive Psychiatry* 70, 25-31.

Rodzinski P, Rutkowski K, Sobanski JA, Murzyn A, Mielimaka M, Smiatek-Mazgaj B, Cyranka K, Dembinska E, Grzadziel K, Klasa K, Mueldner-Nieckowski L, Smiatek-Mazgaj B (2015). Changes in neurotic personality profile associated with reduction of suicidal ideation in patients who underwent psychotherapy in the day hospital for the treatment of neurotic and behavioral disorders. *Psychiatria Polska* 49, 1323-1341.

Romo ML, Abril-Ulloa V, Kelvin EA (2016). The relationship between hunger and mental health outcomes among school-going Ecuadorian adolescents. *Social Psychiatry and Psychiatric Epidemiology* 51, 827-837.

Roush JF, Brown SL, Mitchell SM, Cukrowicz KC (2016). Shame, guilt, and suicide ideation among bondage and discipline, dominance and submission, and sadomasochism practitioners: Examining the role of the interpersonal theory of suicide. *Suicide and Life-Threatening Behavior*. Published online: 20 June 2016. doi: 10.1111/sltb.12267.

Rukundo GZ, Mishara BL, Kinyanda E (2016). Burden of suicidal ideation and attempt among persons living with HIV and aids in semiurban Uganda. *Aids Research and Treatment*. Published online: 16 February 2016. doi: 10.1155/2016/3015468.

Rulliat A (2010). The wave of suicides among Foxconn workers and the vacuity of Chinese trade unionism. *China Perspectives* 2010, 135-137.

Ruutel K, Valk A, Lohmus L (2016). Suicidality and associated factors among men who have sex with men in Estonia. *Journal of Homosexuality*. Published online: 20 September 2016. doi: 10.1080/00918369.2016.1236578.

Ryland HT (2016). Markedly raised risk of attempted suicide in female immigrants and violent criminality in male immigrants in Denmark. *Evidence Based Mental Health* 19, 93-94.

Sadeh N, Wolf EJ, Logue MW, Hayes JP, Stone A, Griffin LM, Schichman SA, Miller MW (2016). Epigenetic variation at SKA2 predicts suicide phenotypes and internalizing psychopathology. *Depression and Anxiety* 33, 308-315.

Saffer BY, Klonsky ED (2016). The relationship of self-reported executive functioning to suicide ideation and attempts: Findings from a large us-based online sample. *Archives of Suicide Research*. Published online: 20 July 2016. doi: 10.1080/13811118.2016.1211042.

Samyde J, Petit P, Hillaire-Buys D, Faillie J-L (2016). Quinolone antibiotics and suicidal behavior: Analysis of the world health organization's adverse drug reactions database and discussion of potential mechanisms. *Psychopharmacology* 233, 2503-2511.

Sankaranarayanan A, Castle D (2016). Burden associated with smoking as a suicidal risk factor in an Australian sample of patients with psychosis. *Australasian Psychiatry*. Published online: 29 April 2016. doi: 10.1177/1039856216646232.

Sansone RA, Elliott K, Wiederman MW (2016). Self-harm behaviors among female perpetrators of intimate partner violence. *Partner Abuse* 7, 44-54.

Santis R, Hidalgo CG, Hayden V, Anselmo E, Jaramillo A, Padilla O, Torres R (2016). Suicide attempts and self inflicted harm: A one year follow up of risk behaviors among out of treatment cocaine users. *Revista Medica De Chile* 144, 526-533.

Sareen J, Afifi TO, Taillieu T, Cheung K, Turner S, Bolton SL, Erickson J, Stein MB, Fikretoglu D, Zamorski MA (2016). Trends in suicidal behaviour and use of mental health services in Canadian military and civilian populations. *Canadian Medical Association Journal*. Published online: 29 April 2016. doi: 10.1177/1039856216646232.

Sattar FA, Bondade S, Kumar KK (2015). Clinical profile of female suicide attempters - a hospital based study. *Journal of Evolution of Medical and Dental Sciences* 4, 15741-15745.

Sawyer SM, Whitelaw M, Le Grange D, Yeo M, Hughes EK (2016). Physical and psychological morbidity in adolescents with atypical anorexia nervosa. *Pediatrics* 137, e20154080.

Schaefer KE, Esposito-Smythers C, Tangney JP (2016). Suicidal ideation in a United States jail: Demographic and psychiatric correlates. *Journal of Forensic Psychiatry and Psychology*. Published online: 16 June 2016. doi: 10.1080/14789949.2016.1193886.

Schapir L, Zalsman G, Hasson-Ohayon I, Gaziel M, Morag-Yaffe M, Sever J, Weizman A, Shoval G (2016). Suicide, satisfaction with life, and insight capacity among adolescents with mental disorders. *Crisis*. Published online: 24 June 2016. doi: 10.1027/0227-5910/a000403.

Schiavone S, Neri M, Mhillaj E, Morgese MG, Cantatore S, Bove M, Riezzo I, Tucci P, Pomara C, Turillazzi E, Cuomo V, Trabace L (2016). The NADPH oxidase NOX2 as a novel biomarker for suicidality: Evidence from human post mortem brain samples. *Translational Psychiatry* 6, e813.

Schimanski ID, Mouat KL, Billinghurst BL, Linscott RJ (2016). Preliminary evidence that schizophrenia liability at age 15 predicts suicidal ideation two years later. *Schizophrenia Research*. Published online: 6 September 2016. doi: 10.1016/j.schres.2016.08.030.

Schneider AL, Hostetter TA, Homaifar BY, Forster JE, Olson-Madden JH, Matarazzo BB, Huggins J, Brenner LA (2016). Responses to traumatic brain injury screening questions and suicide attempts among those seeking veterans health administration mental health services. *Frontiers in Psychiatry* 7, 59.

Schofield P, Das-Munshi J, Becares L, Morgan C, Bhavsar V, Hotopf M, Hatch SL (2016). Minority status and mental distress: A comparison of group density effects. *Psychological Medicine*. Published online: 30 June 2016. doi: 10.1017/S0033291716001835.

Segal DL, Connella A, Miller T, Coolidge FL (2016). Deliberate self-harm among younger and older adults. *Death Studies*. Published online: 6 April 2016. doi: 10.1080/07481187 .2016.1171265.

Selenius H, Leppänen Östman S, Strand S (2016). Self-harm as a risk factor for inpatient aggression among women admitted to forensic psychiatric care. *Nordic Journal of Psychiatry*. Published online: 25 May 2016. doi: 10.1080/08039488.2016.1183707.

Seo JH, Kang JM, Hwang SH, Han KD, Joo YH (2016). Relationship between tinnitus and suicidal behaviour in Korean men and women: A cross-sectional study. *Clinical Otolaryngology* 41, 222-227.

Serafini G, Calcagno P, Lester D, Girardi P, Amore M, Pompili M (2016). Suicide risk in alzheimer's disease: A systematic review. *Current Alzheimer Research* 13, 1083-1099.

Shaikh MA, Lloyd J, Acquah E, Celedonia KL, M LW (2016). Suicide attempts and behavioral correlates among a nationally representative sample of school-attending adolescents in the Republic of Malawi. *BMC Public Health* 16, 843.

Shalit N, Shoval G, Shlosberg D, Feingold D, Lev-Ran S (2016). The association between cannabis use and suicidality among men and women: A population-based longitudinal study. *Journal of Affective Disorders* 205, 216-224.

Shanahan L, Schorpp KM, Volpe VV, Linthicum K, Freeman JA (2016). Developmental timing of suicide attempts and cardiovascular risk during young adulthood. *Health Psychology* 35, 1135-1143.

Shani C, Yelena S, Reut BK, Adrian S, Sami H (2016). Suicidal risk among infertile women undergoing in-vitro fertilization: Incidence and risk factors. *Psychiatry Research* 240, 53-59.

Shearer A, Herres J, Kodish T, Squitieri H, James K, Russon J, Atte T, Diamond GS (2016). Differences in mental health symptoms across lesbian, gay, bisexual, and questioning youth in primary care settings. *Journal of Adolescent Health* 59, 38-43.

Shelef L, Levi-Belz Y, Fruchter E, Santo Y, Dahan E (2016). No way out: Entrapment as a moderator of suicide ideation among military personnel. *Journal of Clinical Psychology*. Published online: 19 April 2016. doi: 10.1002/jclp.22304.

Shrivastava A, Berlemont C, Campbell R, Johnston M, De Sousa A, Shah N (2016). Suicide in hospitalized early psychosis patients at the time of discharge from hospital: An exploratory study of attempters and nonattempters. *Indian Journal of Psychiatry* 58, 142-146.

Shrivastava A, Campbell R, Johnston M, Desousa A, Shah N, Karia S (2016). Predictors of patients with high suicidality during the post discharge period in the early phase of schizophrenia. *International Journal of Medical Science and Public Health*. Published online: 20 May 2016. doi: 10.5455/ijmsph.2016.19042016492.

Sicard S, Mayet A, Duron S, Richard J-B, Beck F, Meynard J-B, Deparis X, Marimoutou C (2016). Factor associated with risky sexual behaviors among the French general population. *Journal of Public Health (Oxford)*. Published online: 24 May 2016. doi: 10.1093/pubmed/fdw049.

Silvers JA, Hubbard AD, Chaudhury S, Biggs E, Shu J, Grunebaum MF, Fertuck E, Weber J, Kober H, Carson-Wong A, Brodsky BS, Chesin M, Ochsner KN, Stanley B (2016). Suicide attempters with borderline personality disorder show differential orbitofrontal and parietal recruitment when reflecting on aversive memories. *Journal of Psychiatric Research* 81, 71-78.

Simoneau H, Menard JM, Blanchette-Martin N (2016). Addiction severity and suicidal behaviors among persons entering treatment. *Archives of Suicide Research*. Published online: 2 May 2016. doi: 10.1080/13811118.2016.1182093.

Sinclair S, Bryan CJ, Bryan AO (2016). Meaning in life as a protective factor for the emergence of suicide ideation that leads to suicide attempts among military personnel and veterans with elevated PTSD and depression. *International Journal of Cognitive Therapy* 9, 87-98.

Singh K, Jindwani K, Sahu RN, Maniram RS, Dubey TN, Sharma VK (2016). A study of psychiatric factors in patients presented with attempted suicide in a state capital medical college hospital in central India. *Journal of Evolution of Medical and Dental Sciences* 5, 117-119.

Skinner KD, Rojas SM, Veilleux JC (2016). Connecting eating pathology with risk for engaging in suicidal behavior: The mediating role of experiential avoidance. *Suicide and Life-Threatening Behavior*. Published online: 2 April 2016. doi: 10.1111/sltb.12249.

Skopp NA, Zhang Y, Smolenski DJ, Reger MA (2016). Risk factors for self-directed violence in US soldiers: A case-control study. *Psychiatry Research* 245, 194-199.

Smith JL, De Nadai AS, Storch EA, Langland-Orban B, Pracht E, Petrila J (2016). Correlates of length of stay and boarding in Florida emergency departments for patients with psychiatric diagnoses. *Psychiatric Services*. Published online: 1 July 2016. doi: 10.1176/appi.ps.201500283.

Smith PN, Selwyn C, D'Amato D, Granato S, Kuhlman S, Mandracchia JT (2016). Life experiences and the acquired capability for suicide in incarcerated men. *Death Studies*. Published online: 6 April 2016. doi: 10.1080/07481187.2016.1171264.

Sobanski JA, Cyranka K, Rodzinski P, Klasa K, Rutkowski K, Dembinska E, Mielimaka M, Mueldner-Nieckowski L, Smiatek-Mazgaj B (2015). Are neurotic personality traits and neurotic symptoms intensity associated with suicidal thoughts reported by patients of a day hospital for neurotic disorders? *Psychiatria Polska* 49, 1343-1358.

Stanley IH, Horowitz LM, Bridge JA, Wharff EA, Pao M, Teach SJ (2016). Bullying and suicide risk among pediatric emergency department patients! *Pediatric Emergency Care* 32, 347-351.

Stephens DB, de Leon J (2016). CYP2D6 ultra-rapid metabolizer phenotype not associated with attempted suicide in a large sample of psychiatric inpatients. *Pharmacogenomics* 17, 1295-1304.

Stockton JG, Tucker RP, Kleiman EM, Wingate LR (2016). How does gratitude affect the relationship between positive humor styles and suicide-related outcomes? *Personality and Individual Differences* 102, 240-244.

Stolz E, Fux B, Mayerl H, Rasky E, Freidl W (2016). Passive suicide ideation among older adults in europe: A multilevel regression analysis of individual and societal determinants in 12 countries (SHARE). *Journal of Gerontology: Social Sciences*. Published online: 5 April 2016. doi: 10.1093/geronb/gbw041.

Strupp J, Ehmann C, Galushko M, Bucken R, Perrar KM, Hamacher S, Pfaff H, Voltz R, Golla H (2016). Risk factors for suicidal ideation in patients feeling severely affected by multiple sclerosis. *Journal of Palliative Medicine* 19, 523-528.

Stubbs B, Wu Y-T, Prina AM, Leng Y, Cosco TD (2016). A population study of the association between sleep disturbance and suicidal behaviour in people with mental illness. *Journal of Psychiatric Research* 82, 149-154.

Sun L, Zhang J (2016). Psychological strains and suicidal intent: An empirical study to relate the 2 psychopathological variables. *Journal of Nervous and Mental Disease* 204, 643-722.

Sun SH, Hu X, Zhang JY, Qiu HM, Liu X, Jia CX (2016). The COMT rs4680 polymorphism and suicide attempt in rural Shandong, China. *Psychiatric Genetics* 26, 166-171.

Supartini A, Honda T, Basri NA, Haeuchi Y, Chen S, Ichimiya A, Kumagai S (2016). The impact of sleep timing, sleep duration, and sleep quality on depressive symptoms and suicidal ideation amongst Japanese freshmen: The EQUSITE study. *Sleep Disorders* 2016, 8737654.

Supraja TA, Thennarasu K, Satyanarayana VA, Seena TK, Desai G, Jangam KV, Chandra PS (2016). Suicidality in early pregnancy among antepartum mothers in urban India. *Archives Women's Mental Health*. Published online: 26 August 2016. doi: 10.1007/s00737-016-0660-2.

Tadrous M, Martins D, Yao Z, Mamdani MM, Juurlink DN, Gomes T, Antoniou T (2016). Varenicline and risk of self-harm: A nested case-control study. *PLoS One* 11, e0163681.

Tan L, Xia T, Reece C (2016). Social and individual risk factors for suicide ideation among Chinese children and adolescents: A multilevel analysis. *International Journal of Psychology*. Published online: 18 April 2016. doi: 10.1002/ijop.12273.

Tanabe S, Terao T, Shiotsuki I, Kanehisa M, Ishii K, Shigemitsu O, Fujiki M, Hoaki N (2016). Anxious temperament as a risk factor of suicide attempt. *Comprehensive Psychiatry* 68, 72-77.

Tanaka E, Tsutsumi A, Kawakami N, Kameoka S, Kato H, You Y (2016). Long-term psychological consequences among adolescent survivors of the Wenchuan earthquake in China: A cross-sectional survey six years after the disaster. *Journal of Affective Disorders* 204, 255-261.

Tang J, Yang W, Ahmed NI, Ma Y, Liu H-Y, Wang J-J, Wang P-X, Du Y-K, Yu Y-Z (2016). Stressful life events as a predictor for nonsuicidal self-injury in Southern Chinese adolescence: A cross-sectional study. *Medicine* 95, e2637.

Taylor CL, van Ravesteyn LM, van denBerg MP, Stewart RJ, Howard LM (2016). The prevalence and correlates of self-harm in pregnant women with psychotic disorder and bipolar disorder. *Archives of Women's Mental Health* 19, 909-915.

Tebbe EA, Moradi B (2016). Suicide risk in trans populations: An application of minority stress theory. *Journal of Counselling Psychology*. Published online: 18 April 2016. doi: 10.1037/cou0000152.

Teevale T, Lee AC, Tiatia-Seath J, Clark TC, Denny S, Bullen P, Fleming T, Peiris-John RJ (2016). Risk and protective factors for suicidal behaviors among pacific youth in New Zealand. *Crisis*. Published online: 9 June 2016. doi: 10.1027/0227-5910/a000396.

Teixeira A, Oliveira A (2016). Exploratory study on the prevalence of suicidal behavior, mental health and social support in female street sex workers in Porto, Portugal. *Health Care for Women International*. Published online: 24 May 2016. doi: 10.1080/07399332.2016.1192172.

Tempier R, Guérin E (2015). Tobacco smoking and suicidal thoughts and attempts: Relationships from a general population survey. *Clinical Epidemiology and Global Health* 3, 137-143.

Thakur D, Gupta A, Thakur A, Mazta SR, Sharma D (2015). Prevalence and predictors of suicidal ideations among school going adolescents in a hilly state of India. *Industrial Psychiatry Journal* 24, 140-143.

Thomassin K, Shaffer A, Madden A, Londino DL (2016). Specificity of childhood maltreatment and emotion deficit in nonsuicidal self-injury in an inpatient sample of youth. *Psychiatry Research* 244, 103-108.

Thompson RG, Jr., Alonzo D, Hu MC, Hasin DS (2016). The influences of parental divorce and maternal-versus-paternal alcohol abuse on offspring lifetime suicide attempt. *Drug and Alcohol Review*. Published online: 19 August 2016. doi: 10.1111/dar.12441.

Thompson RG, Jr., Alonzo D, Hu MC, Hasin DS (2016). Substance use disorders and poverty as prospective predictors of adult first-time suicide ideation or attempt in the United States. *Community Mental Health Journal*. Published online: 16 July 2016. doi: 10.1007/s10597-016-0045-z.

Till B, Tran US, Niederkrotenthaler T (2016). Relationship satisfaction and risk factors for suicide. *Crisis*. Published online: 22 July 2016. doi: 10.1027/0227-5910/a000407.

Tomas-Aragones L, Marron SE (2016). Body image and body dysmorphic concerns. *Acta Dermato-Venereologica* 96, 47-50.

Too LS, Pirkis J, Milner A, Spittal MJ (2016). Clusters of suicides and suicide attempts: Detection, proximity and correlates. *Epidemiology and Psychiatric Sciences*. 9 June 2016. doi: 10.1017/S2045796016000391.

Townsend E, Wadman R, Sayal K, Armstrong M, Harroe C, Majumder P, Vostanis P, Clarke D (2016). Uncovering key patterns in self-harm in adolescents: Sequence analysis using the card sort task for self-harm (CATS). *Journal of Affective Disorders* 206, 161-168.

Trakhtenbrot R, Gvion Y, Levi-Belz Y, Horesh N, Fischel T, Weiser M, Treves I, Apter A (2016). Predictive value of psychological characteristics and suicide history on medical lethality of suicide attempts: A follow-up study of hospitalized patients. *Journal of Affective Disorders* 199, 73-80.

Tran LD, Grant D, Aydin M (2016). California veterans receive inadequate treatment to address their mental health needs. *American Journal of Medical Research* 3, 126-140.

Tran LD, Grant D, Aydin M (2016). The mental health status of California veterans. *Policy Brief UCLA Center For Health Policy Research* 1-10.

Tripp JC, McDevitt-Murphy ME (2016). Trauma-related guilt mediates the relationship between posttraumatic stress disorder and suicidal ideation in OEF/OIF/OND veterans. *Suicide and Life-Threatening Behavior*. Published online: 7 June 2016. doi: 10.1111/sltb.12266.

Tsukahara T, Arai H, Kamijo T, Kobayashi Y, Washizuka S, Arito H, Nomiyama T (2016). The relationship between attitudes toward suicide and family history of suicide in Nagano prefecture, Japan. *International Journal of Environmental Research and Public Health* 13, 623.

Tucker RP, O'Connor RC, Wingate LR (2016). An investigation of the relationship between rumination styles, hope, and suicide ideation through the lens of the integrated motivational-volitional model of suicidal behavior. *Archives of Suicide Research* 20, 553-566.

Turner BJ, Wakefield MA, Gratz KL, Chapman AL (2016). Characterizing interpersonal difficulties among young adults who engage in nonsuicidal self-injury using a daily diary. *Behavior Therapy*. Published online: 14 July 2016. doi: 10.1016/j.beth.2016.07.001.

Turner BJ, Yiu A, Claes L, Muehlenkamp JJ, Chapman AL (2016). Occurrence and co-occurrence of nonsuicidal self-injury and disordered eating in a daily diary study: Which behavior, when? *Psychiatry Research* 246, 39-47.

Unlu G, Cakaloz B (2016). Effects of perpetrator identity on suicidality and nonsuicidal self-injury in sexually victimized female adolescents. *Neuropsychiatric Disease and Treatment* 12, 1489-1497.

Ursano RJ, Kessler RC, Stein MB, Naifeh JA, Aliaga PA, Fullerton CS, Wynn GH, Vegella PL, Ng TH, Zhang BG, Wryter CL, Sampson NA, Kao TC, Colpe LJ, Schoenbaum M, McCarroll JE, Cox KL, Heeringa SG (2016). Risk factors, methods, and timing of suicide attempts among US army soldiers. *JAMA Psychiatric* 73, 741-749.

van Bergen DD, Saharso S (2016). Suicidality of young ethnic minority women with an immigrant background: The role of autonomy. *European Journal of Women's Studies* 23, 297-311.

van de Venne J, Cerel J, Moore M, Maple M (2016). Predictors of suicide ideation in a random digit dial study: Exposure to suicide matters. *Archives of Suicide Research*. Published online: 20 July 2016. doi: 10.1080/13811118.2016.1211044.

Vanyukov PM, Szanto K, Hallquist M, Moitra M, Dombrovski AY (2016). Perceived burdensomeness is associated with low-lethality suicide attempts, dysfunctional interpersonal style, and younger rather than older age. *International Journal of Geriatric Psychiatry*. Published online: 14 June 2016. doi: 10.1002/gps.4526.

Vasiliadis HM, Lamoureux-Lamarche C, Gontijo Guerra S (2016). Gender and age group differences in suicide risk associated with co-morbid physical and psychiatric disorders in older adults. *International Psychogeriatrics*. Published online: 8 September 2016. doi: 10.1017/S1041610216001290.

Velkoff EA, Forrest LN, Dodd DR, Smith AR (2015). Identity, relationship satisfaction, and disclosure: Predicting suicide risk among sexual minority women. *Psychology of Women Quarterly* 40, 261-274.

Velloso P, Piccinato C, Ferrao Y, Aliende Perin E, Cesar R, Fontenelle L, Hounie AG, do Rosario MC (2016). The suicidality continuum in a large sample of obsessive-compulsive disorder (OCD) patients. *European Psychiatry* 38, 1-7.

Verma D, Srivastava MK, Singh SK, Bhatia T, Deshpande SN (2016). Lifetime suicide intent, executive function and insight in schizophrenia and schizoaffective disorders. *Schizophrenia Research*. Published online: 29 August 2016. doi: 10.1016/j.schres.2016.08.009.

Vernham Z, Tapp J, Moore E (2016). Observer ratings of interpersonal behavior as predictors of aggression and self-harm in a high-security sample of male forensic inpatients. *Journal of Interpersonal Violence* 31, 1597-1617.

Viana AG, Dixon LJ, Berenz EC, Espil FM (2016). Trauma and deliberate self-harm among inpatient adolescents: The moderating role of anxiety sensitivity. *Psychological Trauma: Theory, Research, Practice, and Policy*. Published online: 23 June 2016. doi: 10.1037/tra0000161.

Vieira AI, Ramalho S, Brandao I, Saraiva J, Goncalves S (2016). Adversity, emotion regulation, and non-suicidal self-injury in eating disorders. *Eating Disorders*. Published online: 27 June 2016. doi: 10.1080/10640266.2016.1198205.

Voegeli G, Ramoz N, Shekhtman T, Courtet P, Gorwood P, Kelsoe JR (2016). Neurotrophin genes and antidepressant-worsening suicidal ideation: A prospective case-control study. *International Journal of Neuropsychopharmacology*. Published online: 4 July 2016. doi: 10.1093/ijnp/pyw059.

Waesche MC, Clark CB, Cropsey KL (2016). The connection between thwarted belongingness, alcohol consumption, suicidal, and homicidal ideation in a criminal justice sample. *Journal of Addiction Medicine*. Published online: 7 September 2016. doi: 10.1097/ADM.0000000000000257.

Walker KL, Chang EC, Hirsch JK (2016). Neuroticism and suicidal behavior: Conditional indirect effects of social problem solving and hopelessness. *International Journal of Mental Health and Addiction*. Published online: 31 March 2016. doi: 10.1007/s11469-016-9648-4.

Walker R, Francis D, Brody G, Simons R, Cutrona C, Gibbons F (2016). A longitudinal study of racial discrimination and risk for death ideation in African American youth. *Suicide and Life-Threatening Behavior*. Published online: 3 May 2016. doi: 10.1111/sltb.12251.

Wan YH, Liu W, Sun Y, Hao JH, Tao FB (2016). Relationships between various forms of childhood abuse and suicidal behaviors among middle school students. *Zhonghua Liu Xing Bing Xue Za Zhi* 37, 506-511.

Wang M-C, Wong YJ, Nyutu PN, Spears A, Iii WN (2016). Suicide protective factors in outpatient substance abuse patients: Religious faith and family support. *International Journal for the Psychology of Religion*. Published online: 2 May 2016. doi: 10.1080/10508619.2016.1174568.

Wang XL, Yip PSF, Chan CLW (2016). Suicide prevention for local public and volunteer relief workers in disaster-affected areas. *Journal of Public Health Management and Practice* 22, E39-E46.

Wang Y, Bhaskaran J, Sareen J, Bolton S-L, Chateau D, Bolton JM (2016). Clinician prediction of future suicide attempts a longitudinal study. *Canadian Journal of Psychiatry*. Published online: 19 April 2016. doi: 10.1177/0706743716645287.

Ward-Ciesielski EF, Schumacher JA, Bagge CL (2016). Relations between nonsuicidal self-injury and suicide attempt characteristics in a sample of recent suicide attempters. *Crisis*. Published online: 24 June 2016. doi: 10.1027/0227-5910/a000400.

Weeks M, Colman I (2016). Predictors of suicidal behaviors in Canadian adolescents with no recent history of depression. *Archives of Suicide Research*. Published online: 1 September 2016. doi: 10.1080/13811118.2016.1193076.

Wei H-T, Lan W-H, Hsu J-W, Bai Y-M, Huang K-L, Su T-P, Li C-T, Lin W-C, Chen T-J, Chen M-H (2016). Risk of suicide attempt among adolescents with conduct disorder: A longitudinal follow-up study. *Journal of Pediatrics* 177, 292-296.

Welch E, Jangmo A, Thornton LM, Norring C, von Hausswolff-Juhlin Y, Herman BK, Pawaskar M, Larsson H, Bulik CM (2016). Treatment-seeking patients with binge-eating disorder in the Swedish national registers: Clinical course and psychiatric comorbidity. *BMC Psychiatry* 16, 163.

Weng S-C, Huang J-P, Huang Y-L, Lee TS-H, Chen Y-h (2016). Effects of tobacco exposure on perinatal suicidal ideation, depression, and anxiety. *BMC Public Health* 16, e623.

Werbeloff N, Markou M, Hayes JF, Pitman AL, Osborn DPJ (2016). Individual and area-level risk factors for suicidal ideation and attempt in people with severe depression. *Journal of Affective Disorders* 205, 387-392.

Wielgus MD, Aldrich JT, Mezulis AH, Crowell SE (2016). Respiratory sinus arrhythmia as a predictor of self-injurious thoughts and behaviors among adolescents. *International Journal of Psychophysiology* 106, 127-134.

Wiener CD, Molina ML, Passos M, Moreira FP, Bittencourt G, de Mattos Souza LD, da Silva RA, Jansen K, Oses JP (2016). Neuron-specific enolase levels in drug-naive young adults with major depressive disorder. *Neuroscience Letters* 620, 93-96.

Wilson ST, Chesin M, Fertuck E, Keilp J, Brodsky B, Mann JJ, Sönmez CC, Benjamin-Phillips C, Stanley B (2016). Heart rate variability and suicidal behavior. *Psychiatry Research* 240, 241-247.

Wimberley T, Stovring H, Sorensen HJ, Horsdal HT, MacCabe JH, Gasse C (2016). Predictors of treatment resistance in patients with schizophrenia: A population-based cohort study. *Lancet Psychiatry* 3, 358-366.

Windfuhr K, While D, Kapur N, Ashcroft DM, Kontopantelis E, Carr MJ, Shaw J, Appleby L, Webb RT (2016). Suicide risk linked with clinical consultation frequency, psychiatric diagnoses and psychotropic medication prescribing in a national study of primary-care patients. *Psychological Medicine*. Published online: 21 September 2016. doi: 10.1017/S0033291716001823.

Wolford-Clevenger C, Vann NC, Smith PN (2016). The association of partner abuse types and suicidal ideation among men and women college students. *Violence and Victims* 31, 471-485.

Wong MM, Brower KJ, Craun EA (2016). Insomnia symptoms and suicidality in the national comorbidity survey - adolescent supplement. *Journal of Psychiatric Research* 81, 1-8.

Wright MF (2015). Cyber victimization on college campuses: Longitudinal associations with suicidal ideation, depression, and anxiety. *Criminal Justice Review* 41, 190-203.

Wu CS, Liao SC, Tsai YT, Chang SS, Tsai HJ (2016). Comparative risk of self-harm hospitalization amongst depressive disorder patients using different antidepressants: A population-based cohort study in Taiwan. *Psychological Medicine*. Published online: 23 September 2016. doi: 10.1017/S0033291716002257.

Wu D, Rockett IRH, Yang T, Feng X, Jiang S, Yu L (2016). Deliberate self-harm among Chinese medical students: A population-based study. *Journal of Affective Disorders* 202, 137-144.

Xin X, Wang Y, Fang J, Ming Q, Yao S (2016). Prevalence and correlates of direct self-injurious behavior among Chinese adolescents: Findings from a multicenter and multistage survey. *Journal of Abnormal Child Psychology*. Published online: 26 August 2016. doi: 10.1007/s10802-016-0201-5.

Xu H, Qin L, Wang J, Zhou L, Luo D, Hu M, Li Z, Xiao S (2016). A cross-sectional study on risk factors and their interactions with suicidal ideation among the elderly in rural communities of Hunan, China. *British Medical Journal Open* 6, e010914.

Xu Z, Mayer B, Müller M, Heekeren K, Theodoridou A, Dvorsky D, Metzler S, Oexle N, Walitza S, Rössler W, Rüsch N (2016). Stigma and suicidal ideation among young people at risk of psychosis after one year. *Psychiatry Research* 243, 219-224.

Yang FY, Lai CY, Yen CF, Hsu YY, Zauszniewski JA (2016). The depressive symptoms, resourcefulness, and self-harm behaviors of adolescents. *The Journal of Nursing Research*. Published online: 15 June 2016. doi: 10.1097/jnr.0000000000000127.

Yang J, Chen K, Wei Q, Chen Y, Cao B, Burgunder JM, Shang HF (2016). Clinical and genetic characteristics in patients with Huntington's disease from China. *Neurological Research*. Published online: 29 July 2016. doi: 10.1080/01616412.2016.1214555.

Yang Y, Chen J, Liu C, Fang L, Liu Z, Guo J, Cheng K, Zhou C, Zhan Y, Melgiri ND, Zhang L, Zhong J, Chen J, Rao C, Xie P (2016). The extrinsic coagulation pathway: A biomarker for suicidal behavior in major depressive disorder. *Scientific Reports* 6, 32882.

Yao S, Kuja-Halkola R, Thornton LM, Runfola CD, D'Onofrio BM, Almqvist C, Lichtenstein P, Sjolander A, Larsson H, Bulik CM (2016). Familial liability for eating disorders and suicide attempts evidence from a population registry in Sweden. *JAMA Psychiatry* 73, 284-291.

Yaseen ZS, Galynker II, Briggs J, Freed RD, Gabbay V (2016). Functional domains as correlates of suicidality among psychiatric inpatients. *Journal of Affective Disorders* 203, 77-83.

Yi S, Tuot S, Chhoun P, Pal K, Choub SC, Mburu G (2016). Prevalence and correlates of psychological distress among drug users in Phnom Penh, Cambodia. *International Journal of Drug Policy* 36, 25-32.

Yiannakoulias N, Sanchez-Ramirez D, Svenson LW, Voaklander DC (2016). A cohort study of regional migration and the risks of attempted suicide and violent assault injury. *Injury Prevention*. Published online: 9 May 2016. doi: 10.1136/injuryprev-2015-041932.

Yilmaz O, Ateş MA, Semiz ÜB, Tütüncü R, Bez Y, Algül A, Balibey H, Başoğlu C, Ebrinç S, Çetin M (2016). Childhood traumas in patients with bipolar disorder: Association with alexithymia and dissociative experiences. *Anatolian Journal of Psychiatry* 17, 188-195.

Yoo HJ, Hong JP, Cho MJ, Fava M, Mischoulon D, Heo J-Y, Kim K, Jeon HJ (2016). Lifetime suicidal ideation and attempt in adults with full major depressive disorder versus sustained depressed mood. *Journal of Affective Disorders* 203, 275-280.

Yoon J-H, Jeung D, Chang S-J (2016). Does high emotional demand with low job control relate to suicidal ideation among service and sales workers in Korea? *Journal of Korean Medical Science* 31, 1042-1048.

Yoon JH, Kang MY (2016). The crossover effect of spouses' long working hours on depressive symptoms and suicidal ideation. *Industrial Health*. Published online: 5 April 2016. doi: 10.2486/indhealth.2015-0174.

Yoshimi NT, Campos LM, Simão MO, Torresan RC, Torres AR (2016). Social anxiety symptoms in alcohol-dependent outpatients: Prevalence, severity and predictors. *Jornal Brasileiro De Psiquiatria* 65, 117-126.

You J, Jiang Y, Zhang M, Du C, Lin MP, Leung F (2016). Perceived parental control, self-criticism, and nonsuicidal self-injury among adolescents: Testing the reciprocal relationships by a three-wave cross-lag model. *Archives of Suicide Research*. Published online: 19 July 2016. doi: 10.1080/13811118.2016.1199989.

You J, Lin MP, Xu S, Hu WH (2016). Big five personality traits in the occurrence and repetition of nonsuicidal self-injury among adolescents: The mediating effects of depressive symptoms. *Personality and Individual Differences* 101, 227-231.

Yu EA, Chang EC (2016). Optimism/pessimism and future orientation as predictors of suicidal ideation: Are there ethnic differences? *Cultural Diversity and Ethnic Minority Psychology*. Published online: 5 May 2016. doi: 10.1037/cdp0000107.

Yuan X, Devine DP (2016). The role of anxiety in vulnerability for self-injurious behaviour: Studies in a rodent model. *Behavioural Brain Research* 311, 201-209.

Zaborskis A, Sirvyte D, Zemaitiene N (2016). Prevalence and familial predictors of suicidal behaviour among adolescents in Lithuania: A cross-sectional survey 2014. *BMC Public Health* 16, 554.

Zaheer J, Shera W, Tat Tsang AK, Law S, Alan Fung WL, Eynan R, Lam J, Zheng X, Pozi L, Links PS (2016). "I just couldn't step out of the circle. I was trapped": Patterns of endurance and distress in Chinese-Canadian women with a history of suicidal behaviour. *Social Science and Medicine* 160, 43-53.

Zerach G, Levi-Belz Y, Michelson M, Solomon Z (2016). Suicidal ideation among wives of former prisoners of war: A longitudinal dyadic study. *Psychiatry (New York)* 79, 147-163.

Zetterqvist M (2016). Nonsuicidal self-injury in adolescents: Characterization of the disorder and the issue of distress and impairment. *Suicide and Life-Threatening Behavior*. Published online: 2 August 2016. doi: 10.1111/sltb.12283.

Zhang J, Song J, Wang J (2016). Adolescent self-harm and risk factors. *Asia Pacific Psychiatry*. Published online: 25 May 2016. doi: 10.1111/appy.12243.

Zhang SC, Tao FB, Wu XY, Tao SM, Fang J (2016). Low health literacy and psychological symptoms potentially increase the risks of non-suicidal self-injury in Chinese middle school students. *BMC Psychiatry* 16, 327.

Zhong QY, Wells A, Rondon MB, Williams MA, Barrios YV, Sanchez SE, Gelaye B (2016). Childhood abuse and suicidal ideation in a cohort of pregnant Peruvian women. *American Journal of Obstetrics and Gynecology* 215, 501.e1-501.e8.

Zimmerman GM, Rees C, Posick C, Zimmerman LA (2016). The power of (mis)perception: Rethinking suicide contagion in youth friendship networks. *Social Science and Medicine* 157, 31-38.

Zuromski KL, Cero I, Witte TK, Zeng P (2016). The quadratic relationship between body mass index and suicide ideation: A nonlinear analysis of indirect effects. *Suicide and Life-Threatening Behavior*. Published online: 13 June 2016. doi: 10.1111/sltb.12270.

Zvolensky MJ, Jardin C, Garey L, Robles Z, Sharp C (2016). Acculturative stress and experiential avoidance: Relations to depression, suicide, and anxiety symptoms among minority college students. *Cognitive Behaviour Therapy*. Published online: 22 July 2016. doi: 10.1080/16506073.2016.1205658.

Prevention

Delgado-Gomez D, Baca-Garcia E, Aguado D, Courtet P, Lopez-Castroman J (2016). Computerized adaptive test vs. Decision trees: Development of a support decision system to identify suicidal behavior. *Journal of Affective Disorders* 206, 204-209.

Elder H, Karras E, Bossarte RM (2016). Promoting help seeking among veteran households: Associations between exposure to multiple types of health messages and intentions to utilize related public health hotlines. *Military Medicine* 181, 649-654.

Gewirtz AH, DeGarmo DS, Zamir O (2016). Effects of a military parenting program on parental distress and suicidal ideation: After deployment adaptive parenting tools. *Suicide and Life Threatening Behavior* 46, S23-S31.

Hearn S, Wanganeen G, Sutton K, Isaacs A (2016). The Jekkora group: An Aboriginal model of early identification, and support of persons with psychological distress and suicidal ideation in rural communities. *Advances in Mental Health* 14, 96-105.

Hill RM, Pettit JW (2016). Pilot randomized controlled trial of leap: A selective preventive intervention to reduce adolescents' perceived burdensomeness. *Journal of Clinical Child and Adolescent Psychology*. Published online: 17 August 2016. doi: 10.1080/15374416.2016.1188705.

Kasahara-Kiritani M, Masuda F, Ishii A (2015). Qualitative process evaluation of a social support educational program for youths. *Health* 7, 390-396.

Leong C, Alessi-Severini S, Sareen J, Enns MW, Bolton J (2016). Community pharmacists' perspectives on dispensing medications with the potential for misuse, diversion, and intentional overdose: Results of a province-wide survey of community pharmacists in Canada. *Substance Use and Misuse* 51, 1724-1730.

Mascherek AC, Schwappach DLB (2016). Patient safety priorities in mental healthcare in Switzerland: A modified Delphi study. *British Medical Journal Open* 6, e011494.

Metzger MH, Tvardik N, Gicquel Q, Bouvry C, Poulet E, Potinet-Pagliaroli V (2016). Use of emergency department electronic medical records for automated epidemiological surveillance of suicide attempts: A French pilot study. *International Journal of Methods and Psychiatric Research*. Published online: 15 September 2016. doi: 10.1002/mpr.1522.

O'Shea LE, Dickens GL (2016). Role of assessment components and recent adverse outcomes in risk estimation and prediction: Use of the short term assessment of risk and treatability (START) in an adult secure inpatient mental health service. *Psychiatry Research* 240, 398-405.

Ross AM, Kelly CM, Jorm AF (2014). Re-development of mental health first aid guidelines for suicidal ideation and behaviour: A Delphi study. *BMC Psychiatry* 14, 241.

Schembari BC, Jobes DA, Horgan RJ (2016). Successful treatment of suicidal risk what helped and what was internalized? *Crisis* 37, 218-223.

Tyuse SW, Cooper-Sadlo S, Underwood SE (2016). Descriptive study of older adults encountered by crisis intervention team (CIT) law enforcement officers. *Journal of Women and Aging*. Published online: 19 August 2016. doi: 10.1080/08952841.2016.1174513.

Vatne M, Nåden D (2016). Experiences that inspire hope: Perspectives of suicidal patients. *Nursing Ethics*. Published online: 12 August 2016. doi: 10.1177/0969733016658794.

Walker T, Shaw J, Turpin C, Roberts C, Reid C, Abel K (2016). A qualitative study of good-bye letters in prison therapy. *Crisis*. Published online: 22 July 2016. doi: 10.1027/0227-5910/a000411.

Care and support

Ahmed N, John A, Islam S, Jones R, Anderson P, Davies C, Khanom A, Harris S, Huxley P (2016). Investigating the feasibility of an enhanced contact intervention in self-harm and suicidal behaviour: A protocol for a randomised controlled trial delivering a social support and wellbeing intervention following self harm (SWISH). *British Medical Journal Open* 6, e012043.

Barnicot K, Gonzalez R, McCabe R, Priebe S (2016). Skills use and common treatment processes in dialectical behaviour therapy for borderline personality disorder. *Journal of Behavior Therapy and Experimental Psychiatry* 52, 147-156.

Bartgis J, Albright G (2016). Online role-play simulations with emotionally responsive avatars for the early detection of native youth psychological distress, including depression and suicidal ideation. *American Indian and Alaska Native Mental Health Research* 23, 1-27.

Birkbak J, Stuart EA, Lind BD, Qin P, Stenager E, Larsen KJ, Wang AG, Nielsen AC, Pedersen CM, Winslov JH, Langhoff C, Muhlmann C, Nordentoft M, Erlangsen A (2016). Psychosocial therapy and causes of death after deliberate self-harm: A register-based, nationwide multicentre study using propensity score matching. *Psychological Medicine*. Published online: 22 September 2016. doi: 10.1017/S0033291716001872.

Brent DA (2016). Antidepressants and suicidality. *Psychiatric Clinics of North America* 39, 503-512.

Calati R, Courtet P (2016). Is psychotherapy effective for reducing suicide attempt and non-suicidal self-injury rates? Meta-analysis and meta-regression of literature data. *Journal of Psychiatric Research* 79, 8-20.

Chesin MS, Benjamin-Phillips CA, Keilp J, Fertuck EA, Brodsky BS, Stanley B (2016). Improvements in executive attention, rumination, cognitive reactivity, and mindfulness among high-suicide risk patients participating in adjunct mindfulness-based cognitive therapy: Preliminary findings. *Journal of Alternative and Complementary Medicine* 22, 642-649.

Coughlin CG, Jakubovski E, Bloch MH (2016). Time course and predictors of suicidal ideation during citalopram treatment in the STAR*D Trial. *Journal of Clinical Psychiatry*. Published online: 13 September 2016. doi: 10.4088/JCP.15m10075.

Cowles M, Nightingale J (2015). Diagnosis-specific CBT as a stepping stone to transdiagnostic CBT in a complex case. *Cognitive Behaviour Therapist*. Published online: 26 August 2015. doi: 10.1017/S1754470X15000550.

Cox KS, Mouilso ER, Venners MR, Defever ME, Duvivier L, Rauch SAM, Strom TQ, Joiner TE, Tuerk PW (2016). Reducing suicidal ideation through evidence-based treatment for posttraumatic stress disorder. *Journal of Psychiatric Research* 80, 59-63.

Cwik MF, Tingey L, Lee A, Suttle R, Lake K, Walkup JT, Barlow A (2016). Development and piloting of a brief intervention for suicidal American Indian adolescents. *American Indian and Alaska Native Mental Health Research* 23, 105-124.

Diamond G, Russon J, Levy S (2016). Attachment-based family therapy: A review of the empirical support. *Family Process* 55, 595-610.

Dowling S, Doyle L (2016). Responding to self-harm in the school setting: The experience of guidance counsellors and teachers in Ireland. *British Journal of Guidance and Counselling*. Published online: 27 March 2016. doi: 10.1080/03069885.2016.1164297.

Farré A, Portella MJ, De Angel L, Díaz A, de Diego-Adeliño J, Vegué J, Duran-Sindreu S, Faus G, Tejedor C, Álvarez E, Perez V (2016). Benefits of a secondary prevention program in suicide. *Crisis*. Published online: 1 June 2016. doi: 10.1027/0227-5910/a000388.

Forkmann T, Brakemeier EL, Teismann T, Schramm E, Michalak J (2016). The effects of mindfulness-based cognitive therapy and cognitive behavioral analysis system of psychotherapy added to treatment as usual on suicidal ideation in chronic depression: Results of a randomized-clinical trial. *Journal of Affective Disorders* 200, 51-57.

Franklin JC, Fox KR, Franklin CR, Kleiman EM, Ribeiro JD, Jaroszewski AC, Hooley JM, Nock MK (2016). A brief mobile app reduces nonsuicidal and suicidal self-injury: Evidence from three randomized controlled trials. *Journal of Consulting and Clinical Psychology* 84, 544-557.

Gallo JJ, Hwang S, Joo JH, Bogner HR, Morales KH, Bruce ML, Reynolds CF, 3rd (2016). Multimorbidity, depression, and mortality in primary care: Randomized clinical trial of an evidence-based depression care management program on mortality risk. *Journal of General Internal Medicine* 31, 380-386.

Grano N, Kallionpaa S, Karjalainen M, Salmijarvi L, Roine M, Taylor P (2016). Declines in suicidal ideation in adolescents being treated in early intervention service. *Psychosis-Psychological Social and Integrative Approaches* 8, 176-179.

Hetrick SE, Robinson J, Spittal MJ, Carter G (2016). Effective psychological and psychosocial approaches to reduce repetition of self-harm: A systematic review, meta-analysis and meta-regression. *British Medical Journal Open* 6, e011024.

Howson S, Huline-Dickens S (2016). Do interventions reduce the risk of repeat self-harm or suicide in young people? *BJPsych Advances* 22, 287-291.

Huang S-F, Lu C-H, Ju C-L, Lan J-T, Chang C-W, Chang C-L, Kao W-T, Lin C-H, Horng C-T (2015). The benefit of clinical psychologists in prevention from the suicide in one hospital in Taiwan, Republic of China. *Life Science Journal* 12, 138-145.

Idenfors H, Strömsten LMJ, Renberg ES (2016). Non-psychiatric inpatient care preceding admission for self-harm in young people. *Journal of Psychosomatic Research* 88, 8-13.

Ionescu DF, Swee MB, Pavone KJ, Taylor N, Akeju O, Baer L, Nyer M, Cassano P, Mischoulon D, Alpert JE, Brown EN, Nock MK, Fava M, Cusin C (2016). Rapid and sustained reductions in current suicidal ideation following repeated doses of intravenous ketamine: Secondary analysis of an open-label study. *Journal of Clinical Psychiatry* 77, e719-e725.

Kim HS, Shin EJ, Lee SH (2016). Effects of a peer gatekeeper training program in female high school students. *International Journal of Bio-Science and Bio-Technology* 8, 101-110.

Kim JM, Kang HJ, Bae KY, Kim SW, Shin IS, Hong YJ, Ahn Y, Jeong MH, Kang H, Yoon JS (2016). Determinants and escitalopram treatment effects on suicidal ideation in patients with acute coronary syndrome: Findings from the K-DEPACS and EsDEPACS studies. *International Journal of Cardiology* 219, 225-230.

Kline A, Chesin M, Latorre M, Miller R, St. Hill L, Shcherbakov A, King A, Stanley B, Weiner MD, Interian A (2016). Rationale and study design of a trial of mindfulness-based cognitive therapy for preventing suicidal behavior (MBCT-S) in military veterans. *Contemporary Clinical Trials* 50, 245-252.

Kodama T, Syouji H, Takaki S, Fujimoto H, Ishikawa S, Fukutake M, Taira M, Hashimoto T (2016). Text messaging for psychiatric outpatients: Effect on help-seeking and self-harming behaviors. *Journal of Psychosocial Nursing and Mental Health Services* 54, 31-37.

Kohler O, Gasse C, Petersen L, Ingstrup KG, Nierenberg AA, Mors O, Ostergaard SD (2016). The effect of concomitant treatment with SSRIS and statins: A population-based study. *American Journal of Psychiatry* 173, 807-815.

Lahoz T, Hvid M, Wang AG (2016). Preventing repetition of attempted suicide-III. The Amager Project, 5-year follow-up of a randomized controlled trial. *Nordic Journal of Psychiatry* 70, 547-553.

Landes SJ, Matthieu MM, Smith BN, Trent LR, Rodriguez AL, Kemp J, Thompson C (2016). Dialectical behavior therapy training and desired resources for implementation: Results from a national program evaluation in the veterans health administration. *Military Medicine* 181, 747-752.

Law YW, Yip PS, Lai CC, Kwok CL, Wong PW, Liu KS, Ng PW, Liao CW, Wong TW (2016). A pilot study on the efficacy of volunteer mentorship for young adults with self-harm behaviors using a quasi-experimental design. *Crisis*. Published online: 9 June 2016. doi: 10.1027/0227-5910/a000393.

Lee SJ, Osteen PJ, Frey JJ (2016). Predicting changes in behavioral health professionals' clinical practice skills for recognizing and responding to suicide risk. *Journal of the Society for Social Work and Research* 7, 23-41.

Ligier F, Kabuth B, Guillemin F (2016). Mediaconnex: A multicenter randomised trial based on short message service to reduce suicide attempt recurrence in adolescents. *BMC Psychiatry* 16, 251.

Madsen T, van Spijker B, Karstoft KI, Nordentoft M, Kerkhof AJ (2016). Trajectories of suicidal ideation in people seeking web-based help for suicidality: Secondary analysis of a Dutch randomized controlled trial. *Journal of Medical Internet Research* 18, e178.

Mehlum L, Ramberg M, Tormoen AJ, Haga E, Diep LM, Stanley BH, Miller AL, Sund AM, Groholt B (2016). Dialectical behavior therapy compared with enhanced usual care for adolescents with repeated suicidal and self-harming behavior: Outcomes over a one-year follow-up. *Journal of the American Academy of Child and Adolescent Psychiatry* 55, 295-300.

Miller IW, Gaudiano BA, Weinstock LM (2016). The coping long term with active suicide program: Description and pilot data. *Suicide and Life-Threatening Behavior*. Published online: 2 April 2016. doi: 10.1111/sltb.12247.

Milner A, Spittal MJ, Kapur N, Witt K, Pirkis J, Carter G (2016). Mechanisms of brief contact interventions in clinical populations: A systematic review. *BMC Psychiatry* 16, 194.

Nestor BA, Cheek SM, Liu RT (2016). Ethnic and racial differences in mental health service utilization for suicidal ideation and behavior in a nationally representative sample of adolescents. *Journal of Affective Disorders* 202, 197-202.

O'Brien KH, LeCloux M, Ross A, Gironda C, Wharff EA (2016). A pilot study of the acceptability and usability of a smartphone application intervention for suicidal adolescents and their parents. *Archives of Suicide Research*. Published online: 2 May 2016. doi: 10.1080/13811118.2016.1182094.

Rahnama N, Tarkhan M, Khalatbari J, Khalili A (2016). Effectiveness of imagery rescripting and reprocessing therapy on insomnia, nightmare and suicide ideation in depressed persons with suicide attempt history. *International Journal of Medical Research and Health Sciences* 5, 292-296.

Randall JR, Chateau D, Smith M, Taylor C, Bolton J, Katz L, Burland E, Katz A, Nickel NC, Enns J, Brownell M (2016). An early intervention for psychosis and its effect on criminal accusations and suicidal behaviour using a matched-cohort design. *Schizophrenia Research* 176, 307-311.

Reider EE, Sims BE (2016). Family-based preventive interventions: Can the onset of suicidal ideation and behavior be prevented? *Suicide and Life Threatening Behavior* 46, S3-S7.

Rizvi SL, Hughes CD, Thomas MC (2016). The DBT coach mobile application as an adjunct to treatment for suicidal and self-injuring individuals with borderline personality disorder: A preliminary evaluation and challenges to client utilization. *Psychological Services*. Published online: 15 August 2016. doi: 10.1037/ser0000100.

Rogers A, Schmidt P (2016). Emotion talk in the context of young people self-harming: Facing the feelings in family therapy. *Journal of Family Therapy*. Published online: 15 March 2016. doi: 10.1111/1467-6427.12115.

Sandler I, Tein J-Y, Wolchik S, Ayers TS (2016). The effects of the family bereavement program to reduce suicide ideation and/or attempts of parentally bereaved children six and fifteen years later. *Suicide and Life Threatening Behavior* 46, S32-S38.

Sanford R, Cerel J, McGann V, Maple M (2016). Suicide loss survivors' experiences with therapy: Implications for clinical practice. *Community Mental Health Journal* 52, 551-558.

Sankaranarayanan A, Clark V, Baker A, Palazzi K, Lewin TJ, Richmond R, Kay-Lambkin FJ, Filia S, Castle D, Williams JM (2016). Reducing smoking reduces suicidality among individuals with psychosis: Complementary outcomes from a healthy lifestyles intervention study. *Psychiatry Research* 243, 407-412.

Simon GE, Beck A, Rossom R, Richards J, Kirlin B, King D, Shulman L, Ludman EJ, Penfold R, Shortreed SM, Whiteside U (2016). Population-based outreach versus care as usual to prevent suicide attempt: Study protocol for a randomized controlled trial. *Trials* 17, 452.

Singer JB, O'Brien KHM, LeCloux M (2016). Three psychotherapies for suicidal adolescents: Overview of conceptual frameworks and intervention techniques. *Child and Adolescent Social Work Journal*. Published online: 13 August 2016. doi: 10.1007/s10560-016-0453-5.

Suarez E, Jackson DS, Slavin LA, Michels MS, McGeehan KM (2014). Project Kealahou: Improving Hawai'i's system of care for at-risk girls and young women through gender-responsive, trauma-informed care. *Hawai'i Journal of Medicine and Public Health* 73, 387-392.

Teismann T, Forkmann T, Rath D, Glaesmer H, Margraf J (2016). Perceived burdensomeness and suicide ideation in adult outpatients receiving exposure therapy for anxiety disorders. *Behaviour Research and Therapy* 85, 1-5.

Tondo L, Baldessarini RJ (2016). Suicidal behavior in mood disorders: Response to pharmacological treatment. *Current Psychiatry Reports* 18, e88.

Vidot DC, Huang S, Poma S, Estrada Y, Lee TK, Prado G (2016). Familias Unidas' crossover effects on suicidal behaviors among Hispanic adolescents: Results from an effectiveness trial. *Suicide and Life Threatening Behavior* 46, S8-S14.

CASE REPORTS

Abhishek BS, Srinivas SV, Prasad R (2016). A case series of poisonings by insecticides prepared from plant extracts. *Indian Journal of Forensic Medicine and Toxicology* 10, 268-271.

Al-Harrasi A, Al Maqbali M, Al-Sinawi H (2016). Surviving a suicide attempt. *Oman Medical Journal* 31, 378-380.

Alsulaiman SM, Ghazi NG (2016). A case of recurrent, self-inflicted handheld laser retinopathy. *Journal of the American Association for Pediatric Ophthalmology and Strabismus* 20, 168-170.

Aly Z, Rosen N, Evans RW (2016). Migraine and the risk of suicide. *Headache* 56, 753-761.

Amamou B, Salah WBH, Mhalla A, Benzarti N, Elloumi H, Zaafrane F, Gaha L (2016). Use of clozapine for borderline personality disorder: A case report. *Clinical Psychopharmacology and Neuroscience* 14, 226-228.

Arasalingam SAP, Shamsuddin AF, Sidi H, Salleh H (2015). Delayed neuropsychiatry sequelae (DNS) of carbon monoxide (CO) poisoning - a case report. *ASEAN Journal of Psychiatry* 16, 131-134.

Austin S (2016). Working with chronic and relentless self-hatred, self-harm, and existential shame: A clinical study and reflections (paper 2 of 2). *Journal of Analytical Psychology* 61, 411-433.

Barrett M (2016). "Absolutely incapable of 'carrying on:'" Shell shock, suicide, and the death of lieutenant colonel Sam Sharpe. *Canadian Military History* 25, e19.

Bashini MM, Rajavel VP, Rahulan V (2016). Complications and management of attempted suicide by intrapleural injection of prallethrin. *Indian Journal of Critical Care* 20, 182-184.

Baumrucker SJ, Carter GT, McCall-Burton M, Stolick M, Oertli KA, Schmidt LS, Adkins RW (2016). Suicide and self-determination. *American Journal of Hospital Palliative Care* 33, 807-812.

Benmoussa J, Chevenon M, Nandi M, Forlenza TJ, Nfonoyim J (2016). Ibuprofen-induced thrombotic thrombocytopenic purpura. *American Journal of Emergency Medicine* 34, e5-e7.

Berger F, Steuer AE, Rentsch K, Gascho D, Stamou S, Scharli S, Thali MJ, Kramer T, Flach PM (2016). Postmortem computed tomography and magnetic resonance imaging facilitates forensic autopsy in a fatal case of poisoning with formic acid, diphenhydramine, and ethanol. *Forensic Science International* 12, 304-311.

Boumrah Y, Gicquel T, Hugbart C, Baert A, Morel I, Bouvet R (2016). Suicide by self-injection of chlormequat trademark C5SUN(®). *Forensic Science International* 263, e9-e13.

Can SS, Yenilmez D (2016). Suicide with thinner injection. *Journal of Substance Use* 21, 448.

Caride-Miana E (2016). Ingestion of castor seeds in attempting suicide. *Semergen: Medicina De Familia*. Published online: 6 August 2016. doi: 10.1016/j.semerg.2016.06.012.

Carnevale JA, Morrison JF, Choi DB, Klinge PM, Cosgrove GR, Oyelese AA (2016). Self-inflicted nail-gun injury with cranial penetration and use of intraoperative computed tomography. *Surgical Neurology International* 7, S259-S262.

Castellano FJ, Donofrio AM, Ruschelli A, Alcantara ME, Aguirre AI (2016). Isoniazid acute poisoning: Convulsion, acidosis and increased CPK. *Revista De Toxicologia* 33, 56-58.

Cham EYK, Tse JCL, Chong YK, Chen ML, Wong OF, Fung HT (2016). A case of pyrethroid poisoning with clinical presentation mimicking organophosphate poisoning. *Hong Kong Journal of Emergency Medicine* 23, 47-51.

Chandna P, Srivastava N, Adlakha VK, Panthri P (2016). Non suicidal self injury resulting in dental trauma in an adolescent. *Dental Traumatology*. Published online: 29 April 2016. doi: 10.1111/edt.12280.

Chauhan MS, Behera C, Naagar S, Sreenivas M (2016). Ingestion of safety razor blade and delayed hanging in a complex suicide. *Medico-Legal Journals*. Published online: 26 July 2016. doi: 10.1177/0025817216661118.

Cheung G, Sundram F (2016). Understanding the progression from physical illness to suicidal behavior: A case study based on a newly developed conceptual model. *Clinical Gerontologist.* Published online: 28 July 2016. doi: 10.1080/07317115.2016.1217962.

Coffey MJ, Ahmedani BK (2016). Pseudocide: A case report. *Journal of Psychiatric Practice* 22, 333-335.

Combillet F, Saunier V, Rougier MB, Delyfer MN, Korobelnik J-F (2016). Multimodal imaging in a case of self-inflicted laser-induced maculopathy. *European Journal of Ophthalmology* 159, 227-231.

Conde E, Santos T, Leite R, Vicente C, Figueiredo AM (2016). A case of genital self-mutilation in a female - symptom choice and meaning. *Journal of Sex and Marital Therapy.* Published online: 11 July 2016. doi: 10.1080/0092623X.2016.1208699.

de Haan P, Reidinga-Saenen LM, Korporaal-Heijman JA (2016). Intoxication by ingestion of castor beans. *Netherlands Journal of Critical Care* 24, 20-22.

Declercq F, Meganck R, Audenaert K (2016). A case study of paternal filicide-suicide: Personality disorder, motives, and victim choice. *Journal of Psychology.* Published online 18 August 2016. doi: 10.1080/00223980.2016.1211983.

Dura H, Morar S, Cip ian CR (2015). Chemical suicide by inhalation of hydrogen sulfide in Sibiu County, Romania: Case report and literature review. *Romanian Journal of Legal Medicine* 23, 289-292.

Emoto Y, Yoshizawa K, Shikata N, Tsubura A, Nagasaki Y (2016). Autopsy results of a case of ingestion of sodium hydroxide solution. *Journal of Toxicologic Pathology* 29, 45-47.

Fellmeth G, Oo MM, Lay B, McGready R (2016). Paired suicide in a young refugee couple on the Thai-Myanmar border. *British Medical Journal Case Reports.* Published online: 15 September 2016. doi: 10.1136/bcr-2016-215527.

Gadhari RK, Pathak AG, Keoliya AN, Chaudhari KM (2015). Delayed death following attempted suicidal hanging: A case report. *Medico-Legal Update* 15, 17-19.

Glancy DL (2016). ECG of the month: Suicide. *The Journal of the Louisiana State Medical Society: Official Organ of the Louisiana State Medical Society* 168, 66-67.

Gurak KK, Freund B, Ironson G (2016). The use of both prolonged exposure and cognitive processing therapy in the treatment of a person with PTSD, multiple traumas, depression, and suicidality. *Clinical Case Studies* 15, 295-312.

Hasan MN, Sutradhar SR, Ahmed SM, Chowdhury IH (2016). An unusual case of suicide attempt using intravenous injection of kerosene. *Mymensingh Medical Journal* 25, 571-574.

Hashmi AM, Khawaja IS, Shah AA (2016). A 35-year-old man with depressed mood, insomnia, and suicidal ideation. *Psychiatric Annals* 46, 216-218.

Hoizey G, Cheze M, Villa A, Muckensturm A, Pepin G, Garnier R, Deveaux M (2016). Castor bean self-poisoning: Report of a case with blood and urine ricinine measurements. *Toxicologie Analytique Et Clinique* 28, 43-49.

Hunt S (2016). Case 18: Infected self-harm injury on the left ankle. *Journal of Wound Care* 25, S27.

Inyang M, Hua LL (2015). Self-inflicted bilateral ocular perforation in an adolescent patient with major depressive disorder and borderline personality traits. *Adolescent Psychiatry* 5, 64-69.

Jatav OP, Tiwari D, Lahariya D, Varghese J, Kumar S, Jacob J (2016). Amitraz poisoning treated successfully with atropine. *Journal of Association of Physicians of India* 64, 82.

Kim SW, Putzke M, Uhl E, Krishnan KG (2016). Self-inflicted hammer blows to the cranial vault: An interdisciplinary challenge. *The Primary Care Companion for CNS Disorders* 18, 3.

Kitamoto T, Kamijo Y (2016). Rabbit syndrome after taking herbicide containing 2-(4-chloro2-methylphenoxypropionic) acid. *Acute Medicine and Surgery* 3, 190-191.

Kobusiak-Prokopowicz M, Marciniak A, Slusarczyk S, Sciborski K, Stachurska A, Mysiak A, Matkowski A (2016). A suicide attempt by intoxication with taxus baccata leaves and ultra-fast liquid chromatography-electrospray ionization-tandem mass spectrometry, analysis of patient serum and different plant samples: Case report. *BMC Pharmacology Toxicology* 17, 41.

Konecny J, Klvacek A, Simek M, Lonsky V, Santavy P (2016). Complex gunshot injury to the heart as a consequence of suicide attempt in a schizophrenic patient. *International Journal of Surgery Case Reports* 24, 80-82.

Kotera SS, Shankar KCM, Rajagopalan S (2016). Liposuction technique used as a treatment modality for suicide attempt by injection of mercury. *Indian Journal of Surgery*. Published online: 28 July 2016. doi: 10.1007/s12262-016-1534-6.

Kramer L, Nadjem H, Glardon M, Kneubuehl BP, Pollak S, GroSse Perdekamp M, Pircher R (2016). A patterned abrasion caused by the impact of a cartridge case may simulate an atypical muzzle imprint mark. *International Journal of Legal Medicine* 130, 751-757.

Kroning M, Kroning K (2016). Teen depression and suicide: A silent crisis. *Journal of Christian Nursing* 33, 78-86.

Lang J, Felske-Zech H, Veit F, Lasczkowski G, Dettmeyer R (2015). Chronic abuse of hairspray by inhalation and sudden death of a 20-year-old woman. *Romanian Journal of Legal Medicine* 23, 285-288.

Le Garff E, Delannoy Y, Mesli V, Allorge D, Hedouin V, Tournel G (2016). Cyanide suicide after deep web shopping: A case report. *American Journal of Forensic Medicine and Pathology* 37, 194-197.

Levy SA, Russon J, Diamond GM (2016). Attachment-based family therapy for suicidal lesbian, gay, and bisexual adolescents: A case study. *Australian and New Zealand Journal of Family Therapy* 37, 190-206.

Liu G, Liu J, Gao L (2016). An analysis of a suicide case by ingestion of carbofuran. *Australian Journal of Forensic Sciences*. doi: 10.1080/00450618.2016.1177592.

Loo JL, Deena FAS, Hatta S (2016). Is electroconvulsive therapy safe for patient with very low BMI? A case report. *Medicine and Health-Kuala Lumpur* 11, 83-86.

Lubit EB, Fetterman TC, Ying P (2016). Recurrent aspiration in a patient with gastric band undergoing electroconvulsive therapy. *Journal of ECT* 32, 134-135.

Malaga EG, Aguilera EM, Eaton C, Ameerally P (2016). Management of self-harm injuries in the maxillofacial region: A report of 2 cases and review of the literature. *Journal of Oral and Maxillofacial Surgery* 74, 1198.e1-1198.e9.

Malbranque S, Mauillon D, Turcant A, Rouge-maillart C, Mangin P, Varlet V (2016). Quantification of fatal helium exposure following self-administration. *International Journal of Legal Medicine*. Published online: 25 April 2016. doi: 10.1007/s00414-016-1364-x.

Mallik S, Singh SR, Mohanty MK, Padhy N (2016). Attempted suicide by snake bite: A case study. *Medicine Science and the Law*. Published online: 14 July 2016. doi: 10.1177/0025802416659160.

Matthew BJ, Gedzior JS (2016). A disabled army veteran with severe traumatic brain injury and chronic suicidal ideation. *Psychiatric Annals* 46, 157-160.

Mikaszewska-Sokolewicz MA, Pankowska S, Janiak M, Pruszczyk P, Lazowski T, Jankowski K (2016). Coma in the course of severe poisoning after consumption of red fly agaric (Amanita muscaria). *Acta Biochimica Polonica* 63, 181-182.

Misiak P, Jabło ski S, Dziwinska K, Terlecki A (2016). A very unusual case of attempted suicide. *Kardiochirurgia I Torakochirurgia Polska* 13, 145-147.

Okan bilo lu A, Atli A, Demir S, Sir A (2016). A case who had deliberate self-harm by inserting needles to her body for 12 years. *Anatolian Journal of Psychiatry* 17, 38-40.

Osawa M, Matsushima Y, Kumar A, Tsuboi A, Kakimoto Y, Satoh F (2016). Self-inflicted firearm discharge from heating using a gas burner. *Journal of Forensic Sciences* 61, 845-847.

Otonichar J, Mongold D (2016). Precipitously and certainly psychotic- but what's the cause? Ms. L, age 38, rapidly becomes confused and agitated, and expresses suicidal ideation. Her history is not consistent with a typical course of mental illness. How would you treat her? *Current Psychiatry* 15, 62-67.

Patil N, Avinash A, Karthik Rao N, Hande HM, Rao R, Ahmed T (2016). A life saved: One poison neutralizes another. *Research Journal of Pharmaceutical, Biological and Chemical Sciences* 7, 1962-1963.

Petrosellini C, Hameed A (2015). Intrauterine death at term in a cocaine user detained under the mental health act. *British Medical Journal Case Reports*. Published online: 9 December 2015. doi: 10.1136/bcr-2015-212403.

Purg D, Markota A, Grenc D, Sinkovi A (2016). Low-dose intravenous lipid emulsion for the treatment of severe quetiapine and citalopram poisoning. *Arhiv Za Higijenu Rada I Toksikologiju* 67, 164-166.

Rastogi P, Kanchan T (2016). Genital self-mutilation: A case report. *Journal of South India Medicolegal Association* 8, 113-115.

Repplinger DJ, Hoffman RS, Nelson LS, Hines EQ, Howland M, Su MK (2016). Lack of significant bleeding despite large acute rivaroxaban overdose confirmed with whole blood concentrations. *Clinical Toxicology*. Published online: 2 June 2016. doi: 10.1080/15563650.2016.1187736.

Rishi MT, Rishi A, Palesty A (2016). Suicide attempt with a kitchen knife. *Updates in Surgery*. Published online: Published online: 4 June 2016. doi: 10.1007/s13304-016-0377-9.

Rizvi SL, Yu J, Geisser S, Finnegan D (2016). The use of "bug-in-the-eye" live supervision for training in dialectical behavior therapy: A case study. *Clinical Case Studies* 15, 243-258.

Rybojad B, Lukasiewicz A (2016). Neuroinfection or suicide attempt? Difficult diagnosis if lack of anamnesis. *Journal of Child and Adolescent Substance Abuse* 25, 455-457.

Schweitzer J, James C, Jenkins W, Reiff MI, Stein MT (2016). Acute agitation and self-injury in a 5-year old with autism. *Journal of Developmental & Behavioral Pediatrics* 37, 592-594.

Scott S, Diamond GS, Levy SA (2016). Attachment-based family therapy for suicidal adolescents: A case study. *Australian and New Zealand Journal of Family Therapy* 37, 154-176.

Sengupta S, Mungulmare K, Wadaskar N, Pande A (2016). Inverted takotsubo cardiomyopathy after attempted suicidal hanging - two cases. *Indian Heart Journal* 68, S52-S56.

Serafini G, Giordano G, Romano S, Raja M, Girardi P, Amore M, Pompili M (2016). Huntington's disease and suicidal behavior: The importance of lithium treatment. *Clinical Neurology and Neurosurgery* 145, 108-109.

Sevim Y, Ertan T, Tastan B, Topuz O, Sahin R, Karaagac M (2016). Laparoscopic management of gastric outlet obstruction after corrosive ingestion. *Chirurgia (Turin)* 29, 92-94.

Shakoori V, Agahi M, Vasheghani-Farahani M, Marashi SM (2016). Successful management of zinc phosphide poisoning. *Indian Journal of Critical Care* 20, 368-370.

Shapira J, Birenboim R, Shoshani M, Abdel-Kader A, Behar O, Moskovitz M, Ben-Attar Y, Chaushu S, Becker A (2016). Overcoming the oral aspects of -self-mutilation: Description of a method. *Special Care in Dentistry*. Published online: 22 April 2016. doi: 10.1111/scd.12181.

Signorelli JW, Osbun JW, Arias EJ, Reynolds LC, Chyatte D, Reynolds MR (2016). Self-injection of household cleaning detergents into a ventriculoperitoneal shunt reservoir during a suicide attempt: A case report and literature review. *Acta Neurochirurgica* 158, 1655-1660.

Sommerfeld K, Łukasik-Głebocka M, Kulza M, Druzdz A, Panie ski P, Florek E, Zieli ska-Psuja B (2016). Intravenous and oral suicidal e-liquid poisonings with confirmed nicotine and cotinine concentrations. *Forensic Science International* 262, e15-e20.

Su Y-M, Changchien C-H (2016). Self-inflicted, trans-optic canal, intracranial penetrating injury with a ballpoint pen. *Journal of Surgical Case Reports*. Published online: 16 March 2016. doi: 10.1093/jscr/rjw034.

Swain R, Behera C, Kishore S, Krishna K, Gupta SK (2016). Suicidal asphyxiation by carbon monoxide within a polythene bag. *Medico-Legal Journal*. Published online: 12 September 2016. doi: 10.1177/0025817216669286.

Thanuja Nilushi Priyangika SM, Karunarathna WGSG, Liyanage I, Gunawardana M, Dissanayake B, Udumalgala S, Rosa C, Samarasinghe T, Wijesinghe P, Kulatunga A (2016). A rare case of self-injection of elemental mercury. *BMC Research Notes*. Published online: 25 March 2016. doi: 10.1186/s13104-016-1992-8.

Tsai MC, Tsai CF (2016). Experience of caring for a surviving perpetrator of intimate partner homicide-suicide in older adults. *Geriatrics & Gerontology International* 16, 977-978.

Vasama J, Hoppu K, Parry MJ, Kalliomaki J (2016). Fatal outcome after suicidal subcutaneous injection of e-cigarette liquid. *Clinical Toxicology* 54, 371-372.

Vijitharan V, Warnasekare J, Lokunarangoda NC, Farah MF, Siribaddana SH (2016). Fatal poisoning with plant growth regulator - chlormequat. *Ceylon Medical Journal* 61, 89-90.

Wang Y, Kotik V, Fahim G, Alagusundaramoorthy S, Eltawansy SA, Mathis S, Saleh J (2016). Treatment of brodifacoum overdose with prothrombin complex concentrate. *American Journal of Health-System Pharmacy* 73, e14-e17.

Watkins AM, Melde C (2016). Bad medicine: The relationship between gang membership, depression, self-esteem, and suicidal behavior. *Criminal Justice and Behavior* 43, 1107-1126.

Wester KL, Downs HA, Trepal HC (2015). Factors linked with increases in nonsuicidal self-injury: A case study. *Counseling Outcome Research and Evaluation* 7, 3-20.

Winley DM, Ogbaselase F, Kodish T, Okunrounmu E, Ewing ESK (2016). Attachment-based family therapy for teen suicidality complicated by a history of sexual trauma. *Australian and New Zealand Journal of Family Therapy* 37, 177-189.

Wu MS, Storch EA (2016). A case report of harm-related obsessions in pediatric obsessive-compulsive disorder. *Journal of Clinical Psychology*. Published online: 18 September 2016. doi: 10.1002/jclp.22392.

You G, Rhee J, Park Y, Park S (2016). Determination of nicotine, cotinine and trans-3 '-hydroxycotinine using LC/MS/MS in forensic samples of a nicotine fatal case by oral ingestion of e-cigarette liquid. *Journal of Forensic Sciences* 61, 1149-1154.

Zhang Y, Ma H, Wang Y (2016). Case report of body dysmorphic disorder in a suicidal patient. *Shanghai Archives of Psychiatry* 28, 48-5.

MISCELLANEOUS

Anonymous (2014). Antidepressants and suicide in adolescents. *Journal of Paediatrics and Child Health* 50, 836-837.

Anonymous (2015). Correction: Personal experience: Suicide and psychiatric care - A lament (BJPsych Bull (2015) 39 (45-47)). *Psychiatrist* 39, 152.

Anonymous (2016). Age-adjusted death rates for females aged 15-44 years, by the five leading causes of death - United States, 1999 and 2014. *Morbidity and Mortality Weekly Report* 65, 659-659.

Anonymous (2016). Age-adjusted suicide rates for females and males, by method - national vital statistics system, United States, 2000 and 2014. *Morbidity and Mortality Weekly Report* 65, 503.

Anonymous (2016). 'Blue light' volunteers and staff have suicidal thoughts, claims survey. *Emergency Nurse* 24, 6.

Anonymous (2016). Correction to "Bullying, depression, and suicide risk in a pediatric primary care sample" Kodish et al., 2016. *Crisis* 37, 247.

Anonymous (2016). Correction to Morthorst et al., 2016: "Incidence rates of deliberate self-harm in Denmark 1994–2011: A nationwide register study". *Crisis*. Published online: 24 June 2016. doi: 10.1027/0227-5910/a000431.

Anonymous (2016). Corrections to mental health service changes, organisational factors, and patient suicide in England in 1997-2012: A before-and-after study [Lancet Psychiatry (2016), 3, 526-534]. *The Lancet Psychiatry* 3, 498.

Anonymous (2016). Erratum to: Suicidal ideation and mental health of Bhutanese refugees in the United States (Journal of Immigrant and Minority Health, 10.1007/s10903-015-0325-7). *Journal of Immigrant and Minority Health* 18, 1256.

Anonymous (2016). Quickstats: Age-adjusted death rates for males aged 15-44 years, by the five leading causes of death - United States, 1999 and 2014. *Morbidity and Mortality Weekly Report* 65, 815.

Anonymous (2016). Quickstats: Age-adjusted death rates* for females aged 15-44 years, by the five leading causes of death (DAGGER) - United States, 1999 and 2014. *Morbidity and Mortality Weekly Report* 65, 659.

Anonymous (2016). Quickstats: Age-adjusted suicide rates* for females and males, by method - National Vital Statistics System, United States, 2000 and 2014. *Morbidity and Mortality Weekly Report* 65, 503.

Anonymous (2016). Retraction to suicide trends in Upper Egypt. [j forensic sci, 2012;57:1247-51. Doi: 10.1111/j.1556-4029.2012.02247.X]. *Journal of Forensic Sciences* 61, 879.

Anonymous (2016). Self harm and the emergency department. *BMJ* 353, i1150.

Anonymous (2016). Self harm UK. *Nursing Children and Young People* 28, 12.

Anonymous (2016). Sounding the alarm about suicide risk. *ED Management: The Monthly Update on Emergency Department Management* 28, 49-54.

Anonymous (2016). Suicide prevention efforts for the elderly in Korea. *Perspectives in Public Health* 136, 269-270.

Anonymous (2016). 'Worrying' stress levels, poll finds. *Nursing Standard* 30, 9.

Abdollahi A, Carlbring P, Khanbani M, Ghahfarokhi SA (2016). Emotional intelligence moderates perceived stress and suicidal ideation among depressed adolescent inpatients. *Personality and Individual Differences* 102, 223-228.

Abroms M, Sher L (2016). Dual disorders and suicide. *Journal of Dual Diagnosis* 12, 148-149.

Agustina T, Calle A, Fontela E, Toledo MG, Nadile D, Cassara FP, Thomson A, Acosta P, Thomson A (2015). Suicide risk and epilepsy. Four-year follow up. *Neurology* 84, P3.198.

Akhtar U, Syed NM, Malik IA, Rafique I, Bhatti JA (2015). Medical reporting of suspected self-poisoning patients at a teaching hospital in Pakistan. *Suicidology Online* 6, 13-20.

Al-Halabi S, Saiz PA, Buron P, Garrido M, Benabarre A, Jimenez E, Cervilla J, Navarrete MI, Diaz-Mesa EM, Garcia-Alvarez L, Muniz J, Posner K, Oquendo MA, Garcia-Portilla MP, Bobes J (2016). Validation of a Spanish version of the Columbia-suicide severity rating scale (C-SSRS). *Revista Brasileira De Psiquiatria* 9, 134-142.

Alamri Y (2016). Does the choice of religion have an influence on suicidal behaviour? *Acta Psychiatrica Scandinavic.* Published online: 30 August 2016. doi: 10.1111/acps.12634.

Altura KC, Patten SB, Fiest KM, Atta C, Bulloch AG, Jetté N (2016). Suicidal ideation in persons with neurological conditions: Prevalence, associations and validation of the PQH-9 for suicidal ideation. *General Hospital Psychiatry* 42, 22-26.

Alyami M, Alyami H, Sundram F, Cheung G, Haarhoff BA, Lyndon MP, Hill AG (2016). Enhancing suicide risk assessment: A novel visual metaphor learning tool. *Australasian Psychiatry.* Published online: 12 July 2016. doi: 10.1177/1039856216657695.

Ammerman BA, Jacobucci R, Kleiman EM, Muehlenkamp JJ, McCloskey MS (2016). Development and validation of empirically derived frequency criteria for NSSI disorder using exploratory data mining. *Psychological Assessment.* Published online: 12 May 2016. doi: 10.1037/pas0000334.

Andriessen K, Draper B, Dudley M, Mitchell PB (2016). Pre- and postloss features of adolescent suicide bereavement: A systematic review. *Death Studies* 40, 229-246.

Andriuskeviciute G, Chmieliauskas S, Jasulaitis A, Laima S, Fomin D, Stasiuniene J (2016). A study of fatal and nonfatal hangings. *Journal of Forensic Sciences* 61, 984-987.

Anonymous (2016). Research links family problems, bereavement and exams to suicides in children. *Community Practitioner* 89, 7.

Apter A (2016). Commentary: Prospective trajectory research in adolescent suicidal behaviour - a possible basis for the development of empirically based interventions? A reflection on Adrian et al. (2016). *Journal of Child Psychology and Psychiatry* 57, 654-655.

Arensman E, Coffey C, Griffin E, Van Audenhove C, Scheerder G, Gusmao R, Costa S, Larkin C, Koburger N, Maxwell M, Harris F, Postuvan V, Hegerl U (2016). Effectiveness of depression-suicidal behaviour gatekeeper training among police officers in three European regions: Outcomes of the optimising suicide prevention programmes and their implementation in Europe (OSPI-Europe) study. *International Journal of Social Psychiatry.* Published online: 19 September 2016. doi: 10.1177/0020764016668907.

Assadi R, Afshari R (2016). Suicidal attempt with intentional poisoning seems a comorbid illness with an increased burden. *International Journal of High Risk Behaviors and Addiction* 5, e24380.

Aubin HJ, Luquiens A, Berlin I (2016). Smoking and suicide mortality risk in alcohol-dependent individuals. *Journal of Clinical Psychiatry* 77, e906.

Awenat YF, Shaw-Núñez E, Kelly J, Law H, Ahmed S, Welford M, Tarrier N, Gooding PA (2016). A qualitative analysis of the experiences of people with psychosis of a novel cognitive behavioural therapy targeting suicidality. *Psychosis.* Published online: 29 July 2016. doi: 10.1080/17522439.2016.1198827.

Ayer L, Ramchand R, Geyer L, Burgette L, Kofner A (2016). The influence of training, reluctance, efficacy, and stigma on suicide intervention behavior among NCOS in the Army and Marine Corps. *Journal of Primary Prevention* 37, 287-302.

Bakhiyi CL, Calati R, Guillaume S, Courtet P (2016). Do reasons for living protect against suicidal thoughts and behaviors? A systematic review of the literature. *Journal of Psychiatric Research* 77, 92-108.

Balayannis A, Cook BR (2016). Suicide at a distance: The paradox of knowing self-destruction. *Progress in Human Geography* 40, 530-545.

Baldessarini RJ, Lau WK, Sim J, Sum MY, Sim K (2015). Suicidal risks in reports of long-term treatment trials for major depressive disorder. *The International Journal of Neuropsychopharmacology*. Published online: 13 September 2015. doi: 10.1093/ijnp/pyv107.

Barber C, Hemenway D, Miller M (2016). How physicians can reduce suicide- without changing anyone's mental health. *American Journal of Medicine* 129, 1016-1017.

Barbería E, Gispert R, Gallo B, Ribas G, Puigdefàbregas A, Freitas A, Segú E, Torralba P, García-Sayago F, Estarellas A (2016). Improving suicide mortality statistics in Tarragona (Catalonia, Spain) between 2004-2012. *Revista de Psiquiatría y Salud Mental*. Published online: 21 July 2016. doi: 10.1016/j.rpsm.2016.05.004.

Barker E, Kõlves K, De Leo D (2016). Rail-suicide prevention: Systematic literature review of evidence-based activities. *Asia Pacific Psychiatry*. Published online: 14 July 2016. doi: 10.1111/appy.12246.

Barnes SM, Bahraini NH, Forster JE, Stearns-Yoder KA, Hostetter TA, Smith G, Nagamoto HT, Nock MK (2016). Moving beyond self-report: Implicit associations about death/life prospectively predict suicidal behavior among veterans. *Suicide and Life Threatening Behavior*. Published online: 7 July 2016. doi: 10.1111/sltb.12265.

Barnett R (2016). Suicide. *Lancet* 388, 228.

Batterham PJ, Torok M, Krysinska K, Shand F, Calear AL, Cockayne N, Christensen HM (2016). Best strategies for reducing the suicide rate in Australia: Response to Pirkis. *Australian and New Zealand Journal of Psychiatry* 50, 386.

Beard C, Hearon BA, Lee J, Kopeski LM, Busch AB, Bjorgvinsson T (2016). When partial hospitalization fails: Risk factors for inpatient hospitalization. *Journal of Nervous and Mental Disease* 204, 431-436.

Bell J, Stanley N, Mallon S, Manthorpe J (2015). Insights into the processes of suicide contagion: Narratives from young people bereaved by suicide. *Suicidology Online* 6, 43-52.

Benson O, Gibson S, Boden ZVR, Owen G (2016). Exhausted without trust and inherent worth: A model of the suicide process based on experiential accounts. *Social Science and Medicine* 163, 126-134.

Berglund S, Astrom S, Lindgren BM (2016). Patients' experiences after attempted suicide: A literature review. *Issues in Mental Health Nursing*. Published online: 21 June 2016. doi: 10.1080/01612840.2016.1192706.

Betancourt T, Smith Fawzi MC, Stevenson A, Kanyanganzi F, Kirk C, Ng L, Mushashi C, Bizimana JI, Beardslee W, Raviola G, Smith S, Kayiteshonga Y, Binagwaho A (2016). Ethics in community-based research with vulnerable children: Perspectives from Rwanda. *PLoS One* 11, e0157042.

Betz ME, Wintersteen M, Boudreaux ED, Brown G, Capoccia L, Currier G, Goldstein J, King C, Manton A, Stanley B, Moutier C, Harkavy-Friedman J (2016). Reducing suicide risk: Challenges and opportunities in the emergency department. *Annals of Emergency Medicine*. Published online: 21 July 2016. doi: 10.1016/j.annemergmed.2016.05.030.

Binder P, Heintz AL, Servant C, Roux MT, Robin S, Gicquel L, Ingrand P (2016). Screening for adolescent suicidality in primary care: The bullying-insomnia-tobacco-stress test. A population-based pilot study. *Early Intervention in Psychiatry*. Published online: 6 May 2016. doi: 10.1111/eip.12352.

Bishop TM, Maisto SA, Britton PC, Pigeon WR (2016). Considerations in the use of interactive voice recording for the temporal assessment of suicidal ideation and alcohol use. *Crisis*. Published online: 22 July 2016. doi: 10.1027/0227-5910/a000408.

Blasco MJ, Castellvi P, Almenara J, Lagares C, Roca M, Sese A, Piqueras JA, Soto-Sanz V, Rodriguez-Marin J, Echeburua E, Gabilondo A, Cebria AI, Miranda-Mendizabal A, Vilagut G, Bruffaerts R, Auerbach RP, Kessler RC, Alonso J (2016). Predictive models for suicidal thoughts and behaviors among Spanish university students: Rationale and methods of the UNIVERSAL (University & mental health) project. *BMC Psychiatry* 16, 122.

Blickstein D, Younes S, Nakav S (2016). Attempted suicide with rivaroxaban. *Annals of Hematology*. Published online: 14 September 2016. doi: 10.1007/s00277-016-2816-6.

Bloch MH (2016). Editorial: Reducing adolescent suicide. *Journal of Child Psychology and Psychiatry* 57, 773-774.

Bondurant R, Morton N (2016). Implementing change to reduce depression, suicide, and burnout among physicians-in-training. *Missouri Medicine* 113, 16-18.

Bonifazi E (2016). A self-cutting teenager. *European Journal of Pediatric Dermatology* 26, 58-59.

Bossard C, Santin G, Lopez V, Imbernon E, Cohidon C (2016). Surveillance of work-related suicide in France: An exploratory study. *Revue D'epidemiologie et de Sante Publique* 64, 201-210.

Boston P, Cottrell D (2016). Special issue: Adolescent self harm and systemic practice April 2016. *Journal of Family Therapy* 38, 169-171.

Botti P, Gambassi F, Pistelli A, Canzani C, Mocarini A, Masini E, Mannaioni G (2016). Toxic love: A 3-year retrospective analysis of love-related toxicological deliberate self-harm. *Clinical Toxicology* 54, 461-461.

Braithwaite SR, Giraud-Carrier C, West J, Barnes MD, Hanson CL (2016). Validating machine learning algorithms for twitter data against established measures of suicidality. *JMIR Mental Health* 3, e21.

Braun C, Bschor T, Franklin J, Baethge C (2016). Suicides and suicide attempts during long-term treatment with antidepressants: A meta-analysis of 29 placebo-controlled studies including 6,934 patients with major depressive disorder. *Psychotherapy and Psychosomatics* 85, 171-179.

Brausch AM, Muehlenkamp JJ, Washburn JJ (2016). Nonsuicidal self-injury disorder: Does Criterion B add diagnostic utility? *Psychiatry Research* 244, 179-184.

Brent DA (2016). Prevention programs to augment family and child resilience can have lasting effects on suicidal risk. *Suicide and Life Threatening Behavior* 46, S39-S47.

Brent DA (2016). Antidepressants and suicidality. *Psychiatric Clinics North America* 39, 503-512.

Breton J-J, Labelle R (2015). Suicidal behaviour protective factors in adolescents. *Canadian Journal of Psychiatry* 60, S1.

Briscoe J, Webb JA (2016). Scratching the surface of suicide in head and neck cancer. *Journal of the American Medical Association Otolaryngol Head Neck Surgery* 142, 610.

Brüdern J, Berger T, Caspar F, Maillart AG, Michel K (2016). The role of self-organization in the suicidal process. *Psychological Reports* 118, 668-685.

Brundin L, Bryleva EY, Rajamani KT (2016). Role of inflammation in suicide: From mechanisms to treatment. *Neuropsychopharmacology*. Published online: 5 July 2016. doi: 10.1038/npp.2016.116.

Bryan CJ, Kanzler KE, Grieser E, Martinez A, Allison S, McGeary D (2016). A shortened version of the suicide cognitions scale for identifying chronic pain patients at risk for suicide. *Pain Practice*. Published online: 18 June 2016. doi: 10.1111/papr.12464.

Burke TA, Ammerman BA, Hamilton JL, Alloy LB (2016). Impact of non-suicidal self-injury scale: Initial psychometric validation. *Cognitive Therapy and Research*. Published online: 13 September 2016. doi: 10.1007/s10608-016-9806-9.

Button ME (2016). Suicide and social justice: Toward a political approach to suicide. *Political Research Quarterly* 69, 270-280.

Butwicka A, Frisén L, Almqvist C, Zethelius B, Lichtenstein P (2016). Erratum: Risks of psychiatric disorders and suicide attempts in children and adolescents with type 1 diabetes: A population-based cohort study (diabetes care (2015) (38) (453-459)). *Diabetes Care* 39, 495.

Calear AL, Brewer JL, Batterham PJ, Mackinnon A, Wyman PA, LoMurray M, Shand F, Kazan D, Christensen H (2016). The sources of strength Australia project: Study protocol for a cluster randomised controlled trial. *Trials* 17, 349.

Caplan R (2016). The elephant in the room: Suicide in patients with epilepsy. *Epilepsy Currents / American Epilepsy Society* 16, 137-138.

Carasevici B (2016). Dilemmas in the attitude towards suicide. *Revista Medico-Chirurgicală A Societă Ţli De Medici Şi Naturalişti Din Iaşi* 120, 152-157.

Carmel A, Arevalo JB (2016). Integrating suicide risk assessment and management tools into medical student education: A novel clerkship in dialectical behavior therapy. *Academic Psychiatry* 40, 855-856.

Cavazos-Rehg PA, Krauss MJ, Sowles SJ, Connolly S, Rosas C, Bharadwaj M, Grucza R, Bierut LJ (2016). An analysis of depression, self-harm, and suicidal ideation content on Tumblr. *Crisis*. Published online: 22 July 2016. doi: 10.1027/0227-5910/a000409.

Cetin U (2015). Durkheim, ethnography and suicide: Researching young male suicide in the transnational London Alevi-Kurdish community. *Ethnography* 17, 250-277.

Chamberlen A (2015). Embodying prison pain: Women's experiences of self-injury in prison and the emotions of punishment. *Theoretical Criminology* 20, 205-219.

Chan MKY, Bhatti H, Meader N, Stockton S, Evans J, O'Connor R, Kapur N, Kendall T (2016). Predicting suicide following self-harm: A systematic review of risk factors and risk scales. *British Journal of Psychiatry*. Published online: 23 June 2016. doi: 10.1192/bjp.bp.115.170050.

Chang EC, Chang OD (2016). Development of the frequency of suicidal ideation inventory: Evidence for the validity and reliability of a brief measure of suicidal ideation frequency in a college student population. *Cognitive Therapy and Research* 40, 549-556.

Chappell P, Dubrava S, Stewart M, Hartley DM, Alphs L, Brashear HR, Conwell Y, Miller D, Schindler RJ, Siemers ER, Yaffe K (2016). Suicidal ideation and behavior assessment in dementia studies: An internet survey. *Alzheimer's and Dementia: Translational Research and Clinical Interventions* 2, 60-68.

Chesin MS, Stanley B, Haigh EAP, Chaudhury SR, Pontoski K, Knox KL, Brown GK (2016). Staff views of an emergency department intervention using safety planning and structured follow-up with suicidal veterans. *Archives of Suicide Research*. Published online: 20 April 2016. doi: 10.1080/13811118.2016.1164642.

Chiang Y-C, Chung F-Y, Lee C-Y, Shih H-L, Lin D-C, Lee M-B (2016). Suicide reporting on front pages of major newspapers in Taiwan: Violating reporting recommendations between 2001 and 2012. *Health Communication*. Published online: 23 March 2016. doi: 10.1080/10410236.2015.1074024.

Chin EY, Kim HK (2016). Life experience following suicide attempt among middle-aged men. *Journal of Korean Academy of Nursing* 46, 215-225.

Choi YJ, Oh H (2016). Does media coverage of a celebrity suicide trigger copycat suicides? Evidence from Korean cases. *Journal of Media Economics* 29, 92-105.

Christensen H, Cuijpers P, Reynolds CF, III (2016). Changing the direction of suicide prevention research: a necessity for true population impact. *JAMA Psychiatry* 73, 435-436.

Christiansen NP (2016). Re: "Putting an end to it!". *Journal of the National Comprehensive Cancer Network* 14, xliv-xlvi.

Christodoulou C, Efstathiou V, Michopoulos I, Ferentinos P, Korkoliakou P, Gkerekou M, Bouras G, Papadopoulou A, Papageorgiou C, Douzenis A (2016). A case-control study of hopelessness and suicidal behavior in the city of Athens, Greece. The role of the financial crisis. *Psychology, Health and Medicine*. Published online: 30 March 2016. doi: 10.1080/13548506.2016.1164872.

Chu C, Buchman-Schmitt JM, Hom MA, Stanley IH, Joiner TE (2016). A test of the interpersonal theory of suicide in a large sample of current firefighters. *Psychiatry Research* 240, 26-33.

Chung-Do JJ, Goebert DA, Bifulco K, Sugimoto-Matsuda J, Balberde-Kamali'i J, Ka'ae D, Hee LL, Walter L (2016). Insights in public health: Safe messaging for youth-led suicide prevention awareness: Examples from Hawai'i. *Hawai'i Journal of Medicine and Public Health: A Journal of Asia Pacific Medicine and Public Health* 75, 144-147.

Chung Y, Jeglic EL (2016). Detecting suicide risk among college students: A test of the predictive validity of the modified emotional Stroop task. *Suicide and Life-Threatening Behavior*. Published online: 23 September 2016. doi: 10.1111/sltb.12287.

Clegg S, Cunha MPE, Rego A (2016). Explaining suicide in organizations: Durkheim revisited. *Business and Society Review* 121, 391-414.

Close J (2016). Calling on—and grateful for—counseling skills: When a client revealed a suicide attempt, this SLP used techniques she never anticipated she'd actually need. *Asha Leader* 21, 80.

Collins KRL, Best I, Stritzke WGK, Page AC (2016). Mindfulness and zest for life buffer the negative effects of experimentally-induced perceived burdensomeness and thwarted belongingness: Implications for theories of suicide. *Journal of Abnormal Psychology* 125, 704-714.

Condorelli R (2016). Social complexity, modernity and suicide: An assessment of Durkheim's suicide from the perspective of a non-linear analysis of complex social systems. *SpringerPlus*. Published online: 25 March 2016. doi: 10.1186/s40064-016-1799-z.

Conway PM, Erlangsen A, Teasdale TW, Jakobsen IS, Larsen KJ (2016). Predictive validity of the Columbia-suicide severity rating scale for short-term suicidal behavior: A Danish study of adolescents at a high risk of suicide. *Archives of Suicide Research*. Published online: 16 August 2016. doi: 10.1080/13811118.2016.1222318.

Cosco TD, Stubbs B, Prina AM, Wu YT (2016). Religiosity and suicidal behaviour in the national survey of American life. *Acta Psychiatrica Scandinavic*. Published online: 12 May 2016. doi: 10.1111/acps.12592.

Cox KL, Nock MK, Biggs QM, Bornemann J, Colpe LJ, Dempsey CL, Heeringa SG, McCarroll JE, Ng TH, Schoenbaum M, Ursano RJ, Zhang BG, Benedek DM (2016). An examination of potential misclassification of army suicides: Results from the army study to assess risk and resilience in service members. *Suicide and Life Threatening Behavior*. Published online: 22 July 2016. doi: 10.1111/sltb.12280.

Cramer RJ, Akpinar-Elci M (2016). Unclear suicide prevention effects, insufficient large-scale testing of suicide prevention programs. *Journal of Adolescent Health* 59, 128.

Cramer RJ, Bryson CN, Eichorst MK, Keyes LN, Ridge BE (2016). Conceptualization and pilot testing of a core competency-based training workshop in suicide risk assessment and management: Notes from the field. *Journal of Clinical Psychology*. Published online: 26 July 2016. doi: 10.1002/jclp.22329.

Cramer RJ, Bryson CN, Stroud CH, Ridge BE (2016). A pilot test of a graduate course in suicide theory, risk assessment, and management. *Teaching of Psychology* 43, 238-242.

Cramer RJ, Moore CE, Bryson CN (2016). A test of the trait-interpersonal model of suicide proneness in emerging adults. *Personality and Individual Differences* 102, 252-259.

Creed M, Whitley R (2016). Assessing fidelity to suicide reporting guidelines in Canadian news media: The death of Robin Williams. *Canadian Journal of Psychiatry*. Published online: 6 September 2016. doi: 10.1177/0706743715621255.

Cwik JC, Teismann T (2016). Misclassification of self-directed violence. *Clinical Psychology and Psychotherapy*. Published online: 2 August 2016. doi: 10.1002/cpp.2036.

Czyz EK, Horwitz AG, Arango A, Cole-Lewis Y, Berona J, King CA (2016). Coping with suicidal urges among youth seen in a psychiatric emergency department. *Psychiatry Research* 241, 175-181.

Dadasev S, Skruibis P, Gailiene D, Latakiene J, Grizas A (2016). Too strong? Barriers from getting support before a suicide attempt in Lithuania. *Death Studies*. Published online: 3 June 2016. doi: 10.1080/07481187.2016.1184725.

Danylevich T (2016). De-privatizing self-harm: Remembering the social self in how to forget. *Journal of Bioethical Inquiry*. Published online: 28 July 2016. doi: 10.1007/s11673-016-9739-8.

David-Ferdon C, Crosby AE, Caine ED, Hindman J, Reed J, Iskander J (2016). CDC grand rounds: Preventing suicide through a comprehensive public health approach. *Morbidity Mortal Weekly Report* 65, 894-897.

De Carlo A, Dal Corso L, Di Sipio A, Scarcella M, Sorvillo D (2016). Coping with the economic and labor crisis: Models and tools for the evaluation of suicide risk. *Testing, Psychometrics, Methodology in Applied Psychology* 23, 299-317.

De la Cruz-Cano E (2016). Association between FKBP5 and CRHR1 genes with suicidal behavior: A systematic review. *Behavioural Brain Research* 317, 46-61.

Desjardins I, Cats-Baril W, Maruti S, Freeman K, Althoff R (2016). Suicide risk assessment in hospitals: An expert system-based triage tool. *Journal of Clinical Psychiatry* 77, 874-822.

Deuter K, Jaworski K (2016). Assuming vulnerability: Ethical considerations in a multiple-case study with older suicide attempters. *Research Ethics*. Published online: 16 May 2016. doi: 10.1177/1747016116649994.

Dieserud G, Leenaars AA, Dyregrov K (2015). The importance of many informants in PA studies. *Suicidology Online* 6, 47-55.

Diggle-Fox BS (2016). Assessing suicide risk in older adults. *Nurse Practitioner* 41, 28-35.

Dodd P, Doherty A, Guerin S (2016). A systematic review of suicidality in people with intellectual disabilities. *Harvard Review of Psychiatry* 24, 202-213.

Dodson NA (2016). Adolescent gun violence prevention: What we know, and what we can do to keep young people safe. *Current Opinion in Pediatrics* 28, 441-446.

Dodson NA (2016). Teen lives matter: An update on adolescent gun violence. *Current Opinion in Pediatrics* 28, 441-446.

Doherty T, DeVylder J (2016). Identifying risk for suicide. *Health and Social Work* 41, 205-207.

Du CM (2015). The love-suicide mystique of Naxi: Experiential tourism and existential authenticity. *Frontiers of History in China* 10, 486-512

Du S (2012). Epidemic suicide in a Lahu community: Converging qualitative and quantitative methods. *Ethnology* 51, 111-127.

Durand SC, McGuinness TM (2016). Adolescents who self-injure. *Journal of Psychosocial Nursing and Mental Health Services* 54, 26-29.

Dyson MP, Hartling L, Shulhan J, Chisholm A, Milne A, Sundar P, Scott SD, Newton AS (2016). A systematic review of social media use to discuss and view deliberate self-harm acts. *PLoS One* 11, e0155813.

Edwards DC (2016). Suicide in Guyana: A parsonsian corrective to Durkheim's theory of suicide. *Canadian Journal American and Caribbean Studies* 41, 197-214.

Eggertson L (2016). Inuit suicide prevention strategy strives to save lives. *Canadian Medical Association Journal*. Published online: 2 August 2016. doi: 10.1503/cmaj.109-5309.

Eggertson L (2016). Nunavut's new suicide prevention strategy. *Canadian Medical Association Journal*. Published online: 21 March 2016. doi: 10.1503/cmaj.109-5250.

Egnoto MJ, Griffin DJ (2016). Analyzing language in suicide notes and legacy tokens. *Crisis* 37, 140-147.

Ekman I (2016). Beyond medicalization: Self-injuring acts revisited. *Health* 20, 346-362.

Elizabeth Victor S, Davis T, Klonsky ED (2016). Descriptive characteristics and initial psychometric properties of the non-suicidal self-injury disorder scale. *Archives of Suicide Research*. Published online: 7 June 2016. doi: 10.1080/13811118.2016.1193078.

Enja M, Srinivasan K, Lippmann S (2016). Offer these interventions to help prevent suicide by firearm. *Current Psychiatry* 15, e1-e3.

Eppich-Harris M (2015). Hamlet, art, and apoptosis: The Shakespearean artwork of Julie Newdoll. *Interdisciplinary Literary Studies* 17, 540-558.

Erlangsen A (2016). Hospital management of self-harm and later risk of suicide and overall mortality. *Evidence Based Mental Health*. 19 April 2016. doi: 10.1136/eb-2015-102242.

Erlangsen A, Nordentoft M (2016). Psychosocial therapy for people at risk of suicide. *Lancet Psychiatry* 3, 494-495.

Escarment J, Wey PF, Martinez JY, Loheas D (2016). Ketamine: An effective tool for preventing suicide in burned combat veterans. *Journal of Burn Care & Research*. Published online: 29 March 2016. doi: 10.1097/BCR.0000000000000346.

Eskin M, Kujan O, Voracek M, Shaheen A, Carta MG, Sun JM, Flood C, Poyrazli S, Janghorbani M, Yoshimasu K, Mechri A, Khader Y, Aidoudi K, Bakhshi S, Harlak H, Ahmead M, Moro MF, Nawafleh H, Phillips L, Abuderman A, Tran US, Tsuno K (2016). Cross-national comparisons of attitudes towards suicide and suicidal persons in university students from 12 countries. *Scandinavian Journal of Psychology*. Published online: 18 August 2016. doi: 10.1111/sjop.12318.

Evans R, Hurrell C (2016). The role of schools in children and young people's self-harm and suicide: Systematic review and meta-ethnography of qualitative research. *BMC Public Health* 16, 401.

Ewell Foster CJ, Burnside AN, Smith PK, Kramer AC, Wills A, C AK (2016). Identification, response, and referral of suicidal youth following applied suicide intervention skills training. *Suicide and Life-Threatening Behavior*. Published online: 2 July 2016. doi: 10.1111/sltb.12272.

Eylem O, van Bergen DD, Rathod S, van Straten A, Bhui K, Kerkhof AJFM (2016). Canına kıymak – 'crushing life energy': A qualitative study on lay and professional understandings of suicide and help-seeking among Turkish migrants in the UK and in the Netherlands. *International Journal of Culture and Mental Health* 9, 182-196.

Façanha J, Santos JC, Cutcliffe J (2016). Assessment of suicide risk: Validation of the nurses' global assessment of suicide risk index for the Portuguese population. *Archives of Psychiatric Nursing* 30, 470-475.

Fellmeth G, Paw MK, Wiladphaingern J, Charunwatthana P, Nosten FH, McGready R (2016). Maternal suicide risk among refugees and migrants. *International Journal of Gynaecology & Obstetrics* 134, 223-224.

Ferguson M, Baker A, Young S, Procter N (2016). Understanding suicide among Aboriginal communities. *Australian Nursing and Midwifery Journal* 23, e36.

Fernández-Niño JA (2016). Suicide: Incidence or prevalence? Comments on Hernández-Alvarado et al. Increase in suicide rates by hanging in the population of tabasco, Mexico between 2003 and 2012. Int. J. Environ. Res. Public health 2016, 13, 552. *International Journal of Environmental Research and Public Health* 13, e13070671.

Ferrey AE, Hughes ND, Simkin S, Locock L, Stewart A, Kapur N, Gunnell D, Hawton K (2016). Changes in parenting strategies after a young person's self-harm: A qualitative study. *Child and Adolescent Psychiatry and Mental Health* 10, 20.

Finlayson M, Graetz Simmonds J (2016). Impact of client suicide on psychologists in Australia. *Australian Psychologist*. Published online: 11 August 2016. doi: 10.1111/ap.12240.

Fisher J (2016). Perinatal psychiatric care needs of women who die by suicide. *Lancet Psychiatry* 3, 191-192.

Fleischmann A, Arensman E, Berman A, Carli V, De Leo D, Hadlaczky G, Howlader S, Vijayakumar L, Wasserman D, Saxena S (2016). Overview evidence on interventions for population suicide with an eye to identifying best-supported strategies for LMICS. *Global Mental Health*. Published online: 12 February 2016. doi: 10.1017/gmh.2015.27.

Fluegge K (2016). Atomoxetine, ADHD, and the ongoing debate about increased risk of suicidal behaviors: The understudied role of kappa opioid receptor agonism. *Expert Opinion on Drug Safety*. Published online: 27 June 2016. doi: 10.1080/14740338.2016.1200209.

Flynn A, Zackula R, Klaus NM, McGinness L, Carr S, Macaluso M (2016). Student evaluation of the yellow ribbon suicide prevention program in midwest schools. *Primary Care Companion for CNS Disorders* 18, 3.

Fortune S, Cottrell D, Fife S (2016). Family factors associated with adolescent self-harm: A narrative review. *Journal of Family Therapy* 38, 226-256.

Fox KR, Millner AJ, Franklin JC (2016). Classifying nonsuicidal overdoses: Nonsuicidal self-injury, suicide attempts, or neither? *Psychiatry Research* 244, 235-242.

Francis W, Bance LO (2016). Protective role of spirituality from the perspective of Indian college students with suicidal ideation: "I am here because god exists". *Journal of Religion and Health*. Published online: 10 August 2016. doi: 10.1007/s10943-016-0296-6.

Freckelton IQC, Scott R (2016). A psychiatrist's duties in relation to the risks of patient suicide Smith v Pennington 2015 NSWSC 1168 (Garling J). *Psychiatry Psychology and Law* 23, 1-28.

Frey LM, Hans JD, Cerel J (2016). Perceptions of suicide stigma how do social networks and treatment providers compare? *Crisis* 37, 95-103.

Frey RG (1981). Suicide and self-inflicted death. *Philosophy* 56, 193-202.

Ftanou M, Cox G, Nicholas A, Spittal MJ, Machlin A, Robinson J, Pirkis J (2016). Suicide prevention public service announcements (PSAs): Examples from around the world. *Health Communication*. Published online: 16 June 2016. doi: 10.1080/10410236.2016.1140269.

Fuglseth NLD, Gjestad R, Mellesdal L, Hunskaar S, Oedegaard KJ, Johansen IH (2016). Factors associated with disallowance of compulsory mental healthcare referrals. *Acta Psychiatrica Scandinavica* 133, 410-418.

Gamliel E, Levi-Belz Y (2016). To end life or to save life: Ageism moderates the effect of message framing on attitudes towards older adults' suicide. *International Psychogeriatrics* 28, 1383-1390.

Gattone PM (2016). Editorial: Preventing death by suicide. *Epilepsy and Behavior* 61, 292-293.

Gaucher S, Baylé FJ, Magne J (2016). Self-inflicted burns: Are they preventable injuries? *Burns* 42, 1158-1159.

Gelaye B, Kajeepeta S, Williams MA (2016). Suicidal ideation in pregnancy: An epidemiologic review. *Archives of Women's Mental Health* 19, 741-751.

Genovese JM, Berek JS (2016). Can arts and communication programs improve physician wellness and mitigate physician suicide? *Journal of Clinical Oncology* 34, 1820-1822.

Gentry RH, Pickel KL (2016). Jurors' evaluations of a high school bullying case in which the victim attempted suicide. *New Criminal Law Review* 19, 63-92.

Gnanavel S (2016). Mental health policies and suicide rate. *Lancet Psychiatry* 3, 808.

Gokalp G, Anil M, Bal A, Bicilioglu Y, Can FK, Anil AB (2016). Factors affecting the decision to hospitalise children admitted to the emergency department due to non-fatal suicide attempts by pills. *Pakistan Journal of Medical Sciences* 32, 731-735.

Goldblatt MJ, Ronningstam E, Schechter M, Herbstman B, Maltsberger JT (2016). Suicide as escape from psychotic panic. *Bulletin of the Menninger Clinic* 80, 131-145.

Goldney RD (2016). Suicide by health care professionals. *Medical Journal of Australia* 205, 257-258.

Goldstein MR, Mascitelli L (2016). Is violence in part a lithium deficiency state? *Medical Hypotheses* 89, 40-42.

Gontijo Guerra S, Vasiliadis H-M (2016). Gender differences in youth suicide and healthcare service use. *Crisis*. Published online: 1 June 2016. doi: 10.1027/0227-5910/a000387.

Gönülta MB (2016). The description of suicide events investigated by homicide investigation unit between 2011-2015: Sivas example. *International Journal of Human Sciences* 13, 1700-1714.

Gooderham M, Gavino-Velasco J, Clifford C, MacPherson A, Krasnoshtein F, Papp K (2016). A review of psoriasis, therapies, and suicide. *Journal of Cutaneous Medicine and Surgery*. Published online: 5 May 2016. doi: 10.1177/1203475416648323.

Gordon D (2016). From act to fact: The transformation of suicide in western thought. *Historical Reflections* 42, 33-51.

Görzig A (2016). Adolescents' viewing of suicide-related web content and psychological problems: Differentiating the roles of cyberbullying involvement. *Cyberpsychology, Behavior and Social Networking* 19, 502-509.

Grandclerc S, De Labrouhe D, Spodenkiewicz M, Lachal J, Moro MR (2016). Relations between nonsuicidal self-injury and suicidal behavior in adolescence: A systematic review. *PLoS One* 11, e0153760.

Grano N, Oksanen J, Kallionpaa S, Roine M (2016). Specificity and sensitivity of the beck hopelessness scale for suicidal ideation among adolescents entering early intervention service. *Nordic Journal of Psychiatry*. Published online: 14 September 2016. doi: 10.1080/08039488.2016.1227370.

Griffith J, Bryan CJ (2016). Suicides in the US military: Birth cohort vulnerability and the all-volunteer force. *Armed Forces and Society* 42, 483-500.

Gryglewicz K, Chen JI, Romero GD, Karver MS, Witmeier M (2016). Online suicide risk assessment and management training. *Crisis*. Published online: 23 September 2016. doi: 10.1027/0227-5910/a000421.

Gupta S, Gersing KR, Erkanli A, Burt T (2016). Antidepressant regulatory warnings, prescription patterns, suicidality and other aggressive behaviors in major depressive disorder and anxiety disorders. *Psychiatric Quarterly* 87, 329-342.

Ha KM (2016). Managing rumor, looting, and suicide not as breaking news but as community disaster culture. *Impact Assessment and Project Appraisal*. Published online: 1 June 2016. doi: 10.1080/14615517.2016.1176411.

Hagaman AK, Maharjan U, Kohrt BA (2016). Suicide surveillance and health systems in Nepal: A qualitative and social network analysis. *International Journal of Mental Health Systems* 10, 46.

Haghdoost A, Akbari M, Zolala F (2016). Author's reply. *Archives of Iranian Medicine* 19, 235.

Haim M, Arendt F, Scherr S (2016). Abyss or shelter? On the relevance of web search engines' search results when people google for suicide. *Health Communication*. Published online: 19 May 2016. doi: 10.1080/10410236.2015.1113484.

Hakim Shooshtari M, Malakouti SK, Panaghi L, Mohseni S, Mansouri N, Movaghar AR (2016). Factors associated with suicidal attempts in Iran: A systematic review. *Iranian Journal of Psychiatry and Behavioral Sciences* 10, e948.

Hamilton I (2016). Changing healthcare workers' attitudes to self harm. *BMJ* 353, i2443.

Han JS, Lee EH, Suh T, Hong CH (2016). Psychometric evaluation of the Korean version of the suicidal ideation scale in mentally ill patients living in the community. *Scandinavian Journal of*

Caring Sciences. Published online: 10 May 2016. doi: 10.1111/scs.12332.

Hanschmidt F, Lehnig F, Riedel-Heller SG, Kersting A (2016). The stigma of suicide survivorship and related consequences-a systematic review. *PLoS One* 11, e0162688.

Harder HG, Holyk T, Russell VL, Klassen-Ross T (2015). Nges Siy (I love you): A community-based youth suicide intervention in Northern British Columbia. *International Journal of Indigenous Health* 10, 21-32.

Harned MS, Lungu A, Wilks CR, Linehan MM (2016). Evaluating a multimedia tool for suicide risk assessment and management: The Linehan Suicide Safety Net. *Journal of Clinical Psychology*. Published online: 15 June 2016. doi: 10.1002/jclp.22331.

Harper BT, Klaassen Z, DiBianco JM, Yaguchi G, Jen RP, Terris MK (2016). Suicide risk in patients with bladder cancer. *Journal of Wound, Ostomy and Continence Nursing* 43, 170-171.

Harris KM, Lello OD, Willcox CH (2016). Reevaluating suicidal behaviors: Comparing assessment methods to improve risk evaluations. *Journal of Psychopathology and Behavioral Assessment*. Published online: 15 August 2016. doi: 10.1007/s10862-016-9566-6.

Hawton K, Witt KG, Salisbury TL, Arensman E, Gunnell D, Hazell P, Townsend E, van Heeringen K (2016). Psychosocial interventions following self-harm in adults: A systematic review and meta-analysis. *Lancet Psychiatry* 3, 740-750.

Hawton K, Witt KG, Taylor Salisbury TL, Arensman E, Gunnell D, Hazell P, Townsend E, van Heeringen K (2016). Psychosocial interventions for self-harm in adults. *Cochrane Database of Systematic Reviews* 5, CD012189.

Hedman AS (2016). Minnesota clergy's attitudes on suicide prevention and likelihood to inquire about suicidal thoughts and intent. *Mental Health, Religion & Culture*. Published online: 8 August 2016. doi: 10.1080/13674676.2016.1216531.

Hegerl U (2016). Prevention of suicidal behavior. *Dialogues in Clinical Neuroscience* 18, 183-190.

Heintjes EM, Overbeek JA, Penning-van Beest FJ, Brobert G, Herings RM (2016). Post authorization safety study comparing quetiapine to risperidone and olanzapine. *Human Psychopharmacology: Clinical and Experimental* 31, 304-312.

Hemenway D (2016). Firearm legislation and mortality in the USA. *Lancet* 387, 1796-1797.

Henderson SN, Van Hasselt VB, LeDuc TJ, Couwels J (2016). Firefighter suicide: Understanding cultural challenges for mental health professionals. *Professional Psychology: Research and Practice* 47, 224-230.

Hernandez-Alvarado MM, Gonzalez-Castro TB, Tovilla-Zarate CA, Fresan A, Juarez-Rojop IE, Lopez-Narvaez ML, Villar-Soto M, Genis-Mendoza A (2016). Response to the Fernandez-Nino comments on Hernandez-Alvarado et al. Increase in suicide rates by hanging in the population of Tabasco, Mexico between 2003 and 2012. Int. J. Environ. Res. Public health 2016, 13, 552. *International Journal of Environmental Research and Public Health*. Published online: 1 July 2016. doi: 10.3390/ijerph13070672.

Hetrick SE, Goodall J, Yuen HP, Davey CG, Parker AG, Robinson J, Rickwood DJ, McRoberts A, Sanci L, Gunn J, Rice S, Simmons MB (2016). Comprehensive online self-monitoring to support clinicians manage risk of suicide in youth depression. *Crisis*. Published online: 23 September 2016. doi: 10.1027/0227-5910/a000422.

Higgins JP (2016). Suicide prevention by smartphone reply. *American Journal of Medicine* 129, E147.

Hilton C (2016). Unveiling self-harm behaviour: What can social media site twitter tell us about self-harm? A qualitative exploration. *Journal of Clinical Nursing*. Published online: 7 September 2016. doi: 10.1111/jocn.13575.

Hochard KD, Heym N, Townsend E (2016). Investigating the interaction between sleep symptoms of arousal and acquired capability in predicting suicidality. *Suicide and Life Threatening*

Behavior. Published online: 2 August 2016. doi: 10.1111/sltb.12285.

Hodgson K (2016). Nurses' attitudes towards patients hospitalised for self-harm. *Nursing Standard* 30, 38-44.

Hogan MF, Grumet JG (2016). Suicide prevention: An emerging priority for health care. *Health Affairs (Project Hope)* 35, 1084-1090.

Hom MA, Joiner TE (2016). Predictors of treatment attrition among adult outpatients with clinically significant suicidal ideation. *Journal of Clinical Psychology*. Published online: 26 April 2016. doi: 10.1002/jclp.22318.

Hom MA, Podlogar MC, Stanley IH, Joiner TE (2016). Ethical issues and practical challenges in suicide research. *Crisis*. Published online: 26 August 2016. doi: 10.1027/0227-5910/a000415.

Hom MA, Stanley IH, Joiner TE, Jr. (2016). The web-based assessment of suicidal and suicide-related symptoms: Factors associated with disclosing identifying information to receive study compensation. *Journal of Personality Assessment* 98, 616-625.

Hope KJ, Smith-Adcock S (2015). A reason to live: Can understanding close friendships in college prevent suicide? *College Student Affairs Journal* 33, 85-104.

Horgan D (2016). Dexamphetamine and the faltering war against depression and suicide. *Australian and New Zealand Journal of Psychiatry*. Published online: 8 July 2016. doi: 10.1177/0004867416654010.

Hornor G (2016). Nonsuicidal self-injury. *Journal of Pediatric Health Care* 30, 261-267.

Howson S, Huline-Dickens S (2016). Do interventions reduce the risk of repeat self-harm or suicide in young people?: Commentary on... Cochrane Corner. *Advances in Psychiatric Treatment* 22, 287-291.

Hubers AA, Hamming A, Giltay EJ, von Faber M, Roos RA, van der Mast RC, van Duijn E (2016). Suicidality in Huntington's disease: A qualitative study on coping styles and support strategies. *Journal of Huntington's Disease* 5, 185-198.

Hughes JL, Anderson NL, Wiblin JL, Asarnow JR (2016). Predictors and outcomes of psychiatric hospitalization in youth presenting to the emergency department with suicidality. *Suicide and Life-Threatening Behavior*. Published online: 2 July 2016. doi: 10.1111/sltb.12271.

Hunt IM, Appleby L, Kapur N (2016). Suicide under crisis resolution home treatment - a key setting for patient safety. *Transactions of the Korean Institute of Electrical Engineers* 40, 172-174.

Husky MM, Zablith I, Alvarez Fernandez V, Kovess-Masféty V (2016). Factors associated with suicidal ideation disclosure: Results from a large population-based study. *Journal of Affective Disorders* 205, 36-43.

Hvidt EA, Ploug T, Holm S (2016). The impact of telephone crisis services on suicidal users: A systematic review of the past 45 years. *Mental Health Review Journal* 21, 141-160.

Iemmi V, Bantjes J, Coast E, Channer K, Leone T, McDaid D, Palfreyman A, Stephens B, Lund C (2016). Suicide and poverty in low-income and middle-income countries: A systematic review. *Lancet Psychiatry* 3, 774-783.

Ionita A, WyartPsychiatre M (2016). Clinical specificities of suicidal behaviour in the elderly. *Soins Gerontologie* 21, 15-18.

Isaacs AN, Sutton K, Hearn S, Wanganeen G, Dudgeon P (2016). Health workers' views of help seeking and suicide among Aboriginal people in rural Victoria. *Australian Journal of Rural Health*. Published online: 20 May 2016. doi: 10.1111/ajr.12303.

Jackman K, Honig J, Bockting W (2016). Nonsuicidal self-injury among lesbian, gay, bisexual and transgender populations: An integrative review. *Journal of Clinical Nursing*. Published online: 7 June 2016. doi: 10.1111/jocn.13236.

Jahn DR, Quinnett P, Ries R (2016). The influence of training and experience on mental health practitioners' comfort working with suicidal individuals. *Professional Psychology-Research and*

Practice 47, 130-138.

Jin HM, Khazem LR, Anestis MD (2016). Recent advances in means safety as a suicide prevention strategy. *Current Psychiatry Reports* 18, 96.

John A, Hawton K, Gunnell D, Lloyd K, Scourfield J, Jones PA, Luce A, Marchant A, Platt S, Price S, Dennis MS (2016). Newspaper reporting on a cluster of suicides in the UK. *Crisis*. Published online: 22 July 2016. doi: 10.1027/0227-5910/a000410.

Joiner TE, Hom MA, Rogers ML, Chu C, Stanley IH, Wynn GH, Gutierrez PM (2016). Staring down death: Is abnormally slow blink rate a clinically useful indicator of acute suicide risk? *Crisis* 37, 212-217.

Joiner TE, Stanley IH (2016). Can the phenomenology of a suicidal crisis be usefully understood as a suite of antipredator defensive reactions? *Psychiatry (New York)* 79, 107-119.

Jones-Berry S (2016). Nurses facing fitness to practise hearings 'pushed to breaking point'. *Nursing Standard* 30, 12-13.

Jones LM, Cotter R, Birch KM (2016). A review of occupationally-linked suicide for dentists. *New Zealand Dental Journal* 112, 39-46.

Jordan AE, White PH, Patterson KR, Arnold RM (2016). A survey of home hospice staff knowledge of suicide risk factors, evaluation, and management. *Journal of Palliative Medicine* 19, 694-695.

Jørgensen KM, Egeberg A, Gislason GH, Skov L, Thyssen JP (2016). Anxiety, depression and suicide in patients with prurigo nodularis. *Journal of the European Academy of Dermatology and Venereology*. Published online: 9 August 2016. doi: 10.1111/jdv.13827.

Joshi K, Billick SB (2016). Biopsychosocial causes of suicide and suicide prevention outcome studies in juvenile detention facilities: A review. *Psychiatric Quarterly*. Published online: 12 May 2016. doi: 10.1007/s11126-016-9434-2.

Kalesan B, Fagan J, Galea S (2016). Gun violence prevention - Authors' reply. *Lancet (London, England)* 388, 234.

Kanev P (2015). Media, death, dialogue. Social and media values in the discourse about the 'family' suicides in Bulgaria. *Communication Today* 6, 98.

Kapur N, Ibrahim S, Appleby L (2016). Psychiatric beds and increased suicide rates in England - Authors' reply. *Lancet Psychiatry* 3, 604-605.

Kar N (2016). Factors associated with suicides in Wolverhampton: Relevance of local audits exploring preventability. *Medicine Science and the Law*. Published online: 5 July 2016. doi: 10.1177/0025802416657761.

Kaskie BP, Leung C, Kaplan MS (2016). Deploying an ecological model to stem the rising tide of firearm suicide in older age. *Journal of Aging & Social Policy* 28, 233-245.

Kelada L, Whitlock J, Hasking P, Melvin G (2016). Parents' experiences of nonsuicidal self-injury among adolescents and young adults. *Journal of Child and Family Studies*. Published online: 23 August 2016. doi: 10.1007/s10826-016-0496-4.

Kels CG (2016). Firearm access and risk of suicide. *Journal of the American Medical Association* 315, 2124.

Kenedi C, Friedman SH, Watson D, Preitner C (2016). Suicide and murder-suicide involving aircraft. *Aerospace Medicine and Human Performance* 87, 388-396.

Kim B, Jung KJ, Lee SU, Sea J, Kim EY, Kim SH, Jee SH, Park JI, Kim K, Ahn YM (2015). The Korea National Suicide Survey (KNSS): Rationale and design. *Korean Journal of Biological Psychiatry* 22, 1-6.

Kirtley OJ, O'Carroll RE, O'Connor RC (2016). Pain and self-harm: A systematic review. *Journal of Affective Disorders* 203, 347-363.

Knoll Iv JL (2016). Understanding homicide-suicide. *Psychiatric Clinics of North America*. Published online: 6 August 2016. doi: 10.1016/j.psc.2016.07.009.

Ko J, Harrington D (2016). Factor structure and validity of the K6 Scale for adults with suicidal ideation. *Journal of the Society for Social Work and Research* 7, 43-63.

Kodish T, Fein J (2016). Bullying, depression, and suicide risk in a pediatric primary care sample (vol 37, pg 241, 2016). *Crisis-the Journal of Crisis Intervention and Suicide Prevention* 37, 247.

Koenig HG (2016). Association of religious involvement and suicide. *JAMA Psychiatry* 73, 775-776.

Kõlves K, De Leo D (2016). Unclear suicide prevention effects, insufficient large-scale testing of suicide prevention programs reply. *Journal of Adolescent Health* 59, 128-129.

Koweszko T, Gierus J, Mosiołek A, Kami ski M, Janus MD, Szulc A (2016). The development and the structure of the Verbal Suicide Scale (VSS) - measuring attitudes toward suicide in the group of patients hospitalized in the psychiatric unit. *Archives of Psychiatric Nursing* 30, 476-479.

Kozel B, Grieser M, Abderhalden C, Cutcliffe JR (2016). Inter-rater reliability of the German version of the Nurses' Global Assessment of Suicide Risk Scale. *International Journal of Mental Health Nursing.* Published online: 1 May 2016. doi: 10.1111/inm.12193.

Kreuze E, Jenkins C, Gregoski M, York J, Mueller M, Lamis DA, Ruggiero KJ (2016). Technology-enhanced suicide prevention interventions: A systematic review of the current state of the science. *Journal of Telemedicine and Telecare.* Published online: 3 July 2016. doi: 10.1177/1357633X16657928.

Kucuker I, Simsek T, Keles MK, Yosma E, Aksakal IA, Demir A (2016). Our treatment approaches in severe maxillofacial injuries occurring after failed suicide attempts using long-barreled guns. *Journal of Craniofacial Surgery* 27, e133-e138.

Kuipers P, Lindeman MA, Grant L, Dingwall K (2016). Front-line worker perspectives on Indigenous youth suicide in Central Australia: Initial treatment and response. *Advances in Mental Health* 14, 106-117.

Kutcher S, Wei Y, Behzadi P (2016). School- and community-based youth suicide prevention interventions: Hot idea, hot air, or sham? *The Canadian Journal of Psychiatry.* Published online: 12 July 2016. doi: 10.1177/0706743716659245.

Labelle R, Breton JJ, Berthiaume C, Royer C, Raymond S, Cournoyer M, Balan B, Zaloum T, Bibaud A, Gauvin G, Janelle A (2015). Psychometric properties of three measures of protective factors for depression and suicidal behaviour among adolescents. *Canadian Journal of Psychiatry* 60, S16-S26.

Larsen ME, Nicholas J, Christensen H (2016). Quantifying app store dynamics: Longitudinal tracking of mental health apps. *JMIR Mhealth Uhealth* 4, e96.

Larsen ME, Nicholas J, Christensen H (2016). A systematic assessment of smartphone tools for suicide prevention. *PLoS One* 11, e0152285.

Lau E, Hamzah SNZ, Tan SCC, Simonetti B (2016). Suicide and socioeconomic determinants in Canada: Beyond morality and philosophy. *Quality and Quantity.* Published online: 20 June 2016. doi: 10.1007/s11135-016-0370-x.

Lavigne JE (2016). Suicidal ideation and behavior as adverse events of prescribed medications: An update for pharmacists. *Journal of the American Pharmacists Association* 56, 203-206.

LeCloux M, Maramaldi P, Thomas K, Wharff E (2016). Health care resources and mental health service use among suicidal adolescents. *The Journal of Behavioral Health & Services Research.* Published online: 4 May 2016. doi: 10.1007/s11414-016-9509-8.

Lee SH, Tsai YF, Wang YW, Chen YJ, Tsai HH (2016). Development and psychometric testing of the triggers of suicidal ideation inventory for assessing older outpatients in primary care settings. *International Journal of Geriatric Psychiatry* 33, S275-S276.

Levi-Belz Y, Beautrais A (2016). Serious suicide attempts. *Crisis.* Published online: 1 June 2016. doi: 10.1027/0227-5910/a000386.

Lichtenthal WG, Breitbart W, Corner G, Sweeney C, Prigerson HG, Holland J, Roberts K (2016). Development of the Bereavement Risk Inventory and Screening Questionnaire (BRISQ): Item generation and expert panel feedback. *Palliative and Supportive Care*. Published online: 12 August 2016. doi: 10.1017/S1478951516000626.

Lin T-h, Lin Y-l, Tseng W-l (2016). Manufacturing suicide: The politics of a world factory. *Chinese Sociological Review* 48, 1-32.

Lindeman MA, Kuipers P, Grant L (2015). Front-line worker perspectives on Indigenous youth suicide in Central Australia: Contributors and prevention strategies. *International Journal of Emergency Mental Health* 17, 191-196.

Liu RT, Cheek SM, Nestor BA (2016). Non-suicidal self-injury and life stress: A systematic meta-analysis and theoretical elaboration. *Clinical Psychology Review* 47, 1-14.

López-Muñoz F, Cuerda-Galindo E (2016). Suicide in inmates in Nazis and Soviet concentration camps: Historical overview and critique. *Frontiers in Psychiatry* 7, e88.

Louzon SA, Bossarte R, McCarthy JF, Katz IR (2016). The clinical utility of PHQ-9 item 9 for suicide prediction: In reply. *Psychiatric Services* 67, 1042-1043.

Lovell S, Clifford M (2016). Nonsuicidal self-injury of adolescents. *Clinical Pediatrics* 55, 1012-1019.

Lovrecic M, Selb J, Selb K, Lovrecic B (2016). Illicit drug-related suicide mortality and identification of initially unrecognized cases: Experience of Slovenia. *Heroin Addiction and Related Clinical Problems* 18, 51-54.

Luaute JP (2016). Suicides caused by poverty in late nineteenth-century Paris. *Annales Medico-Psychologiques* 174, 485-490.

Lund EM, Nadorff MR, Samuel Winer E, Seader K (2016). Corrigendum to: "Is suicide an option?: The impact of disability on suicide acceptability in the context of depression, suicidality, and demographic factors" [j. Affect. Disord. 189 (2016) 25-35]. *Journal of Affective Disorders* 201, 50.

Lund EM, Schultz JC, Nadorff MR (2016). The factor structure, internal consistency, and convergent validity of two suicide assessment competency measures in vocational rehabilitation counselors. *Rehabilitation Counseling Bulletin*. Published online: 26 July 2016. doi: 10.1177/0034355216660840.

Lytle MC, Silenzio VMB, Caine ED (2016). Are there still too few suicides to generate public outrage? *JAMA Psychiatry*. Published online: 17 August 2016. doi: 10.1001/jamapsychiatry.2016.1736.

Ma J, Batterham PJ, Calear AL, Han J (2016). A systematic review of the predictions of the interpersonal-psychological theory of suicidal behavior. *Clinical Psychology Review* 46, 34-45.

Ma J, Zhang W, Harris K, Chen Q, Xu X (2016). Dying online: Live broadcasts of Chinese emerging adult suicides and crisis response behaviors. *BMC Public Health* 16, e774.

MacDonald J, Scholes T, Powell K (2016). Listening to Australian Indigenous men: Stories of incarceration and hope. *Primary Health Care Research and Development*. Published online: 12 August 2016. doi: 10.1017/S1463423616000256.

Madan A, Frueh BC, Allen JG, Ellis TE, Rufino KA, Oldham JM, Fowler JC (2016). Psychometric reevaluation of the Columbia-Suicide Severity Rating Scale: Findings from a prospective, inpatient cohort of severely mentally ill adults. *Journal of Clinical Psychiatry* 77, e867-e873.

Maki NE, Martikainen PT (2016). Premature mortality after suicide attempt in relation to living arrangements. A register-based study in Finland in 1988-2007. *The European Journal of Public Health*. Published online: 23 August 2016. doi: 10.1093/eurpub/ckw130.

Mallick F, McCullumsmith CB (2016). Ketamine for treatment of suicidal ideation and reduction of risk for suicidal behavior. *Current Psychiatry Reports* 18, 61.

Mann JJ, Michel CA (2016). Prevention of firearm suicide in the United States: What works and what is possible. *American Journal of Psychiatry* 173, 969-979.

Maple M, Pearce T, Sanford RL, Cerel J (2016). The role of social work in suicide prevention, intervention, and postvention: A scoping review. *Australian Social Work*. Published online: 31 August 2016. doi: 10.1080/0312407X.2016.1213871.

Marino E, Wolsko C, Keys SG, Pennavaria L (2016). A culture gap in the United States: Implications for policy on limiting access to firearms for suicidal persons. *Journal of Public Health Policy* 37, 110-121.

Marshall A (2016). Suicide prevention interventions for sexual and gender minority youth: An unmet need. *Yale Journal of Biology and Medicine* 89, 205-213.

Martínez-Aguayo JC, Arancibia M, Concha S, Madrid E (2016). Ten years after the FDA black box warning for antidepressant drugs: A critical narrative review. *Revista De Psiquiatria Clinica* 43, 60-66.

Marzano L, Smith M, Long M, Kisby C, Hawton K (2016). Police and suicide prevention: Evaluation of a training program. *Crisis* 37, 194-204.

Mascayano F, Irrazabal M, D Emilia W, Vaner SJ, Sapag JC, Alvarado R, Yang LH, Sinah B (2015). Suicide in Latin America: A growing public health issue. *Revista De La Facultad De Ciencias Medicas (Cordoba, Argentina)* 72, 295-303.

Matel-Anderson DM, Bekhet AK (2016). Resilience in adolescents who survived a suicide attempt from the perspective of registered nurses in inpatient psychiatric facilities. *Issues in Mental Health Nursing*. Published online: 28 June 2016. doi: 10.1080/01612840.2016.1193578.

May AM, O'Brien KHM, Liu RT, Klonsky ED (2016). Descriptive and psychometric properties of the Inventory of Motivations for Suicide Attempts (IMSA) in an inpatient adolescent sample. *Archives of Suicide Research* 20, 476-482.

Maynard L (2016). Starting out - my self-disclosure helped a patient to open up about her depression. *Nursing Standard* 30, 29.

Mayor S (2016). Half of people seen at English hospitals after self harming do not receive mental health assessment. *British Medical Journal* 353, i2463.

Mayor S (2016). Locking doors in mental health hospitals does not reduce suicide or absconding, shows study. *British Medical Journal* 354, i4198.

Mbekou V, Macneil S, Gignac M, Renaud J (2015). Parent-youth agreement on self-reported competencies of youth with depressive and suicidal symptoms. *Canadian Journal of Psychiatry* 60, S55-S60.

McCall WV (2016). Mediators between sleep problems and suicide: Response to Littlewood et al. *Journal of Clinical Sleep Medicine* 12, 929.

McCarthy M (2016). Suicide rates rise sharply in the US, figures show. *British Medical Journal* 353, i2355.

McCusker PJ (2016). The clinical utility of PHQ-9 item 9 for suicide prediction. *Psychiatric Services* 67, 1042.

McErlean B (2015). Soundness in mind and body. *The Veterinary Record* 177, I-II.

McGinty EE, Kennedy-Hendricks A, Choksy S, Barry CL (2016). Trends in news media coverage of mental illness in the United States: 1995-2014. *Health Affairs (Project Hope)* 35, 1121-1129.

McKenzie SK, Li C, Jenkin G, Collings S (2016). Ethical considerations in sensitive suicide research reliant on non-clinical researchers. *Research Ethics*. Published online: 13 May 2016. doi: 10.1177/1747016116649996.

Mehra A, Sharma N (2016). ECM0: A ray of hope for young suicide victims with acute aluminum phosphide poisoning (AALPP) and shock. *Indian Heart Journal* 68, 256-257.

Merrick J (2016). "It is better to die": Abbé rousseau and the meanings of suicide. *Historical Reflections* 42, 3-31.

Merriott D (2016). Factors associated with the farmer suicide crisis in India. *Journal of Epidemiology Global Health*. Published online: 11 April 2016. doi: 10.1016/j.jegh.2016.03.003.

Meyer D, Abbott JA, Rehm I, Bhar S, Barak A, Deng G, Wallace K, Ogden E, Klein B (2016). Development of a suicidal ideation detection tool for primary healthcare settings: Using open access online psychosocial data. *Telemedicine and e-Health*. Published online: 23 September 2016. doi: 10.1089/tmj.2016.0110.

Meyers J (2016). Pursued by demons: Creativity and suicide. *American Imago* 73, 1-23.

Miller FG (2016). Rational suicide, irrational laws: Examining current approaches to suicide in policy and law. *American Journal of Psychiatry* 173, 736-737.

Milner A, Page A (2016). A rise in Australian suicide? A reflection on the 2016 cause of death statistics. *Australian and New Zealand Journal of Psychiatry*. Published online: 15 July 2016. doi: 10.1177/0004867416659366.

Miner CL, Love HA, Paik SE (2016). Non-suicidal self-injury in adolescents: Addressing the function and the family from the perspective of systemic family therapies. *American Journal of Family Therapy*. Published online: 31 March 2016. doi: 10.1080/01926187.2016.1150798.

Mirick RG, Bridger J, McCauley J, Berkowitz L (2016). Continuing education on suicide assessment and crisis intervention for social workers and other mental health professionals: A follow-up study. *Journal of Teaching in Social Work* 36, 363-379.

Mok K, Ross AM, Jorm AF, Pirkis J (2016). An analysis of the content and availability of information on suicide methods online. *Journal of Consumer Health on the Internet* 20, 41-51.

Mortimer-Jones S, Morrison P, Munib A, Paolucci F, Neale S, Bostwick A, Hungerford C (2016). Recovery and borderline personality disorder: A description of the innovative open borders program. *Issues in Mental Health Nursing*. Published online: 21 June 2016. doi: 10.1080/01612840.2016.1191565.

Moss P, Prince MJ (2016). Helping traumatized warriors: Mobilizing emotions, unsettling orders. *Emotion, Space and Society*. Published online: 27 November 2015. doi: 10.1016/j.emospa.2015.11.001.

Muehlenkamp JJ, Brausch AM (2016). Reconsidering criterion a for the diagnosis of non-suicidal self-injury disorder. *Journal of Psychopathology and Behavioral Assessment*. Published online: 21 March 2016. doi: 10.1007/s10862-016-9543-0.

Mueller AS, Abrutyn S (2016). Adolescents under pressure: A new Durkheimian framework for understanding adolescent suicide in a cohesive community. *American Sociological Review*. Published online: 2 September 2016. doi: 10.1177/0003122416663464.

Mummé TA, Mildred H, Knight T (2016). How do people stop non-suicidal self-injury? A systematic review. *Archives of Suicide Research*. Published online: 16 August 2016. doi: 10.1080/13811118.2016.1222319.

Na K-S, Paik JW, Yun MK, Kim H-S (2015). Psychological autopsy: Review and considerations for future directions in Korea. *Journal of Korean Neuropsychiatric Association* 54, 40-48.

Naji Z, Salamati P, Salamati P (2016). Some ethical challenges regarding self-immolation. *Burns* 42, 1152-1153.

Neha H (2016). Social support: A important psychological factor in farmer's suicide. *International Journal of Research in Social Sciences* 6, 691-698.

Ng KK (2016). Student suicide: What's the role of family physicians? *Hong Kong Practitioner* 38, 50-51.

Nnaji CO (2015). Psychocosmic analysis of suicide. *Open Journal of Philosophy* 5, 163-170.

Nock MK (2016). Recent and needed advances in the understanding, prediction, and prevention of suicidal behavior. *Depression and Anxiety* 33, 460-463.

Norheim AB, Grimholt TK, Loskutova E, Ekeberg O (2016). Attitudes toward suicidal behaviour among professionals at mental health outpatient clinics in Stavropol, Russia and Oslo, Norway. *BMC Psychiatry* 16, 268.

O'Brien KHM, Putney JM, Hebert NW, Falk AM, Aguinaldo LD (2016). Sexual and gender minority youth suicide: Understanding subgroup differences to inform interventions. *LGBT Health* 3, 248-251.

O'Connor N, Paton M (2016). Back-to-base pulse oximetry to prevent inpatient suicide. *Australasia Psychiatry* 24, 204-205.

O'Reilly M, Kiyimba N, Karim K (2016). "This is a question we have to ask everyone": Asking young people about self-harm and suicide. *Journal of Psychiatric and Mental Health Nursing.* Published online: 8 August 2016. doi: 10.1111/jpm.12323.

O'Brien KHM, Aguinaldo LD, Almeida J, White E (2016). The role of parents in safety planning interventions with suicidal adolescents. *International Journal of Emergency Mental Health* 18, 727-729.

Ohnishi M, Koyama S, Senoo A, Kawahara H, Shimizu Y (2016). Suicide prevention and mental health measures for Japanese university students. *Psychiatria et Neurologia Japonica* 118, 22-27.

Oksanen A, Näsi M, Minkkinen J, Keipi T, Kaakinen M, Räsänen P (2016). Young people who access harm-advocating online content: A four-country survey. *Cyberpsychology* 10, 2.

Oliffe JL, Hannan-Leith MN, Ogrodniczuk JS, Black N, Mackenzie CS, Lohan M, Creighton G (2016). Men's depression and suicide literacy: A nationally representative Canadian survey. *Journal of Mental Health.* Published online: 29 April 2016. doi: 10.1080/09638237.2016.1177770.

Oppliger M, Mauermann E, Ruppen W (2016). Reply to: Are transdermal opioids contraindicated in patients at risk of suicide? *European Journal of Anaesthesiology.* Published online: 3 October 2016. doi: 10.1097/EJA.0000000000000483.

Oquendo MA (2016). Subtyping suicidal behavior: A strategy for identifying phenotypes that may more tractably yield molecular underpinnings. *Journal of Clinical Psychiatry* 77, 813-814.

Orsolini L, Valchera A, Vecchiotti R, Tomasetti C, Iasevoli F, Fornaro M, De Berardis D, Perna G, Pompili M, Bellantuono C (2016). Suicide during perinatal period: Epidemiology, risk factors, and clinical correlates. *Frontiers in Psychiatry* 7, e138.

Osteen P, Frey JM, Woods MN, Ko J, Shipe S (2016). Modeling the longitudinal direct and indirect effects of attitudes, self-efficacy, and behavioral intentions on practice behavior outcomes of suicide intervention training. *Suicide and Life-Threatening Behavior.* Published online: 19 August 2016. doi: 10.1111/sltb.12288.

Ostlie K, Stanicke E, Haavind H (2016). A listening perspective in psychotherapy with suicidal patients: Establishing convergence in therapists and patients private theories on suicidality and cure. *Psychotherapy Research.* Published online: 30 May 2016. doi: 10.1080/10503307. 2016.1174347.

Owens C (2016). "Hotspots" and "copycats": A plea for more thoughtful language about suicide. *Lancet Psychiatry* 3, 19-20.

Owens C, Charles N (2016). Implementation of a text-messaging intervention for adolescents who self-harm (TeenTEXT): A feasibility study using normalisation process theory. *Child and Adolescent Psychiatry and Mental Health* 10, 14.

Pan LA, Martin P, Zimmer T, Segreti AM, Kassiff S, McKain BW, Baca CA, Rengasamy M, Hyland K, Walano N, Steinfeld R, Hughes M, Dobrowolski SK, Pasquino M, Diler R, Perel J, Finegold DN, Peters DG, Naviaux RK, Brent DA, Vockley J (2016). Neurometabolic disorders: Potentially treatable abnormalities in patients with treatment-refractory depression and suicidal behavior. *American Journal of Psychiatry*. Published online: 13 August 2016. doi: 10.117/appi.ajp. 2016.15111500.

Park RC, Kam D, Salib A, Gorgy G, Patel TD, Carniol ET, Eloy JA, Baredes S (2016). Scratching the surface of suicide in head and neck cancer-reply. *JAMA Otolaryngology Head Neck Surgery* 142, 611.

Patel S, Batterham PJ, Calear AL, Cryer R (2016). Predictors of comfort and confidence among medical students in providing care to patients at risk of suicide. *Academic Psychiatry*. Published online: 8 July 2016. doi: 10.1007/s40596-016-0583-2.

Patterson S (2016). Suicide risk screening tools and the youth population. *Journal of Child and Adolescent Psychiatric Nursing* 29, 118-126.

Patton CL, Fremouw WJ (2016). Examining "suicide by cop": A critical review of the literature. *Aggression and Violent Behavior* 27, 107-120.

Pauls M, Larkin GL, Schears RM (2015). Advance directives and suicide attempts—ethical considerations in light of Carter v. Canada, SCC 5. *Canadian Journal of Emergency Medicine* 17, 562-564.

Pawan, Rohith S, Rangalakshmi S, Kamat C (2015). A retrospective study of attempted suicide cases admitted into critical care unit of a tertiary care hospital. *Journal of Evolution of Medical and Dental Sciences* 4, 15885-15887.

Peak NJ, Overholser JC, Ridley J, Braden A, Fisher L, Bixler J, Chandler M (2016). Too much to bear. *Crisis* 37, 59-67.

Penberthy JK, Penberthy JM, Harris MR, Nanda S, Ahn J, Martinez CP, Osika AO, Slepian ZA, Forsyth JC, Starr JA, Farrell JE, Hook JN (2016). Are smoking cessation treatments associated with suicidality risk? An overview. *Substance Abuse* 10, 19-30.

Penn CL (2016). Rising suicide rate leads to increased focus on education, prevention. *The Journal of the Arkansas Medical Society* 112, 248-251.

Perreault I, Corriveau P, Cauchie J-F (2016). While of unsound mind? Narratives of responsibility in suicide notes from the twentieth century. *Histoire Sociale/Social History* 49, 155-170.

Perry Y, Werner-Seidler A, Calear AL, Christensen H (2016). Web-based and mobile suicide prevention interventions for young people: A systematic review. *Journal of the Canadian Academy of Child and Adolescent Psychiatry* 25, 73-79.

Petroni S, Patel V, Patton G (2016). Suicide in adolescent girls - Authors' reply. *Lancet* 387, 1814.

Pirkis J, Krysinska K, Cheung YTD, San Too L, Spittal MJ, Robinson J (2016). "Hotspots" and "copycats": A plea for more thoughtful language about suicide reply. *Lancet Psychiatry* 3, 20.

Power J, Smith HP, Trestman RL (2016). 'What to do with the cutters?' - Best practices for offender self-injurious behaviors. *Criminal Justice Studies* 29, 57-76.

Preskorn SH (2016). National Initiative to Prevent Suicide (NIPS): A new proposal to improve the understanding and prevention of suicide. *Journal of Psychiatric Practice* 22, 398-404.

Price JH (2015). The conceptual transfer of human agency to the divine in the second temple period: The case of Saul's suicide. *Shofar-An Interdisciplinary Journal of Jewish Studies* 34, 107-130.

Price JH, Khubchandani J (2016). Firearm violence by the mentally ill: Mental health professionals' perceptions and practices. *Violence and Gender* 3, 92-99.

Pridmore S, Maajid A (2016). 'Suicide is preventable': An unsafe clause. *Asean Journal of Psychiatry* 17, 132-136.

Pridmore S, Pridmore W (2015). Suicide and related behaviour in Dostoyevsky novels. *Asean Journal of Psychiatry* 16, 69-74.

Pridmore S, Varbanov S, Sale I (2016). Suicide and murder-suicide involving automobiles. *Australasian Psychiatry*. Published online: 8 July 2016. doi: 10.1177/1039856216658830.

Pruthi S, Gupta V, Goel A (2015). Medical students hanging by a thread. *Education for Health (Abingdon, England)* 28, 150-151.

Quigley J, Rasmussen S, McAlaney J (2016). The associations between children's and adolescents' suicidal and self-harming behaviours, and related behaviours within their social networks: A systematic review. *Archives of Suicide*. Published online: 7 June 2016. doi: 10.1080/13811118.2016.1193075.

Ralapanawa U, Jayawickreme KP, Ekanayake EM, Dissanayake AM (2016). A study on paracetamol cardiotoxicity. *BMC Pharmacology and Toxicology* 17, 30.

Ramchand R, Jaycox L, Ebener P, Gilbert ML, Barnes-Proby D, Goutam P (2016). Characteristics and proximal outcomes of calls made to suicide crisis hotlines in California. *Crisis*. Published online: 24 June 2016. doi: 10.1027/0227-5910/a000401.

Ramirez J (2016). Suicide: Across the life span. *Nursing Clinics of North America* 51, 275-286.

Rangaiah YKC, Shankar R, Obulesu LC (2015). An analytival study of ligature mark in cases of hanging and ligature strangulation. *Journal of Evolution of Medical and Dental Sciences* 4, 14156-14162.

Rangarajan J, Somanathan GC, Srinivasan MR, Krishnaraj R, Mohanan SS, Pankajakshan APP, Jayachandran S (2016). A study on profile of orally ingested poisons in self harm (attempted suicide) at toxicology unit, Government Stanley Medical College. *Journal of Evolution of Medical and Dental Sciences* 5, 2087-2091.

Rashid A (2016). Yonder: Self-harm, repeat prescribing, deprescribing, and worry. *British Journal of General Practice* 66, 261-261.

Rashid A (2016). Yonder: Suicide, rhinosinusitis, urgent care centres, and favourite patients. *British Journal of General Practice* 66, 473.

Reddy V, Coffey MJ (2016). Plastic surgery and suicide: A clinical guide for plastic surgeons. *Plastic and Reconstructive Surgery Global Open* 4, e828.

Reed VA, Buitelaar JK, Anand E, Day KA, Treuer T, Upadhyaya HP, Coghill DR, Kryzhanovskaya LA, Savill NC (2016). The safety of atomoxetine for the treatment of children and adolescents with attention-deficit/hyperactivity disorder: A comprehensive review of over a decade of research. *CNS Drugs* 30, 603-628.

Rees N, Rapport F, Snooks H, John A, Patel C (2016). How do emergency ambulance paramedics view the care they provide to people who self harm? Ways and means. *International Journal of Law and Psychiatry*. Published online: 27 May 2016. doi: 10.1016/j.ijlp.2016.05.010.

Reising B (2016). Revisiting Ernest Hemingway and baseball: Sanity, success, and suicide. *Journal of American Culture* 39, 165-176.

Rendón-Quintero E, Rodríguez-Gómez R (2016). Experiences of individuals with suicidal ideation and attempts. *Revista Colombiana De Psiquiatría* 45, 92-100.

Rezaeian M, Zarghami M (2016). Algorithm characterization of suicide: Introducing an informative categorization system. *Iranian Journal of Psychiatry and Behavioral Sciences*. Published online: 15 August 2016. doi: 10.17795/ijpbs-4544.

Ribeiro JD, Franklin JC, Fox KR, Bentley KH, Kleiman EM, Chang BP, Nock MK (2016). Suicide as a complex classification problem: Machine learning and related techniques can advance suicide prediction - a reply to Roaldset (2016). *Psychological Medicine* 46, 2009-2010.

Rice S, Robinson J, Bendall S, Hetrick S, Cox G, Bailey E, Gleeson J, Alvarez-Jimenez M (2016). Online and social media suicide prevention interventions for young people: A focus on implementation and moderation. *Journal of the Canadian Academy of Child and Adolescent Psychiatry* 25, 80-86.

Rimkeviciene J, O'Gorman J, Hawgood J, Leo DD (2016). Timelines for difficult times: Use of visual timelines in interviewing suicide attempters. *Qualitative Research in Psychology*. Published online: 28 March 2016. doi: 10.1080/14780887.2016.1170913.

Ringash J (2016). Suicide: A major threat to head and neck cancer survivorship reply. *Journal of Clinical Oncology* 34, 1151-1152.

Ringqvist T, Ambrus L, Träskman-Bendz L, Giwercman A, Giwercman YL, Westrin Å (2016). Mendelian randomization in relation to androgens and suicidal behavior in males. *Psychiatry Research* 245, 414-415.

River J (2016). Diverse and dynamic interactions: A model of suicidal men's help seeking as it relates to health services. *American Journal of Men's Health*. Published online: 29 July 2016. doi: 10.1177/1557988316661486.

Roaldset JO (2016). Listen to the patient - what about patients' perceptions of suicidal risk? *Acta Psychiatrica Scandinavica*. Published online: 2 May 2016. doi: 10.1111/acps.12586.

Rodham K, Gavin J, Lewis S, Bandalli P, St. Denis J (2016). The NSSI paradox: Discussing and displaying NSSI in an online environment. *Deviant Behavior* 37, 1110-1117.

Rogers ML, Ringer FB, Joiner TE (2016). A meta-analytic review of the association between agitation and suicide attempts. *Clinical Psychology Review* 48, 1-6.

Ross V, Sankaranarayanan A, Lewin TJ, Hunter M (2016). Mental health workers' views about their suicide prevention role. *Psychology, Community and Health* 5, 1-15.

Rossom RC, Simon GE, Beck A, Ahmedani BK, Steinfeld B, Trangle M, Solberg L (2016). Facilitating action for suicide prevention by learning health care systems. *Psychiatric Services* 67, 830-832.

Roy W, Roaten K, Downs D, Khan F, Pollio DE, North CS (2016). Suicide risk assessment and management: Real-world experience and perceptions of emergency medicine physicians. *Archives of Suicide Research*. Published online: 16 June 2016. doi: 10.1080/13811118.2016.1199987.

Ruan X, Bydalek K, Kaye AD (2016). Emergency visits for prescription opioid overdose. *Clinical Journal of Pain* 32, 459.

Ruan X, Labrie-Brown C, Kaye AD (2016). Are transdermal opioids contraindicated in patients at risk of suicide? *European Journal of Anaesthesiology*. Published online: 3 October 2016. doi: 10.1097/EJA.0000000000000482.

Russell R, Metraux D, Tohen M (2016). Cultural influences on suicide in Japan. *Psychiatry and the Clinical Neurosciences*. Published online: 13 September 2016. doi: 10.1111/pcn.12428.

Rutt CC, Buser TJ, Buser JK (2016). Evaluating a training intervention for assessing nonsuicidal self-injury: The hire model. *Counselor Education and Supervision* 55, 123-136.

Saini P, Chantler K, While D, Kapur N (2016). Do GPs want or need formal support following a patient suicide?: A mixed methods study. *Family Practice*. Published online: 24 May 2016. doi: 10.1093/fampra/cmw040.

Sakwa R (2015). The Ukraine crisis and the crisis of Europe. *Siberian Historical Research*, 8-39.

Salisbury N (2016). Improving emergency care for people who self harm. *BMJ* 353, i2440.

Sándor K (2016). Autotelic activities aimed at the alteration of the human body from socially accepted to pathological forms: About non-suicidal self-injury. *Neuropsychopharmacologia Hungarica* 18, 21-38.

Sarchiapone M, D'Aulerio M (2015). The role of the culture into the multifactorial approach to suicidal behaviour (editorial). *Suicidology Online* 6, ii.

Saunders KE, Smith KA (2016). Interventions to prevent self-harm: What does the evidence say? *Evidence Based Mental Health*. Published online: 19 July 2016. doi: 10.1136/eb-2016-102420.

Saunders KEA (2016). Risk factors for suicide in children and young people: Common yet complex. *Lancet Psychiatry* 3, 699-700.

Schechter M, Goldblatt MJ, Ronningstam E, Herbstman B, Maltsberger JT (2016). Postdischarge suicide: A psychodynamic understanding of subjective experience and its importance in suicide prevention. *Bulletin of the Menninger Clinic* 80, 80-96.

Scherr S, Arendt F, Schäfer M (2016). Supporting reporting: On the positive effects of text- and video-based awareness material on responsible journalistic suicide news writing. *Archives of Suicide Research*. Published online: 16 August 2016. doi: 10.1080/13811118.2016.1222975.

Schrom K, Nagy T, Mostow E (2016). Depression screening using health questionnaires in patients receiving oral isotretinoin for acne vulgaris. *Journal of the American Academy of Dermatology* 75, 237-239.

Schuman D, Praetorius RT, Barnes DM, Arana AA (2016). Military suicide coverage: AP news wire & suicide guidelines. Death Studies. Published online: 3 June 2016. doi: 0.1080/07481187. 2016.1191559.

Schuman DL, Schuman DL (2016). A value-critical choice analysis of a policy to prevent suicide in veterans and service members. *Social Work in Public Health* 31, 537-548.

Scott R (2016). Risk management and the suicidal patient. *Psychiatry, Psychology and Law* 23, 336-360.

Scott R, Meehan T (2016). Critical incidents during leave from an Australian security hospital - a 12 year audit. *Psychiatry, Psychology, and Law*. Published online: 20 June 2016. doi: 10.1080/13218719.2016.1169572.

Seager M, Sullivan L (2016). Reducing male suicide. *Clinical Psychology Forum* 48-52.

Sellin L, Asp M, Wallsten T, Wiklund Gustin L (2016). Reconnecting with oneself while struggling between life and death: The phenomenon of recovery as experienced by persons at risk of suicide. *International Journal of Mental Health Nursing*. Published online: 15 July 2016. doi: 10.1111/inm.12249.

Selvaggio A, Vars FE (2016). "Bind me more tightly still": Voluntary restraint against gun suicide. *Harvard Journal on Legislation* 53, 671-709.

Serafini G, Pardini M, Pompili M, Girardi P, Amore M (2016). Understanding suicidal behavior: The contribution of recent resting-state fMRI techniques. *Frontiers in Psychiatry* 7, 69.

Seward J (2016). A new national partnership aims to reduce number of construction industry suicides. *Engineering News-Record* 27.

Shah A, Savla-Shah S, Wijeratne C, Draper B (2016). Are elite cricketers more prone to suicide? Further comments on suicides from individual countries of test cricketers. *Australasia Psychiatry*. Published online: 2 September 2016. doi: 10.1177/1039856216665284.

Shain B (2016). Suicide and suicide attempts in adolescents. *Pediatrics* 138, e20161420.

Shannon T (2016). Self-injury in patients with intellectual disability. *Nursing* 46, 61.

Sheehan LL, Corrigan PW, Al-Khouja MA (2016). Stakeholder perspectives on the stigma of suicide attempt survivors. *Crisis*. Published online: 26 August 2016. doi: 10.1027/0227-5910/a000413.

Sher L (2016). Both high and low testosterone levels may play a role in suicidal behavior in adolescent, young, middle-age, and older men: A hypothesis. *International Journal of Adolescent Medicine and Health*. Published online: 7 June 2016. doi: 10.1515/ijamh-2016-0032.

Sher L (2016). Commentary: Help-seeking patterns and attitudes to treatment amongst men who attempted suicide. *Frontiers in Public Health* 4, e88.

Sher L (2016). Commentary: Police and suicide prevention. *Frontiers in Public Health* 4, e119.

Shute N (2016). A plan to prevent gun suicides. *Scientific American* 314, 25-26.

Siegel AJ (2016). Suicide prevention by smartphone. *American Journal of Medicine* 129, e145.

Sikary AK, Swain R, Dhaka S, Gupta SK, Yadav A (2016). Jumping together: A fatal suicide pact. *Journal of Forensic Sciences*. Published online: 19 September 2016. doi: 10.1111/1556-4029.13193.

Silva C, Hagan CR, Rogers ML, Chiurliza B, Podlogar MC, Hom MA, Tzoneva M, Lim IC, Joiner TE (2016). Evidence for the propositions of the interpersonal theory of suicide among a military sample. *Journal of Clinical Psychology*. Published online: 1 August 2016. doi: 10.1002/jclp.22347.

Silva C, Smith AR, Dodd DR, Covington DW, Joiner TE (2016). Suicide-related knowledge and confidence among behavioral health care staff in seven states. *Psychiatric Services*. Published online: 15 June 2016. doi: 10.1176/appi.ps.201500271.

Silverman MM, De Leo D (2016). Why there is a need for an international nomenclature and classification system for suicide. *Crisis* 37, 83-87.

Simon GE, Specht C, Doederlein A (2016). Coping with suicidal thoughts: A survey of personal experience. *Psychiatric Services* 67, 1026-1029.

Simonds S (2016). Ode to suicide, delirium and early REM. *American Poetry Review* 45, 5-7.

Simons R (2016). Use of gene expression biomarkers to predict suicidality. *Aerospace Medicine and Human Performance* 87, 659-660.

Sinclair SJ, Roche MJ, Temes C, Massey C, Chung W-J, Stein M, Richardson L, Blais M (2016). Evaluating chronic suicide risk with the Personality Assessment Inventory: Development and initial validation of the Chronic Suicide Risk Index (S_Chron). *Psychiatry Research* 245, 443-450.

Skerrett DM, Mars M (2014). Addressing the social determinants of suicidal behaviors and poor mental health in LGBTI populations in Australia. *LGBT Health* 1, 212-217.

Smith AR, Dodd DR, Forrest LN, Witte TK, Bodell L, Ribeiro JD, Goodwin N, Siegfried N, Bartlett M (2016). Does the interpersonal-psychological theory of suicide provide a useful framework for understanding suicide risk among eating disorder patients? A test of the validity of the IPTS. *International Journal of Eating Disorders*. Published online: 16 August. doi: 10.1002/eat.22588.

Spiess A, Gallaway MS, Watkins EY, Corrigan E, Wills JV, Weir JC, Bell AMM, Bell MR (2016). The ABHIDE (Army Behavioral Health Integrated Data Environment): A suicide registry. *Military Behavioral Health* 4, 8-17.

Spittal MJ, Bismark M (2016). Reducing suicide through improved quality of care. *Lancet Psychiatry* 3, 491-492.

Squires D, Blumenthal D (2016). Mortality trends among working-age whites: The untold story. *Issue Brief (Commonwealth Fund)* 3, 1-11.

Stallard P (2016). Suicide rates in children and young people increase. *Lancet* 387, 1618.

Stanley IH, Rufino KA, Rogers ML, Ellis TE, Joiner TE (2016). Acute Suicidal Affective Disturbance (ASAD): A confirmatory factor analysis with 1442 psychiatric inpatients. *Journal of Psychiatric Research* 80, 97-104.

Stelzer E (2016). Social implications of love suicide in early modern English drama. *Critical Survey* 28, 67-77.

Sterling AGt, Bakalar JL, Perera KU, DeYoung KA, Harrington-LaMorie J, Haigney D, Ghahramanlou-Holloway M (2016). Perspectives of suicide bereaved individuals on military suicide decedents' life stressors and male gender role stress. *Archives of Suicide Research*. Published online: 25 May 2016. doi: 10.1080/13811118.2016.1166087.

Struck MF, Beilicke A, Hoffmeister A, Gockel I, Gries A, Wrigge H, Bernhard M (2016). Acute emergency care and airway management of caustic ingestion in adults: Single center observational study. *Scandinavian Journal of Trauma, Resuscitation and Emergency Medicine* 24, 45.

Sujith Sreenivas C (2016). Study of atherosclerotic changes of arteries of circle of Willis in suicide - a retrospective autopsy based study. *Medico-Legal Update* 16, 225-227.

Sukhawaha S, Arunpongpaisal S, Hurst C (2016). Development and psychometric properties of the Suicidality of Adolescent Screening Scale (SASS) using multidimensional item response theory. *Psychiatry Research* 243, 431-438.

Suzuki T (2015). How will a risk of income fluctuations influence the suicidal decision making? Insights from a three-period model of suicide. *Eurasian Economic Review* 5, 331-343.

Swanepoel A (2016). Fifteen-minute consultation: Safety assessment prior to discharge of patient admitted for self-harm. *Archives of Disease in Childhood: Education and Practice Edition*. Published online: 13 July 2016. doi: 10.1136/archdischild-2016-310782.

Swanson JW, Bonnie RJ, Appelbaum PS (2016). Firearm access and risk of suicide-reply. *Journal of the American Medical Association* 315, 2124-2125.

Swanson JW, Easter MM, Robertson AG, Swartz MS, Alanis-Hirsch K, Moseley D, Dion C, Petrila J (2016). Gun violence, mental illness, and laws that prohibit gun possession: Evidence from two Florida counties. *Health Affairs (Project Hope)* 35, 1067-1075.

Szyszkowicz M (2016). Visualization of method-specific suicide mortality data. *Letters in Health and Biological Sciences* 1, e1029.

Tait G, Carpenter B (2016). The continuing implications of the "crime" of suicide: A brief history of the present. *International Journal of Law in Context* 12, 210-224.

Tanis J (2016). The power of 41%: A glimpse into the life of a statistic. *American Journal of Orthopsychiatry* 86, 373-377.

Thornton L, Handley T, Kay-Lambkin F, Baker A (2016). Is a person thinking about suicide likely to find help on the internet? An evaluation of google search results. *Suicide and Life Threatening Behavior*. Published online: 25 April 2016. doi: 10.1111/sltb.12261.

Tillman J (2016). The intergenerational transmission of suicide: Moral injury and the mysterious object in the work of Walker Percy. *Journal of the American Psychoanalytic Association*. Published online: 6 June 2016. doi: 10.1177/0003065116653362.

Tingey L, Larzelere-Hinton F, Goklish N, Ingalls A, Craft T, Sprengeler F, McGuire C, Barlow A (2016). Entrepreneurship education: A strength-based approach to substance use and suicide prevention for American Indian adolescents. *American Indian and Alaska Native Mental Health Research* 23, 248-270.

Tollefsen IM, Hem E, Ekeberg O, Zahl PH, Helweg-Larsen K (2016). Differing procedures for recording mortality statistics in Scandinavia. *Crisis*. Published online: 23 September 2016. doi: 10.1027/0227-5910/a000425.

Tøllefsen IM, Thiblin I, Helweg-Larsen K, Hem E, Kastrup M, Nyberg U, Rogde S, Zahl PH, Østevold G, Ekeberg O (2016). Accidents and undetermined deaths: Re-evaluation of nationwide samples from the Scandinavian countries. *BMC Public Health* 16, 449.

Tomicic A, Gálvez C, Quiroz C, Martínez C, Fontbona J, Rodríguez J, Aguayo F, Rosenbaum C, Leyton F, Lagazzi I (2016). Suicide in lesbian, gay, bisexual and trans populations: Systematic review of a decade of research (2004-2014). *Revista Medica de Chile* 144, 723-733.

Torjesen I (2016). Admission for infection is linked to increased suicide risk. *BMJ* 354, i4416.

Ursano RJ, Kessler RC, Stein MB (2016). Suicide attempts in the US army reply. *JAMA Psychiatry* 73, 176-177.

VanSickle M, Tucker J, Daruwala S, Ghahramanlou-Holloway M (2016). Development and psychometric evaluation of the Military Suicide Attitudes Questionnaire (MSAQ). *Journal of Affective Disorders* 203, 158-165.

VanSickle M, Werbel A, Perera K, Pak K, DeYoung K, Ghahramanlou-Holloway M (2016). Principal component analysis of the suicide opinion questionnaire in a U.S. Military sample of Marine Corps Non-Commissioned Officers. *Military Medicine* 181, 672-679.

Veisani Y, Delpisheh A, Sayehmiri K, Moradi G, Hassanzadeh J (2016). Associations of suicide seasonality with rural-urban residence and mental disorders in Ilam, Iran. *Iranian Journal of Medical Sciences* 41, 461-462.

Velentza O, Fradelos E (2016). Mental disorder and suicide in third age individuals. *Sanitas Magisterium* 2, 111-119.

Ventriglio A, Gentile A, Bonfitto I, Stella E, Mari M, Steardo L, Bellomo A (2016). Suicide in the early stage of schizophrenia. *Frontiers in Psychiatry*. Published online: 27 June 2016. doi: 10.3389/fpsyt.2016.00116.

Verberne T (2016). Suicide in adolescent girls. *Lancet* 387, 1814.

Verrocchio MC, Carrozzino D, Marchetti D, Andreasson K, Fulcheri M, Bech P (2016). Mental pain and suicide: A systematic review of the literature. *Frontiers in Psychiatry* 7, e108.

Victor SE, Styer D, Washburn JJ (2016). Functions of nonsuicidal self-injury (NSSI): Cross-sectional associations with NSSI duration and longitudinal changes over time and following treatment. *Psychiatry Research* 241, 83-90.

Viglino D, Bourez D, Collomb-Muret R, Schwebel C, Tazarourte K, Dumanoir P, Paquier C, Danel V, Debaty G, Maignan M (2016). Noninvasive end tidal CO2 is unhelpful in the prediction of complications in deliberate drug poisoning. *Annals of Emergency Medicine* 68, 62-70.e1.

Vijayakumar L (2016). Suicide among refugees - a mockery of humanity. *Crisis* 37, 1-4.

Wang Y-W, Tsai Y-F, Lee S-H, Chen Y-J, Chen H-F (2016). Development and psychometric testing of the protective reasons against suicide inventory for assessing older Chinese-speaking outpatients in primary care settings. *Journal of Advanced Nursing* 72, 1701-1710.

Wang Y, Bhaskaran J, Sareen J, Bolton SL, Chateau D, Bolton JM (2016). Clinician prediction of future suicide attempts: A longitudinal study. *Canadian Journal of Psychiatry* 61, 428-432.

Washington KT, Albright DL, Parker Oliver D, Gage LA, Lewis A, Mooney MJ (2016). Hospice and palliative social workers' experiences with clients at risk of suicide. *Palliative and Support Care*. Published online: 23 May 2016. doi: 10.1017/S1478951516000171.

Wasserman D (2016). Psychosocial interventions to prevent repeated self-harm. *Lancet Psychiatry* 3, 697-698.

Waters S (2016). Suicide voices: Testimonies of trauma in the French workplace. *Medical Humanities*. Published online: 9 September 2016. doi: 10.1136/medhum-2016-011013.

Weinstock LM, Strong D, Uebelacker LA, Miller IW (2016). Differential endorsement of suicidal ideation and attempt in bipolar versus unipolar depression: A testlet response theory analysis. *Journal of Affective Disorders* 200, 67-73.

Westefeld JS, Gann LC, Lustgarten SD, Yeates KJ (2016). Relationships between firearm availability and suicide: The role of psychology. *Professional Psychology: Research and Practice* 47, 271-277.

Wilhelm K, Korczak V, Tietze T, Reddy P (2016). Clinical pathways for suicidality in emergency settings: A public health priority. *Australian Health Review*. Published online: 23 June 2016. doi: 10.1071/AH16008.

Wilkinson ST, Sanacora G (2016). Ketamine: A potential rapid-acting antisuicidal agent? *Depression and Anxiety* 33, 711-717.

Wingren CJ, Ottosson A (2016). Authors reply "association of body mass index and choice of suicide methods". *Journal of Forensic and Legal Medicine* 42, 108-108.

Wise J (2016). CBT may help people who self harm, Cochrane review shows. *BMJ* 353, i2687.

Witte TK, Holm-Denoma JM, Zuromski KL, Gauthier JM, Ruscio J (2016). Individuals at high risk for suicide are categorically distinct from those at low risk. *Psychological Assessment*. Published online: 9 June 2016. doi: 10.1037/pas0000349.

Wolfe-Clark AL, Bryan CJ (2016). Integrating two theoretical models to understand and prevent military and veteran suicide. *Armed Forces and Society*. Published online: 6 May 2016. doi: 10.1177/0095327X16646645.

Wolford-Clevenger C, Smith PN, Kuhlman S, D'Amato D (2016). A preliminary test of the interpersonal-psychological theory of suicide in women seeking shelter from intimate partner violence. *Journal of Interpersonal Violence*. Published online: 25 July 2016. doi: 10.1177/0886260516660974.

Worrall RL, Jeffery S (2016). Survey of attitudes to self-harm patients within a burns and plastic surgery department. *Journal of Burn Care & Research*. Published online: 29 March 2016. doi: 10.1097/BCR.0000000000000350.

Xin X, Ming Q, Zhang J, Wang Y, Liu M, Yao S (2016). Four distinct subgroups of self-injurious behavior among Chinese adolescents: Findings from a latent class analysis. *PLoS One* 11, e0158609.

Xuan Z, Naimi TS, Kaplan MS, Bagge CL, Few LR, Maisto S, Saitz R, Freeman R (2016). Alcohol policies and suicide: A review of the literature. *Alcoholism: Clinical and Experimental Research*. Published online: 12 September 2016. doi: 10.1111/acer.13203.

Yang H, Young AH (2016). Lithium and suicide prevention. *L'Encephale* 42, 270-271.

Yoon HK (2016). Sleep and suicide. *Sleep Medicine and Psychophysiology* 23, 5-9.

Yoshioka E (2016). Suicide, socio-economic inequalities, gender, and psychiatric disorders commentary: Educational levels and risk of suicide in Japan: The Japan Public Health Center Study (JPHC) Cohort I. *Journal of Epidemiology* 26, 277-278.

Young R, Subramanian R, Miles S, Hinnant A, Andsager JL (2016). Social representation of cyberbullying and adolescent suicide: A mixed-method analysis of news stories. *Health Communication*. Published online 26 August 2016. doi: 10.1080/10410236.2016.1214214.

Youssef NA (2016). Exploratory investigation of biomarker candidates for suicide in schizophrenia and bipolar disorder: Preliminary findings of altered neurosteroid levels (vol 36, pg 46, 2015). *Crisis* 37, 77.

Yovell Y (2016). Ultra-low-dose buprenorphine as a time-limited treatment for severe suicidal ideation: A randomized controlled trial (vol 173, pg 491, 2016). *American Journal of Psychiatry* 173, 198.

Zalsman G, Hawton K, Wasserman D, van Heeringen K, Arensman E, Sarchiapone M, Carli V, Höschl C, Barzilay R, Balazs J, Purebl G, Kahn JP, Sáiz PA, Lipsicas CB, Bobes J, Cozman D, Hegerl U, Zohar J (2016). Suicide prevention strategies revisited: 10-year systematic review. *Lancet Psychiatry* 3, 646-659.

Zalsman G, Shoval G, Mansbach-Kleinfeld I, Farbstein I, Kanaaneh R, Lubin G, Apter A (2016). Maternal versus adolescent reports of suicidal behaviors: A nationwide survey in Israel. *European Child and Adolescent Psychiatry*. Published online: 9 May 2016. doi: 10.1007/s00787-016-0862-1.

Zhang J (2016). From psychological strain to disconnectedness: A two-factor model theory of suicide. *Crisis* 37, 169-175.

Zou Y, Leung R, Lin S, Yang M, Lu T, Li X, Gu J, Hao C, Dong G, Hao Y (2016). Attitudes towards suicide in urban and rural China: A population based, cross-sectional study. *BMC Psychiatry* 16, 162.

Zuckerman DM, Kennedy CE, Terplan M (2016). Breast implants, self-esteem, quality of life, and the risk of suicide. *Women's Health Issues* 26, 361-365.

www.ingramcontent.com/pod-product-compliance
Lightning Source LLC
Chambersburg PA
CBHW082352270326
41935CB00013B/1596